Boulettes pour le bouillon

Durée : 10 minutes de préparation
(laisser reposer 1 heure)
1/4 d'heure de cuisson
Egoutter ensuite

Ingrédients

5 œufs
3 cuillères à soupe d'huile
1/2 verre d'eau ou 6 ½ cuillères à soupe d'eau tiède
250 gr. farine de pains azymes
Sel - poivre - herbes de Provence

Marche à suivre

Mousse au chocolat

6 œufs — 1 cuillère café de caféine'
1 tablette chocolat 100 Grammes
3 cuillères à soupe de sucre en poudre
1 sachet sucre vanillé - 1 cuillère de liqueur

- Séparer les blancs des jaunes
- Ajouter aux jaunes les sucres - Battre jusqu'à
  ce que cela devienne blanc
- Ajouter le café - la liqueur
- Ajouter chocolat fondu
- Battre blancs en neige - Mélanger délicatement
  avec 1 cuillère en bois - Mettre au frigidaire

TRUFFES

3 c à soupe sucre en poudre ⎫ environ
250 g chocolat à cuire ⎬ 30 truffes
125 g Beurre ⎭
3 jaunes d'œufs
100 g cacao poudre non sucré

Faites fondre le chocolat au bain-marie
Mélanger avec une cuillère en bois
jusqu'à obtention d'une pâte homogène
Laisser refroidir.
Dans une terrine, mélanger les
œufs, le sucre, le beurre ramolli
et non fondu coupé en morceaux.
Travailler vivement et ajouter petit
à petit le chocolat tiède. Laisser
reposer jusqu'au lendemain
Faites alors des petites boules. Roulez

3/4 l. ... ...
de café - 8 œufs -
sucre

- Verser le café chaud sur
  le sucre.
- Battre 8 œufs entiers, les
- mélanger au café.
- Faire cuire au four (moye...
  bain-marie - Arrêter ...

PESSAH

excellent

Gâteau au Chocolat

160 gr. chocolat noir fondu
160 gr. poudre d'amande
160 gr. sucre
5 œufs inutile de monter
les bla...

à Four moyen ~ 35/mn.
/45
175°c

Recette d'Annie

Gâteau de Grimserlich

Faire caraméliser un moule en
Pyrex - Mettre dans le fond du moule
une couche de pâte à grimser
lich, puis une couche de
pruneaux et d'abricots secs,
à nouveau une couche
...

Quiches, Kugels, and Couscous

Quiches, Kugels, and Couscous

My Search for Jewish Cooking in France

Joan Nathan

ALFRED A. KNOPF NEW YORK 2010

This Is a Borzoi Book
Published by Alfred A. Knopf

www.aaknopf.com

Library of Congress Cataloging-in-Publication Data
Nathan, Joan.
Quiches, kugels, and couscous : my search for Jewish cooking in France / by Joan Nathan.
p. cm.
Includes bibliographical reference and index.
ISBN 978-0-307-26759-7
1. Jewish cooking.   2. Cooking, French.   3. Jews—France—Social life and customs.   I. Title.
TX724.N38 2010   641.5'676—dc22 2010020280

Manufactured in China

First Edition

In memory of Annie (Nanou) Cerf Weil,
July 24, 1944–April 16, 1988,
a dear friend who introduced me to the France she loved so well,
but who died much too early

Contents

Acknowledgments

EACH BOOK I WRITE transports me to new worlds filled with research and human relationships. Without the melding of the two there would never be satisfying results. During this period, which lasts for three to five years, my work becomes my life.

This book took me into homes throughout France. My hope is that the reader will be enriched by my account of these experiences and the recipes gleaned from each adventure. When I started studying French in high school, little did I know how helpful it would prove to be throughout my career. My proficiency in French opened so many doors, as did my lifelong friends and relatives who led me throughout France to otherwise unavailable sources willing to break bread with me.

I have many people to thank, in addition to those appearing throughout the book, to whom I am eternally grateful. During my trips revisiting France in the past few years, I felt like a peeping Tom, watching home cooks and chefs in their kitchens, and forging new friendships.

Thanks to Connie and Dominique Borde, Catherine and Jean-Bruno Dufort, Hélène Goldenberg and Richard Moos, Marthe Layrle, Patrice and Herb Miller, Claudine and Henri Moos, Elie and Gotz Schreiber, Irene and Michel Weil, and Sandrine Weil and Mathias Laurent, who opened their homes to me.

In each city, people have extended themselves to lead me to the right cooks to tell this story and have had the patience to talk with me. Without the help of Yves Alexandre, Gilbert Brenner, Georges Dalmeyda, Marie-Christine Daunay, Lydia Elhadad, Peggy Frankton, Jacqueline Frydman, George Gumpel, Michel Gurfunkiel, Nathalia Hercot, Natan Holchaker, Julie Mautner, Alex Miles, Gérard Monteux, Professor René Moulinas, Lucie Optyker, Jean Paulhan, Gilles Pudlowski, Bernard Saltiel, and Patricia Wells, I could never have been so well accepted into the French Jewish communities.

The staffs of museums and libraries have been invaluable: Carol Ambruster and Peggy Pearlstein of the Library of Congress; Marc Masurovsky of the United States Holocaust Memorial Museum; Rebecca Federman, Roberta Saltsman, David Smith, and Michael Terry of the New York Public Library; the staff of the Alliance Israélite Universelle in Paris; Isabelle Pleskoff at the Jewish Museum of Paris; and the remarkable Philip and Mary Hyman, who let me work in the wonderful world of their private library.

Elizabeth Alpern, Amy Bartscherer, Claire Blaustein, Jan Buhrman, Sandra Di Capua, Krista Gallagher, Maria Gudiel, Merav Levkowitz, Theresa McCulla, Doug Singer, Jennifer Visick, and Rebecca Wall have helped me invaluably in the kitchen and with research.

In addition, I want to thank all these people in the United States, who have led me in the right direction: Howard Abarbanel, Ann Amernick, Daniel Boulud, Lori Chemla, Annick Delacaze, Richard Delerins, François Dionot, Carol Goldberg, Katja Goldman, Barbara Greenwood, Jean Joho, Francis Layrle, Dalya Luttwak, Patty Ravenscroft, Trina Rubenstein, Jonathan Sarna, André Soltner, Jeffrey Steingarten, Cathy Sulzberger, and Paula Wolfert.

Yves Alexandre, Jennifer Breger, Beatrice Fink, Thomas Head, Professor Lisa Leff, Sheila Malovany-Chevallier, Professor Ted Meron, Professor Pamela Nadell, Professor Susan Suleiman, and Eveline Weyl have carefully read over the manuscript. Knowing how busy their lives are, I greatly appreciate the time they spent on me. Thanks, too, to the marvelous MacDowell Colony, where I worked on the introduction.

And, of course, my three children, Daniela, Merissa, and David, and my husband, Allan, once again put up with my obsessions with this fascinating and delicious topic for these past few years.

My agent, Gail Ross, and editors Pete Wells and Nick Fox at *The New York Times* have been 100 percent behind me. I also want to thank the extraordinary people at Alfred A. Knopf. Sonny Mehta first saw the vision for this book. Ken Schneider helped me through various computer glitches, always in good humor, Maria Massey carefully saw the manuscript through production, and Kristen Bearse created the fabulous design of the book.

But most of all my editor, the legendary and phenomenal Judith Jones, went over every word of the manuscript, at least once, encouraging me to tell this amazing story and urging me to craft the book in my own words.

Quiches, Kugels, and Couscous

Introduction

My Gastronomic Journey to France

IT WAS RUTH MOOS WHO first taught me the simple pleasure of sinking my teeth into a slightly melted bar of dark chocolate sandwiched into a crackly baguette. My father had sent me to France as a teenager in the 1950s because he thought fluency in foreign languages should be part of a young girl's education. But my visits with his cousin Rudi Moos and his wife, Ruth, gave me an education beyond mere language. Ruth took me on afternoon hikes in the Alps, with chocolate baguette snacks, and in her kitchen exposed me to dishes such as *gratin dauphinois,* a local regional specialty, and poached fish with a *mousseline* sauce, as well as delicious tarts and tortes made with plums, apples, and other fruits.

At this time in my life, when I began my love affair with France, I was naïvely unaware of the history of Jews in the country. Although I knew that the Moos family had escaped capture during the Nazi occupation by hiding in Annecy, a picturesque lake town in Haute-Savoie, I never felt comfortable asking any questions.

It wasn't until recently that I learned about the terrible ordeal the Mooses went through during the Holocaust. At first they helped Jews fleeing from their native Germany. Robert, their eldest son, remembers nights spent with his father in the basement, wrapping boxes of sardines and old clothes and then shipping them off to Jews confined in the Gurs detention camp. Later, when the Vichy government took control and carried out anti-Semitic measures, the Mooses also had to hide, fleeing from place to place, to save their lives.

A few years after my visit to Annecy, I spent my junior year abroad at the Sorbonne. I frequently visited other Jewish French families, including the Cerfs, Parisians originally from Lorraine, who invited me for the Sabbath and Jewish holidays. On Fridays, their son Bertrand and I would go to a local *boulangerie* for a baguette to be blessed as the challah, and his sister Nanou introduced me to the pleasures of French restaurants and cafés throughout Paris. Seated in the family's Louis XVI dining room, the table appointed with delicate china, we dined on Jewish food cooked with a French flair.

One of the places where Robert Moos was hidden during the war

On Fridays, we would often eat an elegant chicken consommé garnished with matzo balls or, even better, tiny marrow dumplings; an herbed, stuffed veal breast; and golden-brown potatoes. We drank wine—not the sweet Manischewitz that I'd grown up with, but real French wine. For dessert there was sorbet and fruit with tiny French pastries that tasted like a cross between a macaroon and a meringue.

The Passover Seder rituals seemed especially exotic. Prayers were recited mostly in French, or in French-accented Hebrew, making the stories sound throatier, more urgent maybe, and, to my ears, more resonant. It all seemed so familiar, and yet so foreign. I felt a part of something larger, knowing that all over the world, Jews were gathered around Seder tables on the same night, reciting in their own accents the story of the Exodus and eating foods that they called "Jewish."

I later discovered that Jews like my family in Annecy and the Cerfs in Paris were shocked to be thought of as Jews and not simply as French people. When I read the diary of Hélène Berr, the French Anne Frank, who perished in Auschwitz but left her journal behind, I couldn't help thinking of myself at her age, only twenty years before, being young and free and discovering the wonders of Paris. Her journal, a French best seller, shows how she had not even thought of hiding her heritage before the war. But all of a sudden her life changed, and her Jewishness became a point not only of notice but of shame: she had to wear a Jewish star in public, was shoved to the back car of the same *métro* that I traveled on, and endured much, much more.

Since my time in Paris, I have eaten at many Jewish tables throughout the world but have always had a particular fascination with French Jews and their food. Like many American cooks of my age, I worked my way through Julia Child, learning to make the dishes I had tasted while in France. I used my knowledge of the language and the culture to connect with people, mostly chefs, all over the country. But I never really studied the Jews in France, and still knew little about their very long history. In a sense, the delicious food I ate made me hunger for a deeper understanding of the history of French Jews and their food.

Over the course of the past few years, I have broken bread with Jews from different ethnic and religious backgrounds in Alsace-Lorraine, the southwest, Provence and the Côte d'Azur, the Loire Valley, and Burgundy. Given that Paris has the largest concentration of Jews in France, more than half its Jewish population, I spent the bulk of my time there, doing research in libraries and interviewing chefs, shopkeepers, and ordinary home cooks.

In writing this book, I came to understand that French Jews revere the traditions of their region along with the traditions of Jewish cuisine. It has been fascinating for me to learn that within this rich agricultural country, Ashkenazic, Sephardic, and Provençal Jewish food developed side by side and often melded with French regional cooking. Whereas the Jews of Alsace cooked with goose fat and sauerkraut, those of the south cooked with oil and garlic. Since some Jewish families in Provence have been there for over two thousand years, it is hard to differentiate Jewish from Provençal food customs. *Fougasse,* for example, a bread with holes, traditionally mixed, kneaded, and shaped at home, then brought to a communal oven for baking, was the holiday bread for Jews and others from Provence.

Until World War II, France was one of the world's most agriculturally endowed countries, a source of pride for all French people. The produce and specialties of each region affect Jewish cooking as much as the origins of the dishes. And through the centuries, French Jews have adapted their palates to regional favorites.

> During the war we ate what we could, black-market chicken, rations for bread, sugar, coffee. But we had food. Every French person didn't suffer from hunger—we ate bad, but we ate. I didn't know anyone who died of hunger. France is a rich, agricultural country.
>
> —Georges Loinger,
> Jewish Resistance fighter, in an interview with the author

Jewishness in France

The synagogue is a special place for religious Jews, and the ones in France have their own particular character. On a quiet, tree-lined *quai* overlooking the Saône River in Lyon, for example, stands a nineteenth-century building with a façade that looks like any other. Open the doors and go through a courtyard and you will find a large stone structure with stained-glass windows. This hidden synagogue, called the Grande Synagogue, is situated across the river from the Saint-Georges Church, near the Rue de la Juiverie and Jewish ruins, some dating back to the fifth century and perhaps earlier. But from the outside, one would hardly suspect the wonders that lie within.

The Jewishness of the Jews of France is similarly hidden. They tend to practice their religion and eat their meals behind the shuttered windows of their houses, which look from the outside like any other living space. This quiet, inner life is partly the result of the precarious history of Jews in France. It also stems from long-standing assimilation, since Jewish roots in France are almost indistinguishable from the history of the country.

Graham Robb observes in his book *The Discovery of France* that until 1789 France was not a cohesive country at all, but a string of regional identities of language, culture, and cuisine. It was not until the industrial revolution that the national government linked the regions by rail, enhanced education, codified one French language, and tried to create a unified culture in which fine food played a starring role.

From the eighteenth century on, France has been known for its refined cuisine. In drawing on this legacy, France has absorbed and adapted the cuisines of many other countries—pasta and pesto dishes from Italy by way of Catherine de Médicis; eggplants and spices from India and China; tomatoes, peppers, and potatoes from the New World; and myriad dishes from peoples coming to the new promised land of France from all parts of Europe and Africa.

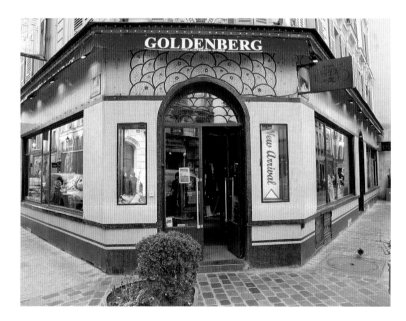

Goldenberg's: A bygone tradition—now a chic boutique

Despite successive waves of anti-Semitic violence, expulsion, and disfavor throughout history, France has nevertheless been more often than not a *pays d'accueil,* a welcoming country for Jews. While its Jewish population has waxed and waned since the first century, and possibly before, there have been continuous Jewish communities in many regions of what is now France. The Jewish community of Paris had its start in the sixth century, worshipping in a synagogue just south of what would later become the Cathedral of Notre-Dame.

With about six hundred thousand Jews living there today, France has the third-largest Jewish population in the world, after Israel and the United States. Even through hard times, the communities have evolved, and for the most part prospered, producing some of the country's most prominent personalities: Marcel Proust, Camille Pissarro, Marcel Marceau, Anouk Aimée, Claude Lelouch, Simone Signoret, Sonia Rykiel, Nostradamus, and Pierre Mendes France. All French; all of Jewish heritage.

The biggest impediment to talking about Jewish cooking is that unlike Italian or Chinese cuisine, which can be discussed in terms of geographic boundaries, Jewish food is mostly diasporic, emerging in many lands and in many forms. It can be defined most easily by kashrut, the dietary laws explained in the books of Leviticus and Deuteronomy and expanded in the Talmud. Throughout the centuries, they have been codified and elaborated upon by scholars and rabbis, including Rabbi Shlomo ben Yitzhak (known as Rashi), who lived in Troyes, in northern France, from 1040 to 1105 C.E.

Among other things, the dietary laws do not allow pork and shellfish, require that blood be extracted from meat, and prohibit milk and meat in the same meal. For French Jews, this means no crustaceans, no eel, no frogs' legs, and no bouillabaisse with its shellfish, as well as no heavy cream sauces or buttery tart crusts accompanying meat meals. But Jews have always improvised and adapted to new diets as they moved from place to place, and in the process have developed a tradition of cooking that blends the influences of their dietary proscriptions with the flavors of the country in which they are living. Likewise, French cooking has benefited from the presence of Jews. Through the ages they have brought new techniques, ingredients, and flavors to the cooking of the various regions.

Jewish ingenuity and activity have been integral to the development of French cuisine and to the economy of food in France. Even earlier than the eighth century, Jews trafficked in wine, cheese, spices, truffles, and later salt cod and herring to satisfy French appetites. Some brought the art of making *foie gras* to France. Others brought African pepper, Madeiran sugar, and cocoa beans, and were the first makers of hot chocolate.

Still, that legacy remains for the most part hidden, even to its inheritors. When I was interviewing Daniel Rose, a young Jewish chef in Paris, for an article for *The New York Times,* I stopped at a table in his restaurant to hear what the patrons were saying about the food. They asked me what I was doing in Paris, and when I told them that I was writing a book about the food of the Jews of France, they began questioning me about French Jewish cooking, as if they knew nothing about it. I learned later that several of the guests at that table were Jewish, something that they likely would have revealed right away had I encountered them in America. It is very French to be reticent about divulging anything personal, but reticence about religion is perhaps a legacy of anti-Semitism, starting with persecution long ago and exacerbated by the lingering scars of the Holocaust.

When I approached French Jews to talk about my research, their first response was often that they didn't know any Jewish dishes. They think of the food they eat as simply French. During the week, they shop at their local markets, buying seasonal produce, and, like all French people, almost obsessing about their next meal. They may go to a kosher butcher or grocery store, but they bring up their children to *se tenir comme il faut,* to have French manners at their beautifully set tables.

Yet, when older French Jews talk about the food of their childhood, the dishes that smell of deep memories and home, they most likely recall their Sabbath and holiday food. Traditional dishes like carp are served cold with a *sauce verte,* a green parsley sauce so French that it is even mentioned in the cookbook of Taillevent, who was one of the first to codify French cooking, in the fourteenth century. Indeed, carp with a *sauce verte* survives to this day mostly as a Jewish holiday dish, and is commonly known as *carpe à la juive* even if it is prepared with other fish.

For observant Jews, the week leads up to the Sabbath and its meals. Starting on Wednesday, home cooks begin planning their menus and working out the logistics so that Saturday can be the day of rest prescribed in the Bible. Shopping is done, and cooked and cold salads as well as cakes are made ahead for the Saturday meals. Kitchens fill up with the smells of slowly simmering stews—Alsatian *choucroute* or *pot-au-feu,* Moroccan chickpea-and-meat Sabbath stews called *adafina* or the warm casseroles of eastern European *cholent.* Everyone has deep memories of childhood dishes—and who has better described the power of food than Marcel Proust, whose mother was Jewish, and for whom the taste of a *madeleine* opens floodgates to the past.

Some fear that these traditional foods, the ones that bind people together and create memories, are being forgotten in almost all French Jewish kitchens. One young Parisian woman pleaded with me to find the old lost recipes before it is too late. But traces of what we would call Jewish cooking crop up in many unexpected places. On one occasion in Paris, at a dinner party, the hostess had prepared a special meal of *pot-au-feu* from her native Alsace, but it was the *knepfle,* or matzo balls, in the broth that brought murmurs of glee from the diners.

Even though some of the oldest Jewish recipes have long since been subsumed into French regional cuisine, you can often recognize ancient cooking in the dishes Jews are serving today. Ratatouille, for example, is similar to the North African *tchoukchouka.* The many *tians* and gratins of vegetables with eggs and rice are found in Sephardic communities throughout the world.

It is these traditions that I am seeking, their origins sometimes obscured or simply unacknowledged. Between intermarriage, travel, expulsion, changing food ways, and different waves of immigration, it is often difficult to trace with precision the path of Jewish cooking in France.

But in the history of the food of Provence and Alsace, I can see relics of recipes such as eggplant dishes and breads that might be linked to Jews. Each one of these associations helps piece together the jigsaw puzzle of French food and everything that influenced it. Each piece of the past enables us to see the present more clearly.

A Culinary History of the Jews in France

The cooking of the Jews of France is inextricably linked to their complex history. It was reflected in their origins. Jews have come in waves from Spain and Portugal, the Balkans, eastern Europe, North Africa, and initially from ancient Palestine, bringing their cooking practices with them. Once settled in France, they traveled back and forth between Spain, France, Italy, and greater Poland, depending on which country was hospitable to them at the time. When they returned to France, they often brought back variations of dishes they had taken with them from France years earlier.

THE FIRST SETTLERS

It is important to realize that Jews were among the very earliest immigrants to what was then called Gaul. Although many scholars think that Jewish merchants came to Gaul as far back as the time of the Babylonian exile, the first recorded settlers arrived with Herod's son King Antipas, who was exiled in 39 c.e., to Lungdunum, which became Lyon. They probably brought with them some dried chickpeas, lentils, and barley, significant additions to the everyday bread, olive oil, and wine basic to the diet in southern Gaul and throughout the Mediterranean area. This tiny community was soon dwarfed by another wave of newcomers that arrived shortly after the destruction of the Temple in Jerusalem, circa 70 c.e. As I drove around the marvelous rocky port of Marseille, so similar in its barren hills and warm climate to the land of Israel, I thought of the early Jewish settlers, who must have felt at home in the ports of Narbonne and Massilia (modern-day Marseille), which once had such a large Jewish population that it was called La Juive. Narbonne grew to be the largest Jewish community in Gaul in the early Middle Ages, and townsmen called the privileged Jewish class there *nasis,* or princes.

As Roman citizens, Franco-Jews farmed, made olive oil, and brought root stock from Palestine, which they used to make wine for their rituals. Jewish peddlers would set out from their towns peppered throughout the south during the week, combing the countryside and selling their wares. They settled with at least nine confrères in small villages, where they formed a minyan (ten men) to pray together on the Sabbath. Merchants transported goods up and down the Rhône River and on the Mediterranean Sea, bringing seeds and dried beans back with them from the journeys they made to seek out musk, *garum* (a fish sauce), and cinnamon, as well as the more important perfumes and furs. Using Hebrew for prayer, the early Jews spoke a Provençal Ladino, called Judéo Provençal or Shuadit, a variation of the Judeo-Spanish spoken among Sephardic Jews. Although the Jewish communities in the small towns are gone, they live on in Jewish last names such as Monteux and Lunel. An important rabbinic figure of this period was Abraham ben David, known as the RABaD of Posquières, today called Vauvert. An influential Talmudic commentator who was born in Provence in 1125, he has a street named after him, Rue Ravad, in present-day Vauvert.

By the twelfth and thirteenth centuries, important scholarly rabbinic centers had sprung up throughout Languedoc and Provence, near Montpellier and Narbonne. The communities in southern France were continually enriched by people traveling from the Iberian Peninsula and the entire Mediterranean region. There was a fertile exchange of foods—dried chickpeas, barley, garlic, lentils—and a sharing of new ideas for curing olives, making olive oil, and producing wine.

CHARLEMAGNE, A GOLDEN PERIOD

In 732 C.E., when Charles Martel, grandfather of Charlemagne, stopped the Muslim advance in Poitiers, the Latin word *mercator* (merchant) was already synonymous with *judaeus* (Jew). Jewish business relationships extended among the entire world then known, including the Arab Andalusia. When Charlemagne sent an ambassador to the Caliph of Baghdad, Isaac the Jew went as an interpreter. All the members of this expedition died on the five-year voyage except Isaac, who returned, causing a sensation with the caliph's gift of an elephant for Charlemagne.

Charlemagne extended special privileges to the Jews, who, as a result, lived comfortably, and were able to own farms and vineyards. The emperor encouraged them to move to the interior and north of what would become France. As international traders, Jewish merchants were the sole avenue whereby products like grain, salt, salted and dried fish, and spices reached France for the next few centuries. Since spices were easy to transport and produced a huge profit margin, they found their way through these Jewish traders to the Christian West. The historian Henri Pirenne comments on this period, "If the Jews were so favoured, it was only because they were indispensable."

At the time and probably earlier, a unique group of Jewish merchants, known as the Radhanites, emerged. First described by an Arab writer, Abu al-Kasim, they brought a revolutionary international trade network to France and beyond. Their four major trading routes began in the Rhône Valley of France or in Iraq, and ended in the silk route of India, Russia, and China, five hundred years before Marco Polo even traveled to the Orient. They traded products like papyrus, spices, textiles, wine, cinnamon, and olive oil.

Jewish physicians used the spices and foods they brought back to cure diseases and to balance the humors, considered in the ancient and medieval worlds as the four major elements of the human body. Charlemagne's son Louis the Pious made use of the doctors and ensured their elevated status in society; but the status didn't come without a price. Jews had to pay higher taxes and still enjoyed little protection in times of trouble.

In this early period, from the eighth to the eleventh century, centers of Jewish commerce and learning sprang up throughout France and present-day Germany. The most famous Talmudic scholar of this period was Rashi. His works are an outstanding example of the vitality of the Jewish communities in northern France in the eleventh century. And he led his son-in-laws, known as the Tosafists, whose approach to Talmudic analysis has shaped the way the Torah has been studied ever since. Through Rashi and the Tosafists we learn about the break between northern and southern French Jewish cooking, to be known later as Ashkenazic and Sephardic. Rashi's home in the wine-growing Champagne region became one of the most important centers of Jewish life in Europe. Rashi founded a religious school that today we might call a commune. His students helped tend his vineyards in order to study with him in the evenings.

Rashi's commentaries on the Talmud and the Torah give fascinating glimpses into the cooking of northern France during this period; he was a thinker who knew about both religion and agriculture. He condemned, for example, the force-feeding of geese to produce *foie gras* and excessive amounts of goose fat, which was essential to Jewish cooking in those days. "Israel will one day pay the price for these geese," he wrote, " . . . for having made these beasts suffer while fattening them." Jews in the south would have eaten salted cod, whereas Rashi would have eaten salted herring as an everyday dish. We know from his writings that Jews and everyone else ate vegetables like cabbage, cucumbers, asparagus, radishes, and turnips, in soups and stews. We also know that almonds were a big part of the diet. Pressed almonds, for instance, were made into a milky substance to drink and were used in sauces during the medieval period.

In addition, Rashi tells us a great deal about the production of another gift of France: wine. In his commentary on the Song of Songs, for example, he writes, "Let us get up early to the vineyards to see whether the vine has budded. . . ." It is evident from his work that Rashi took pleasure in the cultivation of his vines, and that by the eleventh century significant numbers of Jews were following suit, producing their own kosher wine.

Toward the end of Rashi's life, the First Crusade sparked outbursts of violence against Jews living in Metz and Rouen. Anti-Jewish prejudice built up slowly over the centuries. For example, Agobard, Archbishop of Lyon in the ninth century, wrote four epistles denouncing the privileges of the Jews. He led attempts to boycott Jewish-made wine and kosher meat and decried the changing of the Lyon market to Sunday to accommodate the Jews' religious prohibition against working on the Sabbath. Little by little, Jews became the victims of prejudice and violence. In 1171, thirty-two Jews were burned at the stake on the accusation that they had used Christian children's blood to bake matzo at Passover.

Despite these travails, the twelfth-century traveler Benjamin of Tudela, who took the first census of medieval Jewish communities, attested to large Jewish populations in France. He wrote in the *Itinerary of Benjamin of Tudela* that the ruling Jews of Narbonne possessed hereditary privileges and lands "of which no man can forcibly dispossess [them]." These Jewish princes were the descendants of the Jews Charlemagne had protected in the eighth century. The traveler ended his journey in 1173 in Paris and the Île-de-France, where he noted that there were 150 towns with Jews living in them.

> The kingdom of France, which is Zarfath, extends from the town of Auxerre unto Paris, the great city—a journey of six days. The city belongs to King Louis. It is situated on the river Seine. Scholars are there, unequaled in the whole world, who study the law day and night. They are charitable and hospitable to all travelers and are as brothers and friends unto all their brethren, the Jews. May God, the Blessed One, have mercy upon us and upon them!
>
> —*The Itinerary of Benjamin of Tudela*, 1173

THE FIRST EXPULSION OF THE JEWS AND THE JUIFS DU PAPE

As I strolled through the thousand-year-old market in Arles, in the shadow of the Roman theater and forum, I couldn't help thinking how rich Jewish life must have been in 1306, when, of the fifty-two butchers in the town, fourteen were kosher. Throughout the south of France during this period, rabbinic centers flourished where ideas and conversations were exchanged among rabbis in Spain and Morocco.

In Arles, Jews lived in a separate quarter from Christians and had a protected status. They were traders and were valued in the business community. Their prosperity is evident from the way they ate. According to Kalonymus ben Kalonymus, who described the everyday life of the Jews of Arles in the early fourteenth century, holiday dishes included round fried cakes, such as *soufganiyot* or doughnuts, made out of flour, served covered with jam for Hanukkah. Kalonymus also wrote charmingly about the grape harvest in Louis Stouff's *La Table Provençale.* "Everybody goes to the vineyard and transports grapes either by boat or by horses. The weather is very hot. Mosquitoes are numerous. They fall in the wine that we are drinking despite everything. . . ."

But, for the most part, the thirteenth and fourteenth centuries were dark times for Jews throughout France. The 1215 Lateran Council, with strong secular backing, decreed that all Jews wear round fabric badges designating their religion, and pointed yellow hats on their heads. In 1242, Louis IX had the Talmud and twenty thousand other books burned in Paris, and in 1288 a group of Jews was burned alive in Troyes. The culmination of these iniquities came in 1349, when the Jews were accused of causing the Black Death. In 1394, Jews were expelled from France, and "officially" no Jews lived there until after the Revolution.

During these dark times in Provence, many Jews left the country and went to Italy or Alsace. Others went east to Germany and Poland, invited by Casimir I. Some stayed in France and converted, like the family of Michel de Montaigne, the writer, and Michel de Nostredame, the famous seer known as Nostradamus. Called "neophytes" by the Christians, converted Jews were cut off completely from their families.

Even though the Jews had been expelled from the rest of France, the Popes of Avignon officially welcomed them to stay in the Comtat Venaissin, present-day Vaucluse, which includes Avignon, Carpentras, Cavaillon, and L'Isle-sur-la-Sorgue. They were allowed to work only in certain professions, as moneylenders, tailors, and sellers of *brocantes,* or secondhand furniture, something I was reminded of as I rambled through the towns, visiting the synagogues and what little remnants there still are of the Jewish quarters. Today you could not tell a Jew from anyone else in these towns. But in the fifteenth century and earlier, Jews were forced to live in a Jewish quarter and wear a yellow garment to indicate that they were Jewish. By 1650, as the church got stronger in the Comtat Venaissin, until 1790, Jews were locked into their quarter at eight o'clock each night.

The last remnant of the Jewish quarter in L'Isle-sur-la-Sorgue

The thousand so-called Juifs du Pape, or papal Jews, were allowed to live, work, and pray in Les Carrières, the cobblestoned Jewish quarters, like the one in Avignon, literally under the eyes of the popes, who lived in the enormous Palais des Papes just opposite. In return for the protection, they provided the popes with heavy taxes. In Carpentras, for example, in the year 1343, one of the taxes was six pounds of spices per year, three of ginger and three of pepper. They were allowed some measure of protection and safety until 1791, when civil rights were given to Jews, by this time numbering about twenty-five hundred in the Vaucluse, in the aftermath of the French Revolution.

SOUTHWEST AND THE PORTUGUESE MERCHANTS

As I flew into the port city of Bordeaux, I immediately sensed its importance as a center of the wine trade. Vineyards were everywhere, even at the airport. In the city center, with its green-tiled roofs, stood the remains of the *barrière Judaïza* (the Jewish quarter)—a reminder of the longevity of its Jewish community.

Although there were "officially" no Jews in the kingdom of France between 1420 and 1787, the so-called *marchands portugais,* who quietly practiced their Judaism, thrived in the southwest. These Jewish merchants originally migrated to the Iberian Peninsula ("Sefarad" in Hebrew) around the same time as the first Jews came to France. The two groups communicated with each other in French and Spanish Ladino.

A few of these Spanish and Portuguese Sephardic Jews came to Bordeaux, Bayonne, and other places in the southwest of France in the wake of the Inquisition. Their Jewish foods—such as the *cocido madrileño,* a soupy chickpea stew similar to *adafina,* the Moroccan Sephardic Sabbath dish—had been influenced by their long sojourn in Spain. Some of these Jews sailed with Columbus on his voyages, and helped introduce potatoes, chocolate, tomatoes, peppers, and beans to the Old World. Sephardic Jews who first went to the Balkans, Turkey, and especially North Africa had migrated to France in large numbers in the past two centuries. They, too, brought foods with them, such as yogurt, couscous dishes, and *tagines* that are now served on tables throughout France.

The first group to leave Spain and Portugal settled primarily in Saint-Esprit, across the river from Bayonne, and in Bordeaux. While some engaged in local commerce, others traded internationally, bringing, among other products, sugar, rum, and cocoa beans from the Americas to France. Their network reached from Amsterdam and London to the French islands in the Caribbean.

The influence of Jews can be felt in many of the classic dishes of the region. Luckily for me, a few of these Jews from Portugal have preserved their family recipes for *haroset,* chocolate tortes, and duck dishes to this day.

ALSACE-LORRAINE

Around 1000 C.E., another group of Jews settled in Ashkenaz, the valley between the Rhine River and the Vosges Mountains extending beyond into present-day Germany, and developed the Yiddish language, a corruption of German and Hebrew. While they settled there, a local Ashkenazic cuisine evolved that included Germanic-sounding dishes like kugel (g), *knödel* (g) or

Alsatian housewife preparing
for the Sabbath

knepfle (Al) (matzo balls), and *gehackte leber* (g) (chopped liver). With Hebrew remaining the language of prayer, they also spoke a Judeo-German dialect known as Yiddish, transcribed into Hebrew characters. Ashkenazic Jews trace their ancestry to this and other medieval Franco-German communities and their descendants in Europe. In later centuries, Jews from eastern Europe who had settled first in Alsace and Lorraine brought back eastern European variations of the kugels, Sabbath stews, and chopped liver they had taken with them from France hundreds of years earlier. After the French Revolution, when Jews became citizens of France, a huge wave moved mostly to Paris.

Le Juif en Alsace ne mange pas ce qu'il aime, il aime ce qu'il mange.
[The Jew in Alsace doesn't eat what he likes: he likes what he eats.]
—Alsatian Jewish saying

Although France bought Alsace in 1640, it reverted to Germany between 1870 and 1918 and again during World War II, until liberation in 1945. And it is from here, with names like Weil, Hausser, Cahen, and Dreyfus, that many of the old French Jewish families come.

I fell in love with the Alsace region of France, with its rolling farmlands and dense forests. For me, part of the allure was that the food is familiar, coming from the same Germanic roots as my own family's cooking, with its sauerkraut, *charcuterie,* and kuchen. There is such a long Jewish presence in the 150 villages of Alsace that, as one Alsatian told me, everyone here feels part Jewish.

LE IVIF·ERRANT

Since Jews were generally forbidden to own land, they became the go-betweens for the Christian populations. As elsewhere, they lent money, traded in cattle and grain, and raised geese. In towns of any appreciable size, salted, dried, and brined fishes were the stock in trade of "salt-fish mongers," or *herringers,* often Jewish merchants, distinct from purveyors of fresh local fish such as carp or perch.

The history became real to me as I passed through fields dotted with cattle and horses. The Jews here were country people, profoundly marked by rural influences. They were butchers, bakers, cattle dealers, and peddlers, traveling from village to village during the week, returning home only on the eve of the Sabbath, and setting off again once it was over. Their cuisine was rich in meat dishes such as *pickelfleisch,* liverwurst, and stuffed goose neck—dishes that used the less salable parts of the animal.

In almost every village, I saw vestiges of a vibrant Jewish past—a Jewish museum in Bouxwiller, an old synagogue with a *mikveh* in Bischheim, a Jewish cemetery outside of Colmar. By the time of the French Revolution, twenty thousand Jewish peddlers, cattle traders, bakers, butchers, and moneylenders lived in 179 villages throughout Alsace.

MODERN FRANCE

For hundreds of years prior to 1789, Jews lived in isolated pockets dispersed throughout the country. Then, in 1791, after the Revolution, they were granted civil rights and given full citizenship. The Napoleonic Code ensured these rights, setting up a Sanhedrin-like government of consistories, the ruling bodies of the Jewish community. Newly unfettered, Jews left the small villages and moved to Strasbourg, Colmar, Paris, and other cities where they could now live and work in professions opening up to them in the newly democratic nation. By 1831, Judaism was recognized as one of three religions supported by the state, along with Catholicism and Protestantism.

In this newly egalitarian country, Jews tried to become, at least outwardly, French. Many assumed French manners and the French way of eating, and took last names like Laurent, Picart, Bernard, or Garel. Nevertheless, no matter their outer French veneer, they knew and know that they are Jewish. And so do the people of France, which is still essentially a Catholic country.

> The Jewish heritage is love of freedom and love of good cooking.
>
> —Heinrich Heine*

Paris became a magnet for everybody in the new age of industrialization during the second part of the nineteenth century. But it has always had a special pull for Jews. In the late nineteenth century, the Jewish population increased immensely, accommodating Jews flocking in from the provinces and the more than one hundred thousand who came to France fleeing pogroms and the poverty of Russia, Poland, and Romania. In 1870, the Jewish population of Algeria received French citizenship, making it easy for them to leave Algeria for France.

The eastern Europeans brought with them dishes like eggplant caviar, blini or blintzes (familiar to the French as crêpes), and cheesecakes. Because they did not speak French very well, they had a hard time assimilating into the country. Even so, they took advantage of their newfound freedom and entered every profession, including the army. Many of them became furriers and sold hats, leather items, and *schmatteh*s.

A pivotal point in the history of the French Jews was the trial of Alfred Dreyfus, a young French captain of Jewish background on the general staff who was wrongly convicted of treason in November 1894. Dreyfus was first sentenced to life imprisonment, and then cleared of all charges. The case totally divided the French public. Writers like Émile Zola supported Dreyfus, whereas the painters Paul Cézanne and Edgar Degas railed against him. Despite endless controversy over the Dreyfus Affair, as it came to be called, eastern European Jews often said that a country like France, where you could talk openly about anti-Semitism, could not be very anti-Semitic. And, despite the bitterness of the controversy, by the early part of the twentieth century, Jews played a role in every part of the French economy and society.

> *Lebn vi got in Frankraykh.* [Live like God in France.]
>
> —Yiddish saying

The French surrendered quickly after the German invasion in 1940. Before German laws were even in place, the Vichy government rounded up Jews and sent them to deportation camps throughout the country, often camps that had housed refugees from the Spanish Civil War. In all, out of about 350,000 Jews in France, 83,000 were deported, 75,000 of whom were killed at

*Heine never really said, "The Jewish heritage is love of freedom and love of good cooking." Those are his sentiments but not his words. Heine understood Judaism as both a "love of freedom" (*Confessions*) and "an appreciation of good cooking" (Rabbi of Bacherach, Princess Sabath, letter to Moder).

Eating soup at a French detention camp

camps like Auschwitz. Only about 6,000 of the deported Jews came back to rebuild their lives, joining the larger number who had fled France during the war or were hidden by French gentiles throughout the country.

> We had the most severe rationing in Europe, more than Poland, in fact. . . . The food problem became so difficult that it became the main thing of every day. I killed cats to eat them. I killed birds with my sling. I was really a good marksman with my slingshot.
>
> —Oral history at the Holocaust Museum
> of French sculptor Armand

It took about twenty years for people to start admitting to the horrors of World War II. In fact, when I was a student in France in the mid-1960s, there was no public discourse about the German occupation of France under Vichy. It was the student riots at the Sorbonne in 1968 that unleashed discussions about the war years. Three years later, Marcel Ophuls's approximately four-and-a-half-hour documentary *The Sorrow and the Pity* was followed by Robert Paxton's pathbreaking book *Vichy France: Old Guard and New Order, 1940–1944,* in which he argued that Vichy collaboration with Germany was a voluntary program. In 1985, Claude Lanzmann's epic *Shoah,* a nine-hour documentary of the Holocaust, opened up more discussion: so did the 1987 trial of Klaus Barbie, known as the Butcher of Lyon, who helped the Gestapo murder thousands of French Jews.

After World War II, as the colonies of Algeria and subsequently Morocco and Tunisia declared independence, about 250,000 Jews migrated to France from North Africa, almost doubling the Jewish population. Although the North Africans had an easier time than their eastern European predecessors assimilating into French culture because they spoke French, the established French Jews were hesitant to accept them. The North African Jews' openness about their religion, their support for the State of Israel, and their observance of the dietary laws created discomfort among the older French Jewish population.

Chez Bebert, a North African Jewish favorite

As the second generation of North African Jewry has integrated into Jewish life, their presence has given a positive boost to the entire French Jewish community. Marseille, for example, has bounced back from the destruction of World War II to became home to the second-largest Jewish population in France. North African as well as other Jews have moved to new areas of Paris and its suburbs and redefined traditional Jewish neighborhoods, like the Grands Boulevards, the Ninth Arrondissement, and Rue des Rosiers in the Marais. In addition, Lubavitchers and other Hasidic sects have come to France, directing Orthodox schools and kosher restaurants and grocery stores. They supervise kosher runs at wine, cheese, and other facilities throughout France.

Life in France is very different than it was during my student days in the 1960s, when Jews whose families had been there for generations were still in the majority. As their children intermarry with the newcomers and become more and more adventurous about trying different recipes, there is a new and exciting openness in the Jewish population, and in its cooking.

As elsewhere in the world, many traditional recipes are dying out with the older generation, and the youth are spending less time cooking. So I have felt a sense of urgency in trying to recapture these recipes and their stories as the people who cooked them remember them, and to explore their origins.

Since traditional dishes are the last to disappear within a culture, it is usually holiday foods within families that survive even after the language and music have gone. A meal might start with *brik,* progress to a Tunisian meatball couscous for the main course, and end with a French tart for dessert. With more and more intermarriage between Ashkenazic and Sephardic Jews, cross-cultural menus are becoming the norm. But Sephardic cooking, with its emphasis on tasty salads and stews of vegetables, fruit, and meat, is particularly appealing to most families all across France.

Thus, in today's France, as elsewhere in the world, Jewish food is truly an expression of culinary globalism.

"The" falafel joint in the Marais

Kashrut (the Jewish Dietary Laws) and Their Place in French Culture

■

Kosher foods in France fall under the jurisdiction of certifying agencies with rabbinical supervision, similar in purpose to the Orthodox Union in America. Except for Lubavitch, which operates throughout France, most supervision is regional. Each Beth Din, or rabbinical body, is responsible for a region, overseeing the production and distribution of kosher foods, keeping track of the products, and providing certification for kosher shops and restaurants. The rabbis make sure that the laws of kashrut are strictly followed.

Kashrut is the body of Jewish dietary laws outlining which foods can be eaten and how they should be prepared. Observant Jews are permitted to eat meat only from an animal that has cloven hooves and chews its cud. This permits eating the meat of cows, sheep, and goats, and excludes rabbits, horses, dogs, cats, and—of course—pigs. Edible fowl includes turkeys, chickens, geese, and duck, but not birds of prey. In addition, kashrut-observing Jews may eat only fish having both fins and scales, excluding all shellfish.

The book of Leviticus specifies how an animal must be slaughtered. A *shochet,* a ritual slaughterer, makes a quick stroke across the throat with a knife that is perfectly smooth and very sharp, so that the animal does not suffer. The *shochet,* after the kill, ensures that the animal is healthy by examining the lungs and meat for certain types of lesions, cuts, and bruises. Since the Torah absolutely prohibits the consumption of blood, which represents life, the meat must, after the animal is killed, go through a process called *melihah,* in which it is soaked, salted, and then washed again, so that no blood remains. The hindquarters cannot be used unless certain nerves and blood vessels are excised. For the same reason, eggs must be inspected to make sure they do not contain blood spots. The term "*glatt* kosher" refers to meat from animals with smooth, defect-free lungs. Today the very Orthodox also use the term to define extremely strictly processed kosher foods.

Milchig (dairy or dairy products) must be cooked and eaten separately from *fleishig* (meat) dishes, because three times in Exodus and Deuteronomy the Hebrew Bible states that a kid cannot be cooked in its mother's milk. This separation has been gradual. In Rashi's day in northern France, for example, it was specified that milk and meat be eaten with separate spoons, but not from separate plates, as today. To make sure that meat and milk are kept separate, some Jews have two dishwashers and two sets of pots, utensils, and dishes, each of which is used exclusively for either milk or meat meals—and some maintain two entirely separate kitchens.

Pareve (neutral) food, such as fish, eggs, vegetables, nuts, and grains, may be eaten with either milk or meat. I have indicated just above the list of ingredients for each recipe whether the dish is dairy (D), meat (M), or *pareve* (P).

In ritually observant homes, no cooking is permitted on the Sabbath, the day of rest. This rule inspired robust stews, and side dishes like puddings, that could be prepared in advance and allowed to simmer for a long time over a low flame, or in a low oven all night long.

Throughout the years, just as today, Jews have varied greatly in their degree of observance. Although many French Jews do not follow the Jewish dietary laws in their homes, they seem to follow strictly the prohibition against pork.

France being France, and French bread being French bread, the Beth Din consider most French baguettes kosher, since they contain neither milk nor meat. Some very observant Jews reject industrial baguettes, baked in basket molds, and accept only baguettes baked directly on the stones of hearth ovens—and a religious Jew must supervise the lighting of such an oven.

Today Orthodox Jews are producing kosher versions of most regional French cheeses and bringing kosher cooking to the populace through grocery stores and fine-dining restaurants.

Unlike the United States, France has practically no purely kosher food factories. For example, a quenelle factory outside of Lyon, a mustard factory in Dijon, and three *pain-azyme* (unleavened-bread or matzah) factories, one in Agen and two outside of Strasbourg, clean the facilities to make occasional kosher and kosher-for-Passover product runs, supervised by religious Jews who observe the Sabbath and holidays.

Though I have taken all practical measures to assure that these recipes fulfill the requirements of kashrut, it is of course incumbent upon readers to ascertain for themselves that these standards are fully met. Within the many observant communities, there are different views on the dietary laws. Accordingly, although rabbinic authorities have been consulted in the preparation of this text, the ultimate responsibility for ascertaining any particular recipe's conformity with kashrut rests with the reader.

A Note on Kosher Wine

Because France is such a grape-growing country, wine stands front and center. For the past two thousand years, since the first Jews settled there, they have produced kosher wine for themselves. In the olden days, when Jews bought or grew grapes and made their wine at home, there was no question that the wine was kosher, because you knew who was producing it.

To make kosher wine today, however, rabbis specifically trained to be *mashgichim* (kosher supervisors) must take full control of the still-unfermented juice from the first moment of crushing grapes. It is not enough to be Sabbath-observant. Typically, only the rabbis and rabbinical students whose level of piety can be vouched for are permitted to touch the juice.

Kosher law dictates that no animal products or other nonkosher ingredients may be used in the processing. Chlorine or even alcohol, rather than soap, an animal product, is often used to clean the tanks, but practice differs by winery.

Unlike in the United States and Israel, where wineries are either kosher or nonkosher, France has kosher runs at nonkosher wineries, a practice dating at least as far back as the sixteenth century. The head rabbi of each winegrowing region supervises the process. The wines are marketed with the label of the château plus an indication of kashrut. During the eleventh century, making kosher wine was easier. Sages like Rashi, who were also vintners, studied when they were not tending their grapes, and their students helped them make the wine, whose quality and kashrut were known. Nobody needed a kosher seal of approval. Since Jews, who made fine wine, could not own land, they gave part of their wine to the landowner and kept and sold the rest.

Lubavitcher kosher-wine helpers pause to eat lunch in their makeshift *sukkah* in Saint-Émilion.

Because I wanted to see how kosher wine is made in France, I accompanied Claude Maman, the Grand Rabbi of Bordeaux, to several wineries in Médoc and Saint-Émilion that were producing kosher wine. "It wasn't until the 1980s that Jews in France wanted good kosher wine," the rabbi told me as we drove through Saint-Émilion. "In the 1970s, Jews weren't into the culture of wine and wanted to be reassured of quality, so we used known brands, like Perrier-Jouët, as a good quality of champagne. Now they want Margaux, Sauternes, Bordeaux from Médoc, Saint-Émilion, and Pauillac."

Each year, a kosher wine distributor has an oenologist select the wine for kosher runs. That is why we were at Château Bel Air, the vineyard of Philippe Moysson, a grower for twenty years in Saint-Émilion. Until the fall of 2007, Monsieur Moysson had never produced or tasted kosher wine. Because the closely supervised process involving kosher specialists costs a third more, the higher cost of the wine is financially advantageous for the vintner. In recent years there has been a glut of wine in France. Many winemakers have found the kosher market a good avenue to move their excess grape products.

The rabbi and the winemaker taking a cell-phone break from negotiating a kosher-wine run

One condition for making kosher wine is the assurance from the vintner that the quality is as good as that of his nonkosher wine. In the contract to make a certain number of bottles, the vineyard must oversee its production, but it is the rabbi and his assistants who actually do the physical work, with the winemaker there every step of the way.

I visited Château Bel Air in the fall, right in the middle of four days of Jewish holidays—the end of Sukkot, Simchat Torah, and the Sabbath—when production stopped, with the process of fermentation slowed down with artificial ice. This also means that no one can touch the wine— i.e., taste it—for the four days of the Jewish holidays. Despite all these difficulties, we tasted the resulting wine, and found it delicious. Kosher wine, thanks to the French, has come a long way since the story told in Genesis of Noah: "And Noah began to be a husbandman, and he planted a vineyard: and he drank of the wine and was drunken" (Genesis 9:20–21).

Ducks in the Dordogne, the center of *foie-gras* production

Appetizers

Flavored Olives

North African *Brik* with Tuna and Cilantro

Algerian Swiss Chard *Bestel*s, or Turnovers

Harissa (Tunisian Hot Chili Sauce)

Eggplant Caviar

Terrine de Poireaux (Leek Terrine)

Croûte aux Champignons (Wild Mushroom Crusty)

Haroset from Bordeaux

A Thirteenth-Century Provençal *Haroset*

Moroccan *Haroset* Truffles with Almonds and Fruits

Herring with Mustard Sauce

Mango Chutney for *Pâté de Foie Gras*

Françoise's *Foie Haché* (Chopped Liver with a Confit of Onions)

French Chopped Liver Pâté

Buckwheat Blini with Smoked Salmon and Crème Fraîche

Le Monde des Épices

THE WORLD OF SPICES

Many years ago in Paris I discovered Le Monde des Épices, a tiny shop on the Rue François-Miron, near the Marais, which was traditionally the city's Jewish section and is today a hip area overrun with fashion boutiques. As the years pass, this food emporium seems to get better and better. Inside, signs written on cracked pieces of pottery label burlap sacks filled with bulgur for tabbouleh and barrels overflowing with homemade preserved lemons from Morocco.

Israël Solski in his world of spices

There are olives marinated with a variety of pungent flavors—orange peel, fresh garlic, kumquats, cranberries, parsley, Indian Tellicherry pepper, and star anise from Asia.

Whenever I visit, the owner, Israël Solski, a Polish immigrant who looks much like Tevye in *Fiddler on the Roof,* surprises me with new gastronomic treasures. A photographer who came to Paris after World War II, Solski married into the business started by his father-in-law, Samuel Izraël, in 1945.

In the postwar years, the shop catered to a large Jewish clientele, mostly made up of eastern European refugees who came for the homemade pickles. When I first discovered the store, in 1964, it was frequented by recent emigrants from Algeria, Tunisia, and Morocco. Spices like cumin and coriander were completely new to me then. Today most people who walk in don't have a clue that it is a Jewish store; it caters to all lovers of exotic cuisine. The spices themselves illustrate a colorful history of food in France, a history that stretches back for centuries.

Flavored Olives

AT LE MONDE DES ÉPICES, I delight in seeing how simple olives can be turned into a colorful appetizer by melding different kinds and colors of cured olives and doctoring them up with garlic, preserved lemons, oregano, and basil, and serving them in a large, clear bowl. Although the majority of the olives in the shop are grown in Spain and North Africa, many, like the tiny Picholines from Provence, come from the south of France. When I first visited, the olives were simply cured and kept in barrels. Now the many different-flavored varieties are displayed in attractive bowls to tempt the customers.

When doctoring up olives you buy, just make sure to include some red peppers, orange kumquats, or bright-green herbs. I love to serve a variety of sizes and kinds in a clear glass or earthenware bowl. Remember to have a tiny bowl nearby for the pits.

Place the olives and some of their juice in a clear glass bowl.

Stir in the orange zest or kumquat, the cranberries, the mixed herbs, and the cinnamon stick. Serve immediately, or keep in the refrigerator and eat at your leisure.

 YIELD: 2 CUPS

1 pound mixed olives with
  their juice
1 handful of orange zest or
  thin slivers of kumquat
1 handful of dried cranberries
1 cup chopped mixed fresh
  herbs, such as parsley, dill,
  basil, cilantro, and mint
1 cinnamon stick

Fruit and herbs brighten up the salty flavor of olives.

NOTE   You can vary this mix by adding to it six cloves garlic, peeled and kept whole; six red peppercorns, or a few hot red peppers cut into small pieces; or the diced rind of half a preserved lemon (see page 171).

A Cultural Evening with the Jews
of Saint-Rémy-de-Provence

It was Friday, and I was visiting the Provençal town of Saint-Rémy-de-Provence, a big center of Jewish life and learning in the thirteenth and fourteenth centuries, when Jews were merchants, transporting wine and olive oil down the Rhône to the Mediterranean and bringing back spices and silks. The only reminder of this past greatness is the town's fourteenth-century Jewish cemetery, which has two bright-blue Jewish stars emblazoned on the doors.

This cemetery is all that is left of the vibrant Jewish community of the fourteenth century in Saint-Rémy.

That Friday night, a friend brought me to a meeting of the Association Culturelle Juive des Alpilles, an organization created to spread Jewish tradition within the community, which today doesn't even have a synagogue. That night's Sabbath dinner was to be hosted by Algerian-born Hubert and Jocelyne Akoun, who live on the outskirts of town in their charming stucco home, which doubles as a bed-and-breakfast. It was clear that Jocelyne loved every aspect of cooking. Two freezers were stocked with carefully marked dishes: couscous, tomato sauce, roasted peppers. Her summer canning kitchen, built by her husband and located outside, near the swimming pool, held jars for all the preserves and tomato sauces she would make when peppers, tomatoes, and peaches were ripe. To get the best prices on fruits and vegetables, she bought them at the end of the day at the local farmers' markets.

Our dinner, served on the salmon-colored marble sideboard in her kitchen, began with *brik,* a typical North African turnover. It was filled with tuna, hard-boiled egg, and cilantro. I had never tasted *brik* as good as Jocelyne's. The food kept coming: couscous, cooked tomato salad served in little pastry cups, meatballs—some bathed in a tomato sauce (see page 226), others in a sweet raisin-and-onion sauce—eggplant salads, and almond *brik* turnovers dipped in honey for dessert.

"This is typical *pied-noir* food," said Hubert, referring to the French nationals living in Algeria before Algeria's independence. The term *pied-noir* has two possible origins: some say it refers to the fact that white Frenchmen's feet had touched African soil; others say it refers to the distinctive black boots worn by the French living in Algeria. "Unlike the *pieds-noirs,* Jews were in North Africa before the Arabs," Hubert said. "Some Jews arrived there when the first temple in Jerusalem was destroyed and have lived there ever since." Others were converted Berbers or came from Spain during the Inquisition.

As we were leaving, Jocelyne handed us jars of preserves to take back to the United States. When we thanked the Akouns for their hospitality, Jocelyne stopped for a moment and said, "I believe that we are the last generation that will cook like this." I certainly hope not.

Jocelyne Akoun preparing *brik*

North African *Brik* with Tuna and Cilantro

BRIK ARE CRISP, FLAKY APPETIZERS found in Tunisian, Algerian, and Moroccan kitchens in France. The word refers to the dough, similar to the Moroccan *warka,* which one makes by tossing fistfuls of a wet, pastelike batter onto a hot grill. The batter miraculously spreads into a thin, pliable sheet, which may be used as an appetizer or dessert wrapper.

You can find unbaked *feuilles de brik* (*brik* leaves) in Middle Eastern food stores or online (see A Source Guide, page 370). If you can't, use wonton wrappers instead, or even phyllo dough, although your finished product will not have the same grainy texture as real *brik.*

I often make these filled pastries as an appetizer at Hanukkah, instead of potato pancakes.

 YIELD: 48 *BRIK*

Two 6-ounce cans tuna in
   olive oil
2 hard-boiled eggs, diced
1 cup finely chopped fresh
   cilantro
1 small onion, finely diced
   (about ½ cup)
2 tablespoons crème fraîche or
   sour cream
1 tablespoon pine nuts
Salt and freshly ground pepper
   to taste
1 package *brik* leaves cut into
   5-inch squares or 5-inch
   wonton wrappers
1 egg, beaten
Peanut or vegetable oil for
   frying
Harissa for dipping (see
   page 33)

Put the tuna (I prefer the Cento brand of tuna, which is certified kosher) in a mixing bowl, and break it up with a fork. Fold in the hard-boiled eggs, cilantro, onion, crème fraîche or sour cream, pine nuts, and salt and freshly ground pepper. Taste, and adjust seasonings.

Place a teaspoon of the filling along one side of each wrapper. Using your finger, brush the edges of the wrapper with the beaten egg and fold over to enclose the filling. Roll up the package like a jelly roll, sealing by pinching the edges with the beaten egg wash to enclose the filling, pinching the ends together and removing as much air as possible. Put all the turnovers on a baking sheet, and refrigerate or freeze until ready to fry.

Heat at least 2 inches of oil in a wok or large sauté pan until the oil reaches about 375 degrees. Fry the *brik* in batches for 1 to 2 minutes on each side, or until golden. Drain on a paper towel and serve immediately, with a dab of *harissa* on top, or with a bowl of *harissa* alongside for dipping.

NOTE To make potato *brik,* boil 2 pounds of baking potatoes in salted water until tender. Drain and mash them, and mix with ½ cup chopped fresh parsley and one small finely diced white onion. Stir in two diced hard-boiled eggs and salt and pepper to taste.

NOTE To make egg *brik,* place a large *brik* wrapper on a plate. Sprinkle some tuna and diced parsley on top. Then break an egg in the center, quickly fold the wrapper in half, and slide into the hot oil. Serve with *harissa* (see page 33) and preserved lemon (see page 171).

Algerian Swiss Chard *Bestel*s, or Turnovers

ONCE, WHILE VISITING Le Monde des Épices (see page 26), I asked the owner which Jewish cookbook in his large selection he especially liked. His favorite one at the time was *150 Recettes et Mille et Un Souvenirs d'une Juive d'Algérie (150 Recipes and 1,001 Memories of an Algerian Jewish Woman)* by Léone Jaffin, one of the steady stream of North African Jewish cookbooks since the 1970s. This book includes such unusual recipes as these Swiss-chard *bestel*s, traditionally eaten on Rosh Hashanah. North African Jews frequently use the bright-green leaves of beets or Swiss chard, called *blette*. A prayer is recited over the vegetable, called *salek* in Hebrew, meaning to remove or throw out, with the hope that in the coming year enemies will be removed from the community's midst. I have added curry powder, pine nuts, and currants to this tasty turnover, which I sometimes serve with salad as a first course.

YIELD: ABOUT 36 *BESTELS*

2 pounds Swiss chard, beet, or spinach greens, washed and dried

¼ cup pine nuts

2 hard-boiled eggs, mashed

¼ cup currants

1 teaspoon curry powder

½ teaspoon allspice

¼ teaspoon ground cinnamon

Salt and freshly ground pepper to taste

Thirty-six 2-inch wonton wrappers

Peanut or vegetable oil for frying

If the Swiss chard or spinach leaves are small, leave them whole. Otherwise, remove and discard the stems and rough-chop the green leaves. Blanch the leaves for 15 seconds in boiling, salted water. Drain completely, pressing to get rid of any excess water.

Brown the pine nuts in a hot pan for a few minutes. Then mix the leaves with the hard-boiled eggs, the currants, and the pine nuts. Season with the curry, allspice, cinnamon, and salt and pepper to taste.

Place a tablespoon of the stuffing in the center of each wrapper. Moisten the edges with water, fold into a triangle, and crimp the edges with the tines of a fork. Put all the turnovers on a baking sheet lined with wax paper, and refrigerate or freeze until ready to fry.

Heat 2 inches of peanut or vegetable oil in a wok until it reaches about 375 degrees. Fry about five *bestels* at a time on both sides, about 2 minutes on each side, until golden. Drain on paper towels and serve immediately.

NOTE   You can also substitute prepared puff pastry, baking the *bestels* at 350 degrees for 20 minutes. If you like it spicier, add a tablespoon or two of *harissa* (recipe follows) to the filling.

Harissa

(TUNISIAN HOT CHILI SAUCE)

A SIGN OF THE POPULARITY of North African food in France is this hot sauce, which is now prepared and sold in open-air markets and grocery stores throughout the country. In Tunisia, Morocco, and Algeria, the recipes vary slightly from village to village. I have seen it used today in salads, in *bourride*, in *rouille*, and in soups.

Cut the stems from the peppers, remove half the seeds, and soak the peppers in warm water until soft; drain, and squeeze out any excess water. Then grind the peppers—either as North African Jews do, in a meat grinder, or in a food processor using the steel blade with ¼ cup of the olive oil, the garlic cloves, cumin, coriander, and salt. The consistency should be that of a thick purée, and the color bright red. Place in a jar, pour the remaining olive oil over the *harissa,* cover, and refrigerate.

Let sit for a few days before using, until the *harissa* becomes less opaque. Use sparingly, because it is very hot.

P YIELD: ABOUT 1 CUP

2 ounces dried hot red chili peppers, such as tiny New Mexican ones or cayennes

½ cup extra-virgin olive oil, plus more as needed

7 or 8 cloves garlic, peeled

½ teaspoon ground cumin

½ teaspoon ground coriander

1 teaspoon coarse salt, or to taste

NOTE A great source for prepared *harissa* is Pereg Gourmet Spices (pereg-spices.com).

Eggplant Caviar

THE FRENCH CALL THIS APPETIZER *caviar d'aubergine* because the feel of the eggplant seeds on your tongue is similar in texture to that of fish eggs. A delicious and easy-to-prepare dish, it has been in the French Jewish repertoire since at least the turn of the last century, when Romanian immigrants introduced the French to their ways of grilling the eggplant with its dark skin intact, a technique learned in the Middle East via the Caucasus. At about the same time, Russian and Romanian immigrants also brought this so-called poor man's caviar with them to France.

Whereas earlier generations used a hand chopper to make this dish, often blending in either lemon juice and olive oil or tomatoes and green peppers, today most cooks pulse it in a food processor. Although it is easier to roast the eggplants in the oven, oven-roasting will not give you the smoky flavor that comes from grilling over an open flame. This is a recipe to play with. Add diced onion, cilantro, or paprika, if you wish, or a few tablespoons of grapefruit juice or even mayonnaise. I have tasted all kinds of eggplant caviar. The last was at a very upscale French Bat Mitzvah, where the eggplant, laced with pesto, spiced with cumin, and decorated with tiny pansies, was served in an eggshell at the kiddush after the service.

 YIELD: ABOUT 2 CUPS,
OR 6 TO 8 SERVINGS

3 small eggplants (about
  2 pounds), tops removed
⅓ cup extra-virgin olive oil,
  plus more if roasting in
  the oven
Juice of 1½ to 2 lemons
Salt and freshly ground pepper
  to taste

If grilling over a gas stove, make small slits all over the eggplants. Using tongs, hold them over the open flame, rotating them every few minutes, until they are soft and collapsed. If roasting the eggplants in the oven, prick them and put them, cut side down, on a baking sheet. Roast in a preheated 450-degree oven for about 20 minutes, or until very soft.

Put the cooked eggplant in a wooden bowl, and set aside to cool. Peel, discarding the skin and any liquid that has accumulated.

Using a food processor fitted with a steel blade, pulse the eggplant with the olive oil, the lemon juice, salt, and freshly ground pepper in short spurts until blended but still slightly chunky.

Serve as a dip to be eaten with pieces of French *pain de campagne* or with cut-up raw vegetables.

NOTE For a variation from Fez, cut the raw eggplants in half lengthwise. Make a slit in the cut side of each half, and insert an unpeeled clove of garlic in each slit. Brush the cut side with olive oil, place on a baking sheet, cut side down, and roast, along with three red peppers, in a preheated 350-degree oven for 30 minutes, or until the eggplants are very soft and the peppers are charred. Let cool in a bowl, then peel the eggplants and the peppers, discarding the skin and any liquid that has accumulated. Squeeze the garlic cloves from their skin. In a food processor fitted with a steel blade, purée the eggplants, peppers, and garlic along with 2 tablespoons olive oil, 2 teaspoons sweet paprika, ½ teaspoon cumin, and salt, freshly ground pepper, and hot red pepper to taste.

Eggplant caviar served in eggshells at a French Bat Mitzvah

Bain de Marie la Juive

■

I always knew a *bain-marie* as a simmering water bath in which you put a custard or terrine to cook slowly and gently in the oven. To my surprise, I recently learned that the original name was *bain de Marie la Juive,* named after a third-century Greek Jewish alchemist who is said to have invented this process of tempering the heat by water to use in hearth cooking. To achieve this effect, she used metal and glass held together with wax, grease, and a glue made of rice or wheat flour, water, and a little oil of bitter almonds. Today, *bain-marie,* without the addition of *la Juive,* refers to both the technique and the water bath. The German philosopher Albert le Grand (Albrect von Böllstädt) described the process for the first time in the thirteenth century.

Marie la Juive is also identified with Miriam, who was the sister of Moses. At some feminist Passover Seders today, a Cup of Miriam, filled with water, is put on the table next to the traditional Cup of Elijah, filled with wine, to remind Jews of Miriam's well of precious water, which, according to a Midrash, accompanied the Israelites on their journey through the desert to the promised land.

Terrine de Poireaux

(LEEK TERRINE)

"THERE IS NO SUCH THING as Jewish Alsatian cooking. It is Alsatian cooking," Chef Gilbert Brenner told me over lunch at his restaurant, Wistub Brenner, with a view over the Lauch River in Colmar, a charming city in southern Alsace that has had a Jewish presence since at least the eleventh century. "Jewish cooks adapted the dietary laws to what was available here," Monsieur Brenner told me. "France didn't create dishes. Families created the dishes. It is the cooking of their grandparents and great-grandparents."

Looking over the menu at Brenner's popular restaurant, I was taken by this extraordinary leek terrine, which I later learned was put on the menu for Gilbert's Jewish customers and friends who keep kosher or are vegetarians. During the short asparagus season in the spring, Gilbert substitutes asparagus for the leeks. The recipe is a modern version of very old savory bread puddings, like *schaleths* (see page 251).

YIELD: 8 TO 10 SERVINGS

2 tablespoons unsalted butter, plus more for greasing

3 or 4 small leeks, white and light-green parts only, roots trimmed (1 pound)

½ pound morels, *trompettes de la mort,* or conventional button mushrooms, diced (3 cups)

1⅓ tablespoons salt, plus more to taste

¼ teaspoon pepper, plus more to taste

1 cup milk

5 ounces white bread

4 large eggs

1 cup heavy cream or half-and-half

Preheat the oven to 350 degrees. Grease a 5-by-12-inch or 4-by-10-inch terrine pan, and then line it with plastic wrap.

Bring a pot half full of water with a tablespoon of salt to a boil, add the leeks, and boil for 10 minutes, or until fork-tender. Remove them gently from the water, and plunge them into ice water for about 10 minutes. Drain well, pat very dry, and cut the leeks in half lengthwise.

Sauté the mushrooms in the butter in a small frying pan, seasoning them with salt and pepper to taste, until they are golden brown—about 5 minutes. Spread half the cooked mushrooms and any remaining butter evenly in the bottom of the prepared terrine.

Pour the milk into a large bowl. Dip the bread in the milk and squeeze gently to remove the excess liquid. Place the bread, the eggs, the cream, 1 teaspoon salt, ¼ teaspoon pepper, the nutmeg, and the cayenne pepper in the bowl of a food processor equipped with the steel blade. Purée until creamy and uniform, and pour about a third of the mixture into the terrine. Press half of the leeks gently lengthwise into the terrine, cover with another third of the batter, and scatter on the remaining mushrooms. Repeat, using up the remaining leeks and remaining batter.

Cover the terrine with aluminum foil, and place it in a baking pan filled with enough boiling water to come halfway up the sides of the terrine. Bake for about 60 minutes, or until set and no longer wobbly in the center. Once it is cool enough to handle, unmold the terrine by flipping it over onto a serving plate. Slice, and serve warm or at room temperature. You can also cut the terrine into about ten slices in the mold. Then, when ready to serve, just microwave the slices and serve on individual plates.

¼ teaspoon grated nutmeg
Dash of cayenne pepper

NOTE To substitute asparagus for the leeks, boil sixteen large spears in salted water until bright green and barely cooked through. Remove the asparagus from the water, and plunge them into ice water for about 10 minutes. Drain the asparagus and pat them dry, then cut them to fit in the terrine. Cover half of the asparagus with the batter, and proceed as with leeks.

Leek terrine ready for the oven

Croûte aux Champignons

(WILD MUSHROOM CRUSTY)

YVES ALEXANDRE, WHO WAS BORN and raised in Paris, now lives in Strasbourg, where his family's roots go back to 1760. When he is not on the road for his job as a traveling salesman, he does most of the cooking at home. A virtual oral dictionary of gastronomy and French Jewish history, Yves kindly shepherded me around Alsace, where he showed me extraordinary vestiges of a very long past, which went back in some instances to the Roman legions' trip over the Alps and through Lugano, perhaps during the Battle of Bibracte, in the winter of 59–58 B.C.E. It was here that Caesar's army defeated the Helvetii, who were trying to migrate from Switzerland to Aquitaine, in the southwest of France.

Like every Frenchman, Yves cooks by the seasons. This autumn dish, which he prepares when *cèpes* (generally known in the United States by their Italian name, porcini) are in season, can be made any time of the year using whatever mushrooms are available. Serve it as an appetizer, or as a main course over pasta with a salad. You can also use dried morels or dried porcini, soaking them first in warm water for about 30 minutes. Yves warns not to throw away the liquid. "Just filter the liquid, and reduce it to enhance the taste," he told me. When fresh porcini are hard to find, Yves likes using a mix of St. George's mushrooms (fairy-ring mushrooms) and young *pied-de-mouton* mushrooms, a native species that he buys at farmers' markets or gathers in the forests.

D YIELD: AT LEAST 36 SERVINGS AS AN APPETIZER, OR 4 TO 6 AS A MAIN COURSE WITH A SALAD

1 tablespoon vegetable oil
1 tablespoon unsalted butter
1 large shallot, diced
2 pounds fresh seasonal mushrooms, such as porcini, morels, chanterelles, oyster, Paris, or button mushrooms, trimmed and coarsely chopped
Salt and freshly ground pepper to taste

½ cup dry white wine, either Muscadet or Riesling
1 cup heavy cream
1 baguette or *pain de campagne* (French country bread similar to American sourdough), thinly sliced
2 tablespoons finely chopped fresh chives

Heat the vegetable oil and the butter in a medium-sized saucepan, and sauté the shallot very briefly, just until transparent. Add the mushrooms, and cook just until the liquid they release has cooked away. Season with salt and pepper to taste, and remove from the pan to a plate.

Pour the wine into the pan, bring to a boil, and deglaze, reducing the wine by half. Return the mushrooms to the pan, add the cream, and bring to a simmer. Adjust the seasonings to taste.

Meanwhile, toast the bread slices until crispy. Spoon the mushrooms over the bread, and sprinkle with the chives.

Beautiful chanterelle mushrooms

Portuguese Merchants

When I telephoned Hélène Alvarez-Pereyre Sancy, a Sephardic Jew and one of the last members of the *marchands portugais* (New Christians), who have lived in Bordeaux since after the expulsion of the Jews from Spain in 1492, the first thing she said to me was that she knew lots about the cooking of the Portuguese Jews but she was guarding her recipes for her children. I met her anyway, at her home, an early-twentieth-century row house with Art Deco windows, near the Rue Judaïque (Jewish Street) in Bordeaux, a wonderful bourgeois port city. Madame Sancy, a retired teacher of Greek and Latin, has adorned this house with the dark furniture, marvelous brass chandeliers, and pieces of Judaica that she inherited from her parents. The décor only added atmosphere to the stories of the past that she told me.

Hélène and Henri Sancy at home with their handwritten Haggadah

Every Jewish family in France has a story, but Madame Sancy, who was born in Bayonne, has tales that range from the far past, when her ancestors came to France from Amsterdam in 1740, to the near past, when France was occupied by the Nazis.

She told me that her father was a rabbi in Bayonne. At her parents' wedding in 1924, all the townspeople gathered around to see her father, the Alvarez Tre Père or "Priest of the Jews," get married. When her family had to flee the Germans during World War II, her father took a small suitcase with only his *tallith* (prayer shawl), shofar, prayer books, and soil from the holy land. Along the way, as they were talking among themselves about which road to take, an old lady came out of her house, listened to them, and told them not to go to the right. "Go straight," she said. "Otherwise, you will run right into the Germans."

"We didn't know if this was a trap or not, but we listened to her," Madame Sancy told me. They found out later that, indeed, had they gone to the right, they would have headed straight to the Germans and perished like three-quarters of the Jews of Bordeaux. From July 1942 until the end of the war, Madame Sancy hid with her parents, from time to time changing communities. "At the beginning, my father led prayers openly in a big room in Agen, a town south of Bordeaux, because it wasn't necessary to hide in the southwest. When we had to hide, I became, officially, the niece of the peasants. When they saw something happen, they would tap on the window to let us know.

"In 1944, when the Germans came, the police chief told my aunt, 'I can't save you, but I will take the children. I can't take everyone.' He hid us children in the forest for four weeks, until liberation." Although her parents survived, her aunt and uncle died in Auschwitz.

Haroset from Bordeaux

HÉLÈNE SANCY'S *HAROSET* RECIPE goes back to her family's residence in Portugal before the Inquisition. It is probably one of the oldest existing *haroset* recipes in France today, if not the oldest. Her husband's job is to grind the fruits and nuts with the brass mortar and pestle, which they inherited, handed down through the generations.

Although the Sancys do not roll their *haroset* into balls as is called for in other old recipes from Spain and Portugal (recipe follows), they have another fascinating Passover custom. First they say a blessing over the bitter herbs (*maror*)—in their case, romaine lettuce—as a reminder of slavery in Egypt. Then they wrap the romaine around parsley that has been dipped in salt water, a little chopped celery, and about a teaspoon of *haroset*. The Ashkenazi way, in contrast, is to sandwich bitter herbs and *haroset* between two pieces of matzo. Curiously, the Sancys' recipe for *haroset,* in this land of vineyards in the southwest of France, includes no raisins.

YIELD: ABOUT 3½ CUPS

2 apples, peeled and quartered
1¾ cups dates
1¾ cups walnuts
1 cup almonds
¼ cup hazelnuts

Put all the fruits and nuts in a food processor, and pulse until blended, stopping before they become completely puréed. *Haroset* should have some crunch.

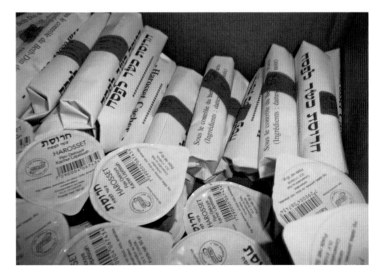

Prepared Moroccan *haroset,*
available at kosher markets
before Passover

Haroset, the Passover Appetizer

■

Then each family prepares the Seder, the ceremony at the center of Passover. On the table is the Seder plate with matzo, lettuce, bitter herbs or maror, and haroset (a mixture of almonds, apples, and ground sugar).

—Alexandre Weill, *Couronne*

To me, no other food represents the wandering of the Jews as do recipes for *haroset,* the relish that symbolizes the mortar used by the Jews in Egypt to build ancient structures—not necessarily the pyramids, as is sometimes believed.

Since biblical times, throughout the Mediterranean, a portion of summer fruit—such as figs, raisins, and dates—has always been set aside at harvest and dried on strings to be prepared for the winter, and a portion for *haroset* at Passover. Before the advent of the food processor, these fruits were pounded with a mortar and pestle, or ground with a manual chopper, often combined with spices, like cinnamon, cardamom, or ginger, and some sweet wine or even vinegar. Spices tend to vary according to the taste buds of the country of origin.

During the period of Rashi and his followers the geographical *haroset* divide developed. In the south of France, where more tropical fruits like dates and pomegranates were available, they became integrated into this Passover "clay" mix. In the north, although in theory all the fruits of the Song of Songs were to be included, only leftover apples from the summer were truly available. The northern Ashkenazic *haroset* developed with apples, nuts, and sweet wine, while in the south of France recipes for *haroset* included dates and other fruits and nuts. This split continues to this day.

At a kosher grocery store in Neuilly, a suburb of Paris, I found packaged versions of Moroccan *haroset* with dates and nuts. And at a Seder in Paris, I ate one very similar to my own family's, with apples, nuts, a little wine, sugar, and cinnamon. The only difference was in the texture, which was less coarse. The *haroset* that the French nineteenth-century writer Alexandre Weill remembers (see above) in his novel *Couronne* also includes apples, almonds, and sugar. *Haroset* in France, as everywhere else, reflects the country from which each family emigrated, often resulting in several variations of *haroset* at one table.

A Thirteenth-Century Provençal *Haroset*

■

I came across a thirteenth-century recipe for *haroset* from Narbonne. It had had been written down by Rabbi Manoah b. Shimon Badrashi and included chestnuts, which are common in that part of France. To make it, all you do is gently pulse about 1 cup each cooked chestnuts, blanched almonds, raisins, figs, and dates along with ¼ cup walnuts and 1 tart apple, peeled and quartered. Season with 1 teaspoon ground ginger and ¼ teaspoon ground cloves, and continue to pulse, adding enough wine vinegar (about 3 tablespoons) to reach the consistency of crunchy clay.

Moroccan *Haroset* Truffles with Almonds and Fruits

THIS *HAROSET* RECIPE ORIGINATED in Toledo, Spain, before the Inquisition, and found its way to Tétouan, near Tangier, in northern Morocco, and then to Paris, where it is served today. Dates, the predominant fruit in most Moroccan *haroset,* are mixed with apples before being rolled into little balls. Sylviane Lévy (see page 65), whose mother gave her the recipe, says to roll them in cinnamon, then serve them in little paper cups. These balls look like chocolate truffles and taste like Passover petits fours!

YIELD: ABOUT 40 *HAROSET* BALLS, SERVING 20

1 pound almonds
1 pound pitted dates
2 apples, peeled, cored, and quartered
1 teaspoon plus ½ cup ground cinnamon
¼ teaspoon powdered ginger

Place the almonds in a food processor with a steel blade, and pulse until finely ground. Add the dates, apples, 1 teaspoon of the cinnamon, and the ginger, and continue pulsing until the apples are chopped fine and the mixture comes together. You might have to do this in two batches. Cover, and refrigerate overnight.

The next day, shape the mixture into balls the size of large marbles. Put about ½ cup cinnamon in a bowl, and roll the balls in it. Serve two per person.

VARIATION Algerian *haroset* balls use ½ pound dried figs, ½ pound dried pitted dates, 1 cup walnuts, ¼ cup dry red wine, ½ teaspoon cinnamon, ¼ teaspoon freshly grated nutmeg, and sugar to taste, pulsed in a food processor, then rolled into balls.

Huevos Haminados
(Hard-Boiled Eggs Jewish Style)

> The mistress of the house [in Paris] asked me what I should like to eat. I replied, some eggs cooked by my servant. They laid the table, we sat down, and I ate some bread with two boiled eggs. I then recited grace and afternoon prayer.
>
> —David Azulai in his journal, 1755

Sometimes, as described above, at a Christian home in Paris, an observant Jew dining with gentiles will ask for a hard-boiled egg. Because it is encased in a hard shell, boiling it in a nonkosher pot does not affect the egg itself.

For Jews, eggs have always had a dual meaning. They symbolize light and life, an egg being the very beginning of life. They are also a symbol of darkness, being the first food eaten at a meal of mourning just after the burial. What is more, eggs are *pareve* (neutral), considered neither meat nor dairy.

For the Jews of Morocco and some other Sephardic Jews, *huevos haminadav* (hard-boiled eggs) are added to *adafina,* their Sabbath meat stew.

In an old French cookbook, *La Cuisine française et africaine pour toutes les familles* by

Eggs baked in sand for Passover

Léon Isnard, I found a Sabbath recipe for eggs Jewish style in which the eggs were buried in the hot sands of North Africa to cook overnight. I tried this in a heavy Dutch oven, covering the eggs in their shells with sand that I had purchased at a garden store. I then baked the eggs in a 200-degree oven for 12 hours. When I cracked them open, the whites had turned light brown and had a delicious creamy texture.

The normal way of boiling *huevos haminados* is to cook them slowly for at least six hours in a large pot of water with the skins of onions and coffee grounds, or in the *adafina* itself, to reach the same effect.

The eggs can be served at your Seder, for Shabbat, or anytime as a first course chopped with sautéed onions.

Herring with Mustard Sauce

SOMETIME IN THE NINTH CENTURY, or perhaps earlier, Baltic fishermen figured out that curing herring in salt would preserve it. Caught and immediately salted to prevent spoilage, the fish was then brought back to French ports to be sold, often by Jewish purveyors who transported it up the Rhône. Salting fish was so important in the medieval period that salt-fish mongers, like fresh-fish mongers, had their own stores for salted, dried, and brined fish such as herring and cod. Because the fish had not in fact been cooked, rabbis considered salted fish to be kosher even if it had been salted by gentiles.

For centuries Jews in northern France, who couldn't eat pork, ate herring as their daily protein. It was prepared in a variety of ways, most often first soaked in milk to remove the excess saltiness, then dressed with vinegar and oil, and served with lots of sliced raw onion and hot boiled potatoes.

Jews in France have put a French touch on their herring dishes, serving them as an appetizer rather than as a main course. They usually prepare the herring with either a horseradish sauce with apples, hard-boiled eggs, and beets, or a mustard-dill sauce with sugar, cream, and vinegar. To break the fast of Yom Kippur, Alsatian Jews use a sweet-and-sour cream sauce with their herring.

D   YIELD: 4 SERVINGS

8 ounces pickled *matjes* herring, cut into 2-inch slices
2 tablespoons white-wine vinegar
1 tablespoon sour or heavy cream
1 teaspoon Dijon mustard
½ teaspoon sugar, or to taste
4 tablespoons vegetable oil
Salt and freshly ground pepper to taste
Chopped fresh dill for garnish

Put the herring slices in a small serving bowl.

In another bowl, whisk together the white-wine vinegar, cream, mustard, and sugar. Gradually whisk in the oil. Add salt and pepper to taste. Pour the dressing over the herring, and sprinkle dill on top. Serve immediately, or refrigerate until serving.

Several kinds of marinated herring in a Paris shop

Kosher *Foie Gras*
from Les Demoiselles de Trémolat

Anne-Juliette Belicha and her husband, Maurice Belicha, are true adventurers. In the 1980s, they moved from Paris to Israel for a few years, and tried to start a *foie-gras* business there. Then, when Israel banned *foie-gras* production, they moved to the Dordogne area of southwestern France.

"Because my family was kosher," Maurice told me, "I wasn't able to eat the nonkosher *foie gras* or pork-based *charcuterie* that is everywhere in France. When I was on vacation on a farm in the southwest of France, I realized that *foie gras* could be made according to the laws of kashrut."

It was 1988 when Maurice visited the Dordogne, one of the main areas for *foie gras* and truffles, and liked the region. To learn the process of making *foie gras,* he first had to look for a good butcher. Stopping one night to sleep in the beautiful town of Trémolat (near the present-day home of the Dalai Lama), he wandered into a butcher shop. There he met Georges Chalivat, a master *boucher-charcutier,* whose accomplished manner impressed him greatly. Maurice, a soft-spoken man, asked the butcher if he would be interested in making kosher *foie gras.* Monsieur Chalivat, who was familiar with Jews and Jewish traditions from his time in the army in Algeria, rose to the challenge. He learned how to raise the temperature of the oven enough to make the blood recede from the liver, according to kosher law. This produced a darker color than that of classic *foie gras,* but a similar flavor.

Georges Chalivat passing on to Maurice Belicha the trick for making high-quality *foie gras* kosher

Foie Gras and Its History

When I was in the southwest of France, I spent hours watching *gavage,* or force-feeding, at a farm in Gers. Although I had seen mechanical force-feeding in Israel and was repulsed by it, here the process seemed very natural. As the farmer told me, the duck, or the goose, like the pelican, has a very muscular neck and feels no pain when corn and water are poured down its throat. In fact, he believes that the bird likes it.

As I watched, the farmer, sitting on a little stool, reached out for a duck, then, holding it with his legs, took a handful of corn kernels, ground them with a little water, and poured them into a funnel, which was gently inserted in the mouth and down the throat of the duck. He soothingly massaged the duck's neck to make the corn go down, and the

A farmer gently feeds his ducks

duck waddled off content. Then he moved on to the next duck. I watched this process for more than an hour and did not hear a quack from any of the ducks. The farmer told me that he does this for fourteen days and then slaughters the birds for the market. In the meantime, they frolic in the fields, living a ducky life.

Legend has it that *gavage* dates from ancient Egypt, where the Israelites may have learned the secret of production during their captivity, to bring it back with them to the land of Canaan. In the tombs of the Pharaohs from the fourth and fifth dynasties, hieroglyphs show farmers holding geese by the neck, feeding them grains and dates. In the third century B.C.E., during the Roman Empire, Cato tells us that geese were force-fed with buckwheat. According to André Daguin, France's king of *foie gras,* the Jews helped develop the technique of *gavage* in France. Rather than trying to produce a delicacy, the Jews wanted to force-feed the geese to produce extra cooking fat, since dietary prohibitions excluded the use of lard. At first the geese were given a diet of dried figs, locally available in the southwest of France, but after Columbus brought corn back to Europe, corn kernels became the preferred feed. As late as the sixteenth century, Jews were seen as the best purveyors of *foie gras*. Bartolomeo Scappi, chef to Pope Pius V, wrote about the fine goose liver produced by Jews in his 1570 work, *Opera dell'Arte del Cucinare.*

Monsieur Daguin told me that *foie gras* used to be made primarily with goose livers, still the source of the best *foie gras* in Alsace. But about sixty years ago, farmers figured out that it could also be made from *mulard* (Moulard) ducks, newly crossbred with the *barbarie* (Muscovy), which became more plentiful than geese. It took about ten years to perfect that process, and now, with increasingly higher demand, the *mulard* represents almost 90 percent of the production. In 2005, the French Parliament voted to give *foie gras* a protected status as a worthy part of the nation's cultural heritage.

Mango Chutney for *Pâté de Foie Gras*

MAURICE AND ANNE-JULIETTE BELICHA, together with their two young daughters, lead a Jewish life, bringing their kosher meat from Paris and only using *bio* (organic) products, in the Dordogne. While Maurice is producing kosher *foie gras* (see page 47), Anne-Juliette is trying to realize her dream of opening a kosher bed-and-breakfast in the Dordogne. She makes this delicious mango chutney, which marries well with both her husband's *foie gras* and with chopped liver.

 YIELD: 2 CUPS

1 tablespoon safflower or
   vegetable oil
1 teaspoon red peppercorns
1 shallot, diced
1 large ripe mango
1 tablespoon sugar
1 tablespoon red-wine vinegar

Heat the oil in a nonstick frying pan. Add the peppercorns and the shallot, and sauté over low heat for 5 minutes.

In the meantime, peel the mango and cut it into ½-inch cubes. Add the mango to the shallot and continue sautéing. Sprinkle the sugar over, splash in the red-wine vinegar, and simmer for 10 minutes. Cover, and cook on very low heat for 40 minutes, or until the mango becomes a marmalade. Cool, discard the peppercorns, and serve as an appetizer with *foie gras*.

Anne-Juliette Belicha and her daughter at work in the kitchen

Gehakte Leber (Chopped Liver)

■

Therefore I say to the Israelite people: No person among you shall partake of blood. . . . Anyone who partakes of it shall be cut off.

—Leviticus 17:12, 14

Kosher dietary laws prohibiting eating blood pose a particular problem with liver, which has more blood than any other part of an animal. In fact, in antiquity, the raw liver was thought of as the soul of man because it held so much blood, which is life itself. The liver was often used to augur the future. In prayer, Jews sometimes say, *"Nefesh habasar bedam hu,"* translated as "The life of the flesh is in the blood."

The first requirement for observant Jews, then, was to remove all the blood from the liver. Sprinkling salt on the meat, the usual form of removing blood in the koshering process, isn't enough for liver. It must be broiled as well, but that tends to dry it out. To become palatable, the liver has to be lubricated with rendered chicken or goose fat and lightened with onions and chopped hard-boiled eggs. Thus the ingenious dish of chopped liver, traditionally eaten for the Sabbath and holidays as an appetizer, was born.

The Jews of Alsace, specializing in the breeding and fattening of geese, made a paste out of the liver, and created a version of *pâté de foie gras,* passing it through a *moulin* (a French grinder). They then added a little brandy, poured it into a terrine, and baked it in a *bain-marie. Voilà:* chopped-liver pâté.

Françoise's *Foie Haché*

(CHOPPED LIVER WITH A CONFIT OF ONIONS)

Chopped liver is a specialty in Michel Kalifa's butcher shop in the Marais.

MICHEL AND FRANÇOISE KALIFA met over a slab of meat. "When I looked at Françoise, I saw only goodness in her eyes," said Michel, a butcher who has a flowing black mustache. "She had a generosity of heart." The two met in Michel's butcher shop on Rue des Écouffes, in the Marais. Françoise's parents came to the Marais after the Second World War, looking for other Jews from Poland who had survived the Nazi occupation. "They all said they would meet in the Pletzl, as the quarter was called," Françoise, a caterer, told me. Now she and Michel, who is from Morocco, live in an apartment above their store with their baby.

When we arrived at their renovated apartment, located in an old courtyard, a large platter of the *charcuterie* that Michel had prepared for us was on the table in the living room. "You should eat with your eyes first," Michel told us. I picked up a thin slice of turkey smoked with beech wood: moist, mellow, and subtle in flavor. As I tasted my way through the platter, I learned to recognize the various flavors that regional differences make in *charcuterie*. And now that so many butchers, like Michel, are coming from North Africa, regional products like *merguez* lamb or beef sausage with its *harissa*-infused flavor are becoming butcher-shop staples.

One of Françoise's amazing specialties is this chopped liver from her Polish family. "On my mother's side, we add onions to almost everything we eat," Françoise told me. Not as finely chopped as most American versions, her liver was laced with finely sautéed sweet onions browned in duck fat and cooked until a caramel color. "The onions are the real secret," Michel added. "They give it the sweet taste." Although the Kalifas wouldn't reveal the recipe, food historians Philip and Mary Hyman, who accompanied me, helped me get close, we believe.

Heat the chicken fat in a frying pan, and sauté the onions over moderate heat, turning frequently, for about ½ hour or more, until soft and almost black. You can add a tablespoon of honey to help caramelize them. Remove from the pan.

Sauté the chicken livers in the fat in which the onions cooked over very high heat to sear well. Do not overcook. The livers may still be red inside, but resist the temptation to cook them further. When cool enough to handle, separate the lobes and cut each into two or three pieces.

Chop the egg, and carefully fold in the onions, the livers, salt, and pepper. Serve with toast or crackers.

YIELD: 8 SERVINGS

¼ cup rendered chicken, goose, or duck fat, or vegetable or canola oil

4 medium onions, peeled and sliced into rounds

1 tablespoon honey (optional)

1 pound chicken livers*

6 hard-boiled eggs

Salt and freshly ground pepper to taste

*If you keep kosher, remove all the blood from the liver first, as described on page 51.

French Chopped Liver Pâté

THE ELEGANT GILBERTE SIMON invited me for tea in her beautiful apartment in Nîmes, a city in the south of France dating back to the Roman Empire.

Born in Lyon, Madame Simon, who is in her late eighties, married a Jewish "Nîmois" whom she met at a dance. But then the Nazis came in 1942 and started taking Jewish families away. "We left before they could find us," she told me. "They were searching for my husband because he was a doctor here, working in the Resistance." When they left Nîmes, the Simons hid in the mountains. "We found a house to live in with our two little girls. The peasants sold us vegetables; sometimes they killed a lamb; they brought us cheese and butter. When we returned to Nîmes, it was very difficult. There were not very many Jews left." Today the majority of Jews are Sephardic, having immigrated to Nîmes in the 1960s from North Africa.

Thinking back to happier and more prosperous times, this is the pâté she made through the years for her own family on Friday nights and the holidays, as well as for Jewish students who stayed with her while studying in Nîmes or nearby Aix-en-Provence.

YIELD: 6 TO 8 SERVINGS

1 pound chicken livers

2 tablespoons rendered chicken fat or vegetable oil

1 medium onion, or 4 shallots, diced

4 large hard-boiled eggs

3 tablespoons Cognac or port

Salt and freshly ground pepper to taste

5 or 6 fresh bay leaves*

*Fresh bay leaves can be obtained through the Web and in many supermarkets. I have a small bay tree in my garden. You can use dried, but fresh look more festive.

Preheat the broiler. Broil the livers on a rack 4 inches from the heat for about 1½ minutes on each side, or until there is no more blood. Drain the livers, and lower the oven temperature to 350 degrees.

Heat the chicken fat or oil in a sauté pan, and sauté the onion or shallots slowly for 10 to 15 minutes, or until very soft and lightly colored. Add the livers, and cook until still lightly pink inside, just a minute or two.

Place the livers, onion or shallots, eggs, and Cognac or port in a food processor fitted with a steel blade. Season with salt and freshly ground pepper to taste. Process until smooth.

Decorate the bottom of a 9-inch loaf pan with the bay leaves, placed shiny side down. Spoon the liver mixture on top of them, tapping gently to get rid of any air bubbles. Set the pan into a *bain-marie,* and bake for 20 minutes. Cool, then unmold. Serve with rye bread.

Buckwheat Blini
with Smoked Salmon and Crème Fraîche

IT WAS IN PARIS in the 1960s that I first tasted buckwheat blini. My friend Nanou took me to a tiny, chic Russian restaurant near the Champs-Élysées. Russians, many of them Jews, came to France at the end of the nineteenth century, not long before the Russian Revolution, and congregated in restaurants like this one. We ordered the elegantly presented blini, and ate them daintily with smoked salmon and crème fraîche.

Twenty years after Nanou died, her son Édouard got married. The wedding party took place at Maxim's, where we drank lots of champagne and danced until the wee hours of the morning. I was touched to taste blini with smoked salmon and crème fraîche, the same appetizer that Édouard's mother and I had enjoyed so many years ago. For me, it was as though she were present at the wedding.

P or D   YIELD: 20 TO 24 BLINI

Put the milk, yeast, and 1 tablespoon of the sugar in a small bowl, and whisk together. Mix the two flours in a large bowl with the remaining sugar and the salt. Whisk in the yeast mixture, the butter, and the egg yolks. Cover the bowl with plastic wrap, and let rise for 1 to 1½ hours, or until bubbly and doubled in bulk. You can also refrigerate overnight until ready to use.

When ready to make the blini, beat the egg whites to stiff peaks, and gently fold them into the risen batter.

Heat a small crêpe pan or griddle to medium, and brush with melted butter. Pour about 3 tablespoons of the batter onto the crêpe pan or the griddle, and fry until golden brown on both sides. Remove from the pan, and keep warm, wrapped in a towel. Brush the pan with additional butter as needed, and continue to make additional blini. Serve with smoked salmon, caviar, and crème fraîche as an appetizer or a breakfast dish.

2½ cups lukewarm milk
1 tablespoon active dry yeast
3 tablespoons sugar
1 cup sifted all-purpose flour
1 cup sifted buckwheat flour
½ teaspoon salt
6 tablespoons unsalted butter, melted and cooled, plus more melted butter for frying
3 eggs, separated
Smoked salmon
Caviar
Crème fraîche

A Provençal fish soup

Soups

Cold Lettuce and Zucchini Soup with New Onions and Fresh Herbs

Soupe au Pistou (Provençal Vegetable Soup with Basil)

Mhamas: Soupe de Poisson (Moroccan Provençal Fish Soup)

Rouille (Garlicky, Peppery Mayonnaise)

French Cold Beet Soup (Borscht)

Soupe aux Petits Pois à l'Estragon (Green Pea Soup with Tarragon)

Soupe à l'Oseille or *Tchav* (Cold Sorrel Soup)

Fava Bean Soup

Spring Chicken Broth

Boulettes de Pâque, Knepfle, or *Kneipflich* (Matzo Balls)

Algerian Julienne of Vegetable Soup for Passover

Consommé Nikitouche (Tunisian Chicken Soup with Tiny Dumplings)

Gemarti Supp (Alsatian Leek and Porcini Soup)

Black Truffle Soup Élysée

Beef Bouillon

Vegetarian Apple Parsnip Soup

Soupe au Blé Vert (Green Wheat Vegetable Soup with Chickpeas)

M'soki (Tunisian Passover Spring Vegetable Ragout
with Artichokes, Spinach, Fava Beans, and Peas)

Cold Lettuce and Zucchini Soup
with New Onions and Fresh Herbs

Sarah Petlin shopping at the *marché* for dinner

ON A LATE-JUNE EVENING, I entered a courtyard in the Fifth Arrondissement, right near the picturesque Rue Mouffetard, one of my favorite streets in Paris when I was a student there so many years ago. Beyond the courtyard, I found myself in a large garden in front of an apartment building. After climbing two flights of stairs, I arrived at the home of Irving Petlin, an American artist, and his beautiful wife, Sarah. The two expats have lived here on and off since 1959.

Sarah frequents the local markets, going to the Place Monge for her onions and garlic, making sure she visits her potato man from North Africa. Having chosen peonies for the table, she arranged them in a vase next to a big bowl of ripe cherries, making her table, with the Panthéon in the background, as beautiful as a perfectly orchestrated still life.

At the meal, I especially liked the soup, which calls for lettuce leaves—a good way, I thought, of using up the tougher outer leaves that most of us discard, but which still have a lot of flavor. The French have a long tradition of herb-and-salad soup, something Americans should be increasingly interested in, given all the new wonderful greens we're growing in our backyards and finding at farmers' markets.

I often replace the zucchini with eggplant and substitute other herbs that are available in my summer garden. This soup is also delicious served warm in the winter.

2 tablespoons olive oil

4 or 5 cloves garlic, peeled and
minced

1 bunch of spring onions or scallions
(about 1 pound), diced

Outer leaves of romaine lettuce or
mature arugula, roughly chopped
(about 4 cups)

4 or 5 small zucchini (about
1½ pounds), roughly chopped

2 stalks celery with leaves, chopped

1 big handful of roughly chopped fresh
parsley (about ½ cup)

1 teaspoon salt, or to taste

½ teaspoon freshly ground pepper, or
to taste

4 to 5 cups vegetable stock or water

2 tablespoons chopped fresh cilantro

2 tablespoons chopped fresh chives or
the tops of scallions

2 tablespoons chopped fresh basil

2 cups Greek yogurt

Heat the olive oil in a big soup pot, and add the garlic and the onions or scallions, stirring occasionally. Once the onions are translucent, add the romaine lettuce, zucchini, celery, parsley, salt, pepper, and vegetable stock or water. Bring to a boil and simmer, covered, for about 10 minutes, or until the zucchini are cooked. Remove from the heat, and cool to room temperature.

Purée the soup in a blender or food processor until smooth. Either serve warm or chill the soup in the refrigerator. Before serving, sprinkle with the cilantro, the chives or scallions, and the basil, and serve with a dollop of Greek yogurt.

Yogurt

Living in France in the 1960s, I loved to eat yogurt served in tiny glass jars and sprinkled with sugar. Although I knew that it was originally a product of the Balkans, I always associated yogurt with France, where it has a long history. Isaac Carasso, a Jew from Thessalonika who came through Spain to France in the 1930s, first peddled his jars of yogurt from a cart on the streets of Paris. During World War II, his family moved his company to New York and called it Danone, in honor of his son, Daniel, who lived to 103, going each day to the office, a living testament to the healthful qualities of his product.

Soupe au Pistou

(PROVENÇAL VEGETABLE SOUP WITH BASIL)

WHEN I STAYED AT LA ROYANTE, a charming bed-and-breakfast in Aubagne just outside of Marseille, I tasted the delicious homemade jam from the fig, cherry, and apricot trees near the terrace, and enjoyed the olive oil made from the olives in the orchard. I talked with Xenia and Bernard Saltiel, the owners, and learned that Bernard is Jewish and traces his ancestry in France to about the thirteenth century, when his people became tax collectors for the king of France in Perpignan. Then they went to Narbonne, and finally to Montpellier, where a Saltiel helped found the University of Medicine. When the Jews were expelled from France, the Saltiel family moved to Greece, and lived in Crete, Macedonia, and then Thessalonika. Ever since Bernard's grandfather returned to France in 1892, Saltiels have lived in the Marseille area.

Today Bernard is a man of Provence, sniffing vegetables at the local market in Aubagne to make sure they are fresh enough for a good *soupe au pistou*. This soup originated in nearby Italy, most probably in Genoa. Provençal Jewish versions include a selection of dried beans as well as fresh green, wax, or fava beans, fresh basil, and an especially strong dose of garlic. Make it in the summer with perfectly ripe tomatoes. In the winter, I substitute good canned tomatoes.

YIELD: 8 TO 10 SERVINGS

1 cup mixed white and red
dried beans

1 large yellow onion, diced

2 stalks celery, diced

1 potato, peeled and diced

3 ripe or one 15-ounce can
tomatoes, peeled, seeded,
and coarsely chopped

7 cloves garlic, diced

3 teaspoons salt, or to taste

½ teaspoon freshly ground
pepper, or to taste

1 pound fresh green beans and
other fresh beans, such as

Put the dried beans in a bowl, cover with water by about 4 inches, and let sit overnight.

The next day, drain the water off and place the beans in a pot filled with about 3 quarts cold water. Bring to a boil, lower to a simmer, and cook, uncovered, for 1 hour.

Add the onion, celery, potato, two of the tomatoes, one garlic clove, 2 teaspoons of the salt, and pepper to taste. Simmer, uncovered, for 20 more minutes. Then add the green beans, the zucchini, and a handful of basil leaves, diced, and cook for 10 more minutes. Add the pasta shells, and cook until *al dente*.

While the pasta is cooking, make the *pistou*. You can do this by using either a mortar and pestle, the way the Provençaux do, or a food processor equipped with the steel blade. If using a mortar, roughly chop the remaining basil leaves and put in the mortar with the remaining garlic and the last teaspoon of the salt. Grind with the pestle, and then add the remaining tomato, slowly incorporating the olive oil, and seasoning, if you like, with a twist of pepper. If using the food processor, put all the ingredients inside, and pulse until puréed with a slight chunk.

When the soup is ready to be served, adjust the seasonings, spoon the soup into bowls, and swirl in the *pistou*. Sprinkle each serving with grated Parmesan cheese.

fava or wax, kept whole or halved crosswise
2 large or 3 small zucchini, cut in half lengthwise and diced into half-moons
1 packed cup fresh basil leaves
½ cup pasta shells
3 tablespoons olive oil
Grated Parmesan cheese

Fava beans at the market in Aubagne

Mhamas: Soupe de Poisson

(MOROCCAN PROVENÇAL FISH SOUP)

IN THE CHARMING TOWN of Cagnes-sur-Mer, whose Jewish population of four hundred comes mostly from Morocco, I tasted a delicious fish soup. This particular recipe is one that painter Pierre-Auguste Renoir, who lived in the town, would have relished.

 YIELD: 6 TO 8 SERVINGS

¼ cup olive oil
2 leeks, cleaned and diced
2 onions, diced
3 cloves garlic, minced
1 stalk celery, diced
Pinch of saffron
1 fennel bulb, diced, plus the fronds
   for garnish
2 or 3 sprigs fresh thyme or
   1 teaspoon dried
1 bay leaf
6 cups prepared fish stock*
½ teaspoon mace
2 tomatoes, diced
1 tablespoon tomato paste

1 half-inch piece orange zest
3 potatoes, peeled and diced
Salt and freshly ground pepper
1 pound oily fish (bluefish, hake,
   pollock, or cod)
1 pound white, meaty fish (sea bream,
   sea bass, yellowtail snapper, or
   halibut)
Juice of 1 lemon or lime
2 tablespoons red wine or *pastis*
2 tablespoons chopped parsley
Rouille (recipe follows)

*Fish stock is available at fish markets and some
   supermarkets.

Heat the olive oil in a large casserole. Add the leeks, onions, garlic, celery, saffron, fennel bulb, thyme, and bay leaf, and sauté until the onions are clear but not browned.

Add the fish stock, bring to a boil, and simmer slowly for 30 to 40 minutes, covered, or until the flavor is mellow. Then stir in the mace, tomatoes, tomato paste, orange zest, and potatoes, and cook for about 15 minutes more, or until the potatoes are cooked.

Fish out the thyme, bay leaf, and orange zest, and purée the other ingredients until smooth.

Return the soup to the casserole, and bring to a boil. Add salt and pepper to taste. Cut the oily fish into 2-inch cubes and add them to the casserole. Simmer, covered, for 5 minutes, shaking the casserole from time to time to prevent sticking; do not stir, or the fish will disintegrate.

Add additional water if needed to cover the fish. After about 2 minutes, add the whitefish pieces to the casserole, setting the most delicate fish on top, and continue to cook until the fish flakes easily with a fork—about 5 minutes more. Stir in the lemon juice and the red wine or *pastis,* and sprinkle with parsley and a few fronds of fennel. Top each serving with a dollop of *rouille.*

Rouille

(GARLICKY, PEPPERY MAYONNAISE)

I HAVE ALWAYS THOUGHT that the best part of fish soup is the *rouille,* a peppery, garlicky sauce that is slathered on toasted rounds of baguette and floated on the surface of the soup. I also like to stir some *rouille* into the broth. Similar to the Provençal aioli, a garlic-flavored mayonnaise, *rouille* is flavored with hot pepper and saffron, which give it its signature rust color. (*Rouille* literally means "rust" in French.) Today I have noticed that North African Jews often spice up their *rouille* even more, by adding a little *harissa* (see page 33) to it.

Traditionally, a mortar and pestle are used to pound the garlic, pepper, and egg yolk, gradually incorporating the oil to make a mayonnaise. Today it is easy to put everything in a food processor and slowly add the oil, drop by drop. Leftover sauce is good on sandwiches or as a dip.

Put the egg yolks and the lemon juice in a small food processor equipped with a steel blade. Drizzle in the oil very slowly, to emulsify into a smooth mayonnaise.

Then peel the garlic and add it to the mayonnaise along with the salt, white pepper, saffron, bread crumbs, and the cayenne or *harissa.* Purée all the ingredients together.

Adjust seasonings to taste. If the *rouille* is not thick enough, blend some cooked potatoes into the sauce.

YIELD : ABOUT 1½ CUPS

2 egg yolks
Juice of ½ lemon
1 to 1¼ cups extra-virgin olive
  oil
3 cloves garlic
Pinch of salt
A few pinches of white pepper
A few saffron strands
½ cup soft white bread crumbs
1 cayenne pepper, dried, or
  ½ teaspoon *harissa*

French Cold Beet Soup

(BORSCHT)

BEETS AND BEET SOUP are as old as the Talmud, in which the dish is mentioned. Borscht, brought to France most recently by Russian immigrants before World War I, is still very popular served either hot or cold, depending on the season. Although there is a meat version, made with veal bones and thickened with eggs and vinegar, I prefer this lighter, dairy beet soup.

The French use a bit more vinegar and less sugar than in American recipes, proportions that allow the beet flavor really to shine through. The soup is traditionally topped with dill or chervil, but I use whatever is growing seasonally in my garden, often fresh mint. The combination of the bright-pink beets, the sour cream or yogurt, and the green herbs makes a stunning dish.

 YIELD: 6 TO 8 SERVINGS

2 pounds raw beets (about 4)

1 pound onions (2 medium)

2 cloves garlic, peeled and left whole

1 tablespoon sugar

Salt and freshly ground pepper to taste

3 tablespoons balsamic vinegar

½ cup sour cream, crème fraîche, or good yogurt

4 tablespoons fresh dill, chervil, or mint cut into chiffonade

Peel the beets and the onions. Cut them into chunks, and toss them together in a large soup pot. Pour in about 2 quarts of water, or enough to cover the vegetables by an inch or so. Add the garlic, sugar, and salt and freshly ground pepper to taste. Bring to a boil, skimming the surface of any impurities that rise. Lower the heat, cover, and simmer for about an hour, or until the beets are cooked.

When the soup has cooled off, ladle the vegetables and some of their broth into a blender, and purée to the consistency of a thick soup. Stir in the vinegar. Adjust the thickness and seasoning of the soup to your taste, adding more beet broth if you want a thinner soup. Serve cold in soup bowls with a dollop of the sour cream, crème fraîche, or yogurt and a sprinkle of the dill, chervil, or mint.

Soupe aux Petits Pois à l'Estragon

(GREEN PEA SOUP WITH TARRAGON)

THIS IS A VERY QUICK RECIPE, even quicker today because of Picard Surgelés, the French chain of grocery stores selling superb frozen food products. Although the vegetables are not certified kosher, even the Beth Din of Paris, the religious governance, approves of their use. I tasted this particular soup at a Shabbat dinner at the home of North African–born Sylviane and Gérard Lévy. Gérard, who is a well-known Chinese-antique dealer on Paris's Left Bank, recited the prayer over the sweet raisin wine sipped on the Sabbath in French homes. Everyone then went into the next room for the ritual hand-washing. When they returned, Gérard said the blessing over the two challahs before enjoying the meat meal, which began with this creamy (but creamless) frozen-pea-and-tarragon soup.

Heat the olive oil in a large pot, and sauté the shallots until translucent. Add the chicken broth, the potato, and a pinch of sea salt. Bring to a boil before adding the peas and the sugar. Simmer, covered, over low heat for about 30 minutes, then uncover and simmer for an additional 15 minutes.

Pour the soup into a blender or food processor and purée. Then, if you like, press through a vegetable mill. Serve in big bowls, garnished with the tarragon. It is also lovely served cold in tiny demitasse cups, laced with mint.

M or P   YIELD: 4 TO 6 SERVINGS

1 tablespoon olive oil
2 large shallots, diced
4½ cups chicken broth
  or water
1 potato, peeled and diced
Sea salt to taste
2 pounds frozen peas
1 teaspoon sugar
2 tablespoons chopped fresh
  tarragon

Pea soup with tarragon

Soupe à l'Oseille or *Tchav*

(COLD SORREL SOUP)

SORREL (EASTERN EUROPEAN *TCHAV*) has been made a little more *soigné* in the hands of the French, by adding herbs and cream. Whereas Jews often substituted spinach and rhubarb to achieve the tangy flavor when they couldn't get sorrel, and ate the soup cold, the French, until recently, ate sorrel soup hot. Austin de Croze, in his 1931 cookbook, *What to Eat and Drink in France,* thought that sorrel soup had come to France with emigrants from eastern Europe.

This particular recipe comes from *Gastronomie Juive: Cuisine et Patisserie de Russie, d'Alsace, de Roumanie et d'Orient,* by Suzanne Roukhomovsky, a book I found years ago while browsing in the Librairie Gourmande, a cookbook store I love to frequent on the Left Bank of Paris. Published by the distinguished house of Flammarion in 1929, it was the first comprehensive cookbook on the Jews of France. Madame Roukhomovsky, also a novelist and poet, called French Jewish cooking *cuisine maternelle.* This recipe surely has its roots in her own Russian background.

If you can't find sorrel, substitute 1 pound of spinach or kale with ½ cup rhubarb to attain that tart flavor, as Jews from Russia did.

YIELD: 4 TO 6 SERVINGS

2 tablespoons unsalted butter

1 leek, diced

1 onion, diced

1 pound sorrel, tough stems removed, and leaves finely chopped

2 cloves garlic, minced

2 tablespoons lemon juice

1 teaspoon salt, or to taste

Freshly ground pepper

½ cup sour cream or crème fraîche

2 hard-boiled eggs (optional)

2 cups croutons

1 English cucumber, thinly sliced

Heat a stockpot, melt the butter, and scatter the leek and onion on top, sautéing until the onion is transparent. Pour in 4 cups water, and bring to a boil. Add the sorrel, garlic, lemon juice, and salt and pepper (about 5 twists of the pepper mill). Simmer for 15 minutes, stirring occasionally, then remove from the heat.

Once the soup has cooled for about 10 minutes, purée, and serve warm with a dollop of sour cream or crème fraîche, or as a cold soup, the way Jews coming to France from Russia did: finely chop the hard-boiled eggs, and stir them into the soup; cool completely in the refrigerator, and serve cold, garnished with the croutons, cucumber slices, and a dollop of sour cream or crème fraîche.

Fava Bean Soup

DRIED FAVA BEANS, A NORTH AFRICAN STAPLE, taste very different from their fresh counterparts, which are only available for a short time in the spring. After they cook for a few hours with garlic, cumin, and *harissa,* they become creamy and take on an earthy heat that is especially comforting on colder days. When served with a hunk of baguette, this soup could very well make an entire weeknight meal.

Rinse the fava beans, and put them in a large bowl. Cover them with 6 cups water, and allow them to soak overnight.

Heat the olive oil in a soup pot. Add the garlic, cumin, and *harissa,* and sauté over medium heat for about a minute, or until fragrant. Add the fava beans along with their soaking water, and pour in another 4 cups water. Season with salt and pepper to taste. Bring to a boil, lower the heat, and cover, simmering for 2 hours. Taste, adjusting seasoning if necessary. Serve garnished with the parsley or cilantro and a squeeze of lemon juice.

 YIELD: 6 TO 8 SERVINGS

2 cups dried fava beans

¼ cup olive oil

2 cloves garlic, peeled and minced

1 teaspoon ground cumin

1 teaspoon *harissa* (see page 33)

Salt and freshly ground pepper to taste

1 tablespoon chopped fresh parsley or cilantro

Juice of 1 lemon

Daniel Rose—An American Chef in Paris

When Daniel Rose (see pages 230, 308, and 110 for more delicious recipes for brisket, *brandade,* and fennel salad), a young chef from Chicago, opened his restaurant Spring in Paris in 2006, he hoped it would lead to a book contract and a Food Network show. Neither panned out, but within a month Spring was a runaway hit. French food critics and the *Michelin Guide* showered it with praise, and getting a reservation was maddeningly difficult. It was one of the smallest restaurants in Paris, with sixteen seats at tiny tables and no frills, not even flowers. At Spring, Daniel cooks a set menu of four courses for forty-two euros, about fifty-eight dollars, nearly unheard-of for a meal of its caliber.

Daniel has a video camera trained on the kitchen and dining room, broadcasting each day's activities in a continuous twenty-four-hour feed. Who watches the video? "My Jewish mother does," Daniel told me when I visited him one day at his restaurant.

While laying out the makings of that evening's menu, Daniel kept musing about how these dishes could be adapted for Hanukkah. In Paris, he told me, people make potato pancakes for small family meals. "How about a kasha risotto with *trompettes de la mort* mushrooms?" he suggested. "Or a kasha crêpe with poached pears for dessert?"

"Paris is such a Jewish city," he told me, but it is something he noticed only after living there for a while. He started to note, for example, how many doors with mezuzahs he passed on his way to the market.

"My landlord is Jewish, my neighbors are Jewish, and it is safe to be Jewish in this neighborhood," he said. When his neighbors learned he was Jewish, he told me, they began to open up to him. The chocolate-maker invited him for Passover, and chided him for not dating Jewish girls. His next-door neighbor, a Moroccan immigrant who is a wedding videographer, once suggested that Daniel open a kosher restaurant, promising that he would provide the customers. "My neighbors tell me that all the time," Daniel said. "But I would only want to do it if it were a fish restaurant, where we wouldn't have to substitute margarine for real butter. Then we could have good, delicious desserts."

Spring Chicken Broth

CHEF DANIEL ROSE STARTS HIS DAY in the kitchen at 7:30 a.m. He begins with the chicken broth, first browning chicken wings, then adding a wine reduction, and then water, leeks, and other aromatics, but never carrots. "This isn't the way my grandmother would have done it," Daniel told me. "But we don't want so much sweetness in our soup." He doesn't bother with a *bouquet garni:* "I just stick the herbs in the pot." Freeze any broth that you don't use right away.

Pour the vegetable oil into a large stockpot and heat. Brown the chicken wings in two or more batches, depending on the size of your stockpot. At this point, the wings should still be raw, but the skin should be slightly brown and lightly caramelized. Remove the chicken, and drain the fat from the pan.

Return the chicken to the pan, and add the wine. Bring to a boil, and simmer for 2 to 3 minutes. Add 6 quarts cold water to the pot and bring to a simmer, skimming off any scum that rises to the top. Stick the clove in the onion and add to the pot, along with the shallots, celery, garlic, leek, parsley, thyme, orange peel, bay leaf, ginger, and salt and pepper. After an hour, add the whole apple.

Simmer for another hour, and remove from the heat. Allow to cool before removing the fat from the top. Then strain, return the soup to the pot, and bring to a boil, reducing to about 4 quarts. Adjust seasonings, and serve either as chicken soup with *quenelles de matzo* (matzo balls; recipe follows) or as a base for other soups or dishes.

M YIELD: 4 QUARTS

3 tablespoons vegetable oil
4 pounds chicken wings
1½ cups dry white wine
1 whole clove
1 onion, peeled and left whole
5 shallots, peeled and halved
2 stalks celery
½ head garlic, peeled and separated into cloves
1 leek, halved and cleaned
1 bunch of fresh parsley
3 branches fresh thyme, or ½ teaspoon dried thyme
Peel of 1 orange
1 bay leaf
One ½-inch slice fresh ginger, peeled
2 teaspoons salt, or to taste
Freshly ground pepper to taste
1 small apple

Boulettes de Pâque, Knepfle, or *Kneipflich*

(MATZO BALLS)

Friday night I got dressed up (I always wear heels here) and took a *métro* to the Cerfs' for dinner. You cannot imagine how nice their family is. There are three children: two boys, Bertrand and Jacques, and a girl, Nanou. We all had dinner together—matzo ball soup and all—and then went to temple for Rosh Hashanah. The temple was in Salle Playel, the largest concert hall in Paris, because the Copernic Temple is too small. They had rented it to fit the 2,000 people who were there. M. Cerf is an officer of Copernic and held the Torah. It was quite impressive.

—The author's diary from 1963

THE RECIPE FOR THESE *KNEPFLE,* also known as *quenelles de matzo* or the more prosaic matzo balls, came from Madame Maryse Weil of Besançon, the late mother-in-law of my friend Nanou, mentioned above. French matzo balls, often called *boulettes* in French and *Knödeln* in German, are made from stale bread or matzo sheets, soaked in water and dried. These dumplings are neither as big as American matzo balls—they are the size of walnuts rather than golf balls—nor as fluffy, since no baking powder is used. Like many middle-class women in her day, Madame Weil rarely cooked but instead guided those who cooked in her kitchen. Her original recipe read, "Take as many eggs as goose fat. Mix well; add salt, pepper, and ginger and enough matzo meal so you can roll them." Many of the old recipes, including this one, often substitute marrow for the goose fat.

I prefer to cook the matzo balls in boiling salted water and then immediately transfer them with a slotted spoon to homemade chicken broth. This way I can make them in advance, and the soup remains clear.

Molding matzo balls in *vieille* Alsace

Put the fat, eggs, water or broth, 2 teaspoons salt, freshly ground pepper, the ginger, and the nutmeg in the bowl of a food processor fitted with a steel blade. Add the matzo meal, and pulse just to mix. Refrigerate for an hour, or overnight.

Bring a pot of water to a boil. Add the remaining teaspoon of salt. Using two teaspoons, dip one into the matzo ball mix and scoop out a spoonful, then push it with the second teaspoon into the boiling water. French matzo balls have a more abstract, irregular shape than American ones. Cover, and simmer for about 20 minutes.

M or **P** YIELD: ABOUT 10 MATZO BALLS

2 tablespoons rendered goose or chicken fat (see note), vegetable oil, or beef marrow

4 large eggs

¼ cup water, or chicken or beef broth

3 teaspoons salt

Freshly ground pepper to taste

½ teaspoon powdered ginger

¼ teaspoon grated nutmeg

1 cup matzo meal

NOTE There are two ways that one can render the fat. The first way is to take the fat off the goose or chicken and melt it down in a frying pan with onions. The second and easiest method is to make chicken soup (using the skin), then cool and refrigerate the soup overnight, and spoon off the fat that accumulates on top.

Algerian Julienne of Vegetable Soup
for Passover

THANKS TO EMIGRANTS FROM NORTH AFRICA, Passover is once again being celebrated in the town of Saint-Rémy-de-Provence, which had a flourishing Jewish community until the fourteenth century. Now Jews reunite for the holidays, and at a recent Passover in one house, several couples got together for a traditional meal.

Jocelyne Akoun, the hostess of this event, told me about a springtime soup filled with fresh vegetables and fava beans. Because I always have vegetarians at my own Seder, I have taken to making this refreshing and colorful soup as an alternative to my traditional matzo-ball chicken soup. If making the vegetarian version, sauté the onion in the oil in a large soup pot, then add 8 cups water, the bay leaf, cloves, peppercorns, and 1 teaspoon salt, and cook for about an hour. Then put through a sieve and continue as you would with the beef broth.

Fresh fava beans are a sign of spring for Moroccan Jews, because the Jews supposedly ate fava beans, poor man's meat, when they were slaves in Egypt.

M OR P   YIELD: ABOUT 10 SERVINGS

1 pound beef shoulder (optional)

1 pound marrow bones (optional)

1 bay leaf

2 whole cloves

5 peppercorns

Salt to taste

2 tablespoons vegetable oil

1 onion, diced

3 leeks, white and light-green parts, thinly sliced

3 carrots, peeled and diced

1 stalk celery, diced

2 large potatoes, peeled and diced (about 1½ pounds)

2 turnips (about 1 pound), peeled and diced

½ small head of cabbage (8 ounces), shredded

½ tablespoon turmeric

Pinch of saffron

1 pound fresh or frozen fava beans, peeled

4 tablespoons chopped fresh parsley for garnish

If using meat, place the beef and bones in a large soup pot. Add the bay leaf, cloves, peppercorns, and 8 cups water. Bring to a boil, add a teaspoon of salt, or to taste, and skim off any scum that rises to the top. Lower the heat, and simmer, covered, for 1 hour.

Remove the bones, pour the liquid through a sieve, and return the broth to a clean soup pot. Discard the bones, but save the marrow to eat—the cook's treat! Cut the beef into 1-inch cubes, and put back into the broth.

Heat the vegetable oil in a frying pan, and sauté the onion until translucent. Transfer to the broth (or the water for vegetarian version; see headnote). Add the leeks, carrots, celery, potatoes, turnips, and cabbage, stirring after each addition. Season with turmeric (about ½ tablespoon, or to taste) and saffron.

Bring the soup to a boil, lower the heat, and simmer, covered, for about 20 minutes, or until the potatoes are cooked. Add the fava beans, and cook for 5 more minutes. Adjust seasonings, sprinkle with parsley, and serve.

Mangeteslégumes.Blogspot.Com— Eat Your Vegetables!

Dr. Yael Ganem is on a mission to have her children lead a healthy life. An internist, she has a blog called "Mange Tes Légumes!" (mangetes légumes.blogspot.com). Her goal is to show tricks for healthy eating to young parents who, like her, are busy. Because her mother worked, Yael learned to cook from her grandmother. As she understood more about nutrition and the increasing obesity in French society—yes, even the French are getting fat—she realized that she had to make a greater effort to lead a healthier life.

Yael, a trim, intense woman, has a refrigerator stocked with fresh fruits and vegetables. She started to cook and test her ideas on her daughters, Emma and Elia, when they were young. "It is between two and ten years of age that you shape the palate of the children," she told me. Yael makes eating fun. "I try to present foods like a game," she said, talking to me in her modern apartment in one of those marvelous old buildings near the Champs-Élysées. "I use yellow, green, and orange spoons to serve vegetables, and cut decorations out of the fruit. I even play with the names of the vegetables to stimulate the children." Green beans become green spaghetti, and razor-thin strips of zucchini and carrots become tagliatelle that she serves raw with soy sauce. "If the texture and the color don't appeal to children, they won't eat it," she told me. She also insists on their eating meals together as a family. "It is very important to share the meal, to speak and exchange ideas." Other mothers learn from her blog, and, more important, her daughters like the healthy food.

Consommé Nikitouche
(TUNISIAN CHICKEN SOUP WITH TINY DUMPLINGS)

THIS TUNISIAN HOLIDAY CHICKEN SOUP that Yael calls *consommé nikitouche* is filled with little dumplings that have become so popular in France because of the growing Tunisian population. *Nikitouches,* similar in size to Israeli couscous, are today prepackaged. When presenting this recipe for her blog, Yael wrote, "It is winter; you are feeling feverish. Nothing replaces the *nikitouche* soup of our grandmothers." Here it is. Just remember that you must start the recipe two nights ahead.

To make the little dumplings, pulse the olive oil, semolina flour, egg yolk, and 1 teaspoon salt in the bowl of a food processor. Stream in 1 tablespoon of water, and continue to pulse until the dough comes together in a ball. Wrap the dough in plastic wrap, and allow to rest in the refrigerator for 2 hours or overnight.

When the dough has rested, take a little bit of dough, about the size of a pea, and roll it into a ball between your thumb and index finger or between your right index finger and left palm. Repeat until all of the dough has been formed into little balls. Place the *nikitouches* on a baking sheet lined with parchment paper, and cover them with a dry towel. Make sure that they are well separated, so that they don't stick together. Let the *nikitouches* dry for at least 8 hours but preferably overnight. Once they are dry, they can be stored in a tightly sealed jar.

To make the bouillon, put the chicken in a pot and cover it with 8 to 10 cups of water. Add the celery, zucchini, onion, cinnamon stick, nutmeg, and salt and freshly ground pepper to taste. Bring to a boil, skim off the scum that rises, and lower the heat, and simmer, partially covered, for about 30 minutes. Add the *nikitouches,* and simmer gently, covered, for 45 more minutes. They should double in size.

To serve, remove the skin from the chicken, break the meat into chunks, and put several chunks in each individual bowl. Ladle the soup and the *nikitouches* over the chicken, and serve hot.

YIELD: 4 TO 6 SERVINGS

2 tablespoons olive oil
1 cup semolina flour
1 egg yolk
1 teaspoon salt, plus more to taste
1 farm-raised chicken (about 3 pounds), cut up into 8 pieces
1 stalk celery, roughly chopped
1 zucchini, cut into rounds
1 onion, roughly chopped
1 cinnamon stick
½ teaspoon grated nutmeg
Freshly ground pepper to taste

Gemarti Supp

(ALSATIAN LEEK AND PORCINI SOUP)

> He spent his evening resoling the shoes of the children with old automobile tires and making a vast tureen of soup for them to eat the next day. At lunchtime he appeared in the schoolyard dragging his wagon with the metal tureen upon it, and he saw to it that each of his children got plenty of the hot soup.
>
> —Philip Hallie, *Lest Innocent Blood Be Shed:*
> *The Story of the Village of Le Chambon and*
> *How Goodness Happened There,* 1979

I LOVE *GEMARTI SUPP,* OR *SELBST GEMARTI SUPP,* which means "homemade soup" in the local Alsatian dialect. Unbeknownst to most Alsatians, this is an ancient Jewish recipe, as its name reveals. *Selbst* means "myself" in German, but *gemarti* is a Hebrew word meaning "I have completed." So this delectable mushroom soup thickened with semolina flour is named "I made it myself."

I found this simple recipe at a tiny Jewish museum (Musée Judéo-Alsacien de Bouxwiller) in Alsace. Similar to *potage bonne femme,* the broth is thickened with a roux made of oil or goose fat and semolina or barley, a common thickening technique brought to the United States and especially to Louisiana by Alsatian immigrants, including many Jews.

"We'd take the leeks out of the ground at the end of summer," recalled Jean Joho, the renowned Alsace-born chef and proprietor of Everest, Brasserie Jo, and Eiffel Tower Restaurant in Chicago. "We would keep them fresh in sand in the root cellar so that we would have them all winter."

In the Middle Ages, people believed that everything that grew in the soil, including mushrooms and truffles, was from the devil. Potatoes at first went into that category, but by the first half of the eighteenth century, potatoes, introduced in about 1673 by Turkish Jews, were well established in France, and this recipe changed. Little by little, *gemarti supp,* with its marriage of mushrooms and leeks, became almost extinct when the mixture of leek, potatoes, and cream became so popular.

2 tablespoons rendered goose fat or
    vegetable oil
1 large onion, finely chopped (about
    1½ cups)
3 tablespoons semolina flour
2 leeks, light-green and white parts
    finely chopped (about 2 cups), and
    dark-green top parts left whole
1 stalk celery, finely chopped (about
    ¼ cup)

3 carrots, peeled and finely chopped
    (about 1 cup)
4 dried porcini mushrooms, soaked in
    hot water for about 10 minutes,
    drained, and then finely chopped
Salt and freshly ground pepper to
    taste
2 tablespoons chopped fresh chives
1 baguette

Heat the goose fat or vegetable oil in a medium-sized pot. Add the onion, and cook over medium heat until golden.

Toast the semolina in a small pan, and add it to the oil and onion. Stir until the oil is absorbed, the onion is coated in the semolina, and it all begins to brown—about 5 minutes.

Pour 6 cups water into the pot, and then add the chopped leeks and leek tops, celery, carrots, and mushrooms. Season with salt and pepper to taste, bring to a boil, and simmer, covered, for an hour. The soup should be thickened, and the vegetables soft.

Remove and discard the leek tops, and serve the soup with a garnish of chives and a hunk of baguette for dunking.

An Alsatian village

Paul Bocuse's Kosher Closet

Lyon, considered the city central to French gastronomy, was near the birthplace of Taillevent, the fourteenth-century French chef who wrote *Le Viandier,* the first cookbook in French. Lyon is also home to Paul Bocuse, the most famous French chef in the world today and the man credited with starting nouvelle cuisine. Most people do not know that during World War II, Bocuse was a staunch supporter of the Resistance. Even fewer people realize that a closet in his banquet hall, whose key is proudly entrusted to the Grand Rabbi of Lyon, contains special plates and other products reserved for kosher events.

Given his location in Lyon, a city with the third-largest Jewish population in

The original kitchen in Paul Bocuse's three-star restaurant. Today there is a tiny kosher closet next door.

France, it was inevitable that some of his customers would be Jewish. In the late eighties, some patrons started asking if they could have their weddings and Bar and Bat Mitzvahs in the elaborate banquet hall of his Abbaye de Collonges, the former site of his mother's restaurant, a converted flour mill that has been in the family since 1765.

Before Bocuse agreed to host kosher events, he met with the Grand Rabbi of Lyon, who explained the constraints of the dietary laws. On the day that I was visiting the *abbaye,* a charming old house painted with bright colors and looking more like Disneyland than a staid French restaurant, the kitchen staff was waiting for the rabbi. To make the kitchen kosher, the rabbi heats a big kettle of water, says a blessing, and boils all the pans and utensils that the cooks want to use. Then he heats the convection ovens to 500 degrees, and when the ovens cool down, he puts tape over them to ensure that they remain kosher until cooking begins. Finally, he cleans the counters, sometimes covering them with aluminum foil. The rabbi keeps the kosher products in a closet close to the kitchen.

One of the difficulties for Bocuse and his staff is to find kosher products that are acceptable to their team. "We don't want to compromise on quality," said Joël Salza, who is in charge of large functions. "It is easy to find kosher mustard from Dijon, kosher meat from Lyon—or, better still, from Strasbourg—but we can't find kosher Bresse chickens for his local specialty *fricassée de volaille de Bresse.*

"For the chefs, cooking kosher is a challenge. Using different products, and not to use cream and butter for a meat meal.

"Other ingredients are easy," continued Joel. "Most of the Jews today in Lyon are from North Africa, so they are accustomed to ingredients such as saffron, coriander, and couscous."

Because Bocuse cannot create his buttery desserts for meat meals, he orders kosher sorbets from Morone Glacier, a Moroccan Jewish ice-cream manufacturer in the Alps, whose quality lives up to his exacting standards.

For kosher life-cycle events celebrated at the restaurants, the women, who are mostly Sephardic, take advantage of the prohibition against using dairy products to make instead their traditional homemade *pareve* North African pastries. (See pages 359 and 362.)

Black Truffle Soup Élysée

HERE IS PAUL BOCUSE'S kosher rendition of his famous soup with black truffles and *foie gras*. He first created it for a dinner in 1975 at the Élysée Palace (the White House of France) when he received the Légion d'Honneur from President Valéry Giscard d'Estaing for valor on the battlefield during World War II. I have omitted the fresh *foie gras*, because obtaining it both fresh and kosher is difficult. This soup is refreshingly delicious, one you can prepare ahead that will still make a grand splash at any dinner. Either make one big soup or use eight 8-ounce ramekins, as the recipe indicates.

YIELD: 8 SERVINGS

8 cups chicken, veal, or beef broth, or any combination thereof

2 carrots, peeled and finely diced (about ½ cup)

1 medium yellow onion, finely diced (about 1 cup)

2 stalks celery, finely diced (about ½ cup)

1 cup button mushrooms, finely diced

4 boneless, skinless chicken breasts

Salt and freshly ground pepper to taste

½ cup white vermouth

7 ounces black truffles, finely chopped

8 disks *pareve* puff pastry, cut slightly larger than the ramekins

4 egg yolks, beaten

Pour the stock into a medium-sized pot and bring to a boil. Add the carrots, onion, celery, mushrooms, chicken, and salt and pepper to taste. Lower the heat until the stock is barely simmering, and cook until the chicken is just cooked through, 15 to 20 minutes. You will have to test with a fork to see if it is done. Remove the chicken from the stock, and set aside.

Preheat the oven to 400 degrees. Then divide the white vermouth, the truffles, the broth, and the vegetables among eight small ovenproof bowls. When the chicken is cool enough to handle, cut it into ½-inch chunks, and divide it among the eight bowls.

Place the puff-pastry rounds on top of the soup-filled bowls, pressing down the edges to form a seal around each bowl.

Brush the puff pastry with the egg yolks, and place in the oven for 18 to 20 minutes, or until the pastry is puffed and golden. Remove from the oven, and serve immediately.

Beef Bouillon

> Today, just as in former times, the special mourning period lasts seven full days. It is during these seven days that one comes to offer one's condolences to the family of the deceased and that one sends them "meals for the grieving," which consist of hard-boiled eggs and bouillon.
>
> —Daniel Stauben, *Scenes of Jewish Life in Alsace*, 1860

BEEF BOUILLON WAS NOT SERVED only at times of mourning. It was and still often is a base for matzo balls, it is served with noodles, and it is perfectly delicious as a broth, served hot, or cold as *consommé gelé* (aspic), at the beginning of any meal.

Put the beef bones in a soup pot, and cover with cold water by at least 3 inches. Bring to a boil, and skim off any scum that rises.

If you want a dark broth, don't peel the onion. If you want a lighter one, peel it. Pierce the onion with the cloves, and add to the pot. Add the leeks, carrots, turnip, parsnip, and the *bouquet garni*. Simmer slowly, covered for 3 hours and uncovered for ½ hour. Add salt and pepper to taste, and heat. Strain the soup, and either remove any fat that might have accumulated and serve, or refrigerate, remove the fat, reheat, and serve.

YIELD: ABOUT 10 CUPS

2 pounds beef shanks or other beef bones

1 onion

4 whole cloves

3 leeks, light-green and white parts chopped, dark-green top parts left whole

3 carrots, peeled and diced

1 turnip, peeled and diced

1 parsnip, peeled and diced

Bouquet garni made of sprigs of fresh thyme and parsley and a bay leaf

Salt and freshly ground pepper to taste

Vegetarian Apple Parsnip Soup

I ONCE KNEW A VERY DISTINGUISHED French ambassador to the United States who felt that soup was the only way to start a dinner. For Jewish people in France, the broth of a stew is often the prelude to holiday and weekday meals, whether it is an Alsatian *pot-au-feu* or a North African *dafina*. A way to give new life to leftover meat and vegetables, soup has always been the food of sustenance for poor people.

When I first tasted this extraordinary soup at a dinner at the French embassy in Washington, I thought that it must have been made with good chicken broth and heavy cream, but to my surprise, it wasn't. Francis Layrle, the ambassador's former chef, made it with fresh vegetable broth, something he used very often for guests at the embassy who kept kosher or were vegetarians. This elegant and light soup has become one of my favorites, with its wonderful vegetarian broth that can be used as a basis for so many other soups. Those who do not keep kosher may, of course, substitute chicken broth. I have separated the ingredients for broth and soup, to facilitate making the vegetarian broth as a separate recipe for other occasions.

 YIELD: 6 TO 8 SERVINGS

VEGETARIAN BROTH

2 tablespoons olive oil

1 onion, peeled and diced

4 carrots, peeled and diced

½ stalk celery

2 leeks, cleaned and diced

2 bay leaves

2 branches fresh thyme

3 plum tomatoes, diced, or 6 ounces
   canned San Marzano plum
   tomatoes

A few sprigs fresh parsley

A few sprigs fresh chervil

Salt and freshly ground pepper to taste

SOUP

1 pound parsnips, peeled and diced

Juice of 1 lemon

2 tablespoons olive oil

2 tablespoons butter or *pareve*
   margarine

6 shallots, diced

4 tart apples, peeled and diced

1 cup cider

8 cups chicken or vegetable broth
   (see headnote)

Salt and white pepper to taste

A few gratings of nutmeg

1 teaspoon cider vinegar (optional)

To make the broth, heat the olive oil very slowly in a large pot. Add the onion, carrots, celery, and leeks, and sauté until the onion is transparent.

Add 10 cups water along with the bay leaves, thyme, and tomatoes. Bring to a boil, and simmer over low heat, half covered, for 45 minutes. During the last few minutes of cooking, add the parsley and chervil, and season with salt and freshly ground pepper to taste. Put everything through a sieve, and set the broth aside.

For the soup, put the parsnips and the lemon juice in a large bowl. Cover with water, and let sit for a few minutes until you are ready to make the soup. Drain and dry the parsnips.

Heat the olive oil and the butter in a heavy soup pot. Add the shallots, parsnips, and apples, and sauté for about 10 minutes, or until the shallots are clear but not golden. Add the cider, and cook, uncovered, for 5 minutes. Then add the broth, bring to a boil, cover, and simmer slowly for 40 minutes. Add salt, white pepper, and nutmeg.

Purée the soup in a blender or food processor, and if you want more acidity, add the cider vinegar. Serve immediately.

Soupe au Blé Vert

(GREEN WHEAT VEGETABLE SOUP WITH CHICKPEAS)

Rudy and Ruth Moos with their daughter, Eveline,
in Annecy, after the war

EVELINE WEYL REMEMBERS GROWING UP in France with a green-wheat soup, served every Friday evening. "We called it *gruen kern* or *soupe au blé vert,* and it was made, basically, by simmering onions and carrots and using green wheat to thicken the broth," she told me. "My mother said it was very healthy for us children."

I asked all over for a recipe for this dish but couldn't find one. Then, watching a Tunisian videographer from Paris taking photographs of his mother making soup, I realized that the soup Tunisians call *shorbat freekeh,* made with parched wheat, is nearly the same as the green-wheat soup for which I had been searching. Young green wheat is available at select health-food stores these days, and made into juice. *Ferik* or *freekeh* is the parched substitute. I like this soup so much that I often use barley, bulgur, wheat berries, or lentils if I can't find the green wheat.

In fourteenth-century Arles, Jews ate many different kinds of grains and legumes. Chickpeas, which came from the Middle East, and green wheat were probably two of them. The original recipe for this soup called for lamb bones, but I prefer a vegetarian version. The tomato paste is, of course, a late addition.

The night before you make the soup, soak the chickpeas or other dry beans in water to cover by about 3 inches.

The next day, pour the olive oil into a soup pot, and sauté the onion, celery, and carrot for about 5 minutes. Drain the chickpeas, and add them to the pan with ¼ cup of the parsley, the bay leaf, the *harissa,* cayenne pepper, salt, and black pepper. Stir in the tomato paste and a cup of water, and cook, stirring, for about 5 minutes.

Add 6 more cups water, and bring to a boil. Add the wheat or other thickeners, stir, and reduce the heat to low. Cover, and simmer for 2 hours, adding water if needed while the wheat cooks. When the chickpeas are soft, and the wheat has thickened the soup or the lentils or grains have cooked, adjust the seasonings. Fish out the bay leaf and discard. Sprinkle with the remaining parsley, and serve with lemon wedges and additional *harissa.*

YIELD: 6 TO 8 SERVINGS

1 cup dried chickpeas or other dry beans

¼ cup olive oil

1 onion, diced

1 stalk celery, finely chopped

1 carrot, peeled and diced

¼ cup plus 2 tablespoons finely chopped fresh parsley

1 bay leaf

1 teaspoon *harissa,* plus more for garnish

½ teaspoon cayenne pepper

1 teaspoon salt, or to taste

½ teaspoon freshly ground black pepper

1 tablespoon tomato paste

1 cup green wheat or parched wheat, picked over for stones and chaff and rinsed, or 1 cup lentils, wheat berries, barley, or bulgur

1 lemon, quartered

M'soki

(TUNISIAN PASSOVER SPRING VEGETABLE RAGOUT
WITH ARTICHOKES, SPINACH, FAVA BEANS, AND PEAS)

WHEN DR. SYLVIANE LÉVY (see page 65), a physician in Paris, got married, she had a Passover dilemma. Her husband's Tunisian family ate *m'soki,* a verdant soupy ragout with spring vegetables—like artichokes (considered a Jewish vegetable), spinach, and peas—and meat; her family, originally from Toledo, Spain, and later from Tétouan, Morocco, ate a thick meat-and-fava-bean soup. So which did she choose? Instead of picking sides, she serves both at her Seder. Now her grown children associate these soups with the taste of home.

M'soki, also called *béton armé* (reinforced concrete) because of its heartiness, is so popular in France today that Tunisians, Algerians, and anyone who has tasted it now prepares it for Passover, and at special events throughout the year. This very ancient soup, probably dating from the eleventh century, would have included lamb, cinnamon, rose petals, and white or yellow carrots. It would not have included *harissa,* as peppers were a New World import.

YIELD: 10 TO 12 SERVINGS

3 tablespoons vegetable oil
1 lamb shoulder, boned (about
   3 pounds)
1 pound beef ribs
2 pounds beef shank
Salt and freshly ground pepper to taste
2 fennel bulbs, cut into ½-inch pieces
3 white or yellow carrots, peeled and
   cut into ½-inch pieces
2 onions, peeled and diced
3 cloves garlic, minced
2 pounds fresh spinach, chopped
Green tops of 3 beets, chopped

2 pounds unshelled fresh fava beans,
   or 1 pound frozen
2 pounds unshelled fresh peas, or
   1 pound frozen
6 artichoke bottoms, fresh or canned,
   quartered
1 cup chopped fresh cilantro, plus
   more for garnish
1 cup chopped fresh mint, plus more
   for garnish
1 teaspoon freshly grated nutmeg
1 teaspoon *harissa* (see page 33)
4 matzos

Heat the vegetable oil in a large soup pot or Dutch oven. Season the lamb shoulder, beef ribs, and beef shank with salt and pepper to taste, and brown in batches on all sides. Remove from the pot. Then toss into the pot the fennel, carrots, onions, and garlic, and sauté, scraping up any bits of meat that have stuck to the bottom. Season with salt and pepper to taste, and cook until slightly softened. Add the spinach and beet tops, and cook until wilted. Return the browned meat to the pot, and add the fava beans and peas. Barely cover with cold water. Bring to a boil, cover, and cook over medium-high heat for 30 minutes.

Add the artichoke bottoms, cilantro, mint, nutmeg, and *harissa.* Lower the heat so that the soup is barely simmering, and cook for 2 more hours, or until the meat is very tender, adding water if needed.

Cut the meat into 1-inch pieces, discarding any bones, and put it back into the soup. Just before serving, break up the matzos into six pieces each. Soak them in salted water until slightly moistened, then press out the water. Serve the soup garnished with the reserved cilantro and mint and the matzo pieces.

A warm bowl of *m'soki*

French green lentils at an open-air market in Bordeaux

Salads

Lettuce with Classic Vinaigrette

North African Roasted Red Pepper Salad with Lemon and Garlic

Salade Juive (Moroccan Confit of Tomato and Peppers with Coriander)

Tchoukchouka (Cooked Algerian Tomato, Pepper, and Eggplant Salad)

Belleville Market's *Mechouia* (Tunisian Lunch Salad
of Tomatoes, Peppers, and Tuna Fish)

Tomato, Almond, and Lettuce Salad with Smoked Salmon,
Walnut Vinaigrette, and Dill

Artichoke and Orange Salad with Saffron and Mint

Salade d'Oranges et d'Olives Noires (Moroccan Orange and Black Olive Salad)

Salade de Blettes (Moroccan Beet Leaf or Swiss Chard Salad)

Tunisian Winter Squash Salad with Coriander and *Harissa*

French Potato Salad with Shallots and Parsley

Beet, Potato, Carrot, Pickle, and Apple Salad

Roasted Beet Salad with Cumin and Cilantro

Fennel Salad with Celery, Cucumber, Lemon, and Pomegranate

Fennel and Citrus Salad

Lentil Salad with Mustard Vinaigrette

Tunisian Carrots with Caraway and *Harissa*

Celery-Root Rémoulade

Salade Frisée with Smoked Duck and Poached Eggs

Lettuce with Classic Vinaigrette

THE FIRST TIME I TASTED a simple French lettuce salad of greens tossed in a mustardy vinaigrette, I marveled at how uncomplicated and delicious it was. Presented after the main course, as is traditional in Europe, the lettuce dish cleanses the palate. In France, with its varied climate and wonderful produce, salad greens are in season all year long and have been eaten forever, both cooked and raw.

Serve as is, or with chopped fresh basil, cilantro, dill, tarragon, or chives sprinkled on top. Tiny slices of radish are a nice addition and, according to the Talmud, help digest lettuce.

 YIELD: 4 TO 6 SERVINGS

2 tablespoons red-wine
   vinegar
½ teaspoon salt, or to taste
A few grinds of pepper
1 clove garlic, minced
1 teaspoon Dijon mustard
¼ teaspoon sugar or honey
4 tablespoons extra-virgin
   olive oil
2 tablespoons finely chopped
   shallots
The leaves of 1 head of lettuce

Mix together the vinegar, salt, pepper, garlic, mustard, and sugar or honey in a salad bowl. Whisk in the olive oil. Add the shallots, and pour the dressing into the bottom of the bowl.

Wash the lettuce, and dry it in a salad spinner or in a paper towel. Tear it up into bite-sized pieces.

Gently place the lettuce on top of the dressing. Just before serving, toss the salad. The French say to toss the dressing thirteen times so you will not become an old maid!

North African Roasted Red Pepper Salad with Lemon and Garlic

THIS IS ONE OF THE SALADS that I make frequently. For some reason, although people always ask me how I make it, I have never put the recipe in any of my cookbooks. Grilling the peppers softens the pulp and brings out the natural sweetness. Sometimes the peppers are mixed with eggplants and tomatoes in North African salads, such as the *salade juive* (recipe follows) or the *tchoukchouka* (see page 94). Sometimes they are served alone. For Rosh Hashanah and dinner parties, I love to serve the colorful combination of red peppers, carrot salad (see page 112), and roasted beet salad (see page 108).

YIELD: 6 TO 8 SERVINGS

8 to 10 red bell peppers

2 cloves garlic

Juice of 1 lemon

4 tablespoons extra-virgin olive oil

4 tablespoons chopped fresh cilantro, basil, or mint

Salt and freshly ground pepper to taste

Put the peppers on a hot grill or a gas grill, turning them with a prong as they char, or put them in a 450-degree oven on a cookie sheet for about 20 minutes. Using tongs, transfer the peppers to a plastic bag and seal it. When they are cool, peel them, and remove the seeds and stems.

Cut the peppers lengthwise into strips, and put them in a medium bowl. Mince the garlic, toss in with the peppers, and sprinkle the lemon juice over all. Gradually add the olive oil. Sprinkle with cilantro, basil, or mint, and salt and pepper to taste.

Salade Juive

(MOROCCAN CONFIT OF TOMATOES AND PEPPERS WITH CORIANDER)

WHEN I EMBARK ON A COOKBOOK, it's like going on a scavenger hunt. One clue leads to another. Sometimes they lead to unexpected findings, such as this wonderful cooked salad of Jewish origins. Someone in Washington had told me that Élisabeth Bourgeois, the chef and owner of Le Mas Tourteron, a restaurant just outside of Gordes, in the Lubéron, was Jewish.

One Sunday afternoon, a friend and I drove two hours from Saint-Rémy-de-Provence to the charming stone house with old wooden beams and antique furniture that is her restaurant. Although I had no idea what *mas tourteron* meant, an atmosphere of bonhomie filled this farmhouse (*mas*) of lovebirds (*tourterons*) as soon as Élisabeth and her husband greeted us. When I explained my quest to Élisabeth, asking her if she was Jewish, she replied, "*Pas du tout*" ("Not at all").

I thought our journey would be for naught, but since we arrived at lunchtime, we sat down to eat. And what a meal we had! Our first course was a trio of tiny late-summer vegetables served in individual cups on a long glass platter: a cucumber salad with crème fraîche and lots of chives and mint; a cold zucchini cream soup; and a luscious ratatouille-like tomato salad, the third member of the trio. When I asked Élisabeth for the recipe for this last dish, she said without hesitation, "*Ça, c'est la salade juive!*" ("That is the Jewish salad!") She explained that the recipe came from a Moroccan Jewish woman who had worked in her kitchen for about thirty years. Now it is part of her summer cooking repertoire and mine.

This recipe calls for *coriandre,* a word that the French use for both the fresh leaves and the seeds of the coriander or cilantro plant. This dish uses both. I serve it either as a salad or as a cold pasta sauce, and make it during every season, even with canned tomatoes in winter. It is always a hit.

YIELD: 8 SERVINGS,
OR ABOUT 4 CUPS

4 pounds bell peppers, red, green, or yellow (8 to 10, depending on size)

One 28-ounce can San Marzano whole tomatoes, drained, or 2 pounds ripe red tomatoes (7 to 8, depending on size)

¼ cup olive oil

2 tablespoons white wine

½ teaspoon ground coriander seeds

½ teaspoon ground cumin

1 teaspoon salt

1 tablespoon tomato paste

1 tablespoon chopped fresh chives

½ teaspoon cayenne pepper

2 tablespoons fresh lemon juice

1 cup chopped fresh cilantro

Put the peppers on a hot grill, turning them as they get charred, roast them over a gas grill using a prong to turn, or put them in a 450-degree oven for about 20 minutes. Using tongs, transfer the peppers to a plastic bag and seal it. When they are cool, peel them, and remove the seeds and stems.

If using fresh tomatoes, bring a pot of water to a boil. Plunge the tomatoes into the boiling water for a minute or two, remove with a slotted spoon, and cool in a bowl of ice water. When cool enough to handle, peel off and discard the skin.

Heat the oil in a large frying pan. Roughly chop the tomatoes and peppers, and add them with the wine, coriander seeds, cumin, salt to taste, tomato paste, and chives to the frying pan. Cook slowly, uncovered, for about 20 minutes, or until most of the liquid is absorbed. Stir in the cayenne pepper and the lemon juice, and sprinkle with the fresh cilantro. Serve as a salad or an appetizer.

Salade juive cooked down to tomato jam

Tchoukchouka

(COOKED ALGERIAN TOMATO, PEPPER, AND EGGPLANT SALAD)

WHEN WE WERE VISITING GALIMARD, one of the perfume factories in Grasse, our guide was an adorable young French girl with huge hazel eyes named Cyrielle Charpentier. After we finished the tour, learning about the flowers from around Grasse that go into perfumes, Cyrielle let us try some of the essences. Noticing a *chai,* the Jewish symbol for "life," on a chain around her neck, we asked her if she was Jewish, and she said that she was. Her father, a Holocaust survivor, and her mother, an Italian Jew who also suffered during the war, lived near Grasse. When I asked her what foods she liked, she immediately named her grandmother's *tchoukchouka,* a North African dish with tomatoes, peppers, and sometimes eggplant.

The purists' versions of *tchoukchouka,* this *salade cuite,* include lots of garlic and no onions, but I have seen some with onions as well. The beauty of this delicious recipe is that it is prepared in advance and tastes even better the next day, especially helpful for the Sabbath and other Jewish holidays, when cooking is prohibited and there is little time to prepare food—you do not have to fuss with a last-minute salad. It can also be used as a base for an egg or sausage dish, and is great as a sauce over pasta.

At work in the flower fields of Grasse

Tchoukchouka at a Shabbat dinner after a civil wedding

Preheat the oven to 450 degrees. Pierce the eggplant all over with a fork, and put it on a baking pan. Roast for about 20 minutes, or until soft, turning once. Allow to cool before scooping the pulp from the eggplant (discard the skin).

On another baking sheet, roast the peppers for 20 minutes. When cool enough to handle, peel them, removing the seeds and any white pith from the peppers. Then cut them into large dice.

If using fresh tomatoes, bring a pot of water to a boil. Plunge the tomatoes into the boiling water for a minute or two, remove with a slotted spoon, and cool in a bowl of ice water. When they are cool enough to handle, peel and dice, keeping most of the liquid but discarding the skin.

Heat the olive oil in a large frying pan. Add the garlic, and cook for a minute or two, until fragrant but not burned. Stir in the eggplant, peppers, and tomatoes, cooking very slowly, uncovered, for about 1 hour, or until almost all the liquid has been evaporated, stirring occasionally and adding additional oil if needed.

Season with salt and pepper to taste and, if you think it is needed, add sugar.

Cool, and sprinkle lemon juice over all. Serve sprinkled with the cilantro.

YIELD: 8 SERVINGS

1 pound eggplant (1 large or about 2 small eggplants)

2 pounds red or orange bell peppers (about 4 large ones)

2 pounds tomatoes, or one 28-ounce can San Marzano chopped tomatoes

6 tablespoons olive oil

6 cloves garlic, minced

Salt and freshly ground pepper to taste

1 to 2 teaspoons sugar (optional)

Juice of 1 lemon

¼ cup chopped fresh cilantro

Belleville Market's *Mechouia*

(TUNISIAN LUNCH SALAD OF TOMATOES, PEPPERS, AND TUNA FISH)

LITTLE TUNIS AND THE MULTICULTURAL and bustling Belleville market in Paris are populated with French farmers and merchants from North Africa. In the restaurants and stores bordering the market, you feel as if you are in North Africa, as Tunisians and others congregate at kosher and halal restaurants, bars, and bakeries. You also feel the influence of the Italian tenure in Tunisia: Italian bread, beignets shaped like the Italian manicotti, and canned tuna in olive oil.

An everyday snack that Jews and Muslims make from the ingredients found in this market is a large *brik* filled with parsley, tuna, and a raw egg, then quickly deep-fried and served with a salad called *mechouia*. The word *mechouia*, which means "grilled" in Arabic, can be applied to grilling an entire lamb or just the vegetables that go with it. Some sprinkle salt on the grill to keep away the evil eye. The trick to making a good *mechouia* is grilling more tomatoes than peppers. To retain the flavor of both vegetables, sprinkle them with salt after they are grilled and peeled, and let them drain overnight, to help the water seep out. In the market, Tunisians use *corne-de-boeuf* peppers, the ones they grew up with in Tunisia, but you can substitute Anaheim peppers, which are very similar, or others.

YIELD: 4 SERVINGS

6 small ripe tomatoes

3 Anaheim, poblano, or green bell peppers

2 cloves garlic

1 teaspoon sea salt, or to taste

2 tablespoons extra-virgin olive oil

Pepper to taste

One 3-ounce can tuna packed in olive oil*

1 hard-boiled egg, quartered

2 tablespoons chopped ripe black olives

*I prefer the Cento brand, which is kosher.

Using a heated grill, a frying pan without oil, or the broiler, grill the tomatoes, peppers, and garlic until the skin is charred and blistered. Remove them, and once the vegetables are cool, peel, making sure to remove all charred parts as well as the seeds of the tomatoes. Cut the vegetables into long strands, place in a sieve, sprinkle with about 1 teaspoon salt, and let the water drain out for an hour or overnight.

Toss the vegetables into a large glass bowl. Using two knives, cut them into little pieces, drizzle with the olive oil, sprinkle with pepper, and adjust seasonings.

Put the tuna in the center of the vegetables, and decorate with the hard-boiled egg and the black olives.

A winery near Bordeaux—a perfect setting for a French salad

Tomato, Almond, and Lettuce Salad with Smoked Salmon, Walnut Vinaigrette, and Dill

Probably the first-ever wedding huppah in this alpine village

WHILE ATTENDING A CATHOLIC-JEWISH WEDDING in Aussois, a quaint French alpine village near the Italian border, I wondered aloud to the bride's uncle if this wasn't the first time most of the villagers had ever met a Jew. In response, he told me this chilling story. During the Second World War, under the Italian occupation of France, 125 Jews were hidden in a house at the base of the town's fortress, which was a confinement center. Villagers brought them a little bread and some potatoes to supplement their meager provisions. When the Italians left, the Jews were sure they were liberated and took a train home, only to run into German soldiers, who sent them all directly to Auschwitz. Even today, stories like this one are often hushed up because they are so painful to hear.

Before the wedding ceremony, my husband and I sat down in a tiny café overlooking the mountains and tasted this salad with fresh lettuce, smoked salmon, tomatoes, and local walnut vinegar, a prized ingredient that I had never tasted but have since found on the Internet.

Dill is such an important flavor in Jewish cooking that the French eleventh-century biblical commentator and Talmudic scholar Rashi wrote that if dill is used for flavor, a special blessing over the earth must be recited before tasting it. If, however, it is simply added to decorate the dish, it is not intended for food value, so just a general prayer over food must be recited.

 YIELD: 4 SERVINGS

¼ pound smoked salmon,
   cut into 1-inch pieces
2 tomatoes, cut into wedges
4 cups mixed salad greens
¼ cup slivered almonds, toasted
2 tablespoons walnut wine vinegar

1 teaspoon Dijon mustard
½ teaspoon mustard powder
3 tablespoons vegetable oil
Salt and freshly ground pepper to taste
2 tablespoons chopped fresh dill
2 tablespoons chopped fresh chives

Gently toss together the smoked salmon, tomatoes, greens, and toasted almonds in a salad bowl.

Whisk together the vinegar, mustard, mustard powder, oil, and salt and freshly ground pepper to taste in a small bowl. Pour over the salad, mix, and sprinkle with the dill and chives just before serving.

Artichoke and Orange Salad with Saffron and Mint

ARTICHOKES, ONE OF MY FAVORITE VEGETABLES, are edible thistles that were prized by the ancient Romans as food of the nobility. They have been a springtime food in the Mediterranean for thousands of years and particularly loved by Jews. Usually the French serve artichokes as a cold salad appetizer with a vinaigrette.

Although I have seen this recipe in many Jewish cookbooks from North Africa, I hadn't tasted it until Paula Wolfert cooked it for me on my PBS show, *Jewish Cooking in America*. It was a *merveille,* as my French friends would say.

In the years since, I have eaten many different versions of this salad. Céline Bénitah, who lives in Annecy but came from Berkane, on the Algerian border of Morocco, said that all North African Jews who grew up in this orange-growing region have their own versions of this recipe. Hers includes saffron. Of course, this salad tastes best when fresh artichokes are used, but frozen artichoke hearts or bottoms work as well.

 YIELD: 6 TO 8 SERVINGS

1½ lemons, juiced
15 fresh baby artichokes, or
    15 frozen artichoke hearts
    or bottoms
2 tablespoons olive oil
2 cloves garlic, peeled and
    thinly sliced
1⅓ cups orange juice
Salt and freshly ground pepper
    to taste
4 Valencia or other thin-
    skinned oranges
1 tablespoon sugar, or to taste
Pinch of saffron
2 tablespoons chopped fresh
    cilantro
2 tablespoons chopped fresh
    mint

If using fresh artichokes, pour about 4 cups water and the juice of half a lemon into a large bowl. Break off the outer leaves of the artichokes, leaving only the tender inner ones. Trim off the tips and the rough parts of the stems, and drop the artichokes into the acidulated water.

Heat the olive oil in a sauté pan over medium heat, and cook the garlic for about a minute, or until fragrant. Stir in the remaining lemon juice, 1 cup of the orange juice, and salt and freshly ground pepper to taste. Bring the liquid to a boil, and add the artichokes. Reduce the heat to low, and cook the artichokes, covered, for about 10 minutes for frozen hearts and 20 minutes for fresh, or until tender. Remove the artichokes with a slotted spoon to a serving dish, reserving the cooking liquid.

While the artichokes are cooking, section the oranges by cutting off the skin and white pith and cutting in between the white membranes. Put the orange segments in a small skillet with the remaining ⅓ cup orange juice, the sugar, and the saffron. Cook over medium heat for about 5 minutes. With a slotted spoon, transfer the glazed orange segments to the serving dish. Reduce the liquid in the pan until syrupy, about 5 more minutes.

Pour the artichoke-cooking juices into the syrup skillet. Reduce over high heat to a few tablespoons, adjust the seasonings, and drizzle over the artichokes and oranges. Cool to room temperature. Just before serving, garnish with the cilantro and mint.

Purple-hearted artichokes, or *artichauts poivrades*, are often eaten raw in the south of France.

Shabbat with the
Grand Rabbi of Bordeaux

On a Friday night I prayed at the Grande Synagogue in Bordeaux, where, more than sixty years ago, the Jews were held in detention by the Nazis. First built in 1810, then rebuilt in 1873, after a great fire, the synagogue, with its towering columns made of Carrara marble, is the largest in France, with a seating capacity of fifteen hundred.

Rabbi Claude Maman, the king of kosher wine in the Bordeaux region (see page 22), invited us to dinner. We walked to his home, an apartment in a turn-of-the-century limestone building with wooden moldings, located down the street from the synagogue where he was the Grand Rabbi until he retired a few years ago.

On the mantelpiece was a large magnum of 2000 red Médoc—kosher, of course—given to him by one of his wine associates. After the blessing over the wine, we sipped the Médoc, and glasses of Pomerol and Saint-Émilion from bottles that he opened and set out on a table for us. It was in Bordeaux that Rabbi Maman became interested in French wines. For centuries, in fact, this particular rabbinical job description has included the supervision of the production of kosher wines.

The rabbi, born in Fez, came to France in 1957, after Morocco's independence. A few years later, he met his wife, Arlette, who continues to make the French Moroccan food of her childhood for his family, just as she did for us. My favorite part of this copious Friday night meal was the salads, made in advance for the Sabbath.

Salade d'Oranges et d'Olives Noires

(MOROCCAN ORANGE AND BLACK OLIVE SALAD)

"I SO MISS SHABBAT MEALS IN FRANCE," a young North African man from Marseille living in Washington told me when we were seated next to each other on a plane. "My mother never makes fewer than ten to fifteen salads." One of these salads might be a combination of oranges and olives. It is very refreshing, and looks beautiful as one of many Moroccan salads. The black and orange colors remind me of black-eyed Susans. Prepared with argan oil, which comes from argan pits harvested from the argan tree, the salad is balanced with the oranges and grapefruit. These are all 2,000-year-old Moroccan flavors.

Segment the oranges and grapefruit: first remove the outer skin, then the white pith, and cut in between the white membranes to free the segments.

Toss the oranges and grapefruit and their juice with the olives, scallions, lemon juice, olive or peanut oil, and salt and freshly ground pepper to taste. Garnish with the parsley before serving. Serve in a bowl or on salad plates.

YIELD: 4 TO 6 SERVINGS

4 oranges, peeled
1 grapefruit, peeled
1 handful of cured black olives, pitted
3 scallions, finely chopped
1 teaspoon lemon juice
1 tablespoon argan, extra-virgin olive, or peanut oil
Salt and freshly ground pepper to taste
2 tablespoons chopped fresh parsley

Salade de Blettes

(MOROCCAN BEET LEAF OR SWISS CHARD SALAD)

MOROCCAN COOKS USUALLY MAKE this tasty salad with Swiss chard, but I have seen it also with beet leaves. Eaten all year round, it is prepared by Moroccans on Rosh Hashanah for their Sephardic Seder, when they say a series of blessings over squash, leeks, dates, pomegranates, black-eyed peas, apples, the head of a fish or a lamb, and Swiss chard and beet greens.

YIELD: 4 TO 6 SERVINGS

⅓ cup peanut, grapeseed, or
  vegetable oil
4 cloves garlic, minced
2 bunches of Swiss chard or
  beet leaves with stems,
  coarsely chopped
  (about 1 pound)
Salt to taste
1 teaspoon sweet paprika
1 teaspoon ground cumin
1 teaspoon *harissa* (see
  page 33), or to taste
¼ cup white vinegar or lemon
  juice
Freshly ground pepper to taste

Heat the oil in a medium skillet. Toss in the garlic, sautéing until just fragrant, then add the chard and cook for a few minutes. Sprinkle on a little salt, the paprika, cumin, and *harissa,* and cook for another minute, stirring. Pour the vinegar or lemon juice into the pan, and cook for another minute, or until it has begun to evaporate. Season with salt and freshly ground pepper to taste. Serve at room temperature.

Tunisian Winter Squash Salad
with Coriander and *Harissa*

THIS IS A SURPRISING and appealing melding of squash, coriander, and *harissa* that I tasted with couscous when I was recently in Paris. It is also served on Rosh Hashanah.

Bring about 6 cups water to a boil in a large pot. Then add the squash, salt, and garlic clove. Lower the heat, and simmer until the squash is very tender, about 20 minutes.

Remove the squash to a mesh strainer, and squeeze the garlic out of its skin into the strainer. Mash the two together to get rid of any water. Transfer them to a large bowl, and stir in the *harissa,* salt to taste, the coriander, lemon juice, and olive oil. Taste, adjust the seasonings, then serve.

 YIELD: 4 SERVINGS

1 pound butternut or kabocha squash, peeled and cut into large chunks

1 teaspoon salt, plus more to taste

1 clove garlic, unpeeled

1 teaspoon *harissa* (see page 33)

¼ teaspoon ground coriander

Juice of ½ lemon

1 tablespoon extra-virgin olive oil

Kabocha squash

French Potato Salad with Shallots and Parsley

THIS CLASSIC FRENCH POTATO SALAD is very simple. A non-Jewish version might include *lardons* (a type of bacon) and shallots, but instead I use a tart mayonnaise. For a North African touch, you can add sliced hard-boiled eggs and cured black olives. I often add julienned basil with the parsley, or other compatible herbs.

YIELD: 6 SERVINGS

8 large or 16 small new
  potatoes (about 2 pounds)
Salt to taste
½ cup finely chopped shallots
1 egg yolk
¼ cup red-wine vinegar
½ cup vegetable or extra-virgin
  olive oil
Freshly ground pepper to taste
½ cup chopped fresh parsley

Wash the potatoes under running water, removing any dirt with your hands. Peel them, cut into quarters or eighths, depending on their size, and drop into a pot of water. Bring the water to a boil, add salt to taste, and cook until tender but still firm, 8 to 10 minutes. Drain.

Toss the potatoes and the shallots together in a salad bowl.

Using a food processor fitted with a steel blade, blend the egg yolk and vinegar. With the motor running, slowly stream in the vegetable or olive oil. Season with salt and freshly ground pepper to taste. Fold the dressing into the warm potatoes, sprinkle with parsley, and serve warm or at room temperature.

Beet, Potato, Carrot, Pickle, and Apple Salad

WHEN I VISITED MY COUSINS IN ANNECY, they served me this unusual salad. Its variety of colors and textures is stunning. As with many other cooked salads, it tastes even better the next day, making it a great dish for dinner parties or picnics. The kosher dill pickles came from shopping trips to Geneva and were a big treat.

Preheat the oven to 350 degrees, and line a baking sheet with aluminum foil.

Cut off the tops of the beets, scrub them, and place them on the baking sheet. Coat them with 1 tablespoon of the olive oil, and roast them in the oven for an hour. Remove from the oven, and when they are cool enough to handle, peel and cut them into ½-inch cubes.

Bring a small pot of salted water to a boil, and cook the potatoes until they are tender, about 15 minutes. Remove from the water, and allow to cool before peeling and cutting into ½-inch cubes. Cook the carrot for about 5 minutes in that same boiling salted water. Remove with a slotted spoon, cool, and cut into ½-inch rounds.

Whisk together the vinegar, garlic, mustard, sugar, and salt and freshly ground pepper to taste in a salad bowl. Stream in the remaining 4 tablespoons olive oil. Toss in the beets, the potatoes, the carrot, the pickle, the apple, and the eggs. Stir until everything is just coated with the vinaigrette. Serve at room temperature, or refrigerate and serve the next day, either way garnished with fresh dill.

YIELD: 6 TO 8 SERVINGS

2 medium beets
5 tablespoons olive oil
Salt to taste
2 small (not tiny) russet potatoes
1 large carrot, peeled
2 tablespoons red- or white-wine vinegar
1 clove garlic, minced
1 teaspoon Dijon mustard
Dash of sugar
Freshly ground pepper to taste
1 large kosher sour pickle, diced
1 tart green apple, diced
2 hard-boiled eggs, peeled and roughly chopped
1 tablespoon chopped fresh dill

Roasted Beet Salad with Cumin and Cilantro

IN MARKETS ALL OVER FRANCE, I saw stalls with freshly boiled and peeled beets, which saves cooks from dyeing their hands the telltale pink that comes from handling beets. Since we seldom have this convenience in America, I prefer to roast my beets to intensify their earthy flavor, and then carefully peel and cut them. Beets and cumin marry well and look beautiful when sprinkled with lots of green cilantro.

YIELD: 6 TO 8 SERVINGS

9 medium beets in your choice of colors

½ cup olive oil

Juice of 1 lemon

Juice of 1 orange

3 tablespoons balsamic vinegar

2 cloves garlic, peeled and minced

1 teaspoon ground cumin, or to taste

1 teaspoon sweet paprika, or to taste

½ teaspoon sea salt, or to taste

¼ teaspoon freshly ground pepper, or to taste

6 tablespoons finely chopped fresh cilantro or parsley

Preheat the oven to 350 degrees, and line a baking sheet with aluminum foil.

Scrub the beets, and, keeping them whole with an inch or so of the bottoms still attached, place on the baking sheet. Drizzle with 2 teaspoons of the oil, and roast for an hour, or until tender when pierced with a fork. Cool, peel, and cut into bite-sized pieces.

To make the vinaigrette, purée two-thirds of the cooked beets with the lemon and orange juice, the balsamic vinegar, the garlic, the cumin, the sweet paprika, the salt, the pepper, and the remaining olive oil. This can be done a day in advance.

Just before serving, toss the rest of the beets with the vinaigrette. Adjust the seasonings and garnish with the cilantro or parsley. Serve alone or as one of several colorful salads, such as the red *salade juive* (see page 92) and the orange Tunisian carrot salad (see page 112).

Fennel Salad with Celery, Cucumber, Lemon, and Pomegranate

THE SEEDS OF CULTIVATED FENNEL, like eggplant, are said to have been brought to France by Jews and other merchants. Of course, wild fennel grows everywhere in the south of France.

I have tasted this salad in many North African French homes. It is very simple, and a lovely counterpoint to all the more elaborate salads of the North African tradition. Once the fennel and celery have begun to wilt a bit, the flavors all come together. If pomegranates are not in season, substitute dried cranberries or cherries.

Cut the fennel bulb in quarters, then lengthwise into ½-inch-thick slices. Snip 2 tablespoons of the fronds, and set aside. Toss the fennel, 1 tablespoon of the fronds, the celery, the cucumber, and the onion together in a medium-sized salad bowl.

Squeeze the lemon over the vegetables, and drizzle on the olive oil. Season with salt and pepper to taste, and toss to coat. Serve, sprinkled with the remaining tablespoon of fennel fronds, and the pomegranate seeds.

YIELD: 6 SERVINGS

1 large fennel bulb, fronds intact

2 stalks celery, cut into ½-inch pieces

1 cucumber, sliced into rounds

¼ cup diced red onion

Juice of 1 lemon

4 tablespoons extra-virgin olive oil

Salt and freshly ground pepper to taste

2 tablespoons pomegranate seeds

Pomegranate

NOTE To peel the pomegranate without staining yourself with juice, gently score the outer skin in quarters. Then place the entire pomegranate in a large bowl filled with water. With your hands under the water, gently pull off the skin and remove the arils (the seeds, with their fleshy covering), which will fall to the bottom. Drain off the water and discard everything but the arils. Dab them dry and leave on paper towels until ready to serve. You can also cut the pomegranate in two, then, holding one half in your hand with seeds down over a bowl, whack the outer shell with a mixing spoon, letting the seeds fall through your hands and into the bowl. Keep whacking the shell until all the seeds are out; remove any pith that falls into the bowl. Repeat with the other half of the pomegranate.

Fennel and Citrus Salad

CHEF DANIEL ROSE (see page 68) served the following salad with *brandade* potato latkes (see page 308) at his Spring Restaurant during Hanukkah. The secret to this colorful winter salad is to keep the fennel very cold. This recipe, and all Daniel Rose's recipes, may change according to the market and *ses humeurs* (the chef's moods).

YIELD: 6 TO 8 SERVINGS

1 fennel bulb, trimmed

4 grapefruit

5 oranges

1 teaspoon sugar

3 tablespoons sherry vinegar

½ cup extra-virgin olive oil

Freshly ground pepper to taste

2 handfuls of baby arugula

Sea salt to taste

Finely grated zest of 1 lemon

2 tablespoons finely chopped fresh dill

1 tablespoon chopped fresh parsley

1½ tablespoons chopped fresh mint

Using a mandoline or a sharp knife, slice the fennel very thin. Place it in a bowl of ice water, and refrigerate for at least an hour or until ready to use.

Cut off the tops and the bottoms of the grapefruit and oranges. Slice off the peel and white pith, and cut in between the white membranes to yield individual segments. Put in a large bowl, and stir in the sugar, vinegar, olive oil, and pepper to taste.

Arrange the arugula on a serving platter. Drain the fennel well, pat dry, and season to taste with salt and pepper. Toss into the bowl of citrus segments and their vinaigrette, and toss to mix.

Scoop the citrus-fennel mixture on top of the arugula. Sprinkle with lemon zest, dill, parsley, and mint. Serve immediately.

Lentil Salad with Mustard Vinaigrette

GUY WEYL WAS A LITTLE BOY during World War II, when his parents fled the Nazis, first hiding in the Dordogne and then crossing the border into Spain when France became too dangerous. They then went to Portugal, and from there took a boat to New York, where they stayed through the rest of the war. The whole time Guy was in the United States, he missed the green lentils from France. During the war, lentils were just beginning to gain popularity in New York as a wartime alternative to meat, but they still were not the delicacy they were in France. So, when Guy returned to France and went to school, he was thrilled to eat lentils again, but his schoolmates laughed at his fondness for them, because that was all they had had to eat during the war. This hasn't lessened his ardor for the tiny green pulses, and Guy's wife, Eveline, makes a wonderful lentil salad.

Rinse the lentils, and discard any pebbles you may find.

Put the lentils in a saucepan with water to cover. Set the saucepan over medium heat, and bring to a boil. Add the teaspoon of salt, the celery, quartered onion, garlic, bay leaf, and 1 teaspoon of the fresh thyme. Simmer the lentils, uncovered, for about 20 minutes, or until *al dente*. (Cooking time for lentils can vary greatly.) When cool enough to handle, fish out the celery, onion, and bay leaf, and discard.

Whisk together, in a salad bowl, the mustard, vinegar, oil, salt, and freshly ground pepper to taste. Drain the lentils while warm, and put them in the bowl with the vinaigrette. Toss with the diced onion, parsley, and remaining teaspoon of thyme.

YIELD: 4 TO 6 SERVINGS

1 cup green lentils or lentils from Puy

1 teaspoon salt, plus more to taste

1 stalk celery with leaves, cut into ½-inch dice

1 onion, quartered, plus ½ onion, diced

1 clove garlic

1 bay leaf

2 teaspoons fresh thyme, or 1 teaspoon dried thyme

1 teaspoon Dijon mustard

1 tablespoon red-wine vinegar

2 tablespoons extra-virgin olive oil

Freshly ground pepper to taste

1 bunch of fresh parsley, finely chopped

Tunisian Carrots with Caraway and *Harissa*

WHEN ALEXANDRE ZBIROU CAME TO FRANCE from Tunisia in 1966 to study marketing, there were few good kosher restaurants in Paris. In 1976, he opened a French restaurant, called Au Rendez-vous/La Maison du Couscous, in the Eighth Arrondissement near the Champs-Élysées. Four years later, he turned it into a kosher Tunisian restaurant, the only one of its kind in the quarter. Today, there are more than thirty-eight in the Eighth Arrondisement. "I saw Jews arriving in the quarter," he told me over lunch at his restaurant. "They came, and I was waiting for them. It was home cooking for Tunisians and Ashkenazim. After all, there are lots of mixed marriages here in France."

In 1988, his mother, Jeanne Zbirou, immigrated to Paris, and is now directing the cooking in the kitchen. Well into her eighties, she comes to the restaurant every day to work with her son. His restaurant, although technically kosher, does not close on Friday night or Saturday. "I feel that we are rendering a service to kosher clientele, to give them a kosher meal for the Sabbath," he said. Other restaurants, under the supervision of the Parisian rabbinical authority, the Beth Din, are either closed for the Sabbath or open only to customers who pay in advance.

Carrots for Rosh Hashanah

Sitting down at the restaurant, we were first served an array of *kemia,* similar to the ubiquitous *mezze* at Arab restaurants. We began with flaky *brik,* filled with potatoes, parsley, and hard-boiled eggs (see page 30). At least a dozen salads followed, served on tiny plates, all brimming with bold colors and flavors. Some of my favorites were raw artichoke slivers with *harissa,* oil, and onions; turnips with bitter orange; and this delicious carrot salad with *harissa* and caraway seeds. When I asked how much salt they used to cook the carrots, Jeanne said, "Enough salt to make a raw egg rise in water." In my own kitchen, I prefer roasting the carrots, because it brings out the sweetness of the vegetable.

Preheat the oven to 350 degrees, and toss the carrots and the garlic with half of the olive oil in a small roasting pan. Roast in the oven for about 50 minutes, or until the carrots are fork-tender. Remove from the oven.

While the carrots are roasting, whisk together the lemon juice, remaining olive oil, *harissa,* caraway seeds, cumin, salt, and sweet paprika.

After the carrots have cooled slightly, cut them into ½-inch rounds and toss them with the dressing. Transfer to a shallow bowl, and sprinkle with cilantro, parsley, or chives.

YIELD: 8 SERVINGS

2 pounds carrots, peeled

4 cloves garlic, peeled and sliced into slivers

⅓ cup olive oil

2 tablespoons lemon juice

1 teaspoon *harissa* (see page 33)

1 teaspoon caraway seeds, whole or ground in a spice grinder

½ teaspoon ground cumin

1 teaspoon salt, or to taste

½ teaspoon sweet paprika

2 tablespoons chopped fresh cilantro, parsley, or chives

Celery-Root Rémoulade

AT A RECENT KIDDUSH AFTER a Bat Mitzvah service in France, the wine was French, unlike the sweet wine usually served at American synagogues. The food was elegantly prepared, as only the French can do it: spread out on a large table were thin slices of smoked salmon on toast, eggplant rolled and filled with goat cheese, a North African sautéed-pepper salad, squash soup served in tiny cups, and celery-root rémoulade.

If you have never eaten celery-root salad, then start now! And if you've never made mayonnaise before, it's an exhilarating and rewarding experience that I highly recommend. Any leftover mayonnaise can be kept in a jar in the refrigerator for a few days.

 YIELD: 4 TO 6 SERVINGS

1 pound celery root (also called celeriac), peeled
2 carrots, peeled
1 green apple (optional)
1 tablespoon salt, plus more to taste
3 tablespoons plus 1 teaspoon freshly squeezed lemon juice
1 large egg
1 teaspoon Dijon mustard
½ cup vegetable oil
½ cup light olive oil
Freshly ground pepper to taste

Cut the celery root, carrots, and the optional apple into julienne matchsticks. The best way to do this is to use a julienne disk on a food processor. Work quickly, so the celeriac doesn't change color. Toss the sticks in a large bowl with 1 tablespoon salt and 3 tablespoons lemon juice. Add enough cold water to the bowl just to cover the mixture, and let it steep for 30 minutes. Drain, and discard the water.

Using a food processor fitted with a steel blade, pulse together the egg, the remaining 1 teaspoon lemon juice, and the mustard. With the motor running, slowly stream in the oils. When you finish pouring in the oil, you should have a thick, yellowish mayonnaise. Season with salt and freshly ground pepper to taste.

Put the celery root, carrots, and apple together with 2 heaping tablespoons of your prepared mayonnaise into a large bowl, and fold together. Cover, and refrigerate until ready to serve. This tends to taste best when it sits for a day or two in the refrigerator.

Salade Frisée with Smoked Duck and Poached Eggs

THIS IS A RECIPE THAT NATAN HOLCHAKER, an avid cook, makes in Bordeaux. In a take on the classic *frisée* and *lardons,* Natan uses duck instead of the prohibited pork. I have found that in France even the most secular French Jews avoid pork, substituting smoked duck instead. You can also substitute turkey bacon or kosher beef fry (akin to pastrami).

Put the eggs in a small saucepan filled with water. Bring to a boil, and cook for 4 minutes, then drop the eggs into ice water for a minute.

While the eggs are cooking, arrange all the lettuce and greens on eight individual plates.

Sauté the duck, turkey bacon, or beef fry in a little oil in a frying pan. Add the shallot and cook until the meat is crisp.

As soon as the eggs are ready, shell them and cut them in half. Arrange one half of each egg on a bed of lettuce. The yolk will spill over onto the salad. Top with the diced meat and the shallot and a sprinkling of sea salt and freshly ground pepper. Repeat with the other servings. Serve warm.

 YIELD: 8 SERVINGS

4 large eggs

8 cups greens, either baby lettuce or mâche

1 cup purslane, arugula, escarole, or other bitter salad greens

3 ounces smoked duck, diced turkey bacon, or kosher beef fry, cut into small chunks

Oil for sautéeing

1 large shallot, finely chopped

Sea salt and freshly ground pepper to taste

A world of Jewish baked goods in Paris's Marais

Breads, Both Sacred and Secular

Fougasse (An Old Ladder Bread)

Alsatian *Barches* or *Pain au Pavot* (Braided Sabbath Bread with Poppy Seeds)

Pain Pétri (Moroccan Anise-Flavored Challah with Sesame Seeds)

Tunisian *Bejma* (Friday Night Bread)

Rabbi's Wife's Challah

Brioche for Rosh Hashanah

Babka à la Française (*Babka* Rolls with Olive Tapenade)

Parisian *Pletzl* (A Big Bialy)

Alsatian Pretzels with a Moroccan Touch

Brassados (Provençal Boiled and Baked Rolls with a Hole)

Oatmeal Bread with Fig, Anise, and Walnuts

Hutzel Wecken (Alsatian Hanukkah Fruit Bread)

Quick Goat Cheese Bread with Mint and Apricots

A Baker in Provence

Fougasse

In Marcel Pagnol's famous movie *The Baker's Wife,* the baker Aimable gives his wife, Aurélie, a bread shaped like a heart. The bread is a *fougasse,* a very old bread, which comes from the Italian word *focaccia.* Gérard Auzet, a fourth-generation retired breadbaker in Cavaillon, pointed this out to me during lunch at his house in nearby Beaucaire. We sat in an arbor, nestled between white-oak trees, overlooking vineyards from which the wine we were sipping was made. "The history of bread," he said, "is the history of men and of all time."

Gérard's great-grandfather, also a baker, traveled on a donkey to farmers' houses in the countryside, bringing with him flour and his starter—a fermentation of flour, grapes or other fruit, and water—and would make bread that was good for eight days. At that time, most bread was formed in round country loaves. One of Gérard's specialties, which used to be baked on Sundays and for special occasions at his bakery in Cavaillon, was these handmade *fougasses,* which he still makes at home, sometimes studded with olives or anchovies, sometimes with *herbes de Provence,* and sometimes with the spices used in bouillabaisse. According to Gérard, who is not Jewish, *fougasse,* a very old flatbread, was traditionally made from November to the end of March with olive oil, and in the summer months with butter. He showed me with his fingers how the designs differ—crosses poked in the bread for olive-oil, and oblong holes for butter *fougasse.*

Fougasse

(AN OLD LADDER BREAD)

Maman! Oin pan a oli
Uje me fait goi!
Mama! Make bread with oil
Or I become a goy!

—Old Provençal Jewish song

KALONYMUS BEN KALONYMUS, a Provençal Jewish philosopher, writer, and translator who wrote in the early part of the fourteenth century, satirized the Jewish community of Arles for dreaming, while at synagogue, about the honey, milk, and flour that they would use to make their ladder breads for Shavuot. Although *fougasse* was and is usually made with oil, at this Jewish holiday celebrating the giving of the Torah and the abundance of dairy products at the time of the barley harvest, the Jews used milk. The *fougasse* was baked in the shape of a so-called ladder, with holes, and candied cherries or candied orange peel hung or embedded in the dough. Ladders to heaven are a common metaphor for holiday breads in Judaism.

The *fougasse,* kneaded and shaped by hand at home for the Sabbath and holidays, was then carried on a board to the baker, sometimes Jewish and sometimes Christian, depending on the size of the Jewish community in the town.

Put the yeast, olive oil, and 2½ cups lukewarm water in the bowl of a standing mixer and blend. Add 6 cups of the flour and the salt gradually to the yeast mixture, stirring with the dough hook and adding more flour as necessary until the dough comes together. Form the dough into a ball and let rise in a bowl, covered, for one hour, then divide the dough into two portions. Roll each out into an oval about ¼ inch thick.

Preheat the oven to 400 degrees, scatter some semolina on a cookie sheet, and transfer the dough onto the prepared sheet. Let rise for 30 minutes.

Brush with additional olive oil, and bake in the oven for about 20 minutes. Eat when warm, if possible.

P YIELD: *2 FOUGASSES*

2 teaspoons active dry yeast
½ cup olive oil, plus more for brushing
6 to 8 cups all-purpose flour
1 tablespoon salt
Semolina for dusting

NOTE to make a butter *fougasse*, substitute ½ cup softened butter for the oil and 1½ cups milk for the water, and add ¼ cup honey.

Alsatian *Barches* or *Pain au Pavot*

(BRAIDED SABBATH BREAD WITH POPPY SEEDS)

> In the kitchen, the fire crackling joyously in the oven and under the cooking pots; they are cooking the weekly bread and the *barches* for the Sabbath, to be blessed at the table.
> —George Stenne, *Perle* (Paris, 1877)

DANIEL HELMSTETTER LIVES HIS LIFE by the sign that hangs above his bakery in Colmar: "*Le talent et la passion.*" A fourth-generation baker, he told me that he "fell into the mixer and never came out." The Helmstetter Bakery was started by his grandfather in 1906 in the central square of Colmar, a town once known for its large Jewish population. Each Thursday and Friday, Daniel still makes *barches au pavot,* an oval-shaped challah with poppy seeds and a thin braid on top, for his Jewish clientele. *Barches* (also spelled *berches*), which means "twisted," is also a derivation of the Hebrew word *birkat* (blessing), from the verse in Proverbs 10:22, *Birkat Adonai hi ta-ashir,* "The blessing of the Lord, it maketh rich."

An Alsatian mother making noodles for Friday night noodle soup

"A local rabbi said that the braid represents the tribes of Israel," Daniel told me over coffee and pastry at his home near the bakery. "And the poppy seeds, the manna in the desert." Poppy seeds, once grown in the region, may have disappeared from the fields, but the taste from them lingers on.

For his *barches,* Daniel makes a dough that is tighter than his baguette dough, so that it can be easily braided. In a few nineteenth-century versions, boiled potatoes were substituted for some of the flour in the dough, perhaps to help preserve the loaf over the course of the Sabbath.

Pour 2 cups lukewarm water into the bowl of an electric mixer fitted with a dough hook. Stir in the yeast and the sugar.

Add one of the eggs, the vegetable oil, and the salt. With the mixer on low speed, add about 7 cups of the flour. When the dough is still sticky, turn it out onto a floured board and knead it, adding the remaining flour as necessary to prevent the dough from sticking to your hands or the board. Continue kneading the dough until it is smooth and elastic, then put it in a greased bowl and cover it. Let it rise for about an hour, or until the dough has doubled in size.

Punch the dough down, and let rise again, covered, for another hour. Meanwhile, preheat the oven to 400 degrees, and dust a baking sheet with semolina flour.

Punch the dough down once more, and turn it out onto a lightly floured board. Divide it into two balls, and set one aside. Separate out about a fifth of one ball of dough. Mold the remaining, larger piece of dough into a smooth oblong loaf about 10 inches long, and place on a parchment-lined baking sheet. Then take the smaller piece of dough, cut it into three long thin strips, and braid them. The braid can be stretched or shortened, as needed to cover the loaf. Carefully place the braid onto the loaf, and gently press down to attach, using a little water as glue if needed. Repeat with the second ball of dough, and put onto the baking sheet.

Break the remaining egg into a small bowl, beat well, and brush the wash over both loaves. Let rise for ½ hour, and then brush again with the egg wash. Sprinkle poppy seeds all over, and bake for about 30 minutes, or until golden and firm.

YIELD: 2 LOAVES

1½ tablespoons active dry
  yeast
2 tablespoons sugar
2 large eggs
3 tablespoons vegetable oil
1 tablespoon salt
8 cups all-purpose flour
Semolina for dusting
2 tablespoons poppy seeds

Arranging poppy seeds
on *pain de pavot*

Challah from Heaven

One Friday night, at the home of Claude Maman, the Grand Rabbi of Bordeaux, I tasted an anise-flavored challah that one guest remarked was so delicious it must have come from heaven. When I asked who made it, Rabbi Maman told me that Georgette Hamier, the caterer who cooks for events at the synagogue, had baked it.

A few days later, I headed for her nineteenth-century stone building, just a short distance from the Grande Synagogue.

After greeting me at the door of her sprawling fifth-floor walk-up apartment, Madame Hamier ushered me into the tiny, spotlessly clean kitchen overlooking the city of Bordeaux. "I am a maniac cleaner-upper," she said in French. "I don't want anyone working with me."

As I watched, she told me stories about life in the Jewish quarter of Fez. Known as the Mellah, from the Arabic word for "salt," it was established as the Jewish quarter in 1438 on land that used to be called al-Mallah, or the "saline area," where salt could be found.

Madame Hamier's mother was a baker there and ran a restaurant and bar called Au Tout Va Bien. "*Maman* made the bread for us and croissants for the men who came in for coffee in the morning," she told me. "When we went to school, she made cakes and everything. An Arab apprentice would come early in the morning to take the bread and cakes to the public oven. Everybody ate our bread and my mother's almond-and-date cakes to break the fast of Yom Kippur."

After Morocco became independent in 1956, Madame Hamier's family went to Israel, and later to France, where she lived in Périgord before settling in Bordeaux. She has been cooking for the Jewish community in Bordeaux ever since, making ten challahs a week for the rabbis.

As we started working, she carefully sifted her flour. Then she broke her eggs in a clear glass bowl, one at a time, to make sure that there was no blood. Madame Hamier used neither measuring cups nor an electric

Georgette Hamier forms her challah into a spiral.

mixer to make her bread. "I use my hands and my eyes," she told me. *"C'est comme ça; c'est une vue d'oeil."* ("It is like that; I do everything by sight.")

What was so remarkable to me was how quickly she made the bread— she told me that the entire process would take one hour, and I didn't believe her. "It's quick with me," she said. "It doesn't take a long time." After she poked a hole in her dough, she just let it rest for about five minutes. Next she rolled a wad of dough and threw it in the oven as the symbolic offering in remembrance of the priest's portion in the Temple in Jerusalem. Then she rolled the dough into a spiral, brushed it with egg yolk, and popped it right into the oven. And guess what? The challah was quick and delicious.

Pain Pétri

(MOROCCAN ANISE-FLAVORED CHALLAH WITH SESAME SEEDS)

The finished product:
anise-flavored challah from Bordeaux

IN THE MIDDLE AGES, *pain pétri* (kneaded bread) got its name because women kneaded and formed the bread at home and then baked the loaves in public ovens, a tradition that remained in Morocco until recent years. Even in the late Middle Ages, when bread could be easily purchased from a baker, Jewish women still made the *pain pétri* as one of the three *mitzvoth* that a woman performs for the Sabbath. (The other two are to light candles, and to go to the ritual bath, or *mikveh*.) The Sabbath tables of even Reform and Liberal Jews have two loaves of bread. These represent the double portion of manna that was gathered on the eve of the Sabbath during the forty years of wandering in the wilderness. Except on the eve of the Sabbath, manna had to be gathered daily, for it spoiled overnight.

Madame Hamier made her recipe using cake yeast, something not readily available in the United States these days, so I have substituted dry yeast here.

Preheat the oven to 375 degrees, and line two baking sheets with parchment paper.

Put the yeast in the bowl of an electric mixer equipped with a dough hook, and pour in 2 cups lukewarm water. Stir, and when the yeast is dissolved, whisk in the two whole eggs, then add the oil.

Add 7 cups of the flour, the salt, sugar, and anise seeds to the bowl, and knead with the electric mixer until smooth and elastic, adding more flour as necessary. Form into a round loaf, and poke a 1-inch hole all the way through the center. Let the dough rest, uncovered on a floured board, for about 10 minutes.

Divide the dough into four pieces, using a knife or a dough cutter. Flour the board and your hands, and roll each piece of dough into a long cylinder, about 20 inches long. With the palms of your hands, flatten the cylinder, then roll it into a long rope, about 2 feet long, making sure that there are no seams in the dough. Then bring the two ends next to each other and twist to form a loose spiral. Place on one of two lined baking sheets. Do this with the other three pieces of dough, two to a baking sheet.

Beat the two egg yolks in a bowl, and add about a tablespoon of water. Stir well, and brush all of the egg glaze over the loaves. Then sprinkle the sesame seeds on top.

Bake in the oven for 10 minutes. Reduce the temperature to 350 degrees, and bake for another 30 minutes, or until the loaves sound hollow when tapped.

YIELD: 4 CHALLAHS

2 tablespoons active dry yeast

2 large eggs, plus 2 large egg yolks

½ cup peanut or vegetable oil

8 cups all-purpose flour, plus more for dusting

1 tablespoon salt

⅓ cup sugar

2 heaping teaspoons anise seeds

1½ tablespoons roasted sesame seeds

NOTE You can also make two larger challahs, or twist two cylinders together to make one long braid and twist that into a round challah, but the baking time will be a bit longer.

Tunisian *Bejma*

(FRIDAY NIGHT BREAD)

WALKING THROUGH THE COLORFUL Belleville market in Paris one Friday morning, I came across a Jewish bakery. Glancing in the window, I was surprised to see a triangular Tunisian Friday night bread called *bejma,* made out of three balls of dough. It was similar in flavor to a good eastern European challah. A few years later, I passed by a branch of Charles Traiteur, on the Boulevard Voltaire, and there was the *bejma* again, this time placed right next to the eastern European challah.

YIELD: 3 LOAVES

2 tablespoons active dry yeast
¼ cup sugar
4 large eggs
¼ cup vegetable oil
2 teaspoons salt
7 cups unbleached all-purpose
   flour

Dissolve the yeast and 1 teaspoon of the sugar in 1½ cups lukewarm water in a large bowl or the bowl of an electric mixer fitted with the dough hook.

Add three of the eggs, the vegetable oil, the salt, and the remaining sugar. Slowly work in enough flour to make a soft, tacky dough. Beat in the mixer, or knead by hand on a floured surface for 10 minutes, or until smooth. Place the kneaded dough in a large greased bowl, and let it rise, covered, for 1 hour.

Preheat the oven to 375 degrees, and grease a cookie sheet.

Punch down the dough, and divide it into nine pieces about the size of tennis balls. Arrange three rounds together, touching, on the greased cookie sheet, to form a triangle. Repeat with remaining dough. Let rise, uncovered, for about 30 minutes.

Beat the remaining egg with a little water, and brush the dough with the egg wash. Bake for about 20 minutes, or until golden.

Bejma, Tunisian challah,
made at home

Jews, the Specialists in Grains

> The Lord spoke to Moses, saying: Speak to the Israelites and say to them: When you enter the land to which I am taking you and you eat of the bread of the land, you shall set some aside as a gift to the Lord: As the first yield of your baking you shall set aside a loaf as a gift.
>
> —Numbers 15:7–19

"If there is no flour there is no Torah; if there is no Torah there is no flour" (Chapter 3, Mishnah 21[b]). In the Middle Ages this quote became associated with Rabbi David Kimchi of Narbonne, France, an influential scholar and grammarian, whose name, Kimchi, derives from the Hebrew word for flour, *kemach*.

As the historian Louis Stouff tells us, during the Middle Ages Jews were specialists in the commerce of grains in the Vaucluse. They could store wheat and other grains in their silos after buying them from the farmers, and they would sell and export them as needed throughout the year.

Sometimes this middleman position could fuel anti-Semitism. Haquinus Callot, a Jew in Manosque, in Provence, for example, was accused of having wanted to poison Christian bread. During his interrogation, he declared that he simply threw a piece of dough into the oven in which the bread was baking according to the instructions from Numbers, cited above. He added that such a gesture must be done in every oven in which Jewish bread is baked. Sometime later, he was acquitted on the grounds that he was only following the law of Moses.

Rabbi's Wife's Challah

"LOOK AT THAT BEAUTIFUL BRIOCHE," I overheard a guest saying at a Bat Mitzvah in Geneva. The brioche was the glistening round challah made by Nicole Garai, the rabbi's wife. During the service at the hidden Quai du Seujet Synagogue, located near the Rhône River, Nicole helps her husband by escorting assigned readers to the *bima* (platform). The Garais, French Jews, came to Switzerland to start this synagogue in the 1980s.

Nicole told me that she bakes challah for people of whom she is fond, like her congregant, Juliette Laurent, braiding it in a round to signify the circle of life for Rosh Hodesh (the first of the month); she also makes it for the new year, and for Bar and Bat Mitzvahs.

I especially liked the way she decorated the challah, by first liberally sprinkling a thick band of sesame seeds, then poppy seeds all over the top of the bread. Another trick she uses is to brush the bread twice: once at the beginning of the second rise, after the bread is braided, and again just before she pops it into a cold oven. The procedure of turning on the heat after the bread is in the oven must date back a long time, at least to the beginning of home wood ovens.

Rabbi's Wife's Challah

 YIELD: 1 LARGE ROUND
CHALLAH

2 tablespoons active dry yeast
2 tablespoons sugar
1 large egg, plus 1 egg yolk
⅓ cup vegetable oil
7 to 8 cups all-purpose flour
1 tablespoon salt
Sesame seeds
Poppy seeds

Dissolve the yeast and the sugar in 2 cups warm water in the bowl of a standing mixer equipped with a dough hook. Add the whole egg and the oil, and mix.

Gradually add 7 cups of the flour and the salt to the bowl, and blend well. When the dough starts to come together, turn it out onto a floured work surface and knead with your hands, adding more flour until the dough is smooth and doesn't stick to your hand.

Put the dough in a greased bowl, cover it with a cloth, and set it in a dry place. Let it rise for 45 minutes.

Punch down the dough and separate it into three balls. Roll each out to a long strand, then braid the three strands. Pinch the ends together to form a circle with a diameter of at least 9 inches. Cover a baking sheet with parchment paper, and carefully transfer the dough to the sheet. Beat the egg yolk in a little bowl, and paint the dough with it.

Let the dough rise for 45 minutes in the closed oven.

Remove the dough, paint again with more egg yolk, and sprinkle some sesame seeds heavily in a 2-inch band, then sprinkle a band of poppy seeds, continuing to make five or six wide strips of poppy seeds and sesame seeds around the dough.

Put the challah back in the oven, turn the oven temperature to 400 degrees, and cook for 30 minutes, or until the challah sounds hollow when tapped. Remove, and let cool.

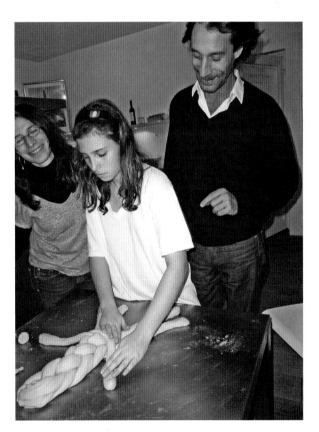

Juliette Laurent learns to braid challah with her mother and uncle.

Brioche for Rosh Hashanah

WHEN HUGUETTE UHRY MARRIED a local butcher from the town of Ingwiller in Alsace, her sister-in-law lived with her, helping with the cooking. They usually had eighteen people for lunch and dinner, including children, friends, and workers. Today, retired and living in nearby Bollwiller, Madame Uhry is known throughout Alsace as a great cook. Some of her recipes appear on the Web site judaisme.sdv.fr. Here is her brioche, which she starts one day and bakes Rosh Hashanah morning for breakfast, before the family goes to synagogue.

 YIELD: 1 BRIOCHE CAKE

DOUGH

1 tablespoon active dry yeast

½ cup lukewarm milk

4 cups all-purpose flour, plus
   more for sprinkling

½ cup granulated sugar

2 teaspoons salt

4 large eggs, at room
   temperature

1 stick (½ cup) unsalted
   butter, at room temperature

FILLING

¾ cup ground almonds

4 tablespoons (½ stick)
   unsalted butter

¼ cup almond paste

1 cup crumbs made from cake,
   pound cake, or bread

1 teaspoon vanilla extract

1 cup raisins or dried
   cranberries (optional), or
   8 ounces good bittersweet

Dissolve the yeast in the warm milk in a small bowl.

Place the flour in the bowl of a heavy-duty electric mixer, then pour in the sugar and salt and, using a dough hook, start beating slowly as you pour in the dissolved yeast.

Add the eggs one by one, and continue beating, on the slowest speed, for about 15 minutes. (This may seem like a long time, but it takes that long for the eggs to mix with the flour and to attain a smooth, shiny texture.) Add the butter, little by little, continuing to beat until it is totally absorbed and the dough is smooth, about 3 minutes. Sprinkle additional flour on top.

Let the dough rise, covered, in the mixing bowl for 3 hours at room temperature. Punch it down, and let it rise again, for 2 more hours.

Meanwhile, make the filling by placing the almonds, butter, almond paste, cake crumbs, and vanilla in a food processor and pulsing until combined.

Grate the chocolate, if you are using it, or macerate the raisins or cranberries in 2 tablespoons of the brandy for a few minutes.

Butter a Bundt or *kugelhopf* pan. Form the dough into a cylinder, then roll it out into a 10-by-16-inch rectangle. Spoon the filling onto the dough, sprinkling on top either the raisins and dried cranberries, or the chocolate; roll up tightly, like a jelly roll, on the long side; and gently stretch to a length of about 18 inches. Gently press the roll, seam side up, into the Bundt or *kugelhopf* pan. Let the dough rise, covered, in the refrigerator overnight.

The next morning, take the dough out of the refrigerator and let rise for about 45 minutes. Preheat the oven to 350 degrees, and bake for about 50 minutes, or until the brioche is golden on top and a toothpick comes out clean when inserted in the center.

Stir the confectioners' sugar and 2 remaining tablespoons brandy in a small bowl. Remove the cake from the mold, and with a spoon, paint the top with the sugar glaze.

chocolate, preferably imported (optional)
2 or 4 tablespoons *eau-de-vie* or brandy
1 cup confectioners' sugar

Contemplating *Baba, Babka,* and Brioche

One of my greatest pleasures in Paris is to spend time with Philip and Mary Hyman, who have devoted their entire adult lives to the study of French culinary history. Their apartment in the Eighteenth Arrondissement is lined with French cookbooks, some going back several centuries. When I was pondering *babka* and *baba,* Mary shared with me what she had written for the forthcoming *Oxford Companion to French Food,* which she and her husband are writing.

According to Mary, *baba* means different things to different people. In many parts of France, including Paris, a *baba* is a small, cork-shaped cake often soaked in rum. In Lorraine, however, where it was brought as a large turban-shaped cake by Stanislaw Leszcyński, the deposed king of Poland and father-in-law of King Louis XV in the middle of the eighteenth century, it is considered a regional specialty.

The word *baba,* which means "old woman" in Polish, also refers to a large saffron-flavored cake, presumably so named because grandmothers make it.

Babka, which means "grandmother," is a sort of first cousin to the brioche—both are yeast-risen breads enriched with eggs, butter, and sugar.

Babka à la Française

(*BABKA* ROLLS WITH OLIVE TAPENADE)

ONCE, I ASKED TWO-STAR MICHELIN CHEF Thierry Marx of Cordeillan-Bages in Pauillac, the greatest wine-producing area of France, why he uses beets in so many of his dishes—beets for color, beets for sweetness, beets for texture, and beet borscht purée. He replied that he likes to play with the flavors and shapes of his childhood, reminding him of his Jewish grandmother from Poland, who raised him in Paris. "Cooking is a transmission of love," he told me.

Two-star chef Thierry Marx

One wouldn't necessarily think of the food Thierry serves in his stunning restaurant as particularly Jewish—it is so molecular, so Japanese (because of where he studied), and so French (because of where he grew up).

The dining room of the château, decked out in sleek black-and-white furniture with hints of red, looks out on a vineyard laden with ripe dark grapes ready for picking. But when the bread basket arrived, it contained what looked like a miniature chocolate or poppy-seed *babka*. My first bite, though, told me that I had still been fooled. This *trompe l'oeil* was in fact a savory *babka*, filled with olives, anchovies, and fennel—a delicious French take on a sweet Polish and Jewish classic.

YIELD: 24 *BABKA* ROLLS

2½ to 3 cups all-purpose
  flour
⅛ teaspoon salt
¼ cup sugar
2½ teaspoons active dry yeast
½ cup whole milk, at room
  temperature
1 large egg, plus 3 to 4 egg
  yolks (enough to make
  ½ cup egg and egg yolks
  total)

To make the dough, put 2½ cups of the flour, salt, and all but 1 tablespoon of the sugar in the bowl of an electric mixer fitted with the dough-hook attachment.

Put the yeast and 1 tablespoon warm water and the reserved tablespoon of sugar in a small bowl, and stir just until the sugar and yeast have dissolved. With the mixer, using the dough hook on low speed, pour into the bowl the yeast mixture, the milk, and the egg and egg yolks. Knead the dough until it is smooth, shiny, and elastic, about 10 minutes, adding more flour as needed.

Add the pieces of butter a little at a time, until it is incorporated, then knead the dough on low speed for about 5 minutes, until it is silken and rich. Transfer it to a large, greased bowl, cover with plastic wrap, and allow it to rise for 2 hours. When the dough has risen, press it down, and put it in a plastic bag or wrap it in plastic wrap. Refrigerate for 1 to 2 hours or overnight.

To make the tapenade filling, put the olives, half the anchovies, the fennel seeds, and 1 tablespoon of the olive oil in the bowl of a food processor fitted with a steel blade. Purée the mixture until it is smooth. Taste, and if you want, add more anchovies or salt, and another tablespoon of olive oil if the filling is not smooth enough.

When ready to assemble the *babka*s, grease two 9-inch round pans. Take the dough from the refrigerator and divide it in half. On a lightly floured surface, roll out one piece into a 16-by-12-inch rectangle.

Using a knife or an offset spatula, spread half of the olive-anchovy filling very thinly over the dough, leaving a ½-inch border all around. Beginning with the long side, tuck in the ends and roll the dough up tightly. Cut the rolled-up dough into twelve equal pieces, and place them, with one of the cut sides of each facing up, in one of the pans in one layer. Repeat with the remaining dough and filling in the other pan.

Allow the *babka*s to rise, covered with a towel, for 2 hours before brushing with the reserved 2 tablespoons melted butter.

Preheat the oven to 350 degrees, and bake for 25 to 30 minutes, or until golden. Once the rolls are cool enough to handle, pull them apart gently into individual *babka*s.

½ cup (1 stick) unsalted butter, cut in small pieces, plus 2 tablespoons melted butter

1¼ cups pitted black picholine olives

2 canned anchovies, drained

1 tablespoon fennel seeds, pulverized

1 to 2 tablespoons olive oil

Thierry Marx's olive-anchovy *babka*

Parisian *Pletzl*

(A BIG BIALY)

Florence Finkelsztajn (*far right*) and her family, with their *pletzlach*

ON A RECENT VISIT TO THE MARAIS, I stopped in at Florence Finkelsztajn's Traiteur Delicatessen, as I always do. The quarter has two Finkelsztajn delicatessens, one trimmed in yellow (Florence's ex-husband's) and one in blue (Florence's—now renamed Kahn). According to Gilles Pudlowski, the gastronomic critic of Polish Jewish origin who writes the popular *Pudlo* restaurant guides, Florence's store is the best place to satisfy a nostalgic craving for eastern European cooking. In addition to Central European Yiddish specialties, like herring, chopped liver, and pastrami, Florence also sells *pletzlach,* baked in the back of the shop. I have made her recipe, which she gave me a few years ago, and I can assure you it is delicious.

Pletzl, short for *Bialystoker tsibele pletzl,* refers to a circular eastern European flat onion bread, often studded with poppy seeds, that came from the city of Białystok, Poland. The bread is known in America in a smaller version as the bialy.

Try it as a snack hot from the oven, or make a "big *pletzl* sandwich," as Florence does. Her fillings vary as much as the different ethnicities of Jews living in Paris today: Alsatian *pickelfleisch* (corned beef), Romanian pastrami, Russian eggplant caviar (see page 34), North African roasted peppers, and French tomato and lettuce.

Pour 1 cup lukewarm water into a large bowl. Stir in the yeast and the sugar until dissolved. Add 4 cups flour, the eggs, ¼ cup of the oil, and the salt. Mix well, and knead for about 10 minutes, or until smooth, adding more flour if necessary. Or use a food processor or a standing mixer with a dough hook. Transfer the dough to a greased bowl, and let rise, covered, for 1 hour. Preheat the oven to 375 degrees, and grease two cookie sheets.

Divide the dough into twelve balls, and roll or flatten them out into rounds about 6 inches in diameter. Put the rounds on the cookie sheets, and make thumbprints in the centers. Brush the dough with cold water, and sprinkle about ¼ cup of onion in each indentation. Brush the rounds with the remaining vegetable oil, and sprinkle the poppy seeds on top. Let sit for 15 minutes, uncovered.

Bake for 20 minutes. Then, if you like, slip the *pletzlach* under the broiler for a minute, to brown the onions. Serve lukewarm, as is or in a big *pletzl* sandwich.

YIELD: 12 *PLETZLACH*

1 scant tablespoon active dry yeast
4 tablespoons sugar
4 to 5 cups all-purpose flour
2 large eggs
¼ cup plus 2 tablespoons vegetable oil
2 teaspoons salt
3 cups diced onions
¼ cup poppy seeds

Paris's Pletzl

The heart of Jewish Paris is a central square called by the Yiddish word *pletzl*. It sits near the *métro* station Saint-Paul, in the part of the Marais that has been the Jewish quarter since the thirteenth century. When the Jews were expelled from the city of Paris, they moved to this area, which was then outside the city.

As holidays approach, Parisian Jews flock here to buy skullcaps, prayer books, challahs, and cakes. "It is the only part of Paris where the bakers make the sweet twisted challah, cheesecake, and honey cake I remember from my mother," the Polish-born author Marek Halter told me.

These days, like the Lower East Side of New York City, the Marais is filled with chic fashion boutiques and gay bars, transforming it from a quaint shtetl into an up-and-coming neighborhood. Many of the old bookshops and restaurants have closed, but the shops that are left in this ancient quarter, with its narrow streets, overflow with delicacies from eastern Europe, France, Israel, and North Africa. Today you'll find homemade farfel (tiny bits of pasta) and great falafel as well as *fijuelas* and other Sephardic delicacies.

In the past, the Pletzl has also served as a meeting place for Jews in less auspicious circumstances. Escaping the pogroms of eastern Europe in 1881, Jews came here in large numbers, more than half of them from Poland. During the Second World War's police *rafles* (roundups) of Jews, many called out to one another, as they were separated, to meet in the Pletzl if they survived.

Alsatian Pretzels with a Moroccan Touch

LIKE MANY MOROCCAN JEWS WHO CAME to France after Morocco became independent in 1956, Deborah Lilliane Denino, a psychologist, and her family were welcomed by the Jewish community in Strasbourg. Down the street from her apartment is a kosher bakery, grocery, and butcher shop called Délices Cacher, where she buys *merguez* lamb and beef sausage and other Moroccan items on which she grew up in Marrakesh.

When she is busy, she asks one of her three children or the American students with the Syracuse University Junior Year Abroad program who live with her to fetch the groceries. She teaches those not familiar with a kosher kitchen about the color-coded forks, towels, and other utensils, to identify and keep separate the meat and milk dishes she cooks in her apartment.

For Shabbat, this great cook with a fun-loving family always makes Moroccan challah. But because her children, who were born in Strasbourg, like soft pretzels (as do most Alsatian children—they call them *bretzeln*), she sets aside some of the dough, forms long fingers out of it, twists them into pretzels, and bakes them as a snack.

Preheat the oven to 400 degrees, and line a baking sheet with parchment paper or a Silpat.

Take the challah dough and separate it into six small pieces. Roll each piece out into a cylinder 9 inches long and about ¾ inch in diameter. Fold both ends into the center, crossing them in the middle and pressing them down into their opposite corners, to form a pretzel. The result should look like two hands praying. You can also make long fingers of straight dough.

Whisk the egg yolk with 1 teaspoon water. Brush the pretzels with this egg wash, and sprinkle with coarse salt. Bake for 20 minutes, or until golden brown.

YIELD: 6 SMALL PRETZELS

¼ leftover Moroccan challah
  dough (see page 124)
1 egg yolk
Kosher or sea salt to taste

Brassados

(PROVENÇAL BOILED AND BAKED ROLLS WITH A HOLE)

NO BREAD FORM IS SO COMPLETELY IDENTIFIED with Jews as the bagel, which came from eastern Europe with immigrants, mostly from Łódź, Poland, at the turn of the last century. Unlike American bagels, French bagels were rather like rolls that were baked but not boiled. When Euro Disney and the United States Army in Europe wanted bagels in the late seventies, they asked Joseph Korcarz, whose family ran a bakery in the Marais, to go to the United States to learn the commercial technique of boiling the dough before baking.

Two older bread forms, however, might shed new light on the origins of the bagel. In the mountains of Savoie, near the Swiss border, an area with few if any Jews today, there is a specialty of the region—an ancient anise-flavored bread called *riouttes,* which were boiled before baking, a technique that kept the bread fresher a longer time. *Riouttes* might have come to the mountains with Jews or with Arabs, who make *ka'ak* ("bracelet" in Arabic), small, round, crispy rolls with a hole, flavored with anise and sesame seeds.

Probably the oldest bagel-like roll in France, however, dating back to antiquity, is the Provençal *brassado,* also called *brassadeau.* Sweet and round, with a hole in the center, they are also first boiled and then baked, much like bagels. The word *brassado* is related to the Spanish and Portuguese words for the physical act of an embrace or a hug. The unusual inclusion of floral scents like orange-flower and rose water could be the influence of Jews involved in the perfume industry in Grasse. This particular recipe is an adaptation of *brassados* found by Martine Yana in her *Trésors de la Table Juive.*

 YIELD: ABOUT 1 DOZEN
BRASSADOS

1 tablespoon active dry yeast
¾ cup sugar
2 large eggs
2 teaspoons salt
Zest of ½ orange
Zest of ½ lemon
2 tablespoons orange-blossom
 water
1 teaspoon orange extract

Put the yeast, 1 tablespoon of the sugar, and ½ cup warm water in the bowl of an electric mixer fitted with a dough hook. When the yeast and sugar are dissolved, whisk in the eggs, the salt, the rest of the sugar, the zests, the orange-blossom water, and the butter or margarine.

Gradually add the flour, beating with the dough hook to incorporate. When the dough holds together, turn it out onto a floured surface and knead until smooth.

Place the dough in a greased bowl, cover with a kitchen towel, and let rise in a warm place for 3 hours.

Remove the dough from the bowl. Pull off two small pieces of the dough, each about the size of a walnut, and roll them out with the palms of your hands into two snakes about 8 inches long. Pinch the two strands together at one end, and twist one strand over the other until you have a long chain. Squeeze the two ends together to make a ring. Repeat with the remaining dough, to make twelve rings.

Bring a large pot of water to a boil, preheat the oven to 350 degrees, and line two baking sheets with parchment paper.

Drop four of the *brassados* into the boiling water, and cook for about 30 seconds. Remove to a rack, and repeat with the rest of the dough, cooking four at a time.

Once the rings have all been boiled and left to dry for a few minutes, gently transfer them to the lined baking sheets. Bake in the center of the oven for about 25 minutes, or until golden and crisp. Let cool on a baking rack.

3½ tablespoons butter or
  pareve margarine, cut into
  small pieces
About 3 to 3½ cups all-
  purpose flour

Friday night dinner before a Bat Mitzvah

Matzo: Bread of Freedom

Hadassa Schneerson Carlebach moved to New York after World War II, and she could not bring herself to share her tale and that of her father, Rabbi Zalman Schneerson, until recently.

Born in Russia, he moved to France in the early 1930s. In 1944, with help from the French Resistance, the rabbi found hiding places in farmhouses dispersed throughout the countryside near Grenoble for about sixty people, mostly children whose parents had been sent to Auschwitz. "We had a little wheat, which we milled into flour for Passover," Hadassa, who now lives in Brooklyn, told me. In their village, the farmers used a communal oven for baking. "It was too dangerous for us to go there during the day, so in the middle of the night we went in, heated the oven very high to make it kosher, and baked the matzo in a hurry, while the dogs were barking," she said. "I was so scared, but we had one matzo per person for Pesach with the wine that we made ourselves from raisins. In spite of the danger, we celebrated with the sincere hope that we were going to be liberated."

Rabbi Schneerson saved sketches of a matzo oven he constructed in 1941, when he and his daughter were hiding in a derelict château near Marseille. "We were all mobilized to help with the rolling out, baking, packing, and shipping of the matzo for the camps," Hadassa said. "One day, the Gestapo came and took away sixteen of the fifty-nine children. I have never forgotten their pain."

As hungry as most people were throughout the war, they were starving in 1944. "Everything was black-market," said Hadassa. "We had no bread for quite a while, so we got wheat berries; we took turns grinding them in a hand-cranked coffee mill. The flour came out very coarse, but we mixed it with water and some salt and let it stand, baked it in an old woodstove, and it tasted divine. I would love to have a taste of it now."

Oatmeal Bread with Fig, Anise, and Walnuts

THE FRENCH LOVE THEIR BREAD, but they usually buy it in *boulangeries*. In many homes I visited, though, people would make a quick bread like the goat-cheese-and-apricot bread on page 145. When they had a bit more time, on a weekend morning perhaps, they would make a heartier bread and eat it throughout the week. This recipe, which I tasted at a friend's house in Paris, is very forgiving and can withstand additions and variations. I often add bits of leftover nuts and dried fruit. Great for breakfast with goat cheese or preserves, it is also a wonderful sandwich bread.

Dissolve the yeast in 3 cups lukewarm water in the bowl of an electric mixer fitted with a dough hook.

Once it is dissolved, turn the mixer on low and slowly add the honey, rolled oats, steel-cut oats, wheat germ, salt, anise seeds, walnuts, and dried figs. Stir in the whole-wheat flour and 3½ cups of the all-purpose flour and knead.

Put the slightly sticky kneaded dough in a large greased bowl, and cover with plastic wrap. Let it rise for 1 hour, or until it is doubled in volume.

Preheat the oven to 375 degrees. Grease a baking sheet, or line it with parchment paper.

Punch down the dough, and turn it out onto a lightly floured surface. Divide it in half, and form two round loaves. Place them on the baking sheet and using a sharp knife or a razor blade, make a few long, shallow gashes across each of the loaves. Let rise another ½ hour.

Bake for 40 minutes, or until the loaves sound hollow when tapped. Allow to cool before slicing.

YIELD: 2 LOAVES

2 tablespoons active dry yeast
½ cup honey
2 cups old-fashioned rolled oats
1 cup steel-cut oats
1 cup toasted wheat germ
1 tablespoon kosher salt
2 teaspoons anise seeds
1 cup roughly chopped walnuts
1 cup diced dried figs
2 cups whole-wheat flour
4 cups all-purpose flour, plus more as needed

Hutzel Wecken

(ALSATIAN HANUKKAH FRUIT BREAD)

MOST JEWS IN FRANCE PRIOR TO the twentieth century used handwritten cookbooks passed down from mother to daughter. And since Alsace-Lorraine was under German occupation between 1871 and 1918, the majority of the Jews living there read German, using many of the dozen or so kosher cookbooks published in Germany in the late nineteenth and early twentieth centuries.

Combing through these German books and her mother's handwritten cookbook, Agar Lippmann, a caterer in Lyon, came across a recipe she had been trying to track down for years. *Hutzel wecken,* which literally means hat- or dome-shaped little rolls in German, is a very old Hanukkah and To B'Shevat (the new year of trees) fruitcake rarely made today. I prefer it treated more as bread, sliced very thin and served with cheese or really good butter. My guess is that the peanuts were a later addition. If you don't have all the different dried fruits and nuts, just use what you have. The recipe is very flexible. Once, when I made it for a party, some of the guests liked it so much that, unbeknownst to me, they took home little slices hidden in paper napkins for their breakfast!

Caterer Agar Lippmann uses old and new recipes in Lyon.

Put the pears and plums in a saucepan with water to cover by an inch. Bring the water to a boil, and simmer for 2 to 3 minutes, or until soft. Drain, reserving both the fruit and the liquid.

Toss the pears and plums in a large bowl with the raisins, currants, figs, dates, walnuts, peanuts, hazelnuts, almonds, orange zest, and lemon zest. Add the kirsch, and toss again.

In a separate bowl, dissolve the yeast in ½ cup of the reserved fruit liquid, and then add ½ cup of the flour, and 2 tablespoons of the sugar. Cover, and let rise for 1 hour. Stir in the remaining 2 cups flour, ¼ cup sugar, and the salt.

Knead the dough in the bowl of a standing mixer with a dough hook. Add the fruits and nuts, and, using a low setting, slowly stir into the dough. When everything is incorporated, turn the dough out onto a heavily floured surface, incorporating enough more flour to make the dough smooth and elastic. Even so, it will be a wet dough. Shape into a large ball, put in a greased bowl, cover with plastic wrap, and let the dough rest for about 1 hour.

Preheat the oven to 400 degrees, and line a baking sheet with parchment paper. Divide the dough into two pieces. Form each piece into a round ball, and put both on the baking sheet. Let rest for 20 minutes. Bake, turning the temperature down to 375 degrees after 20 minutes, until the crust is golden and the dough is cooked through, 40 to 45 minutes.

If you want, while the breads are baking, make a glaze by whisking together ½ cup of the fruit water and the confectioners' sugar. As soon as the breads come out of the oven, spoon the glaze over them. Serve warm or at room temperature.

 YIELD: 2 LOAVES

2 cups chopped dried pears

1 cup chopped dried pitted plums

1 cup golden raisins

1 cup dried currants

1 cup roughly chopped dried figs

1 cup roughly chopped pitted dates

½ cup roughly chopped walnuts

⅓ cup salted peanuts

⅓ cup roughly chopped hazelnuts

⅓ cup roughly chopped almonds

Grated zest of 1 orange

Grated zest of 1 lemon

¼ cup kirsch

1 tablespoon active dry yeast

2½ to 3 cups all-purpose flour

2 tablespoons plus ¼ cup granulated sugar

1 teaspoon salt

6 tablespoons confectioners' sugar (optional)

Quick Goat Cheese Bread with Mint and Apricots

WHEN I ATE DINNER AT THE HOME of Nathalie Berrebi, a Frenchwoman living in Geneva, she served this savory quick bread warm and sliced thin, as a first course for a dinner attended by lots of children and adults. For the main course, Nathalie prepared *rouget* (red mullet) with an eggplant tapenade on top, something all the children loved. The entire dinner was delicious, but I especially liked that savory bread with the unexpected flavor combination of goat cheese, apricots, and fresh mint. Now I often make this quick bread for brunch or lunch and serve it with a green salad.

Preheat the oven to 350 degrees, and grease a 9-by-5-inch loaf pan with some of the oil.

Crack the eggs into a large bowl, and beat well. Add the milk and oil, whisking until smooth.

Mix the flour, baking powder, salt, and pepper in another bowl, and add to the wet mixture, stirring until everything is incorporated and the dough is smooth.

Spread the batter in the prepared baking pan, sprinkle on the grated Gruyère, Cheddar, or Comté, crumble the goat cheese on top, and then scatter on the apricots and the mint. Pull a knife gently through the batter to blend the ingredients slightly. Bake for 40 minutes. Cool briefly, remove from the pan, peel off the foil or parchment paper, slice, and serve warm.

YIELD: 6 TO 8 SERVINGS

⅓ cup olive oil, plus some for greasing

3 large eggs

⅓ cup milk

2 cups all-purpose flour

1 teaspoon baking powder

½ teaspoon salt

Freshly ground pepper to taste

2 ounces grated Gruyère, aged Cheddar, or Comté cheese

4 ounces fresh goat cheese

1 cup chopped dried apricots

2 tablespoons roughly minced mint leaves or 2 teaspoons dried mint

Exotic kosher fish

Fish

Salmon with Pearl Onions, Lettuce, and Peas

Alsatian Sweet and Sour Fish

Carpe à la Juive, Sauce Verte (Carp with Parsley Sauce)

Gefilte Fish (Polish-Style Fish Balls)

Sauce au Raifort (Horseradish Sauce)

Cabbage Stuffed with Gefilte Fish

Couscous de Poisson (Tunisian Fish Couscous)

Saumon à l'Oseille (Salmon with Sorrel Sauce)

Choucroute de Poisson au Beurre Blanc
(Fish Sauerkraut with Wine and Butter Sauce)

Passover Moroccan Shad with Fava Beans and Red Peppers

Turkish "Red Sea" Mackerel with Tomato and Parsley

Dorade Royale (Sea Bream with Preserved Lemon,
Tamarind, Ginger, and Cilantro)

Citrons Confits (Preserved Lemons)

Bourride (Provençal Fish Stew with Vegetables and Wine)

Grilled Cod with *Raïto* Sauce

Passover Provençal Stuffed Trout with Spinach and Sorrel

Kosher Fish in France Today

The Angel who has redeemed me from all harm bless the lads. In them may my name be recalled. And the names of my fathers Abraham and Isaac. And may they be teeming multitudes upon the earth.

—Genesis 48:16

As early as the ninth century, Louis the Pious granted Jews special dispensation to fish in the royal rivers, thus allowing traveling Jews who couldn't find ritually slaughtered meat to eat fish.

In the eleventh century, the French sage Rashi told us in his commentary on the book of Genesis that Jews should multiply just like fish, who "proliferate and multiply and are unaffected by the evil eye." In Rashi's day, fish, considered an aphrodisiac because it helped a man to please his wife on the Sabbath, was a favorite delicacy for Friday evenings. It may have helped that, like most Jewish dishes of the Middle Ages, fish was usually highly seasoned with pepper and garlic, substances also thought of as aphrodisiacs.

Although the variety of fish in France was far more limited in the eleventh century, when Rashi lived, the globalized seafood market today supplies an abundance of sea life with fins and scales—which are acceptable according to the laws of kashrut. And, given the predominance of North African immigrants in France, the fish dishes are often prepared with cumin, saffron, and other tantalizing spices.

Despite the exotic fish preparations that exist today, I still prefer the simplest ones. I remember a very fresh poached fish that I had at a home in Hossegor, on the Atlantic coast of France, near Bayonne. We biked to the local fish market on the wharf, where I noticed a couple strolling arm in arm, looking with delight at the choices for their Sunday lunch. After selecting our fish, a plump turbot, we pedaled back home. There we steamed it, and served it whole alongside boiled potatoes and a simple lettuce salad (see page 90). So delicious. So simple. Who needs more?

Salmon with Pearl Onions, Lettuce, and Peas

AS A SIGN OF SPRING, this salmon dish, made with the first peas of the season, has been handed down from generation to generation since the first Jews left Spain during the Inquisition. I tasted it in Biarritz, at the lovely villa of Nicole Rousso, who comes from a Portuguese merchant family from Bayonne.

Bring a small saucepan of water to a boil. Drop in the pearl onions, and boil for 3 minutes. Turn off the water, and remove the onions with a slotted spoon to a bowl of cold water. When they reach room temperature, cut the root ends and pop onions out of the skin.

Melt the butter over medium heat in a Dutch oven or other heavy-bottomed pan. Stir in the onions and the lettuce, and sauté for 2 to 3 minutes. Stir in the peas, sugar, thyme, savory, parsley, salt and freshly ground pepper to taste, and ¼ cup water. Cover, and simmer slowly for about 5 minutes.

Gently nestle the salmon in among the peas, onions, and herbs. Cover and cook for 10 to 15 more minutes, or until the salmon is just barely cooked through. Pluck out the herb sprigs and serve.

YIELD: 4 TO 6 SERVINGS

10 ounces pearl onions

1 tablespoon butter

5 large lettuce leaves (preferably romaine or Bibb), washed and halved

2 cups shelled peas, fresh or frozen

2 teaspoons sugar

3 sprigs fresh thyme

3 sprigs fresh summer savory

2 tablespoons chopped fresh parsley

Salt and freshly ground pepper to taste

2 pounds salmon fillets, cut into 4 to 6 servings

Salmon with Pearl Onions, Lettuce, and Peas

Alsatian Sweet and Sour Fish

All the pious, wise, and upright
Chosen souls from everywhere—
And the Lord God's favorite fish will
Furnish out the bill of fare,

Partly with white garlic gravy,
Partly in a well-browned roux
Made with spicy wine and raisins—
Something like a seafood stew.

Sizzling in the garlic gravy,
Bits of radish fizz and hiss—
I would wager, friar, you would
Relish fish prepared like this!

Or the brown one—it's delicious
Raising sauce right off the fire;
It would make a little Heaven
In your belly, dearest friar.

God's cuisine is haute cuisine. . . .

—Heinrich Heine,
Jewish Stories and Hebrew Melodies

HEINRICH HEINE, THE AUTHOR OF the above poem (which is often sung to the tune of Beethoven's "Ode to Joy"), wrote in a letter that he especially liked "the carp in brown raisin sauce which my aunt prepared on Friday evenings to usher in the Sabbath." Ernest Auricoste de Lazarque, the famous nineteenth-century folklorist, was also impressed by this dish. In his 1890 *La Cuisine Messine* (*Cooking from Metz*), he includes a recipe for *carpe à la juive* from Lorraine.

I have seen variants that use nutmeg and saffron as well. Taillevent has a recipe in *Le Viandier* of 1485 for the sweet-and-sour *cameline* sauce, so named for its tawny camel color, which includes ginger, cinnamon, cloves, grains of paradise, pepper, mastic, galangal, nutmeg, saffron, sugar, anise, vinegar, wine, and sometimes raisins. Most of the spices were trafficked from far corners of the world by Jewish and other merchants. Mastic, also known as gum arabic, is the resin from the acacia tree and has a sweet, licorice flavor; grains of paradise, sometimes used in making beer today, have an aromatic peppery taste, almost like cardamom and coriander; and galangal, a rhizome related to ginger, has a hot, peppery flavor.

The carp with its sweet-and-sour sauce became a Jewish staple, brought out for the Sabbath and holidays, and surviving, as traditional recipes do, in the Jewish community to this day.

Although the original recipe calls for a 3-pound carp, washed, cut into steaks, and then arranged back into the original shape of the fish, I often use a single large salmon or grouper or bass fillet instead.

YIELD: 8 TO 10 SERVINGS

Heat the olive oil in a pot or poacher large enough to hold the fish, and sauté the onion, seasoned with salt and freshly ground pepper to taste, until translucent.

Dissolve the sugar in 2 tablespoons water in a heavy skillet over low heat, stirring with a heat-resistant spoon. Raise the heat to medium and stir constantly until large bubbles start to form, about 5 minutes. Then stop stirring and carefully rotate the pan over the heat until a golden-brown color is reached, brushing down any crystals that might form with a brush dipped in cold water. Pour this caramel over the onion.

Pour 2 cups water over the caramel and onion and bring to a boil. Stir in the cinnamon, vinegar, ginger, salt and freshly ground pepper to taste, the bay leaves, the raisins, and the almonds. Place the fish on top, cover, and simmer over very low heat for about 15 minutes, or until the fish is barely cooked through. Carefully remove the fish to a serving plate, and boil the sauce down to reduce by half. Pour the sauce over the fish, cool, and refrigerate. Serve the fish at room temperature.

3 tablespoons olive oil

1 medium onion, peeled and thinly sliced

Salt and freshly ground pepper to taste

1 cup sugar

½ teaspoon ground cinnamon

2 tablespoons cider vinegar

½ teaspoon ginger

6 bay leaves

½ cup golden raisins

½ cup slivered almonds

One 3-pound fillet of carp, salmon, grouper, bass, rockfish, or sea bream

Carpe à la Juive, Sauce Verte

(CARP WITH PARSLEY SAUCE)

Carpe à la juive is such an unexpected pleasant surprise for the non Jew. The fish is served cold in a succulent jell. . . . If the women of Israel had presented this dish to Titus, he never would have had the courage to destroy the Temple of Jerusalem.

—C. Asserolette, *Ma Cuisine*, 1890

CARP, ORIGINALLY FROM CHINA, were unknown west of the Rhine until the middle decades of the thirteeth century, when the French started farming fish in ponds. They used holding tanks for live storage in a world without refrigeration or canning methods and in areas that had no access to the sea. Said to have been brought to France by Jews, carp became the most popular fish in Europe during the Middle Ages, and the Sabbath fish par excellence for the Jews of Alsace-Lorraine, in eastern France.

Carpe à la juive, or "carp in the Jewish style," as described above in C. Asserolette's charming "letters" to a friend in which she recounted watching the preparations for a Rosh Hashanah dinner in an Alsatian home in Paris, is poached in advance and served cold. The evolution of the sauces used for this weekly fish reflects the culinary and cultural continuity of the Jewish people.

In medieval France and southern Germany two sauces were very popular: the sweet-and-sour sauce (see preceding recipe) and this green parsley sauce, still used today in many homes at Passover. The green sauce is a simple one, often made with ginger, parsley, bread crumbs, and vinegar.

Today few people in France except Jews use carp, since there are so many more *poissons nobles* (noble fish), as one Frenchman told me. Whatever fish you choose—carp, grouper, salmon, sea bream, pike, or cod—you can, for ease of preparation, use fillets or slice the fish into steaks, cook them on a bed of sautéed onions, then poach them in water and wine. When they are done, you may reduce the cooking liquid and pour it over the fish slices, arranged on a platter to resemble the whole fish, and serve the dish cold or at room temperature.

YIELD: 6 SERVINGS

One 3-pound fillet of carp, grouper, sea bream, or salmon

Rinse the fish under cold water, and dry it off.

Heat the olive oil in a medium-sized frying pan. Add the onions, shallots, fennel, leek, garlic, and ginger, and sauté without browning for 2 to 3 minutes. Stir in the flour or matzo meal with a whisk, and cook until it browns slightly.

Put the vegetable mixture in a heavy casserole or fish poacher large enough to hold the fish fillet in one piece. Add the wine, bay leaf, thyme, salt and freshly ground pepper to taste, the fish stock or water, and 2 tablespoons of the parsley. Bring to a boil, and simmer for about 20 minutes over medium heat. Gently lower the fish into the casserole or poacher, cover, and simmer for 15 to 20 minutes, or until just cooked.

Leaving the liquid in the pan, gently lift out the fillet and put it on a serving platter. Over high heat, reduce the liquid by half. Correct the seasoning, and pass the liquid through a fine sieve over the fish. Let the fish cool, then refrigerate for at least 2 hours. Serve cold, sprinkled with the remaining chopped parsley and accompanied by grated horseradish.

2 tablespoons olive oil

2 large onions, peeled and sliced

3 medium shallots, peeled and thinly sliced

1 fennel bulb, thinly sliced

1 leek, cleaned and sliced into thin rounds

3 cloves garlic, peeled and sliced

½-inch piece of ginger root, peeled and grated

2 tablespoons flour or matzo meal

2 cups dry white wine

1 bay leaf

A few sprigs fresh thyme

Salt and freshly ground pepper to taste

2 cups strong fish stock or water

1 cup chopped fresh parsley

Horseradish for garnish

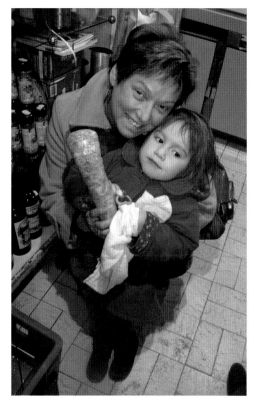

Helping Grandma buy horseradish for Passover in the Marais

How Sarah Wojnaski Learned Tradition

Most gefilte-fish recipes are handed down from generation to generation by word of mouth. But not this one.
Sarah Wojnaski, whom I met at a tea party at her sister-
in-law's home in Paris, learned no recipes from her
mother, because her parents were taken away by the
Gestapo in the summer of 1942, when she was only
nine years old. This is her story and the story of her
gefilte-fish recipe.

"If my brother, Joseph, and I are living, it is because
Marie Fricker, our Catholic nanny, came to find us.
After hours of tears and pleading with the French police,
she convinced them to let her take us. Finally, they

Sarah Wojnaski, one of Paris's
gefilte-fish mavens

Straining the fish broth

allowed this woman with a big heart to take us home, but not my mother, who was sent to Auschwitz. Many years later, after my adopted parents' death, Marie and Georges Fricker's children received the medal of the Just Among Nations from Jacques Chirac, then mayor of Paris. It is very important to remember that 11,400 Jewish children were deported from France. But 60,000 were saved, especially thanks to the French gentile population. We do not forget.

"Since my mother died when I was so young, I knew nothing of Jewish cooking. My mother-in-law taught me all I know. She understood that I needed to take advantage of her knowledge and helped me as much as she could. The history of this recipe corresponds with the history of my perfect accord with this unusual woman, who died at the age of 101. For fifty-four years, there was only love between us. She was extraordinarily tender, while never trying to take the place of my own mother."

The finished product

Gefilte Fish

(POLISH-STYLE FISH BALLS)

ONE OF THE EARLIEST PRINTED RECIPES for stuffed fish was in a volume entitled *Le Cuisinier Royal et Bourgeois* by François Massialot, published in Paris in 1691. The author suggested that the fish be cleaned and the skin filled with the chopped flesh of carp, along with chopped mushrooms, perch, and the nonkosher eel. The skin of the stuffed carp was stitched or tied together, and the fish was then left to cook in an oven in a sauce of brown butter, white wine, and clear broth; it was served with mushrooms, capers, and slices of lemon. In Alsace today there is still a special stuffed fish cooked in white wine, *carpe farcie à l'alsacienne,* which is similar. But by and large, gefilte fish came to France with the waves of emigrants from eastern Europe.

Sarah Wojnaski's Parisian version of gefilte fish from Poland uses pike, haddock, cod, whiting, sole, and carp, and sautéed onions. Although she makes her gefilte fish into balls, she also stuffs some of the chopped-fish mixture into the head of the fish and encloses more of it in the skin. I have divided Sarah's recipe in half, but the amounts might still be too big for you. If so, just divide them again. I have a big Seder and always give some gefilte fish away.

YIELD: 36 PATTIES

8 pounds whole fish with bones and skin, such as carp, mullet, rockfish, haddock, whiting, sole, whitefish, or pike, filleted and ground*

2 tablespoons salt, or to taste

7 peppercorns, plus freshly ground pepper to taste

4 onions, peeled

6 medium carrots, peeled

*Ask your fishmonger to grind the fish, reserving the tails, fins, heads, and bones. Be sure he gives you the bones and trimmings.

Put the reserved bones, skin, and at least one of the fish heads (see footnote) in a wide, very large saucepan with a cover. Pour in water to cover by about 5 inches. Add 1 tablespoon of the salt and the peppercorns, and bring to a boil. Remove any scum that accumulates with a slotted spoon.

Cut one onion into quarters, and add along with five of the carrots and the parsnip. Add the sugar, and bring to a boil. Cover, and simmer for about 2 hours. Long cooking will ensure a broth with jelly. Turn off the heat, strain the broth, and discard the bones and vegetables, reserving the carrots. Refrigerate overnight.

The next day, take the remaining three onions, slice thinly into rounds, and sauté in the oil in a medium-sized frying pan until they are golden. Pulse to grind in a food processor equipped with the steel blade.

Put the ground fish and onions in a large bowl. Grate the remaining raw carrot into the bowl and add the eggs, one at a time, the remaining tablespoon of salt, the ground pepper, and about

½ cup of cold water. Mix thoroughly. Stir in enough matzo meal to make a light, soft mixture that will hold its shape. Either taste the raw fish to see if the seasonings need to be adjusted, or if you are uncomfortable tasting uncooked fish and eggs, heat the broth and dip a small amount in the broth to cook before tasting.

Wet your hands with cold water, scoop up about ¼ cup of the fish mixture, and form it into an oval shape about 3 inches long. Repeat until you have made oval patties out of all the mixture except for a handful to stuff the cavity of the reserved fish head or heads. Gently put the fish patties and the fish heads in the simmering fish stock, adding more water if necessary almost to cover. Cover loosely, and simmer for 20 to 30 minutes. Taste the liquid while the fish is cooking, and add seasoning to taste. Shake the pot periodically, so the fish patties won't stick. When the gefilte fish is cooked, remove from the water and allow to cool for at least 15 minutes.

Using a slotted spoon, carefully remove the fish patties and the heads, and arrange on a platter with the fish head or heads in the center. Strain some of the stock over the fish, saving the rest in a bowl. Slice the cooked carrots into rounds cut on the diagonal about ¼ inch thick. Put a piece of carrot on top of each gefilte-fish patty. Chill until ready to eat. Serve one gefilte-fish patty with a sprig of parsley and a dollop of horseradish.

1 parsnip, peeled and chopped

2 tablespoons sugar, or to taste

3 tablespoons peanut or vegetable oil

3 large eggs

About ⅓ cup matzo meal

Horseradish for garnish

NOTE   Gefilte fish freezes well.

Sauce au Raifort

(HORSERADISH SAUCE)

ACCORDING TO THE TALMUD and the French sage Rashi, beets, fish, and cloves of garlic are essential foods to honor the Sabbath.

French Jews also use horseradish, sliced as a root or ground into a sauce, and served at Passover to symbolize the bitterness of slavery. It was probably in Alsace or southern Germany that the horseradish root replaced the bitter greens of more southerly climes as the bitter herbs at Passover dinner.

For hundreds of years, local farmers would dig up horseradish roots and peel and grate them outdoors, by their kitchens, making sure to protect their eyes from the sting. Then they would mix the root with a little sugar and vinegar and sometimes grated beets, keeping it for their own personal use or selling it at local farmers' markets. In 1956, Raifalsa, an Alsace-based company, began grating horseradish grown by the area's farmers in the corner of a farm in Mietesheim, near the Vosges Mountains. A few years ago, Raifalsa, still the only manufacturer of prepared horseradish in France, agreed to produce a batch of kosher horseradish. They had the rabbi of Strasbourg come to the factory to supervise the operation, which resulted in the production of six thousand 7-ounce pots, all stamped with a certification from the Grand Rabbinat de Strasbourg.

Before grating the horseradish, just remember to open a window and put on a pair of goggles.

YIELD: ABOUT 2 CUPS

1 fresh horseradish root, about ½ pound, peeled
2 medium beets, boiled and peeled, cooking liquid reserved
3 to 4 tablespoons lemon juice
½ teaspoon kosher salt
¼ cup sugar, or to taste
¼ cup white vinegar or beet-juice water

Finely grate the horseradish and the beets with a hand grater, or in a food processor fitted with a shredding disk, into a large bowl. Toss with the lemon juice and salt.

Put the sugar in the vinegar or beet-juice water in a small pan, and set over medium heat to dissolve. Bring slowly to a boil, and turn off after about 3 minutes. Stir this liquid into the horseradish and beets. If too dry, stir in some of the reserved beet-cooking liquid.

Put the horseradish and some of the liquid in a jar, and keep tightly closed in the refrigerator for a day. Then remove and taste, adding more salt, sugar, or beet liquid as needed.

Cabbage Stuffed with Gefilte Fish

EVERY YEAR AT PASSOVER, I make too much gefilte fish. In fact, when I made gefilte fish one year with Jackie Lyden on National Public Radio's *All Things Considered,* I used 27 pounds of fish!

Hadassa Schneerson Carlebach, a fascinating woman (see page 140) who worked with her late father making and providing matzo and other kosher food for observant Jews in detention camps in France, gave me this recipe for gefilte-fish-stuffed cabbage. Flavored with slowly cooked peppers and tomatoes, it is a great way to use up leftover patties. Even avowed gefilte-fish detesters love this dish. A cooking tip: I put the cabbage in the freezer for two days, defrost it for a day, and then use the limp leaves to wrap the fish.

Remove eight leaves from the head of defrosted cabbage, keeping them whole. (It's easiest to do this by cutting out the cabbage heart and then peeling away the leaves.) If the leaves aren't limp and pliable, place them in a large bowl with ½ cup water, and microwave, covered, for 3 minutes. Drain and set aside. Shred about 2 cups of the remaining cabbage.

Heat the olive oil in a Dutch oven or other medium-sized, oven-safe casserole. Add the shredded cabbage, tomatoes, peppers, celery, jalapeño, and salt and freshly ground pepper to taste. Lower the heat, and simmer, covered, for about an hour, stirring occasionally.

Preheat the oven to 325 degrees.

Put a gefilte-fish patty in the center of a cabbage leaf. Wrap it like an envelope—first the bottom up, then the sides into the middle, then the top down. Repeat with the remaining seven cabbage leaves and gefilte-fish patties.

When the tomato-and-pepper mixture has finished cooking, nestle the stuffed cabbage, seam side down, into this sauce. Bake, covered, for about 90 minutes. Serve with the fresh parsley sprinkled on top.

P YIELD: 8 SERVINGS

1 head of green cabbage, frozen, then defrosted (see headnote)

2 tablespoons olive oil

4 tomatoes, cut into 1-inch pieces

6 red, green, yellow, or orange bell peppers (or any combination thereof), cut into 1-inch pieces

8 stalks celery, cut into ½-inch pieces

½ jalapeño pepper, finely diced

Salt and freshly ground pepper to taste

8 gefilte-fish patties (see page 156)

2 tablespoons chopped fresh parsley

Saint-Germain Sushi

Ramble down Boulevard Saint-Germain toward Odéon and you will stumble upon Sushi West, nestled between Armani and Sonia Rykiel. From the outside it looks like any other upscale French sushi restaurant, but as you walk through the door, a mezuzah hangs to your right. Inside, a young Israeli in a yarmulke watches to make sure that everything is okay. "Seventy percent of the diners are kosher," he told me, "fifteen percent tourists, and the rest regular French people who just want sushi." Run by two Jews, one from Morocco and the other from Tunisia, the chain has ten kosher sushi restaurants in Paris alone. Kosher French wine is served with all kinds of sushi: salmon, tuna, and mahimahi, and the glorious *yamaka*—tuna and salmon on a bed of sticky rice.

Bringing Tunisian Fish
in Your Carry-On Luggage

When Annie and André Berrebi left their native Tunisia for Paris after their country became independent in 1956, they sold their shirt factory but never really left their home in Tunis. The elegant apartment they settled into in Paris's Sixteenth Arrondissement, near the chic Avenue Foch, reflects this double identity: beautiful wood pieces from Tunisia are interspersed with Louis XV furniture. Most of the Berrebis' friends are Tunisian Jews who, like themselves, were displaced after Tunisia's independence. At that time there were 130,000 Jews in Tunisia; today there are barely 1,300.

But even with a long history of intermittent prosperity and persecution, many Tunisian Jews are still very much connected to their birthplace. Although

Annie and André Berrebi at table

André, after forty years in Paris, likes grocery shopping at the Belleville market, he still prefers going to the market in Tunis, which he does every few weeks or so, bringing back with him goodies that his cook in Tunis makes for him. He particularly cherishes her *harissa* and salads made from fresh, seasonal artichoke hearts (see page 100). But most beloved is the *mérou,* a kind of grouper. This he brings back in his carry-on, packed in ice, kept fresh for Annie's *couscous de poisson,* a Tuesday lunch specialty in Tunis.

Couscous de Poisson

(TUNISIAN FISH COUSCOUS)

IN HER MODERN KITCHEN, with its sleek mauve cabinets and red-and-purple tiles, Annie Berrebi showed me how to make this landmark dish. The stew can be prepped in advance and finished with a few minutes of simmering. Annie often freezes leftover grains of cooked couscous and then pops them into the microwave before using. Unlike Moroccan Jews, who serve their food in courses as the French do, the Berrebis serve everything at once (couscous, salads, and hot sauce). During this absolutely delicious meal, Annie told me, "I miss the sun in Tunis. But I love Paris. We have made our lives here."

You can either serve the couscous, fish balls, and vegetables on different plates, as Mrs. Berrebi does, or, if you want to make a big splash, as I like to do when presenting such a grand dish, pile the couscous in a pyramid on a big serving platter, then arrange the fish balls and the vegetables around it. Ladle the broth all over, and garnish with the cilantro. Pour some extra *harissa* into a little bowl, and put that on the table alongside cooked salads such as carrot salad (see page 112) or a tomato salad.

YIELD: AT LEAST 10 SERVINGS

FISH BALLS

1 pound grouper or other meaty white fish

1 pound fresh soft-flesh white fish, such as sole, flounder, or whiting

8 spring onions or large scallions, diced

1 bunch of fresh parsley, chopped

2 teaspoons salt, or to taste

¾ baguette, soaked in water and drained

¼ teaspoon freshly ground pepper, or to taste

2 teaspoons *harissa* (see page 33), or to taste

5 large cloves garlic, 4 of them minced

3 large eggs

Olive oil for frying

2 fresh tomatoes, peeled and diced, or one 6-ounce can

1 heaping tablespoon tomato paste

BROTH

¼ cup olive oil

1 onion, peeled and diced

2 large cloves garlic, minced

2 tomatoes, fresh or canned, peeled and diced

2 teaspoons tomato paste

2 teaspoons *harissa* (see page 33), or to taste

2 cups fish stock or water

Salt and freshly ground pepper to taste

1 leek, halved lengthwise and cleaned

2 zucchini, cut in half lengthwise

2 medium potatoes, peeled and cut in half

2 stalks celery, cut in half

3 carrots, peeled and cut into thirds

1 yellow winter squash (such as butternut), peeled and cut in large chunks

1 cup chickpeas, cooked fresh or rinsed and drained from a can

1 pound couscous (see page 270)

2 tablespoons chopped fresh cilantro for garnish

To make the fish balls, grind both kinds of the fish in the bowl of an electric food processor fitted with a steel blade. Set aside in a medium bowl.

Put the spring onions or scallions and the parsley in a strainer, and sprinkle with 1 teaspoon of the salt. Let sit for about ½ hour, and press out the liquid. Rinse, and press again. (According to Annie, the salt helps get rid of the smell of the onion.)

Using your hands, mix the ground fish with the spring onions and parsley and the drained bread. Sprinkle in the remaining teaspoon salt, the pepper, 1 teaspoon of the *harissa,* and the minced garlic. Add the eggs, and mix again. The texture should be paste-like but not mushy. If it's too thin, add some more bread; if too thick, add a little water. Refrigerate the fish mixture for at least ½ hour.

Dip your hands into cold water, then mold the fish mixture into balls a little larger than walnuts, and place them on a large plate. You should have about three dozen balls.

Heat ½ inch of olive oil in a large, heavy frying pan, and sauté the fish balls until they become golden. Depending on the size of your pan, you might want to do this in two or even three batches. Remove with a slotted spoon, and drain on paper towels.

Discard all but about ¼ inch of the oil from the pan. Add the tomatoes, pressing them down, and the remaining garlic clove. Cook for about 5 minutes. Pour in about 2 inches of water, and stir in the tomato paste and the remaining teaspoon of *harissa.* Bring to a boil, and add the fish balls. Reduce the heat and simmer, uncovered, for a few minutes, coating them with the sauce. Set aside.

To make the broth, heat the oil in a soup pot. Sauté the onion and one of the minced garlic cloves until the onion is translucent. Add the tomatoes, the tomato paste, and the *harissa,* stir, and continue cooking over low heat. Then add the fish stock or water, salt and freshly ground pepper to taste, the leek, zucchini, potatoes, celery, and carrots. Cook for about 5 minutes, then add the squash and the chickpeas. Bring to a boil, cover, and simmer for about 15 minutes, or until the squash is cooked. Remove the pot from the heat, and set aside.

Just before the broth has finished cooking, reheat the fish balls and prepare the couscous according to the package directions (or see page 270). Follow the serving suggestions in the headnote at left.

Pierre Troisgros
and His Jewish Connection

One of my favorite food memories is the meal I was privileged to cover for *The New York Times* in celebration of the three thousandth year of the city of Jerusalem. The meal, prepared by twelve chefs, including seven three-star chefs from France, was strictly kosher. The image that remains with me still is of a beautiful young *sabra,* an Israeli-born student at the Hadassah College of Technology, seated next to one of the doyens of French cooking, Pierre Troisgros of Restaurant Troisgros in Roanne.

Three-star chef Pierre Troisgros

Several years later, I found myself in Roanne and ate at Troisgros. Over dessert and coffee in one of the restaurant's lounges, Pierre explained to me that in 1933 the restaurant received its first star from the Michelin rating system (established in 1899, with the advent of the automobile). In 1965, it received two stars; every year since 1969, it has received three stars.

Located across the street from the railroad station, the restaurant was a natural meeting point for businessmen (many of whom were Jewish) from the jewelry and textile industries in Roanne. They would have lunch with their clients at Troisgros, visit the factories, where they would take orders, and then put their clients back on the trains heading for Paris and elsewhere.

But some of the restaurant's guests were less welcome. During World War II, German officers arriving at the same station in leather coats also frequented the town's best restaurant. "To this day, when I smell leather I get sick," Monsieur Troisgros told me.

Saumon à l'Oseille

(SALMON WITH SORREL SAUCE)

THE SLIGHT TARTNESS OF SORREL and the richness of salmon are two flavors that Jews have always loved in their cooking. Eastern European Jews eat cold sorrel soup, which they call *tchav*; Greek Jews eat a tart rhubarb-and-spinach sauce over fish, and French Jews are drawn to Pierre Troisgros's now classic salmon with sorrel sauce. Pierre told me that this seminal, simple, and delicious recipe came about because he had grown an abundance of sorrel and had to do something with it. With its subtle interplay of tartness and creaminess, this dish is sometimes made with kosher white wine and vermouth for Jewish weddings held at the restaurant.

YIELD: 4 SERVINGS

1 cup dry white wine, preferably Chardonnay

⅓ cup dry vermouth

¼ cup finely minced shallots

1 cup heavy cream

4 cups fresh young sorrel, washed, stemmed, and torn into ½-inch pieces

1 tablespoon fresh lemon juice

Salt and freshly ground pepper to taste

One 12-ounce center-cut salmon fillet, boneless, with skin on

Pour the wine and the vermouth into a small saucepan over medium heat. Scatter the shallots over them and cook. When reduced by half, add the cream. Bring the mixture to a simmer, stirring frequently, and cook for about 20 minutes. Remove from the heat, and strain the sauce through a fine-mesh sieve into a clean saucepan.

Reserving a small handful for garnish, stir the sorrel into the sauce a handful at a time. Add the lemon juice, and salt and freshly ground pepper to taste, and cook briefly, stirring. Remove from the heat and keep warm.

Cut the salmon fillet in half crosswise. Then cut each piece into two rectangles; you should have four portions. Gently pound each piece with the flat end of a cleaver to make the salmon pieces thinner.

Season the skin side of the salmon with salt and freshly ground pepper. Heat a nonstick pan over medium heat, and cook the fillets, skin side first, for 30 seconds. Flip, and cook for another 30 seconds.

Distribute the sorrel sauce evenly among the centers of four warm serving plates. Place a salmon fillet over each, arranging some sorrel pieces around them. Serve immediately.

Choucroute de Poisson au Beurre Blanc

(FISH SAUERKRAUT WITH WINE AND BUTTER SAUCE)

ONE MORNING, AS MY EDITOR, JUDITH JONES, and I were wandering around the streets of Strasbourg looking for a cell-phone store, I bumped into three young men having a smoke outside a restaurant. I saw "Crocodile" written on their chefs' jackets and asked if Emil Jung, the chef-owner and a friend of a friend, was in the restaurant. They said he was and told me just to go knock on the door to say hello. We did; three hours later, we left the restaurant having been wined and dined beautifully by him and his lovely wife, Monique.

One of their Alsatian specialties is fish *choucroute* (sauerkraut) with heavenly *beurre-blanc* sauce, a dish appreciated by customers who follow the laws of kashrut. In Strasbourg, where everybody eats sauerkraut, there is even a Choucrouterie theater and restaurant built on an old sauerkraut factory. Roger Siffert, the affable director of this bilingual (Alsatian dialect and French) cabaret theater, says that they serve seven varieties of *choucroute,* including fish for observant Jews. "With words like *pickelfleisch* and *shmatteh* existing in both Yiddish and Alsatian," said Siffert, "people should reach out to what is similar, not separate. In Alsace we call Jews 'our Jews.' "

YIELD: 6 TO 8 SERVINGS

2 tablespoons olive oil

1 medium onion, diced

6 ounces Savoy cabbage
  (*chou frisé*)

12 ounces sauerkraut, rinsed
  in cold water and drained

1⅓ cups Riesling white wine

¼ teaspoon juniper berries,
  crushed, or 1 teaspoon
  gin

4½ cups fish stock

A few sprigs fresh thyme

1 bay leaf

Freshly ground black pepper to
  taste

Heat 1 tablespoon of the oil in a frying pan, and sauté the onion and the cabbage until the cabbage is wilted and the onion is translucent.

Stir the sauerkraut into the onion and cabbage. Add 1 cup of the white wine, the juniper berries, ½ cup of the fish stock, the thyme, the bay leaf, and the freshly ground black pepper to taste. Simmer, uncovered, for about 15 minutes, or until most of the liquid is absorbed but the cabbage is still crunchy. Fish out the bay leaf, stir in the cilantro, and transfer to a flat ovenproof casserole.

To make the *beurre blanc,* sauté the shallots in 1 tablespoon of the butter in a saucepan for a few minutes. Add the remaining ⅓ cup white wine, the vinegar, and the remaining 4 cups fish stock, and cook, whisking, to reduce by more than half. Then add the remaining butter, piece by piece, whisking all the time. Add the lemon juice, and salt and freshly ground white pepper to taste. Set aside.

Season the fish with salt and freshly ground pepper to taste.

Quickly sear the fillets in a nonstick frying pan in the remaining tablespoon of olive oil. Place on top of the sauerkraut, and heat in the oven for about 5 minutes, or until the fish is cooked through. While the fish is baking, reheat the *beurre-blanc* sauce. Serve topped with the warm sauce, with steamed potatoes on the side.

2 tablespoons chopped fresh cilantro

4 shallots, finely chopped

6 ounces (1½ sticks) butter, cut in small pieces and chilled

4 teaspoons white-wine vinegar

Juice of 1 lemon

Salt and freshly ground white pepper to taste

6 to 8 fillets of salmon, haddock, sole, or cod, with the skin (3 pounds)

8 potatoes, steamed

Passover Moroccan Shad
with Fava Beans and Red Peppers

TYPICALLY PREPARED AT PASSOVER by French Moroccan Jews, this is one of the most colorful and delicious fish dishes I have ever tasted. Today most French Jews buy their fava beans, a sign of spring, twice peeled and frozen, from Picard Surgelés. Frozen is easier, but in this dish, fresh tastes even better.

YIELD: 4 TO 6 SERVINGS

½ cup plus 2 tablespoons olive oil

4 to 6 cloves garlic, sliced

3 red bell peppers, cut in 1-by-2-inch slices

1 bunch of fresh cilantro, finely chopped

1 teaspoon salt, plus more to taste

2 pounds fresh fava beans, shelled

1½ teaspoons sweet paprika

Freshly ground pepper to taste

½ teaspoon cayenne pepper (optional)

2 pounds boneless shad fillets, including intact roe if you like (salmon or rockfish can be substituted for the shad)

Heat ½ cup of the oil in a large, wide sauté pan with a cover. Stir in the garlic and the red peppers. Sauté slowly, stirring occasionally, for about 2 minutes. Add about 2 cups water, and bring to a boil. Reduce to medium heat, add half the cilantro, and continue cooking, covered, for about 30 minutes, adding a little more water if necessary.

While the peppers are cooking, bring about 6 cups water with 1 teaspoon salt to a boil. Toss in the fava beans, and cook for about 4 minutes, or until the beans are *al dente*. Remove, plunge into ice water, drain, and slip the thin outer skin off the beans.

Add the fava beans to the peppers with 1 teaspoon of the paprika, salt and freshly ground pepper to taste, the cayenne pepper, shad, and the roe, if using. Drizzle the remaining 2 tablespoons olive oil over the fish, as well as the remaining ½ teaspoon paprika and all but 2 tablespoons of the remaining cilantro. Simmer, covered, until the shad is cooked through, 7 to 10 minutes, adding more water if necessary. Remove the fish, vegetables, and sauce to a serving plate, and sprinkle the reserved fresh cilantro on top.

Turkish "Red Sea" Mackerel with Tomato and Parsley

THIS DISH COMES FROM SUSIE MORGENSTERN, the Judy Blume of France. When she is not writing novels for teenagers or lecturing around France, she is cooking in her marvelous nineteenth-century house, high up in the hills above Nice, overlooking the Mediterranean. When I visited her, she told me I'd need to climb a hundred steps to reach her home. I did, only to find that they were the wrong hundred stairs! So down I went, and up again. But the two climbs were worth it, and I was rewarded with a spectacular view from the house.

Although Susie, who greeted me warmly, does not consider herself a good cook, she is known for her Passover Seders, always welcoming people from Nice's diverse cultures.

She learned this Turkish Jewish dish, which marries sautéed parsley with mackerel, from her mother-in-law, who came to France from Constantinople. Susie calls it "Red Sea" mackerel because of the red color of the dish. Served at Passover, it evokes the story of the Jews crossing the Red Sea during their exodus from Egypt. When I suggested adding garlic to the dish, Susie paused. "My mother-in-law was no garlic miser, but she didn't put it in this; there must have been a reason." This confirms my belief that traditional foods, handed down from generation to generation, are the last to change within a culture.

YIELD: 6 TO 8 SERVINGS

⅓ cup olive oil

1 bunch of fresh parsley, finely chopped (about 4 cups)

2 cups puréed peeled fresh or canned tomatoes

Salt and freshly ground pepper to taste

1 tablespoon sugar

2 fresh mackerel, 2 to 2½ pounds each

Juice of 1 lemon

Heat the olive oil in a large skillet over medium heat. Sprinkle on the parsley and brown for about 5 minutes, watching carefully, because the parsley can burn easily.

Stir in the tomatoes, salt and freshly ground pepper to taste, and the sugar. Simmer, stirring occasionally, for about ½ hour.

Cut off the heads and the tails of the mackerel, and carefully remove the fins. Then slice each fish through the bone into four pieces. Nestle the pieces in the sauce, and simmer, uncovered, for about 20 minutes, making sure to spoon the sauce over the fish as it cooks. Remove from the heat, and place the mackerel on a plate. Check the sauce; if it's too thin, cook it down a bit more. Spoon the sauce over the fish, and squeeze the lemon over all. Eat at room temperature.

Dorade Royale

(SEA BREAM WITH PRESERVED LEMON, TAMARIND, GINGER, AND CILANTRO)

WHILE IN NICE, I HAD LUNCH WITH Irene and Michel Weil at their charming house, with fig trees growing in their garden and nasturtiums on their deck. Although Irene quietly confessed to me that she wasn't much of a cook, she treated us to a delectable and creative meal. It began with the last tomatoes from their garden served with a little olive oil, sea salt, and a sprinkling of fresh herbs, including mint, basil, and cilantro, from her garden; then we had a Mediterranean *dorade royale* (sea bream) with preserved lemons, tamarind, and ginger. Comté cheese brought from Michel's native Besançon, fresh pomegranate seeds from the yellow pomegranates growing in their garden, raspberries, and fresh walnuts in the shell finished the meal, all attractively presented as only the French can do.

When I asked about the seasonings for the *dorade,* Irene said that she loves the flavor contrasts of the preserved lemon, tamarind, and ginger.

YIELD: 6 SERVINGS

3 tablespoons olive oil

6 branches fresh cilantro

One 3-to-4-pound whole *dorade royale* (gilt-head bream), snapper, or grouper, or 2½ pounds fillets

1 heaping tablespoon tamarind paste, or 1 teaspoon tamarind concentrate

2 tablespoons brown sugar

2 teaspoons soy sauce

¼ cup white wine

One 6-inch knob of ginger, half peeled and grated, half cut in 2 pieces

1½ preserved lemons (recipe follows), diced

Preheat the oven to 425 degrees, and smear 1 tablespoon of the olive oil in a 13-by-9-inch ovenproof glass baking pan. Stick the cilantro inside the belly of the fish, or scatter around the fillets and slide into the pan.

Stir together the tamarind paste or concentrate, the brown sugar, and the soy sauce in a small mixing bowl, adding enough water to thin until runny. Stir in the white wine, and spoon the sauce over the fish. Scatter the grated and cut ginger and the preserved lemons around the fish, and drizzle the remaining oil on top. Bake in the oven for 20 to 30 minutes, or until just cooked through. Remove the ginger knobs and serve.

Citrons Confits

(PRESERVED LEMONS)

PRESERVED LEMONS ARE AN indispensable item in my pantry cupboard. I use them all the time and believe they are best made at home. Although I have tasted lemons preserved in water or an equal mix of lemon juice and water, I much prefer them preserved in pure lemon juice. Many people scrape out and discard the pulp when using the lemons, but I often include the preserved pulp. I blend a preserved lemon in with my hummus, sprinkle the rind on grilled fish, and stuff my chicken with a whole lemon, and I dice preserved lemons and mix them into salads, rice dishes, and vegetables. In addition to regular lemons, you can also use Meyer lemons or, as Irene Weil does, even kumquats.

Cut off the very ends of each lemon. Cut each one lengthwise into quarters, cutting to but not through the opposite end. Sprinkle 2 tablespoons of salt into the cut sides of each lemon.

Put the lemons in a large jar (it's fine if you have to squeeze them in, because they will shrink), and cover completely with lemon juice. Let sit for a day.

The next day, if they are not covered with lemon juice, pour a thin film of olive oil over the lemons. This will help keep them sealed while they preserve. Put the jar in the refrigerator and allow to cure for 2 to 3 weeks. Before using, scrape off the pulp if desired.

YIELD: 8 PRESERVED LEMONS

8 lemons (about 1½ pounds)
About ½ cup kosher salt
1 cup fresh lemon juice, plus more if necessary
2 tablespoons olive oil

NOTE You can shorten the curing period by about 2 weeks by freezing the lemons for a few days after cutting them. Defrost and cure as above in salt and lemon.

Bourride

(PROVENÇAL FISH STEW WITH VEGETABLES AND WINE)

CHEZ PAUL, LOCATED NEAR THE PORT of Marseille, stands at a crossroads with three other fish restaurants. But the license from the Beth Din of Marseille, hanging on the wall, certifying that the restaurant is kosher, sets this one apart. When I visited Chez Paul, Fathi Hmam, the Tunisian Muslim chef, was busy prepping bouillabaisse for the evening's dinner.

Technically, his bouillabaisse stew is a *bourride,* because it only has fish with fins and scales—those that swim near the magnificent rocky shore of this ancient port city of France. But he does not use *lotte* (monkfish), also a nonkosher fish, central to fish *bourrides* in Marseille.

Bourride is one of the oldest dishes in France, said to have been brought by the Phoenicians in the sixth century B.C.E. Of course, the tomatoes and potatoes arrived much later. It is also said that a few Jews came with the Phoenicians on this voyage. Is that why, perhaps, there is no shellfish in the *bourride*?

The success of this simple dish depends on knowing at what moment the fish is perfectly cooked. And, of course, don't forget the *rouille* (see page 63), which North African Jews and Muslims alike make their own by adding a Tunisian touch: *harissa.*

 YIELD: 8 SERVINGS

2 tablespoons olive oil

2 cups white wine

8 to 10 cups fish broth or water

Sea salt and pepper to taste

Peel of 1 orange

Pinch of saffron

1 large onion, peeled and diced

3 cloves garlic, minced

1 leek, cleaned and chopped

1 fennel bulb, diced

1 teaspoon anise seeds

4 tomatoes, peeled and diced, or one 15-ounce can tomatoes

2 carrots, peeled and diced

A few branches fresh thyme

1 sprig fresh parsley, plus 1 cup diced parsley

2 pounds potatoes, peeled and cut into 1-inch chunks

4 pounds mixed fish fillets, such as mahimahi, bluefish, striped bass, sea bream, or codfish, cut in big chunks

1 baguette

Rouille (see page 63)

Put the olive oil, the wine, 8 cups of fish broth or water, salt, pepper, the orange peel, saffron, onion, garlic, leek, fennel, anise seeds, tomatoes, carrots, thyme, and parsley sprig in a 6-quart casserole, and bring to a boil. Simmer for about 15 minutes.

Add the potatoes, and cook for about 10 minutes, or until they are almost done. Then add the fish in two batches, starting with firmer fish and waiting about a minute to put in the next batch. Simmer, covered, for 5 to 7 minutes, until done, adding more broth if necessary. Fish out the orange peel, the thyme, and the parsley; use a knife to slice the fish carefully, adjust seasonings with salt and pepper; and sprinkle on the diced parsley. Serve immediately in one big bowl with some of the broth. Place the fish and ladle the broth on top. Slice the baguette into small rounds, toast, and serve with a teaspoon or so of *rouille* on top. Serve the remainder of the baguette and the *rouille* on the side.

Seaport of Cassis, near Marseille

Grilled Cod with *Raïto* Sauce

RAÏTO, ALSO SPELLED *RAITE* OR *RAYTE,* is a very old sauce, traditionally served by Provençal Jews on Friday night over cod, either simply grilled or baked. Some people add a small whole fresh or canned anchovy, a few sprigs of fennel, and/or about ¼ cup of chopped walnuts or almonds. Similar in taste to a *puttanesca* sauce, it can also be served over grilled tuna or pasta.

YIELD: ABOUT 2 CUPS SAUCE TO SERVE 4

4 cloves garlic, minced

2 onions, peeled and chopped

4 tablespoons olive oil

1 tablespoon flour

5 ripe tomatoes, peeled and chopped

2 cups fruity red wine, such as Côte de Provence

A *bouquet garni* of 3 branches each of thyme, rosemary, parsley, and tarragon tied together with 2 cloves in cheesecloth

Salt and freshly ground pepper to taste

⅓ cup black picholine olives, pitted and halved

1 tablespoon capers, drained

3 pounds grilled cod or tuna

Sauté the garlic and the onions in the olive oil in a heavy soup pot until the onions are transparent. Whisk in the flour until brown and smooth.

Add the tomatoes, wine, and 2 cups water. Bring to a boil, then add the *bouquet garni* and a little salt and pepper. Simmer slowly, uncovered, for about an hour, until the sauce is reduced by half.

Remove the *bouquet garni,* purée the tomatoes and onion in a food processor or blender, and return to the pot. Add the picholine olives and capers. Adjust the seasonings, and serve over grilled cod or tuna, or over pasta.

NOTE Don't make this dish unless good fresh ripe tomatoes are available. Don't use canned.

Passover Provençal Stuffed Trout
with Spinach and Sorrel

THIS DELIGHTFUL JEWISH RECIPE adapted from one by the famous Provençal food writer Jean-Noël Escudier in his *La Véritable Cuisine Provençale et Niçoise* uses matzo meal to coat the trout, which is stuffed with spinach and sorrel, or, if you like, Swiss chard. Trout was and still is found in ponds on private property in Provence and throughout France. This particular recipe is served at Passover by the Jews of Provence.

Preheat the oven to 425 degrees, and use 1 tablespoon of the butter or olive oil to grease a 9-by-12-inch glass baking pan.

To make the stuffing, put the spinach, parsley, and garlic in a food processor, and pulse to chop. Heat a frying pan with 2 tablespoons of the butter, and sauté the shallots for a minute or two. Then add the chopped vegetables, and sauté until they are soft. Season to taste with salt and pepper, and cool. Now add the chopped sorrel.

Season the trout inside and out with salt and pepper, and carefully stuff each of the trout with the vegetables. Close each with a long skewer.

Brush some butter or oil on the outside of each of the trout. Put the matzo meal in a wide plate, carefully dip each fish into the matzo meal, and then put in the baking pan. Surround the trout with any leftover vegetables. Bake for 15 to 20 minutes, or until done.

D OR P YIELD: 6 SERVINGS

7 tablespoons melted butter or olive oil

Two 10-ounce bags fresh spinach

½ cup chopped fresh parsley

5 cloves garlic, crushed

2 shallots, chopped

Salt and freshly ground pepper to taste

1 pound sorrel, chopped

Six 6-ounce trout, cleaned and boned

1½ cups matzo meal

A weekend retreat in Burgundy

Chicken, Duck, and Goose

Rosh Hashanah Chicken with Cinnamon and Apples from Metz

Tagine au Poulet et aux Coings (Algerian Chicken and
Quince *Tagine* for Rosh Hashanah)

Roast Chicken Stuffed with Rosemary and Thyme
(and Sometimes Truffles)

Honey-Coated Baked Chicken with Preserved Lemon

Friday Night Chicken Provençal with Fennel and Garlic

Poulet à la Bohémienne (Chicken with Peppers,
Tomatoes, Onion, and Garlic)

Terrine of Chicken Flavored with Pistachio Nuts, Curry, and Hazelnuts

Friday Night Algerian Chicken Fricassee

Moroccan *Tagine* of Chicken with Prunes, Apricots, and Almonds

Poulet à la Juive

Moroccan Chicken with Olives and Preserved Lemons

Southwestern *Cassoulet* with Duck and Lamb

Tunisian Chicken with Onions, Peas, and Parsley

Canard aux Cérises (Roast Duck with Cherries)

Gala Goose

Rosh Hashanah Chicken
with Cinnamon and Apples from Metz

WHEN I WAS A STUDENT IN FRANCE, Rose Minkel was a fixture at Friday night dinners at my friend Nanou's home. Called Mémé, an endearing term for "Grandmother," she brought with her the recipes from her family's native Metz, a city in the province of Lorraine with a long Jewish presence.

Though the Jews had been in Metz for many generations (some say the first Jews settled there in 221 C.E.), up until the eighteenth century they lived a very different life from non-Jews in the town. They paid extra taxes on meat, wines and liqueurs, and other provisions. It was easy to spot a Jew on the street, because the men wore yellow hats to distinguish them from the black-hat-wearing gentiles. But over time they did assimilate, and already at the beginning of the eighteenth century, the Jews of Metz began to speak French instead of Yiddish.

One Rosh Hashanah recipe that I remember most fondly was this simple roast chicken with peeled apple quarters, cinnamon, sugar, and wine.

YIELD: 4 TO 6 SERVINGS

One 3½-to-4-pound roasting chicken

Salt and freshly ground pepper to taste

1 teaspoon ground cinnamon

1 onion, peeled and cut into chunks

1 cup chicken broth

1⅓ cups white wine

3 apples, cored and cut horizontally into 4 pieces (the French would use *reine-des-reinettes* apples or pippins, but Fuji apples are fine)

2 tablespoons sugar

Preheat the oven to 375 degrees.

Season the chicken with salt and freshly ground pepper to taste and ½ teaspoon of the cinnamon. Put in a roasting pan with the onion. Pour the chicken broth and wine over the chicken, and roast in the oven for 45 minutes.

After the chicken has been cooking for 45 minutes, surround it with the apples sprinkled with the remaining cinnamon and the sugar. Baste with the wine, and roast for about 45 more minutes, or until the apples are very soft and the chicken is cooked.

Rosh Hashanah chicken from Metz

Tagine au Poulet et aux Coings

(ALGERIAN CHICKEN AND QUINCE *TAGINE* FOR ROSH HASHANAH)

WHILE HER HUSBAND WAS ON A fall Sunday ramble with friends, Anne-Juliette Belicha gave me a cooking lesson in their fifteenth-century house overlooking the fields in the Dordogne countryside. The house is located on the outskirts of Montagnac, right near the caves of Lascaux, renowned for their prehistoric animal paintings. In the kitchen hang photos of the woman who owned the house at the turn of the century, who tended geese for *foie gras* and to provide goose fat for the winter.

Because quinces were in season, Anne-Juliette decided to cook us one of her Algerian husband's beloved Rosh Hashanah dishes, from a book that is also one of my favorites—*150 Recettes et Mille et Un Souvenirs d'une Juive d'Algerie* by Léone Jaffin.

The quince, believed to be the Biblical "apple" of the Garden of Eden by some scholars, is a complex fruit. Hard to peel and quarter, quinces require careful handling. Once peeled, they darken rather quickly, so you need to keep them in water mixed with a little lemon juice.

Anne-Juliette picked the quinces from a friend's tree and used an old variety of onions—a cross between onions and shallots—that she bought at a nearby farmers' market. As she cooked, first frying the onions and then the kosher chickens that she buys in Paris, she told us about her dream: to open a kosher bed-and-breakfast in the Dordogne.

YIELD: 4 TO 6 SERVINGS

One 3-to-4-pound chicken, cut up into 8 pieces
Salt and freshly ground pepper to taste
1 cup all-purpose flour
Safflower oil for frying
1 pound onions, peeled and diced
1 heaping tablespoon brown sugar
1 pound quinces
Juice of 1 lemon
¼ teaspoon grated nutmeg
1 teaspoon ground cinnamon

Season the chicken with salt and freshly ground pepper to taste, and roll the pieces in the flour. Heat a thin film of oil in a heavy frying pan, and brown the chicken pieces until golden. Remove, and drain on paper towels.

Sauté the onions and the brown sugar in the same frying pan until the onions are translucent but not caramelized, about 5 minutes.

Peel the quinces, cut each into six pieces, and sprinkle the lemon juice over them. Season them with the nutmeg and the cinnamon.

Put the chicken, onion, and quinces in a 6-quart casserole. Cover, and simmer over low heat for 1½ hours. Serve with rice.

Truffles

Jews have been eating truffles since at least the fifth century, when one rabbi wrote in the Talmud that they "emerge as they are in one night, wide and round like rounded cakes."

Bonjues ben Isaac de Monteux was the head of a yeshiva in Monteux, Provence, until 1276. In addition to his scholarly tasks, he gathered truffles with the help of his two dogs, cleaned them, and laid them in willow baskets on top of green leaves. Then he sold them in Carpentras, at the Friday truffle market from late autumn to early spring. This little business enabled his family to live decently, the work lasting perhaps three months each year. The rest of the time he could study.

The Jews from North Africa have brought a different truffle to France. *Terfezia,* known as desert truffles, are found in the sand and considered a delicacy at Passover. Said to be born when lightning strikes the desert, they do not have the same woodsy flavor as the more costly forest truffles but have the pleasant flavor of potatoes, garlic, and smoke. They are also more affordable, a fraction of the cost of other truffles.

Roast Chicken Stuffed with Rosemary and Thyme (and Sometimes Truffles)

SANDRINE WEIL AND MATHIAS LAURENT represent to me how France has changed in a generation. Their apartment at the time, overlooking the Bois de Boulogne, was very modern, very relaxed. With three young girls, they didn't care if everything was in order, and the place had a wonderful warm feeling of welcoming chaos.

On one special Shabbat, Mathias was the cook, and gave me a present of a meal with truffles.

After the blessings were recited over the wine and the challah, made by Sandrine and her daughters, we tasted scrambled eggs with truffles as a first course, followed by an extraordinary dish of chicken with truffles stuffed under the skin, called in French *poularde demi-deuil* (chicken in half-mourning), and truffled gelato for dessert.

Here is Mathias's recipe for roast chicken. Since truffles are rare and expensive, I often instead scatter around the chicken some carrots, potatoes, Brussels sprouts, green beans, or whatever is seasonally available. It is delicious, and a snap to prepare.

If you are lucky enough to have a truffle, however, omit the rosemary, thyme, and preserved lemon the night before, and carefully slide a small, sharp knife under the skin of the chicken, separating the skin from the meat. Then cut the truffle into six to eight thin slices and slide them under the skin. Leave in the refrigerator overnight. Continue with the roasting as I describe below.

The night before roasting, rub the chicken with the garlic and olive oil. Season with salt and freshly ground pepper to taste. Stuff the cavity with rosemary and thyme sprigs, the preserved lemon, the garlic cloves, and the onion. Place in a Pyrex baking dish, cover, and leave in the refrigerator overnight.

Two hours before cooking, take the chicken out of the refrigerator. Remove the lemon and squeeze its juice over the skin, then return it to the cavity. Put the chicken in a cold oven. Then raise the heat to 375 degrees, and cook for 1½ to 2 hours, basting occasionally, until golden and cooked through.

YIELD: 4 TO 6 SERVINGS

One 3½-to-4-pound chicken
2 cloves garlic, sliced in 2 pieces each
2 tablespoons olive oil
Salt and freshly ground pepper to taste
2 sprigs fresh rosemary
2 sprigs fresh thyme, or ½ teaspoon dried thyme
1 lemon or preserved lemon (see page 171), cut in half
1 onion, cut in half lengthwise
Juice of 1 lemon

Honey-Coated Baked Chicken
with Preserved Lemon

SWEETLY GLAZED AND FLAVORED WITH preserved lemons, this chicken, a recipe from Irene Weil, brings a Moroccan flavor to a classic French roasted chicken. Recipes like this represent the new France, with its influences from all over the world. Irene, married to a Frenchman for more than thirty years, was born in the United States to parents who came from Vienna. Even though she raised her children in France, she still has an American sense of adventure in her cooking.

YIELD: 6 TO 8 SERVINGS

2 tablespoons olive oil

2 onions, peeled and cut in rings

Two 3½-to-4-pound chickens, each cut into 8 pieces

Salt and freshly ground pepper to taste

½ cup acacia or other flavorful honey

3 cups white wine

4 whole preserved lemons (see page 171), the skin (including pulp, if you wish) cut in 12 slices each

1 handful of black pitted Niçoise olives

1 handful of chopped fresh cilantro

Preheat the oven to 375 degrees.

Heat the olive oil in a sauté pan, and fry the onions until golden. Spoon them into a 9-by-13-inch casserole.

Season the chicken pieces with salt and freshly ground pepper to taste, and brown them in the same pan. Put the pieces, skin side up, on top of the onions in the casserole. Smear a little honey on the chicken.

Pour the wine and remaining honey into a saucepan, and bring to a boil. Reduce by half, and pour over the chicken. Scatter the lemon pieces and the olives around the chicken.

Bake, uncovered, for 40 minutes, or until the chicken pieces are cooked through. Sprinkle with the fresh cilantro before serving.

Friday Night Chicken Provençal
with Fennel and Garlic

CHICKEN FLAVORED WITH FENNEL AND GARLIC is a very Jewish Friday night dish, one eaten by Rashi and his family in the eleventh century. I have found recipes for it in many historical cookbooks, but the inspiration for this version was a particularly tasty one from the late Richard Olney, who lived in Provence. There is something very comforting about the long-simmered fennel and garlic topped by the sautéed chicken.

Heat the olive oil in a large skillet. Add the fennel bulbs and the garlic, and sauté slowly over medium heat for about 30 minutes, turning occasionally with tongs. Season with salt and pepper, and carefully transfer to a baking pan, shaking the excess oil back into the skillet.

Preheat the oven to 375 degrees and season the chicken with salt and pepper. Sauté in the oil until browned on all sides.

Arrange the chicken on top of the fennel and garlic. Deglaze the skillet with the wine, scraping the sides and bottom with a wooden spoon. Reduce the wine and juices by half, and pour over the chicken. Then cover the chicken with aluminum foil, and bake in the oven for 35 minutes. Remove the foil, and continue cooking for another 5 to 10 minutes, until the chicken is tender and the fennel cooked. Serve sprinkled with the parsley.

 YIELD: 6 SERVINGS

¼ cup olive oil

3 large fennel bulbs (about 4 pounds), cut in half, with 2 tablespoons of the chopped fronds

1 whole head garlic, peeled and separated

Coarse salt and freshly ground pepper to taste

About 3½ pounds chicken thighs and drumsticks

½ cup white wine

1 tablespoon chopped fresh parsley

Coffee with the Baroness de Rothschild

Seated on a fox-fur throw, Baroness Nadine de Rothschild offered me a cup of coffee. We were at her Château de Pregny, our feet resting on a Louis XIV rug, surrounded by Italian Renaissance paintings. Château de Pregny is located on a hilltop near the United Nations compound in Geneva, overlooking Lake Leman.

A redhead with a big smile, the baroness (widow of Edmond de Rothschild) runs a school of etiquette and cooking in Geneva and also directs Château Clark, her branch of the Rothschilds' vineyard near Bordeaux. "I passed the test of etiquette with my mother-in-law on the first rendezvous with her," she said. "Although I didn't know it, she made a test of how I ate. She told my husband that I had a *ravissante manière de table*. To the others, who didn't pass the test, she said they ate *comme un caniche* [like a poodle]," she told me in a mixture of French and English. "My manners were correct."

Since the Revolution of 1848, which made James de Rothschild (her husband's great-grandfather) realize how much anti-Jewish sentiment there was in French society and how much he was disliked by poor Jews, the Rothschilds have made an effort to be generous and involved in the French Jewish community. They established a Jewish hospital in 1850, became leaders in the Consistory of Paris (the governing body of French Jewry), and established a permanent soup kitchen in the Rue de Rivoli.

The baroness is still personally involved in Jewish causes. L'OPEJ (Oeuvre de Protection d'Enfants Juifs) in Paris has a special place in her heart. Started during World War II as a home for children from three to eighteen whose parents were deported and killed, the school now serves as a refuge for battered women and for Jewish children whose parents are drug addicts and alcoholics. "You don't think of Jews that way," she told me, "but there are many." Each Passover, the baroness goes to l'OPEJ to tell them the story of the Exodus and to join them for a meal.

Although she loves eating, she rarely cooks. "How can I? I have houses everywhere. With some of the best chefs in the world as the cooks, what would I do?"

Poulet à la Bohémienne

(CHICKEN WITH PEPPERS, TOMATOES, ONION, AND GARLIC)

THIS IS ONE OF THE DOWN-TO-EARTH recipes Baroness Rothschild loves. When I made the dish for a friend, he said that, like stuffed cabbage, this Bohemian chicken recipe tasted better on the second day. Holding it only enhances the flavor, making it a perfect dish for Shabbat.

Season the chicken with salt and freshly ground pepper to taste.

Heat 2 tablespoons of the oil in a Dutch oven or other large pot, and brown the chicken on all sides. Remove it from the pan, and discard the fat. Pour the remaining tablespoon of oil into the pan, put the chicken back in, pour on half of the white wine, and reduce it by half.

Scatter the peppers, tomatoes, onion, garlic, fennel, and paprika around the chicken, and season with salt and freshly ground pepper to taste. Stir, bringing to a boil, then cover, lower the heat, and cook for 30 minutes. Add the rest of the white wine and continue to cook, uncovered, for 15 minutes. Once the chicken is cooked through, serve whole, surrounded by the vegetables and lemon slices. Carve at the table.

Baroness
Nadine de Rothschild

YIELD: 4 TO 6 SERVINGS

One 3-to-4-pound chicken
Salt and freshly ground pepper
   to taste
3 tablespoons olive oil
¾ cup white wine
4 bell peppers, roasted (see
   basic technique on page 91),
   peeled, seeded, and cut into
   long strips
2 tomatoes, peeled, seeded,
   and cut into large chunks,
   or one 15-ounce can stewed
   tomatoes
1 onion, diced
1 clove garlic, minced
½ fennel bulb, diced
1 tablespoon sweet paprika
1 lemon, sliced into 6 pieces

Terrine of Chicken Flavored with Pistachio Nuts, Curry, and Hazelnuts

AFTER A RECENT TRIP TO FRANCE, I told chef Daniel Boulud that I wanted to learn more about *charcuterie*. He suggested that I spend a day with Sylvain Gasdon, the *charcutier* at his newly opened Bar Boulud in New York. It turned out that some of the trends I had been noticing in French restaurants were the foundation of the menu at Bar Boulud, featuring *charcuterie* and lighter terrines. I asked Sylvain, who came from Paris to help Daniel, if he would teach me how to make a terrine, one for those who eschew pork. This is it!

 YIELD: 8 TO 10 SERVINGS

Vegetable oil for greasing

6 boneless skinless chicken-breast halves (about 3 pounds total)

Salt and freshly ground pepper to taste

2 cups flavorful chicken broth, or as needed

A few sprigs fresh thyme, or ½ teaspoon dried thyme

3 bay leaves

4 tablespoons olive oil

1 cup minced shallots (about 6 large ones)

1 tablespoon balsamic vinegar

½ cup (or more) very roughly chopped pistachio nuts

½ cup (or more) very roughly chopped hazelnuts

3 teaspoons curry powder

2 tablespoons kosher powdered gelatin

1 apple, thinly sliced

Preheat the oven to 325 degrees, and grease a 5-by-12-inch porcelain terrine, or equivalent-sized rectangular baking dish, with the vegetable oil.

Put the chicken breasts in the dish, and season with salt and freshly ground pepper to taste. Add chicken broth to cover, as well as the thyme and bay leaves. Cover the dish, and put in the oven for 30 minutes, or until the breasts are almost cooked through. Remove from the broth, reserving it, and carefully cut the breasts horizontally into three or four ½-inch-thick wide, flat scaloppini. Lower the oven temperature to 300 degrees. Strain the reserved chicken broth through a cotton kitchen towel; set aside 2 cups, and save the rest for another use.

Heat the olive oil in a sauté pan, and sauté the shallots until translucent. Then pour in the balsamic vinegar to deglaze the pan, using a wooden spoon to scrape up any bits that have stuck to the bottom. Season with salt and pepper, and set aside.

Put a layer of chicken slices in the bottom of the terrine or baking dish, cutting some slices into pieces to make an even layer. Sprinkle over the top a third of the shallots, a third of the pistachio nuts, a third of the hazelnuts, and 1 teaspoon of the curry powder. Make two more layers like that of the chicken, shallots, nuts, and curry, ending with a fourth layer of chicken.

Mix the 2 cups reserved chicken broth with the gelatin. Stir to dissolve, about 2 minutes of stirring. Once dissolved, pour the broth over the layered chicken, up to ½ inch from the top of the terrine. Cover with a piece of parchment paper, and place weights on top of the parchment. Put the terrine in a larger baking dish, and pour about 4 cups boiling water all around, to make a *bain-marie.*

Carefully set in the oven and bake for 45 minutes. Cool, and refrigerate, with the weights in place, for 1 day, to allow the gelatin to set.

When ready to serve, run a knife around the edges of the terrine to loosen it from the pan, then put a plate over the terrine and flip it over to unmold. Cut into ½-inch slices, and serve with slices of the apple on the side. I also like to serve it with lettuce salad tossed with a red-wine vinaigrette.

Free-range kosher chickens

Friday Night Algerian Chicken Fricassee

WHEN I WAS IN BORDEAUX, I received a call from Yaël Nahon, a young woman in public relations who loves to cook. We decided to meet at the Place des Quinconces, a beautiful square near the harbor with shimmering water where children play in the summer. In her spare time she is trying to re-create the dishes of her mother and grandmother, who came from Oran, in Algeria. Like many other North Africans, she uses *spigol* (an Algerian spice combination of hot pepper, saffron, and cumin, now packaged in Marseille) to enhance the flavor of her chicken dishes.

This is a dish Yael ate every Friday night of her childhood. It was always preceded by several salads and followed by cookies and fruit.

 YIELD: 4 TO 6 SERVINGS

6 boneless, skinless chicken breast halves

Salt and freshly ground pepper to taste

1 cup all-purpose flour

2 large eggs, beaten

Vegetable oil for frying

2 cloves garlic, peeled and left whole

Pinch of saffron

Pinch of ground cumin

½ teaspoon cayenne pepper, or to taste

1½ teaspoons grated fresh ginger

¼ teaspoon grated nutmeg

1 sprig fresh thyme

1 bay leaf

Juice and rind, chopped, of 1 lemon

Season the chicken breasts with salt and freshly ground pepper to taste. Put the flour in one bowl and the eggs in another, and season both with salt and freshly ground pepper. Heat about ½ inch of oil in a large frying pan. Roll the chicken first in the egg, then in the flour. Fry in the oil until golden on each side, just a minute or two. Drain the chicken on paper towels.

Discard all but a thin film of the oil. Add the garlic, and sauté briefly over medium heat. Return the chicken to the pan, and add about 1 cup water, or enough almost to cover the chicken. Sprinkle on top a pinch of saffron, a pinch of cumin, cayenne pepper, the ginger, and the nutmeg, and toss in the thyme and bay leaf. Sprinkle the lemon juice over all, then add the rind to the liquid. Bring to a boil, cover, and simmer for about 20 minutes, or until the chicken is cooked through and tender. Serve with rice or boiled potatoes.

Moroccan *Tagine* of Chicken
with Prunes, Apricots, and Almonds

IN THE HEART OF DIJON, at the Municipal Museum, right next door to the majestic stone kitchen of the dukes of Burgundy, Alette Lévy checks coats. Once the owner of Dijon's only kosher butcher shop, she talks food between customers, such as this chicken-*tagine* recipe she makes for her French friends.

The trick to this recipe is to put the almonds in the microwave for 3 minutes, to make them crackly. This way you don't run the risk of burning them, the way I always seem to do when I forget them in the oven or frying pan. Alette told me you can substitute lamb for the chicken.

M YIELD: 4 TO 6 SERVINGS

Heat the oil in a Dutch oven or other large, heavy frying pan with a cover. Add the onions, and sauté slowly until golden. While the onions are cooking, season the chicken pieces well with salt and pepper, and sprinkle with cinnamon. Push aside the onions and tuck the chicken pieces into the pan. Brown them well on all sides.

Add the prunes, raisins, and apricots to the chicken pieces, along with the saffron, cumin, and paprika, and a cup of water. Simmer, covered, stirring occasionally, for about 40 minutes, or until the chicken is cooked and most of the liquid has evaporated. (Add more water if necessary.)

Just before serving, toast the almonds in the microwave for 3 minutes, and sprinkle them over the chicken. Serve with saffron rice (see page 278).

¼ cup vegetable oil

2 onions, peeled and sliced in thin rings

One 3½-to-4-pound chicken, cut into 8 pieces

Salt and freshly ground pepper to taste

1 teaspoon ground cinnamon

1 cup pitted prunes

¼ cup raisins

½ cup dried apricots

A few saffron strands

½ teaspoon ground cumin

½ teaspoon hot paprika

½ cup blanched almonds

Poulet à la Juive

THIS JEWISH-STYLE STEWED CHICKEN COMES FROM *Gastronomie Pratique,* a cookbook published in 1907 by Ali-Bab. Born Henri Babinski to Polish Christian immigrants to France, he was by profession a mining engineer, but he loved to cook and travel.

Using the pseudonym Ali-Bab, he wrote the book for fun and included a long description of kosher cuisine as well as two Jewish recipes, one for *choucroute,* and one for *poulet à la juive.* Basically, he's making a *pot-au-feu,* substituting chicken for beef and using fresh rendered chicken fat or veal-kidney suet. Since he finishes the dish off with butter, a no-no in kosher cooking, I have omitted this step.

When serving this, I sometimes remove the skin and bones from the chicken for a more refined dish. I pile the chicken over white rice and spoon the gravy on top. Others, who like the meat on the bone, serve it as is. Sometimes called *poule au bouillon* or *poule au pot,* it is a comfort dish, and one often served in France for Friday night dinner or for the meal before the fast of Yom Kippur.

YIELD: 4 TO 6 SERVINGS

1 large onion, peeled and quartered

2 leeks, halved and rinsed

2 large carrots, peeled and cut into 1-inch pieces

1 medium turnip, peeled and cut into 8 pieces

1 stalk celery, cut into 1-inch pieces

3 tablespoons vegetable oil

Salt to taste

One 3½-to-4-pound chicken, cut into 8 pieces

3 large shallots, finely diced

1 clove garlic, minced

2 tablespoons flour

Freshly ground pepper to taste

1 tablespoon chopped parsley

Sauté in a large saucepan or small stockpot the onion, leeks, carrots, turnip, and celery in 2 tablespoons of the vegetable oil. Season with salt to taste, and cook, stirring occasionally, until the vegetables are golden brown. Add 3 cups water, bring to a boil, and reduce the vegetable stock to a simmer, then cook for 40 minutes.

Rinse the chicken pieces and pat dry. Heat the remaining tablespoon of oil in a Dutch oven, and sear the chicken in batches on all sides until it is a deep golden brown. Set aside.

Pour off all but 2 to 3 tablespoons of the fat. Lower the heat, and add the shallots and garlic. Stir constantly for 2 to 3 minutes. Sprinkle the flour over the shallots and garlic, and cook, stirring, for about 3 minutes, or until light brown.

Add the vegetables and their stock, and, using a wooden spoon, scrape up all of the bits that have stuck to the bottom of the pan. Return the chicken to the pot, season with salt and freshly ground pepper, cover, and simmer slowly for 1 hour. Just before serving, garnish with the fresh parsley.

Lyon, the City of Silk
and the City of Immigrants from North Africa

After Morocco became independent in 1956, Céline Bénitah, like many others, came to France with her parents. "The change was very brutal," she told me during a cooking session at a friend's home. "We had lived in Oujda and vacationed near the sea. When we arrived in Lyon, we lived in an attic apartment with two rooms for nine people, without a toilet or shower. It was so cold in the winter that my mother had to put blankets on the walls. In the middle of the winter, two old people died because of the cold in the apartment. When some journalists saw that we didn't even have heat, they wrote about it. Luckily, the mayor of Lyon read the article and helped us. And, luckily, my mother made clothes for us. . . . Don't forget, Lyon is the city of silk." Today, with some twenty thousand Jews, Lyon has the third-largest Jewish population in France, the majority of whom, like Madame Bénitah, came from North Africa.

Judaica at a home in Lyon

Moroccan Chicken with
Olives and Preserved Lemons

WHEN CÉLINE BÉNITAH COOKS THIS DISH, she blanches the olives for a minute to get rid of the bitterness, a step that I never bother with. If you keep the pits in, just warn your guests in order to avoid any broken teeth! Céline also uses the marvelous Moroccan spice mixture *ras el hanout,* which includes, among thirty other spices, cinnamon, cumin, cardamom, cloves, and paprika. You can find it at Middle Eastern markets or through the Internet, or you can use equal amounts of the above spices or others that you like.

To make my life easier, I assemble the spice rub the day before and marinate the chicken overnight. The next day, before my guests arrive, I fry the chicken and simmer it.

 YIELD: 4 TO 6 SERVINGS

4 large cloves garlic, mashed

Salt and freshly ground pepper to taste

1 teaspoon ground turmeric

1 to 2 tablespoons *ras el hanout*

1 bunch of fresh cilantro, chopped

4 tablespoons olive oil

One 3½-to-4-pound chicken, cut into 8 pieces

1 teaspoon cornstarch

1 cup black Moroccan dry-cured olives, pitted

Diced rind of 2 preserved lemons (see page 171)

Mix the mashed garlic with salt and freshly ground pepper to taste, the turmeric, the *ras el hanout,* half the cilantro, and 2 tablespoons of the olive oil. Rub the surface of the chicken pieces with this spice mixture, put them in a dish, and marinate in the refrigerator, covered, overnight.

The next day, heat the remaining 2 tablespoons olive oil in a large pan. Sauté the spice-rubbed chicken until golden brown on each side.

Stir the cornstarch into 1 cup water, and pour over the chicken. Bring to a boil, and simmer, covered, for about 20 minutes. Add the olives, and continue cooking for another 20 minutes. Sprinkle on the preserved lemon, and continue cooking for another 5 minutes. Garnish with the remaining cilantro. Serve with rice or couscous (see page 270).

Preserved lemons make this chicken an outstanding dish.

A Farm in the Southwest of France

When a friend learned about my latest project, he suggested that I visit his mother, Marthe Layrle, who had hidden Resistance fighters during World War II on her farm in the southwest of France.

So I followed my friend's advice and drove up a dusty dirt road to her hilltop farm, outside the town of Masseube, which housed a detention center during the war.

Marthe Layrle feeds chickens on her farm in Masseube.

Marthe, an extraordinary woman in her seventies, raised four children after her husband died in an accident. Today telephone poles and paved roads connect the sparsely placed houses, linking neighbors to the outside world with cars, televisions, telephones, and the Internet. But during the war, Marthe told me, her town was a different place. No telephones, no electricity. Everyone kept to himself; locals could not even trust their neighbors, who might denounce any farmer sheltering a fugitive.

Although she mostly stays close to her farm, Marthe has visited Toulouse and Hossegor and goes once a week to the farmers' market in town, about a mile away.

The rhythm of each day is determined by the animals. At eight in the morning and six-fifteen in the evening, she feeds them, starting with the rabbits, then the chickens, then the pigs, then the geese, then the sheep, ending by carefully plucking the chicken eggs from the nests made in the hay. Since I arrived around six in the evening, we worked together to gather the day's production. She marks the date on the eggs with a pencil and distributes them to her family. In the basement of her home are shelves filled with jams, pickles, *foie gras,* confit, ham, *cassoulet,* and preserved vegetables.

Staying with her for a few days, I realized how much luckier Jews who found shelter at farmers' homes during the war were, because they had something to eat. Marthe's family hid people in her barn during the day and gave them food to take back to their comrades at night.

After a dinner of southwestern specialties of *foie gras, cassoulet* with white beans, and a local *pastis (croustade)* of apples made with a phyllo crust, we went to sleep. When I crawled into my bed, I found that Marthe had warmed it up with an old-fashioned hot-water bottle, a gesture of such kindness, and so typical of this selfless and caring woman.

Southwestern *Cassoulet* with Duck and Lamb

FAVA BEANS AND CHICKPEAS were brought to France in the thirteenth century with the opening of trade routes by the Crusaders. Before white beans came from the New World, the French used fava beans for *cassoulet* and called it *févolade*. *Cassoulet* could well be a variation of the overnight Sabbath stews such as *dafina* or *hamim*, which means "warm." *Cassoulet* could also have come from the Arabs, who made a similar dish, *skeena*. All I know is that, in a land where there is lots of pork, in a land where the Jews played a role in developing the art of fattening goose livers, *cassoulet* looks suspiciously like the ubiquitous Sabbath stews, and often has no pork in it at all.

This *cassoulet* calls for lamb shoulder and a great deal of duck or goose fat instead in which to cook the duck legs and sausage and lamb (it is not all consumed). You can use vegetable oil, but it will not taste the same. E-mail Aaronsfood@aol.com for a place to obtain rendered kosher duck fat, or roast a duck and make your own.

YIELD: 10 TO 12 SERVINGS

12 whole duck legs (about 10 pounds)

3 cups kosher salt, plus salt for flavoring

5 cups dry white beans (about 2 pounds)

2 bay leaves

3 carrots, peeled

2 stalks celery

2 leeks, cleaned

2 whole onions, peeled

6 cloves

½ head garlic, peeled and diced

6 cups duck or goose fat

2 pounds boneless lamb shoulder, cut into chunks

Freshly ground pepper to taste

The day before serving, put the duck legs in a bowl, sprinkle the salt over them, and refrigerate. Pour the beans into a large bowl, cover with cold water, and let soak overnight.

The next day, rinse the legs in cold water, drain, and dry them.

Drain the beans, put them in a pot with water to cover by 4 inches, and bring to a boil. Spoon off any scum that accumulates and discard. Add the bay leaves, one of the carrots, a celery stalk, and a leek. Stud one of the onions with the cloves, and add to the pot. Cover with water by 4 inches, and cook, uncovered, for about an hour, adding about a teaspoon of salt after 45 minutes. Taste after an hour, and if not tender, cook a little more. Drain the beans, and reserve the broth.

Dice the remaining carrots, celery, leek, and onion, and the garlic. Heat a thin film of duck fat in a heavy Dutch oven, and add the lamb shoulder, to brown gently. Then add the diced vegetables, and sauté them for a few minutes. Season with salt and freshly ground pepper to taste. Add the tomatoes and about 2 cups water, or enough to cover. Bring to a boil, and simmer slowly, uncovered, for 1 hour, adding more water if needed. Taste after an hour and adjust seasonings.

Preheat the oven to 275 degrees. Heat the remaining duck fat in a large, wide pot. Add the duck legs and the sausage, and cook in the oven for an hour or so, removing the sausage with tongs after 45 minutes. When the legs are cooked, they will float. Remove them from the fat, reserving all but 1 cup of fat for another use.

Pour the 1 cup of fat into the bottom of a large, wide casserole. Scatter the lamb on the bottom. Drain the beans, saving the water, and add them to the pot. Submerge the duck sausage in the beans, and put the duck legs on top of the casserole, gently pressing them into the beans. Add enough bean broth to cover the beans. Sprinkle the duck legs with the bread crumbs, and return the casserole to the oven for an hour. The *cassoulet* will be even better if you let it cool and store it overnight in the refrigerator. Reheat it the next day, adding more bean broth. Serve from the casserole.

One 14-ounce can San
    Marzano tomatoes
2 pounds duck sausage
¼ cup bread crumbs

Ducks taking a drink in the south of France

Tunisian Chicken
with Onions, Peas, and Parsley

LIKE MANY OTHER COMMUNITIES IN FRANCE, the town of Annecy had few Jews living there until the late 1950s. Then, one day, the town's mayor assembled the Catholic archbishop, the head of the Protestants, and the leader of the tiny Jewish community, who happened to be my relative Rudi Moos (see page 3), and asked them to welcome emigrants from North Africa. Rudi sponsored about forty Moroccan, Tunisian, and Algerian Jewish families and built a synagogue in this town that had none.

Cécile Zana and her husband were one of these families. They left Tunisia and went first to the Congo, and then, in 1968, to Annecy, where they live today. And, perhaps not surprisingly in this small Jewish world, Cécile's daughter married Rudi's grandson. Cécile showed me how to make this delicious spring dish with lots of parsley and peas.

 YIELD: 4 TO 6 SERVINGS

One 3½-to-4-pound chicken, cut up into 8 pieces

Salt and freshly ground pepper to taste

4 tablespoons olive oil

4 medium onions, peeled and diced

4 large cloves garlic, chopped

½ tablespoon honey

½ teaspoon ground cinnamon

2 bunches of fresh Italian parsley, finely chopped

Juice of ½ lemon

2 tomatoes, peeled and diced

2 cups chicken broth

1 teaspoon tomato paste

1 pound shelled fresh or frozen peas

Season the chicken with salt and pepper to taste. Heat the olive oil in a Dutch oven or other heavy sauté pan. Add the chicken pieces, sautéing just to brown the skin on both sides. Remove the chicken pieces, and drain on paper towels.

Stir the onions, garlic, and honey into the same pan. Sauté over medium heat until the onions are almost caramelized. This may take about 20 minutes.

Return the chicken pieces to the pan, skin side up, and sprinkle on ¼ teaspoon more pepper, the cinnamon, and the parsley, stirring to incorporate. Add the lemon juice and the tomatoes. Pour in chicken broth, enough just to cover the chicken, and stir in the tomato paste. Simmer the chicken, covered, for about 40 minutes, then stir in the peas. Cook for 5 minutes, or until the peas are done. Taste, adjust the seasonings, and serve with rice or wheat berries (see page 266).

Canard aux Cérises

(ROAST DUCK WITH CHERRIES)

> Jewish cooking is homey, down-to-earth, without ambition, without hope of being domineering. Jewish cooking is neither a model, nor exceptional. It is accessible to everyone . . . aware of its democratic simplicity. It is not pretentious, prepared as simply or magnificently as you want. It is clearly conscious of its possibility and of its limits in the service of man.
>
> —Juliette Herz in the introduction to *La Tradition de la Cuisine Juive*

THE COOKBOOK CITED ABOVE INCLUDES several recipes for roast duck and sweet red cherries, the variety that grows in Alsace being Reverchon or Coeur de Pigeon (Pigeon's Heart). I use Bing or Montmorency cherries, and you can also substitute peaches or rhubarb. If using rhubarb, just increase the amount of sugar to taste. I use cherries with pits, because they add more flavor, but remember to warn your guests!

Put the margarine or vegetable oil in a small saucepan. Sprinkle in the sugar, and stir. Toss in the cherries, coating them well, and simmer for just a few minutes. Add ⅓ cup water and the kirsch, stirring as you bring it just back to a boil. Remove from heat and set aside.

Preheat the oven to 375 degrees, and sprinkle the duck with salt and pepper. Put it in a casserole with the onion, shallot, carrot pieces, cayenne pepper, ginger, and *bouquet garni*. Cook, covered, for about one hour in the oven, removing the fat that accumulates.

After one hour, stir the cherries and their sauce into the casserole. Cook for another 20 minutes, or until the legs move easily when wiggled.

Just before serving, remove the *bouquet garni*. Put the carrot, onion, and shallot in the food processor and purée. Stir them into the sauce, and serve.

 YIELD: 4 TO 6 SERVINGS

4 tablespoons *pareve* margarine or vegetable oil

½ cup sugar

1 pound sweet red cherries, unpitted

1 tablespoon kirsch

1 young duck (about 3 pounds), giblets removed and reserved

Salt and freshly ground pepper

½ onion, diced

1 shallot, diced

1 carrot, peeled and halved

Cayenne pepper to taste

1 tablespoon grated fresh ginger

Bouquet garni of a sprig each of rosemary, thyme, parsley, and marjoram

Gala Goose

RASHI TEACHES US A GREAT DEAL about cooking in the eleventh century. In the Talmud a rabbi "told his attendant: roast a goose for me, and be careful of burning it." Rashi explains that "they would roast geese in their small ovens which opened on top. The food would be suspended from the opening, which would then be sealed until the food was roasted."

One hundred fifty years ago, goose was the meat par excellence in the Jewish communities of Alsace-Lorraine and southern Germany. In my grandmother's notes in German on roast goose, she includes a recipe for "hurt goose," meaning goose roasted without its outer skin and the fat underneath, which of course was used to render the fat and to make *gribenes,* crispy rinds, my grandfather's favorite treat. They also carefully separated the skin from the long neck, stuffed it with meat, onions, flour, and spices, and cooked it as a Sabbath delicacy.

Ariane Daguin, head of D'Artagnan Foods, had me try this crispy recipe from her mother, a French-Polish Jew. To make the goose less fatty, Ariane cooks it very slowly, leaves it overnight in the kitchen so that the fat can jell, then roasts it in a hot oven to crisp the skin, the absolutely most delicious part of the goose.

YIELD: 6 TO 8 SERVINGS

One 10-to-12-pound goose
Salt to taste
Juice of 1 lemon
1½ cups coarsely chopped carrots
1½ cups coarsely chopped onions
1½ cups coarsely chopped celery
6 tablespoons all-purpose flour
4 cups chicken broth
2 cups dry white wine
4 sprigs flat-leaf parsley
Peelings from 1 green apple
1 large bay leaf

Remove the giblets and the neck from the cavity of the goose. Pull off any loose fat, and cut off the first two wing joints, if still attached, and reserve. Wash the goose, tie the legs together, prick the bird all over with a sharp fork, and season with salt and the juice of a lemon.

Put the loose goose fat in a large sauté pan over medium-high heat, and render about 3 tablespoons of fat. Remove and discard the remaining fat (or use later). Add to the pan the giblets, wing pieces, and neck, and the carrots, onions, and celery. Sauté until the vegetables are browned, about 5 minutes, turning frequently. Sprinkle on the flour, adjust the heat to medium, and continue stirring until the flour is lightly browned, about 5 minutes.

Pour the chicken broth and the white wine into a roasting pan large enough to hold the goose and able to be used on the stovetop, and bring to a boil. Lower the goose into the pan, breast side down, and strew the pieces of browned goose, the cooked vegetables, the parsley, the apple peelings, and the bay leaf all around. Pour in enough water to cover the goose by about two-thirds, and bring to a simmer. Whisk a cup of this liquid into the sauté pan that had the vegetables and the goose parts, then scrape the seasoned liquid back into the roasting pan. Cover the pan, and cook very gently, regulating heat to keep it just at a simmer.

After an hour, turn the goose over, by inserting a set of prongs into the cavity of the chicken, being careful not to break the skin. Wearing a pair of rubber gloves makes this relatively easy. Poach the goose about 2 more hours, or until the meat is tender when pierced with a fork. Turn off the heat, cool, cover the pan, and refrigerate overnight.

The next day, remove the layer of fat from the liquid. Gently lift out the goose, and bring the liquid to a boil over high heat. Reduce to a simmer, then reheat the goose in the stock for about 10 minutes while preheating the oven to 450 degrees.

Remove the goose from the liquid, drain, and place on a rack, breast side up, in a shallow roasting pan. Roast until the skin is brown and crispy, about 30 minutes. Take the goose out of the oven, and let it stand for about 15 to 20 minutes.

While the goose is resting, skim the grease from the pan liquid and strain to remove the pieces of goose, the vegetables, and the seasonings. Purée the vegetables in a blender or food processor, and put them back into the pan with the juices. Boil quickly to reduce the liquid by half, and put in a gravy bowl. Serve the goose on a bed of sautéed red cabbage with chestnuts (see page 304), with the sauce on the side.

A rabbi examines a goose to make sure it is kosher.

Beef, Veal, and Lamb

Alsatian *Pot-au-Feu* (Sabbath Beef Stew)

Adafina (Sabbath Meat Stew with Chickpeas and Rice)

Cholent (Sabbath Beef Stew with Potatoes, Beans, and Barley)

Pickelfleisch (Corned Beef)

Alsatian *Choucroute* (Sauerkraut with Sausage and Corned Beef)

Alsatian Mustard Sauce

Beef Cheek Stew with Cilantro and Cumin, Algerian Style

Alsatian Sweet and Sour Tongue

Tongue with Capers and Cornichons

Faux Poisson or Fake Fish (Sweet Meatballs)

Almondeguilles (Algerian Meatballs with Tomato Sauce)

Stuffed Breast of Veal with Parsley and Onions

Brisket with Ginger, Orange Peel, and Tomato

Tunisian Stuffed Vegetables with Meat

Membre d'Agneau à la Judaïque (Roast Lamb Jewish Style)

Provençal Lamb with Garlic and Olives

Moroccan Braised Lamb with Couscous

Suzon's *Harissa* Sauce

Römertopf (Lamb with Potatoes, Zucchini, and Tomatoes)

Kosher Meat in France

◼

> Any animal that has true hoofs, with clefts through the hoofs, and that chews the cud—such may you eat.
>
> —Leviticus 11:3

Kosher slaughterhouses, under the jurisdiction of the Jewish consistory of each city, exist throughout France. Kosher veal, lamb, and kid are butchered to include only the front portion of the animal, with special attention paid during slaughtering to removing as much blood as possible, as described in detail on page 20.

But by far the most popular meat is beef. Today French Jews who observe the dietary laws eat many cuts: beef cheeks and shanks are often used for braising, as American Jews use brisket, and the more delicate *côte de boeuf* (a bone-in rib-eye steak) is often grilled and roasted. Many portions of the animal that would be set aside as trim in the United States, and used only for making ground meat, are sold as braising cuts in France. And the so-called fifth quarter—the tongue, lungs, spleen, etc.—is still prized in Jewish kitchens. Beef marrow and tongue, in particular, have always been a special treat.

During the Middle Ages in Saint-Rémy-de-Provence, the Jewish butchers had a monopoly on beef butchering in the town. Kosher butchers did all the slaughtering and kept the kosher cuts, selling the nonkosher ones to non-Jews. Today Jewish butchers from North Africa have largely taken over the kosher trade. So the meat is cut slightly differently, and beef sausages with traditional Alsatian spices have been replaced by *merguez* sausage. Using lamb and mutton or beef ground with fat, butchers flavor the sausage with robust spice combinations, often including allspice, ground fennel, coriander, sumac, and *harissa* to give flavor and a reddish color.

American and French butchers alike favor a bit of fat on their large cuts of meat. But whereas American roasts are sold with the fat in place, the French carefully remove the fat, then cover the piece of meat with it, tying it on for roasting. The fat slows moisture loss while the meat roasts and imparts a small amount of flavor; it is then removed before serving. In kosher butcher shops in Paris, you may see beautiful roasts encased in beef fat and decorated with olives.

The Last Jew of Bergheim

One spring evening, while visiting southern Alsace, my editor, Judith Jones, and I stopped in a charming village called Bergheim, next to Ribeauvillé, on the Alsatian wine route. Because we were hungry, we went into a *winstub,* a bistro selling local wine and simple country dishes. When I asked the owner if any Jews still lived in this town, she said that a Madame Hausser, a retired woman, lived there, and that a synagogue was just down the street. After dinner we strolled over to the large temple, which was recently converted into the town's cultural center. Originally built in 1398, when there was a thriving Jewish community in the town, it was rebuilt in 1883 on the same site.

The next morning, we knocked on Jacqueline Hausser's door. Inside, her television was on, and she explained to us that each morning she watched her daughter, Anita, a commentator for LCI TV, who reported on the political news from Paris.

Jacqueline, in her mid-eighties, also told us that she and her late husband, Sylvain, were two of the ten Jews who returned to the town after World War II. Before the war, Bergheim, with a long history of a Jewish presence, was a rather important village, where many Jews were active in the wine trade. According to a document from 1430, Jews could live in Ribeauvillé and the surrounding area but had to pay their taxes (two measures of wine from their grapevines) for protection.

In 1940, as soon as the Germans crossed over the French border and annexed Alsace, the Jews fled to the free zone of France. Jacqueline and Sylvain, who were teenagers then, went with their families to the still-French Loire valley and Dordogne. Most did not return to Bergheim. But Sylvain, whose family were cattle merchants and then butchers for centuries, came back, because they had left behind a home and a butcher shop.

After the war was over, the two married and started life anew. Sylvain went to the synagogue every Saturday, praying alone all morning without a *minyan* (the requisite ten men needed to fulfill a public religious obligation). When he returned home, his wife would make him *pot-au-feu* and *matze knepfle,* the Alsatian Sabbath stew and matzo balls.

When I asked Jacqueline why she didn't go live with her son in nearby Sélestat, or with her daughter in Paris, she replied, *"Je suis chez moi ici"* ("I am at home here").

Alsatian *Pot-au-Feu*

(SABBATH BEEF STEW)

WHEN I WAS IN PARIS, I got in touch with Anita Hausser, Jacqueline's daughter. We met at a café in Paris to chat. The conversation turned into lunch, then finally extended into a dinner on another occasion in her charming and very French apartment, near the Maison de la Radio in Auteuil.

For dinner, the first course was Alsatian goose liver spread on grilled bread, accompanied by champagne. Sometimes, she told me, she slathers the marrow from the cooked bones on the toast instead, sprinkling it with coarse salt.

At the dinner we ate as a first course the broth from the *pot-au-feu* with tiny *knepfle* (matzo balls), to the delight of her very assimilated French Jewish guests.

A century or so ago, in small villages of Alsace, the *pot-au-feu* cauldron of vegetables and meat would hang on a hook in the chimney to simmer slowly all night. I imagine religious Jews placing it there before the Sabbath began, and going to sleep with the tantalizing aromas of meat and vegetables as the fire slowly turned to embers and died out, leaving the pot still warm.

When Anita makes her *pot-au-feu,* she cooks the meat slowly with the vegetables, which she discards toward the end. She then adds fresh carrots, leeks, and turnips, cut in chunks, for the last 30 minutes of cooking. She always accompanies her *pot-au-feu* with horseradish, mustard, and gherkins. This slow-cooked dish is traditionally made in Jewish homes for Rosh Hashanah and the Sabbath.

YIELD: 8 TO 10 SERVINGS

STEW

6 pounds beef shoulder, chuck, and/or ribs

3 chicken wings

1 large onion, peeled and left whole

6 cloves

2 leeks, cut lengthwise, cleaned, and halved

2 large carrots, peeled and left whole

1 stalk celery, halved crosswise

Place the beef and the chicken wings in a large casserole. Cover with about 3 quarts water. Bring to a boil, and skim off the scum that rises to the top. Pierce the onion with the cloves, and add it to the water. Simmer, partially covered, for about an hour.

Add to the casserole the leeks, the carrots, the celery stalk, and salt and freshly ground pepper to taste. Continue simmering, covered, for another 1½ hours, or until the beef is tender.

Cool, strain the meat and vegetables, and refrigerate the broth and the meat separately overnight, discarding the chicken wings and the vegetables. The next day, skim the fat that has congealed on top of the bouillon, and discard. Cut the meat against the grain into bite-sized pieces, and return it to the broth. Add the leeks, carrots, turnips, and marrow bones, and simmer for about 30 minutes, or until the vegetables are soft and the marrow pulls away from the bones.

To make the marrow toast as an appetizer, cut the baguette diagonally into ten rounds, and grill. Remove the bones from the broth, scoop out the marrow, and spoon onto the grilled bread. Sprinkle the parsley and a little coarse salt on top, and serve.

For the first course, ladle the broth from the *pot-au-feu* into soup bowls with the *knepfle* (matzo balls). Then serve the meat and vegetables as a main course, accompanied by grated horseradish, mustard, and cornichons.

NOTE   Although Anita does not serve potatoes as another garnish with this dish, many people do.

Salt and freshly ground pepper
to taste

VEGETABLES FOR GARNISH
2 leeks, cut lengthwise,
cleaned, and cut into thirds
3 carrots, peeled and cut into
3-inch rounds
2 turnips, quartered

MARROW BONES
2 pounds marrow bones
One baguette
2 tablespoons chopped fresh
parsley
Coarse salt to taste

Matzo balls (see page 70)
Horseradish as garnish
Mustard as garnish
Cornichons as garnish

Anita Hausser serving her guests *pot-au-feu*

Sabbath Stew—*Adafina* and *Cholent*

■

You shall kindle no fire throughout your settlements on the sabbath day.
—Exodus 35:3

Adafina and *cholent,* Sabbath bean-and-meat dishes that are cooked slowly overnight, probably go back to biblical times. Around 200 C.E., rabbis codified the practice in the Mishnah, a
compendium of Jewish laws that prohibited the lighting of fire on the Sabbath, the day of rest,
when no work, not even cooking, is permitted. The rule for cooking an overnight Sabbath stew
is to make sure it is "technically" cooked before sundown and then to keep it warm while the
flavors continue to develop until lunch on the Sabbath. The dish became known as *hamim,* from
the Hebrew meaning "warm," and later, in Spain and Morocco, as *dafina* or *adafina,* from the
Arabic meaning "covered" or "buried."

As Jews traveled, so did their Saturday dish. By the Middle Ages, it often included cabbage
and other vegetables in France, eventually becoming *choucroute.*

Later, Jews who moved to eastern Europe adapted their long-cooking stew to the potatoes
and broad beans available in their own culture and sealed the dish with a dough crust and then
a cover. This *cholent* comes from the old French words *chaud* (warm) and *lent* (slow). As the
cooking vessels changed over time from clay pots in the Middle Ages to iron during the industrial revolution to aluminum and steel pots in modern ovens, the ingredients in the slowly
cooked stew also changed, with Jews moving from Metz to Moscow and Massachusetts.

Shabbat Lunch in Paris

It was one o'clock on a fall Saturday afternoon, and I was invited for lunch at the home of my cousin David Moos, an investment banker, and his wife, Carène, a divorce lawyer. As I walked to their home on the outskirts of Paris, in Boulogne, I passed by the Edmond de Rothschild Park and the Albert Kahn Gardens and Museum, both reminding me of the Jewish presence in this lovely suburb. David, Carène, and their three adorable children, Hanna, Simon, and Nathan, live in a top-floor duplex strewn with the happy clutter of children's playthings.

Hanna at Shabbat lunch

Eagerly, the children gathered around to say the prayers, looking forward to this family ritual and to the chance to sing for the guests. First they recited the blessing over the wine, and then the blessing over the challah, a slightly sweet twisted bread bought at a nearby supermarket. Like other Jews living in this neighborhood, the Moos family came here for the religious school and the synagogue. With a large Jewish population, the area has also attracted three kosher restaurants and two kosher supermarkets, one of which is a chain called Naouri with about thirty branches in Paris.

Carène comes from very humble Jewish origins in Algeria, where her grandmother was a cleaning lady for the rich French colonists, but her food is not humble at all. David, whose family is of southern-German and French Jewish background, loves her North African food. At this Sabbath lunch, Carène prepared many salads for the first course: fennel (see page 110), avocado with lemon and cilantro, sautéed eggplant, eggplant caviar (see page 34), sautéed mushrooms, and *tchoukchouka* (grilled peppers and tomatoes slowly cooked to a jamlike consistency; see page 94).

The entrée was an *adafina,* a Moroccan Sabbath dish, cooked all night long. *Adafina* varies according to the cook. Algerians who live near Tunisia, for example, might add white beans, whereas some Tunisians add spinach. For dessert we had strawberries and raspberries topped with meringue. Afterward we sipped our coffee on the rooftop, from which we could hear the sound of the children playing outside on the terrace and enjoy a lovely view of the Eiffel Tower. All in all, it was a beautiful and relaxing Shabbat lunch in Paris.

Adafina

(SABBATH MEAT STEW WITH CHICKPEAS AND RICE)

IN SOUTHERN MOROCCO, this Sabbath stew was cooked first over a wood fire and then kept warm in a pot tucked under the hot sand. In Spain and northern Morocco, it was cooked in communal ovens in the Jewish quarter of cities. Called by the Jewish youth of France today "*daf marocaine*," this flavorful stew, also known as *skeena*—meaning "hot" in northern Morocco—is preferred by many young people to ordinary *cholent* (see page 213) for Sabbath lunch.

Today in France the meat is usually beef rather than the lamb or mutton more commonly used in North Africa. For this one-pot meal, the rice and/or wheat berries or white beans must be kept apart for cooking, so that they can be served separately. Carène Moos encloses the seasoned rice and wheat berries in pieces of gauze or cheesecloth, knotting the cloth to make two individual bundles.

 YIELD: 8 TO 10 SERVINGS

1 cup dried chickpeas

3 cups wheat berries

½ cup vegetable oil

2 onions, roughly chopped

⅓ cup raisins*

2 tablespoons sugar

2¼ teaspoons sea salt, plus
  more to taste

¾ teaspoon ground turmeric

½ teaspoon sweet paprika

½ teaspoon cayenne pepper

½ teaspoon crushed red-pepper
  flakes

3 pounds chuck roast or brisket

12 small Red Bliss, Yukon
  Gold, or new potatoes

½ teaspoon ground cumin

*In Alsace and the south of France,
  prunes or dates are often substituted for
  the raisins.

Two days before serving, fill two bowls with warm water. Pour the chickpeas in one bowl and the wheat berries in the other. The next morning, drain both and set aside separately.

The day before or on the day of serving, heat 4 tablespoons of the oil in a large ovenproof casserole. Add the chickpeas, onions, raisins, and sugar, and sauté for about 5 minutes.

Make a rub of ¼ teaspoon each of the salt, turmeric, paprika, cayenne pepper, and red-pepper flakes, and rub on the meat. Put the meat in the casserole, and scatter the potatoes around; then fill the pot with enough water to cover, and bring to a boil.

In a separate bowl, mix the wheat berries with another 2 tablespoons of the oil, 1 teaspoon salt, and the cumin. Then place the berries in cheesecloth and loosely tie it up, keeping in mind that the wheat berries will expand as they cook.

In another bowl, mix the rice with the remaining 2 tablespoons oil, another teaspoon of salt, the garlic clove, and the remaining turmeric, paprika, cayenne, and red-pepper flakes. Tie the rice up in another piece of cheesecloth, as you did for the wheat berries, again leaving room to expand.

Place the sacks in the casserole, and add the head of garlic, the sweet potatoes, and the eggs. Bring the stew to a boil, and simmer, covered, for 1 hour and 45 minutes.

Preheat the oven to 250 degrees. Remove the casserole cover, drizzle honey over all, and cook in the oven for at least 5 hours, or until the vegetables are reddish brown. (You can also cook the *adafina* in a 200-degree oven overnight.)

To serve, remove the bundles of rice and wheat berries. Spoon the meat and vegetables onto a platter with a slotted spoon, and pile the grains around them.

2 cups long-grain rice

1 clove garlic, peeled, plus
   1 whole head garlic

2 sweet potatoes, peeled and
   halved

4 large eggs in the shell

½ cup honey

A colorful row of spices at an outdoor market

"Being Nice to One Another"

> Who is the man that desireth life. And loving days, that he may see good therein? Keep thy tongue from evil, and thy lips from speaking guile.
>
> —Psalm 34:13–14

During World War II, a Lithuanian Orthodox rabbi hid in Aix-les-Bains. He belonged to a sect whose members pattern their lives after the above psalm, devoting themselves to good works and kind words. When the war ended, the rabbi was so grateful to the people for saving him that he settled in the ancient town, known for its Roman sulfur baths, but certainly not for Bar Mitzvahs. Today it is home to a community of about a hundred of this sect of ultra-Orthodox Jews, studying at the Yeshiva Chachmei Tzorfas.

Though kindness is the rule in this community, personal histories include memories of great violence. Caroline Moos, one of the rabbi's followers, told me this story. During the war, her parents and fourteen other family members were hidden in La Brutagne, a tiny village near Limoges. Four days after the Allies landed at Normandy, German soldiers came to Oradour-sur-Glane, the next village, announcing that weapons were hidden there and demanding that the mayor choose hostages. When he refused to give up any of the townspeople, the Germans shot the men, put the women in the church, doused the foundation with gasoline, and set the church on fire.

"My mother watched the smoke in the distance all night long," said Caroline. "The baker was burned to death in his own oven, perhaps in part because he brought flour to my parents and others each week." In all, 642 people died, including many Jews who were hidden in the village.

Caroline can't help thinking of this story each time she goes to her local bakery. She and her husband, Philippe, like their fresh-baked baguettes, but now eat only kosher bread, which means that the baking is under rabbinical supervision. Since a hundred families are just too few to support an entirely kosher bakery, the rabbi found a solution. After all, a French baguette, made from flour, yeast, salt, and water, has no nonkosher ingredients within it and is baked on a hearth, not even in a greased mold. But to really make sure, each day at 5:00 a.m. a member of the community goes to light the oven of a neighborhood bakery and checks the facility to be sure it is kosher. This way, the families have their baguettes, and the baker sleeps a little later. By acting in kindness to one another, the whole community continues the teachings of the hidden rabbi.

Cholent

(SABBATH BEEF STEW WITH POTATOES, BEANS, AND BARLEY)

ONE FRIDAY MORNING WHEN I ARRIVED at Philippe and Caroline's home, the family was in full Shabbat swing. Four of Caroline's nine children were nearby to help with preparations for the Sabbath. Caroline was assembling ingredients for *cholent*, based on a recipe that came with her family from Poland.

Caroline makes *cholent* each week, cooking it all night in a slow cooker and serving it at lunch on Saturday. She simmers the meat in red wine, adds some barley and sometimes bulgur, and uses vegetable oil instead of the traditional chicken shmaltz.

 YIELD: AT LEAST 12 SERVINGS

Two days before you plan to serve ths stew, put the dried beans in a pot with water to cover by about 2 inches. Let soak overnight. Drain and rinse the next morning.

The day before serving, heat the oil in a frying pan, add the onions, and sauté until translucent. Then add the beef (not the bones), and brown on all sides. Remove the meat and the onions to a 4-quart slow cooker or a large, heavy cast-iron pan with a cover.

Put the carrots, potatoes, and the meat bones on top of the meat. Sprinkle on the paprika and the sugar. Spoon the tomato paste and the red wine over the meat, and top with the drained beans. Pour on the beef broth or water, filling the pot to cover the vegetables and meat by at least an inch. Dissolve the potato starch in ½ cup water, and stir into the pot.

Cover the slow cooker or pan, and simmer for 30 minutes. Then turn to low, and, before the Sabbath starts, stir in the barley and cook overnight, or for at least 5 hours if you are less observant. If you look at the *cholent* in the morning and it is dry, pour in a little water. If it is too watery, let it sit for a bit uncovered before you serve it for lunch. Just remember, if you are religious you cannot even stir the *cholent* from sunset to sunup after the Sabbath begins. Stirring is considered work. Just spoon it out and serve.

1 cup dried white or red kidney beans

3 tablespoons vegetable oil

3 onions, peeled and cut into large chunks

3 pounds plate, brisket, flank steak, or beef shanks, and the bone

4 carrots, peeled and cut into thick rounds

10 medium-sized potatoes, peeled and cut in half

1 tablespoon hot paprika, or to taste

2 teaspoons sugar

2 tablespoons tomato paste

2 cups red wine

About 6 cups beef broth or water

1 tablespoon potato starch

1 cup whole barley

Jews and Pork

When I wanted to research the art of cooking for the Jews, the most ancient people of the world, I found them to be people of rather bad taste, and I believe that their primate dirtiness is preserved because of this tradition. One may read about this in the history of their meals: these large stewpots, dripping with disgusting grease into which these Levites would dive, each in his turn, to pull out the best morsels, do not give a good image of the refinement of the *Chosen People.* Moreover, they eat unleavened bread with wild lettuce, which may be very healthy, but whose unbearable bitterness does nothing to enhance the taste. This diet, together with the abstinence from pork, and from an infinitude of other good dishes which are forbidden to them by law, would not suit Christians at all.
—François Marin, Préface, *Suite des Dons de Comus* (1742 edition)

In the 2008 movie *Roman de Gare,* the character played by Dominique Pinon calls himself Louis Goldberg when he visits a farm family in the Auvergne. When the host hears Goldberg's name, he asks if he is one of those Jews who won't eat pig, an animal that has no cloven hooves and does not chew its cud, as said in the Bible. Goldberg responds that only his father is Jewish, so he can eat pork. A similar thing happened to me. I spent a delightful day with a rugby player in the southwest of France. Suddenly he asked, "You seem so much like us. But tell me, why is it that you Jews don't eat pork?"

Throughout history, there have been questions about the Jews and their differences, as the quote above from the most popular cookbook of the eighteenth century shows. Not only have Jews not accepted Christianity, but they don't eat like Christians. They have not evolved and are stubborn about it. Today the French are more tolerant of the Jews' culinary peculiarities, as they are of other ethnic food peculiarities.

Professor René Moulinas, a historian from the University of Avignon, explained to me medieval Christian reasoning: "Jews killed Jesus, but more than that they were guilty of not having recognized Jesus as Christ. They should have disappeared by becoming Christians but they did not. Christians could show their goodness by allowing the Jews to live in France, but punished them for their not following the true faith." Following the dietary laws is a constant reminder of their failure to assimilate totally in a country that takes its food seriously.

Pickelfleisch

(CORNED BEEF)

Jewish *charcuterie,* where there isn't the slightest scrap of pork, is most delicious. Enter a Russian or Alsatian Jewish pastry-*charcuterie* shop and see beautiful beef tongues, pink and velvety smoked meat or *pickelfleisch* veined with yellow fat, preserved goose breasts, *griebens,* goose liver with a rare finesse, salamis and pyramids of sausages! Smell the appetizing aroma of salty cornichons and of the good *choucroute* mixed with fat herrings dripping in fat and their milk bath.
—Suzanne Roukhomovsky, *Gastronomie Juive,* 1929

ALSACE IS THE ONLY PART of France with a tradition of both pork and beef *charcuterie.* When I asked a butcher in Strasbourg about *pickelfleisch* (corned beef) and pickled tongue, he paused to think a minute. Yes, he told me, both are eaten primarily by Jewish clientele.

Of that *charcuterie, pickelfleisch* is the crown prince. Basically corned beef cured for eight to ten days with salt, sugar, spices, and saltpeter and then baked or boiled, it is more garlicky, with more varied spices, than that in America. Try making your own corned beef. It is great fun. Eat it as is or in a *choucroute garni* (sauerkraut dressed with meat and potatoes).

YIELD: 8 SERVINGS

One 4-to-5-pound brisket of beef
2 onions, coarsely chopped
1 teaspoon peppercorns
2 teaspoons powdered ginger
½ teaspoon ground cloves
2 bay leaves, crumbled
⅛ teaspoon grated nutmeg
⅛ teaspoon hot paprika
7 cloves garlic, minced
6 tablespoons coarse kosher salt
3 tablespoons brown sugar
1 tablespoon saltpeter (optional)
1 carrot, peeled and chopped
1 stalk celery, coarsely chopped
Garnish: Mustard and horseradish

Wash and remove most of the fat from the brisket. Mix together one of the chopped onions, the peppercorns, ginger, cloves, bay leaves, nutmeg, paprika, and garlic in a small bowl.

Bring 1 cup water to a boil. Dissolve the salt, sugar, and, if using, the saltpeter for coloring, in it. Cool, putting a few ice cubes in the water, and mix with half the mixed spices.

Rub the other half of the spices into the meat. Carefully move the meat to a gallon-sized resealable plastic bag, then pour on the liquid, close, and place in a 9-by-13-inch pan. Place two weights on top of the meat, and refrigerate for 10 days, turning every 2 days.

After 10 days, remove from the brine and rinse well under cold water. Put the brisket in a pot just large enough to hold the meat. Add the remaining onion, the carrot, and the celery, and cover with water by 2 inches. Bring the water to a boil, and simmer slowly, covered, for about 3 hours, or until the meat is tender. Remove from the heat, cool, slice thin, and place on a platter. Serve with mustard and horseradish.

Alsatian *Choucroute*

(SAUERKRAUT WITH SAUSAGE AND CORNED BEEF)

ONE-DISH SABBATH MEALS LIKE *choucroute* and *pot-au-feu* are for Alsatians what *cholent* is for Jews from eastern Europe. In the nineteenth century, the author Alexandre Weill mentioned the Sabbath lunch meal of his childhood, which included a dish of pearl barley or beans, *choucroute,* and kugel, made with mostly dried pear or plum.

Choucroute with sausage and corned beef is also eaten at Purim and has particular significance. The way the sausage "hangs" in Alsatian butcher shops is a reminder of how the evil Haman, who wanted to kill all the Jews, was hanged. Sometimes Alsatians call the fat hunk of corned or smoked beef "the Haman."

Michèle Weil, a doctor in Strasbourg, makes sauerkraut on Friday, lets it cool, and just reheats it for Saturday lunch. She varies her meal by adding *pickelfleisch,* duck confit, chicken or veal sausages, and sometimes smoked goose breast. You can make this dish as I have suggested, or vary the amounts and kinds of meats. *Choucroute* is a great winter party dish; the French will often eat it while watching rugby games on television. When you include the corned beef, you can most certainly feed a whole crowd.

YIELD: 8 TO 10 SERVINGS

2 pounds sauerkraut

2 tablespoons duck fat or vegetable oil

5 whole duck legs, cut into thighs and drumsticks

Salt and freshly ground pepper to taste

2 medium onions, peeled and chopped (about 2½ cups)

3 cloves garlic, chopped

2 carrots, peeled and cut into large rounds

10 juniper berries, or ½ cup gin

6 peppercorns

2 bay leaves

Wash the sauerkraut in cold water, and drain. Wash and drain again, squeezing it to eliminate as much water as possible.

Preheat the oven to 325 degrees, and heat the duck fat or oil in a large ovenproof casserole.

Season the duck legs with salt and freshly ground pepper, and brown them on both sides. Remove the duck legs to a plate, leaving the duck fat that has accumulated in the pan. Add the onions, the garlic, and the carrots, and sauté for about 5 minutes, or until the onions are translucent. Scatter the sauerkraut over the vegetables, and stir to incorporate. Tuck the duck legs into the sauerkraut, then add the juniper berries or gin, peppercorns, and bay leaves. Pour in the white wine and enough chicken broth almost to cover the sauerkraut. Bring to a boil on top of the stove, cover, and remove to the oven to cook for 2 hours, or until the liquid is absorbed by the sauerkraut.

While the sauerkraut is cooking, cook the potatoes in boiling salted water, and then peel. Sauté the sausages or hot dogs in a hot pan, or boil them for about 5 minutes.

Take the sauerkraut out of the oven and taste, adjusting the seasoning if necessary. Add the potatoes, sausages or hot dogs, and corned beef to the casserole, and return to the oven for about 20 minutes, or until the potatoes are tender. Remove the corned beef and slice against the grain. Serve on a large platter with piles of sauerkraut, duck legs, sausages, corned beef slices, and potatoes, and with a variety of mustards or mustard sauce and horseradish alongside.

2 cups dry white wine

2 cups chicken broth, plus more if necessary

12 small Red Bliss or Yukon Gold potatoes

5 garlic-chicken sausages, beef sausages, or hot dogs

One 3-to-4-pound corned beef (see preceding recipe)

Mustard or mustard sauce (recipe follows) as garnish

Horseradish as garnish

Alsatian *Chourcroute*

Alsatian Mustard Sauce

THIS TYPICAL ALSATIAN MUSTARD SAUCE is served with pickled or smoked tongue or *pickel-fleisch*; it has been eaten with fresh and salted meat or fresh and dried fish for centuries by the northern Jewish communities in France.

 YIELD: ABOUT 2 CUPS

2 tablespoons strong French
  Dijon mustard
⅔ cup red-wine vinegar
Salt and freshly ground pepper
  to taste
1 scant cup peanut or
  safflower oil
2 large shallots, diced
2 tablespoons chopped fresh
  chives
2 tablespoons chopped fresh
  parsley
1 French cornichon or Russian
  gherkin, diced (optional)

Put the mustard and the vinegar in a small bowl and stir together. Season with salt and freshly ground pepper, and slowly whisk in the oil.

Just before serving, stir in the shallots, chives, parsley, and, if you like, the pickle.

Mustards galore at a Paris market

Beef Cheek Stew
with Cilantro and Cumin, Algerian Style

"TO BE JEWISH IS TO BE CONSCIOUS of what one says and what one does," Jacqueline Meyer-Benichou, who cooks some of Paris's most elegant kosher food, told me. The head of a real-estate company, with a degree from Les Beaux Arts in architecture, Jacqueline treats cooking as her avocation and considers the presentation of food to be as important as the menu.

Living near branches of great gourmet stores in Paris, such as Lenôtre, she window-shops, looking at their food preparations and presentations, and tries to replicate the recipes for kosher dinners at her home. For dessert, she often fills little golden cups with soy-based iced soufflés, as Lenôtre does. "I love perfection," she said.

At Passover, Jacqueline makes beef cheeks or even veal shanks seasoned the Algerian way, with hot pepper and cilantro, and serves them as a main course, accompanied by her Algerian take on cabbage with cilantro and hot pepper. If you can't find beef cheeks, use veal shanks, stew meat, or flanken—any slightly fatty cut will do. Slow cooking makes the meat tender and delicious. Since it tastes even better prepared a day in advance, reheat just before serving.

Heat 3 tablespoons of the oil in a heavy pan, add the onions and garlic, and cook until the onions are golden, adding more oil if needed. Remove from the pan, and set aside.

Add the remaining oil, and brown the meat on all sides. Return the onions and garlic to the pan, stir in the bay leaves, salt and freshly ground pepper to taste, the cumin, and all but 2 tablespoons of the cilantro. Pour the chicken broth over the meat. Bring to a boil, cover, and simmer very slowly for 1½ to 2 hours, or until the meat is tender. Take the pan off the heat, let cool, then remove the meat with a slotted spoon and cut into 1-inch cubes.

Return the meat to the pan, and refrigerate overnight. The next day, remove any fat that has accumulated, reheat the stew over low heat, adjust seasonings, and sprinkle with the 2 tablespoons of reserved fresh cilantro leaves before serving.

YIELD: AT LEAST 8 SERVINGS

5 tablespoons vegetable oil
3 large onions, peeled and chopped
4 cloves garlic, crushed
2 pounds beef cheeks, beef or veal shanks, stew meat, or flanken, cut into 2 pieces
2 bay leaves
Salt and freshly ground black pepper to taste
1 tablespoon ground cumin
1 bunch of fresh cilantro, chopped
2 cups chicken broth

Alsatian Sweet and Sour Tongue

IN FRANCE, FOR ROSH HASHANAH AND PASSOVER, tongue, with its velvety texture, is often served with a sweet-and-sour ginger sauce. In some homes the tongue is put on the table as a symbol of the wish for success in the New Year.

Spicy-sweet sauces often accompanied pickled meats in Alsace, where sugar was first used as a condiment rather than as a dessert sweetener. By the time the meat had been pickled, desalted, and then cooked, it had lost much of its flavor, so sugar, ginger, and other spices ensured a good taste.

Jews have a long history of treating tongue, an often scorned cut of meat, as a delicacy. It is preserved and pickled in a salt brine with garlic, pepper, spices, sodium nitrite, and sodium erythorbate. The tongue is then boiled, the skin peeled off, and slices of meat are served with a sauce.

YIELD: 10 TO 12 SERVINGS

One 4-to-5-pound pickled beef tongue
3 onions, quartered
6 bay leaves
3 teaspoons whole peppercorns
1 teaspoon whole cloves

SWEET AND SOUR SAUCE
2 tablespoons vegetable oil
1 onion, peeled and diced
Salt and freshly ground pepper to taste

½ teaspoon ground mace
½ teaspoon ground cloves
½ teaspoon allspice
10 gingersnaps, crumbled
2 to 3 tablespoons cider vinegar
½ cup raisins
½ cup blanched slivered almonds
4 or 5 thin lemon slices
1 tablespoon chopped fresh parsley
  for garnish

Fill a pot with cold water. Add the tongue, onions, bay leaves, peppercorns, and cloves. Bring to a boil, and simmer, covered, for 2½ to 3 hours, allowing about 20 minutes per pound, until the meat is tender when pierced with a knife. Allow the tongue to cool to room temperature in the cooking water. Using a sharp knife, peel off the outer skin and any extra fat or gristle. Return the tongue to the cooking water, cover, and refrigerate. This may be done a day in advance.

To make the sauce, heat the oil in a medium-sized frying pan. Sauté the diced onion until golden. Add salt and freshly ground pepper to taste, the mace, cloves, allspice, and 1½ cups water. Bring to a boil, and add the gingersnaps, cider vinegar, raisins, almonds, and lemon slices. If the sauce gets too thick, thin with a little more water. The sauce may be made a day in advance; cover and refrigerate.

Preheat the oven to 350 degrees. Remove the tongue from the cooking water, and place in a roasting pan. Brush with the sauce, and bake for 45 minutes, basting the tongue occasionally. Cut the tongue on the diagonal into slices about ¼ inch thick, and serve garnished with the parsley and the sauce on the side.

A glimpse of an Alsatian village

Tongue with Capers and Cornichons

BECAUSE THE JEWS WERE A SOURCE of income to the Popes of Avignon until the Revolution, they were squeezed whenever money was needed. A story goes that in Carpentras, the home of the largest number of Jews in the thirteenth century, a 1276 agreement forced the Jews to deliver to the bishop's table a prized delicacy, the tender tongue of all the animals that they slaughtered in the kosher manner.

The Jewish tradition of smoking or pickling tongue is a perfect example of my definition of a culinary lag—using pickled tongue even when refrigeration makes it no longer necessary, and at a time when we focus on eating fresh foods without preservatives. But because these are traditional family recipes, people are hesitant to tamper with them. After tasting fresh tongue at Le Mas Tourteron (see page 92) just outside Gordes, I have always opted for fresh, because of its amazing flavor and texture. Including garlic and saffron adds a North African touch to this dish, which is often served at weddings and Bar Mitzvahs in North Africa.

A kosher butcher in Paris

Bring a large pot of water to a boil. Add the tongue, and simmer, covered, for about 20 minutes. Remove the tongue and discard the water. Rinse the pot.

Pour fresh water into the same pot. Pierce the onion with the cloves, and add to the pot, along with the carrot, celery, leek, orange zest, 1 tablespoon of the white vinegar, the bay leaves, saffron, thyme, peppercorns, and salt. Lower the tongue into the pot, making sure the water almost covers the meat. Bring to a boil, and simmer, covered, for about 2 hours, depending on the weight of tongue, until it is tender when pierced with a knife. As it cooks, replenish the water as needed so the tongue remains almost covered.

While the tongue cooks, heat the oil in a sauté pan. Add the flour, stirring, over low heat without browning for about 4 minutes. Strain in about 1 cup of the tongue-cooking water, whisk, and add the tomato, white wine, remaining tablespoon vinegar, capers, cornichons, and a little salt and pepper. Bring to a boil, and simmer for about 15 minutes over a low heat, until the sauce reduces a bit. Adjust the salt and pepper to taste.

When the tongue is done, turn off the heat. When it is cool enough to handle, remove the tongue from the water, and peel the skin off with a sharp knife. Cut on the diagonal into slices about ¼ inch thick, and arrange on a serving platter. Discard the vegetables or use for soup. Pour the sauce over the slices, and sprinkle parsley over all.

 YIELD: 8 TO 10 SERVINGS

One 3-to-4-pound fresh beef tongue, washed, or 2 veal tongues

1 medium onion, peeled

6 cloves

1 medium carrot, peeled

1 stalk celery, halved

1 leek, trimmed, cut lengthwise, and cleaned

Grated zest of 1 orange

2 tablespoons white vinegar

3 bay leaves

Pinch of saffron

4 sprigs fresh thyme, or 1 teaspoon dried thyme

A few peppercorns, plus freshly ground pepper to taste

2 tablespoons coarse salt, plus more to taste

⅓ cup vegetable oil

1 tablespoon flour

½ small tomato, peeled and puréed

½ cup white wine

2 tablespoons drained capers

2 tablespoons finely diced cornichons (gherkin pickles)

1 bunch of fresh parsley, minced

One War Story

Some of the most poignant memories I have from interviewing people for this book are the haunting tales of their experiences during World War II.

When Danielle Fleischmann's daughter Sandrine heard about my project, she asked me to interview her mother, who lives now in Montmartre. She wanted to make sure that her mother's stories and recipes would not die with her.

Danielle's Polish family first went to Belgium during the war, then fled to the Free Zone in the south of France. In 1942 and 1943, it was falsely rumored among Jewish refugees that families with three children wouldn't be deported, so Danielle, the third child, was conceived and born. Because her parents had to work and life was still dangerous, Danielle was sent to the Montalibets, a Christian family in the mountains who agreed to hide her. "The Montalibets had an inn and a café," she told me. "Lili, their nineteen-year-old daughter, took care of me. My parents came to visit me from time to time in the night. When I left after we were liberated, Lili was devastated. Later, I made sure that the family received the 'Righteous Gentile' awards given by Yad Vashem Memorial in Jerusalem to non-Jews who saved or hid Jews in Europe during the Holocaust.

"When I joined my family," Danielle told me, "I clung to my mother. I was always afraid she would go away again. Maybe that is why I make her food today."

Faux Poisson or Fake Fish

(SWEET MEATBALLS)

IT IS COMMON KNOWLEDGE THAT Jews should usher in the Sabbath with a little bit of fish. But in the village in Poland from which Danielle's mother hailed, they often could not get carp in the winter, because the lake was frozen. The story goes that the Jews thought they could make an arrangement with God to create *falshe fish* (Yiddish for "fake fish"). So they made meat patties, shaped in ovals or balls, depending on the family tradition, and simmered them in a broth with salt, sugar, pepper, and a little carrot, so they would look and taste like sweet-and-sour gefilte fish. "Because the intentions were good, the benevolent God agreed with the Jews and said that he would make believe that it was fish," said Danielle. (In this recipe, sugar is used as a seasoning, as it was in past centuries.)

Gently mix together the veal, beef, eggs, matzo meal, salt, pepper, 5 tablespoons of the sugar, and the diced onion in a mixing bowl.

Bring 6 cups water to a boil in a medium pot. When the water boils, add the chopped onion and the carrots. Season with salt to taste and the remaining sugar.

Dip your hands into cold water, and shape the meat mixture into fifteen little rounds the size of Ping-Pong balls. Slip them into the boiling water, and simmer, half covered, for about 30 minutes. Serve at room temperature with horseradish, as you would gefilte fish.

YIELD: 15 MEATBALLS

½ pound ground veal

¼ pound ground beef

2 large eggs

2 heaping tablespoons matzo meal

½ teaspoon salt, plus more to taste

½ teaspoon freshly ground pepper, or to taste

⅔ cup sugar

½ onion, peeled and finely diced, plus 1 onion, peeled and roughly chopped

2 carrots, peeled and cut into rounds

Horseradish for garnish

Almondeguilles

(ALGERIAN MEATBALLS WITH TOMATO SAUCE)

> [Friday night was] meatballs simmering in garnet-red tomato sauce.
>
> —Albert Cohen, *Livre de Ma Mère*

JOCELYNE AKOUN (see page 28) also served me meatballs with tomato sauce for Friday night dinner, a typical Sephardic dish for the eve of the Sabbath. I had found centuries-old recipes for these *almonde-guilles* or *albondigas,* but without tomato sauce. For me, the post–Columbian Exchange marriage of tomatoes and meatballs greatly enhances the flavor of this dish!

 YIELD: ABOUT 2 CUPS SAUCE

 YIELD: ABOUT 18 MEATBALLS

TOMATO SAUCE

4 pounds fresh tomatoes, or two 28-ounce cans whole peeled San Marzano tomatoes, chopped

¼ cup olive oil

8 cloves garlic, minced

Salt and freshly ground pepper to taste

1 teaspoon ground cumin

¼ cup chopped fresh cilantro, basil, or parsley, or 2 tablespoons dried *herbes de Provence*

MEATBALLS

6-inch section of a baguette, cut into pieces

1 pound ground beef

1 medium onion, finely diced

3 large cloves garlic, diced

1 bunch of fresh cilantro, finely chopped (at least 1 cup)

2 large eggs

Salt and freshly ground pepper to taste

1 tablespoon ground cumin

1 tablespoon sweet paprika

1 cup semolina

Vegetable oil for frying

To make the sauce, if using fresh tomatoes, bring a large pot of water to a boil. Drop in the tomatoes and leave for a minute. Using a slotted spoon, carefully remove the tomatoes, and, when cool, peel off the skin.

Heat the olive oil in a large pan. Add the tomatoes (fresh or canned), the garlic, salt and freshly ground pepper to taste, the cumin, and the herbs. Simmer over slow to medium heat for about 30 minutes, until the sauce is thickened and well reduced.

To make the meatballs, soak the bread in a bowl of water for a few minutes, then remove from the bowl and squeeze to remove as much water as possible. Cut up the baguette, and gently mix in a large bowl with the beef, onion, garlic, cilantro, eggs, salt and freshly ground pepper to taste, cumin, and paprika. Dip your hands into cold water, and shape the meat mixture into little rounds the size of golf balls.

Put the semolina in a wide bowl, and roll the meatballs in it. Heat about an inch of vegetable oil in a frying pan over medium heat. Brown the meatballs, and drain them on paper towels.

Heat the tomato sauce, add the meatballs, and simmer about 15 minutes, or until the meatballs are cooked through.

A kosher butcher makes meatballs for Shabbat.

Turckheim's Jewish Butcher

The charming Alsatian wine village of Turckheim, located on the eastern slopes of the Vosges Mountains, produces some of the best Gewürztraminer and Rieslings in the world and is the starting point of the famous Route des Vins. Inside the medieval walls of this small town is the picturesque Geismar Traiteur, Boucherie, Charcuterie, dating back to 1784, just before the start of the French Revolution. The oldest surviving Jewish butcher shop in Alsace, it is an important landmark from the time when Turckheim had a thriving Jewish population.

"Before World War II, my family only sold beef and veal," said Jacques Geismar, in his early fifties, now the head of the company. "After World War I, we started making *charcuterie,* because the Jewish rural community started to leave. After the Second World War, with only a handful of Jews left in the town, we sold everything, even pork." Geismar, which still has a kosher catering arm of its company, is also known for traditional meat products like *knoblewurst* (garlic sausage), *tierfleisch* (smoked meat), *lungenwurscht* (a wurst made out of lungs, heart, and onions), as well as garlic-and-liver sausage and the famous *pickelfleisch*. "Alsatian *charcuterie* is traditionally German and French," Raymond, Jacques's father, told me. "But when Polish and Russian butchers came here in the nineteenth century, they brought their own traditions."

When World War II broke out, Jacques's grandfather Gaston took his family to the Ardèche, where he rented a house until 1945. Like many Jewish butchers, Gaston knew what to do with the lesser cuts like the guts, heart, tripe, head, and feet, turning them into delicacies like *lungenwurscht* and *knoble* sausage for a Jesuit seminary in the mountains.

In 1943, just before Rosh Hashanah, the Geismars were on their way to the synagogue when they heard the Germans coming. With nowhere to go, they fled to the seminary. "I will hide your children," said the priest. The children then got on a truck, hiding behind a wine tank, and stayed at the seminary until the end of the war, in August 1944, when liberation came to France. Unlike many others, however, the Geismars returned to Turckheim in 1945, to continue the family tradition.

Stuffed Breast of Veal with Parsley and Onions

THIS VEAL DISH IS A BIG FAVORITE of butcher Jacques Geismar's Jewish clientele. You can substitute matzo for the bread at Passover, and, if you like, add raisins and apples to the stuffing. This dish is popular for the Sabbath or the high holidays in France, the way brisket or stuffed turkey is in America. Try the stuffing for your next turkey.

 YIELD: 6 TO 8 SERVINGS

Mix the soaked baguette, garlic, parsley, one of the diced onions, the eggs, and salt and freshly ground pepper to taste in a medium bowl.

Season the outside and the pocket of the veal with salt and freshly ground pepper. Place the stuffing in the veal pocket. Using skewers or large toothpicks, close off the pocket to seal in the stuffing.

Heat a thin film of oil in a heatproof casserole large enough to hold the veal, and slide the stuffed veal on top. Sear the veal on all sides until golden brown, then remove to a plate.

Spoon the remaining onions, the carrots, tomatoes, and ginger into the casserole. Season with salt and freshly ground pepper to taste, and cook until the onions are translucent. Return the veal to the casserole, and add enough water to cover the veal halfway. Simmer, covered, for 1½ hours, or until tender.

Cool, and refrigerate overnight. The next day, remove the fat that has accumulated, and slice the veal with its stuffing. Heat the veal slices in the veal juices with the vegetables for about 20 minutes, or until heated through and serve on a plate with green beans and onions (see page 315).

½ baguette, soaked in warm water and squeezed to remove as much water as possible, and cut into little pieces

3 cloves garlic, minced

1 bunch of fresh parsley, finely chopped

3 large onions, peeled and finely diced

2 large eggs

Salt and freshly ground pepper to taste

3 pounds veal breast, without the bone, with a pocket cut into the meat

3 tablespoons vegetable oil, or enough to coat the bottom of the casserole

2 or 3 carrots, peeled and cut into rounds

1 or 2 tomatoes, peeled and diced

1 teaspoon powdered ginger

Brisket with Ginger, Orange Peel, and Tomato

TO THE HORROR OF CHEF DANIEL ROSE (see page 68) of Spring Restaurant in Paris, it is impossible to find an American brisket in France. It just doesn't exist.

American butchers tend to cut larger pieces of meat. Five- or six-pound briskets (*poitrines*) or huge rib-eye steaks (*entrecôtes*) are the result of sawing through the muscle or the shoulder section of the animal. French butchers, by contrast, cut around the contours of the muscles to yield more tender but much smaller pieces. French Jews tend to use a breast of veal that usually has a pocket inside it for stuffing for their brisket. In this version, Daniel applies French techniques to make a perfectly delicious brisket with a subtle hint of orange in the sauce. I always make this dish a day in advance.

YIELD: 6 TO 10 SERVINGS

One 3-to-5-pound veal or beef
  brisket
Salt and freshly ground pepper
  to taste
2 tablespoons vegetable oil
12 small spring onions,
  trimmed and halved, or
  2 medium onions, thickly
  sliced
6 carrots, peeled
8 cloves garlic, peeled
1 tablespoon cider vinegar
1 cup dry white wine
3 cups veal, beef, or chicken
  stock
3 small tomatoes, halved
2 sprigs fresh thyme, or
  ½ teaspoon dried thyme
1 bay leaf
5 sprigs fresh parsley, plus
  ¼ cup chopped fresh parsley

Preheat the oven to 325 degrees. Season the brisket with salt and freshly ground pepper to taste.

Pour the oil into a Dutch oven over medium heat. Brown the meat for about 4 minutes on each side. Remove, and set aside. Add the onions, carrots, and garlic cloves to the Dutch oven, cooking until they are just beginning to soften, adding more oil if necessary. Raise the heat, pour in the cider vinegar, and stir with a wooden spoon to scrape up any bits that have stuck to the pan. Add the white wine and continue stirring, allowing the liquid to reduce for a few minutes.

Put the meat back in the pot, along with the stock. Bring to a simmer, and add the tomatoes, thyme, bay leaf, parsley sprigs, ginger, and leek top.

Using a straight peeler, remove the zest in long strips from one of the lemons and one of the oranges. Add to the pot. Cover, and place in the oven for 45 minutes.

Lower the oven temperature to 275 degrees, and continue cooking for 2 to 2½ more hours, or until tender.

Remove the meat and vegetables from the pot. Discard the citrus peels, thyme and parsley sprigs, ginger, bay leaf, and leek top. If cooking in advance, let the pot cool, and refrigerate the brisket in the sauce.

Before serving, remove the meat, and slice on the bias. Put

the meat back in the sauce, and reheat in a warm oven or on the stovetop. Arrange the meat on a serving platter along with the vegetables.

Strain the sauce into a pan, and reduce it over high heat to concentrate the flavor and thicken. Pour the sauce over the sliced brisket, and, before serving, sprinkle with the grated zests of the remaining lemon and orange and the chopped parsley.

One ½-inch slice of fresh ginger
Green top of 1 leek
2 lemons
2 oranges

Daniel Rose in his kitchen

Tunisian Stuffed Vegetables with Meat

FOR WOMEN, COOKBOOKS ARE OFTEN memories of their mothers. Daisy Taïeb, the mother of two daughters, wrote *Les Fêtes Juives à Tunis Racontées à Mes Filles* (*Jewish Holidays in Tunis as Told to My Daughters*). "My daughters wanted to learn the religious customs in Tunis, like the *fête des filles,* a festival where the girls go to the synagogue all in white," she told me. "Soon, with rapid Frenchification and assimilation, you will be able to learn about these traditions only in museums."

One day when I was in Nice, I watched Madame Taïeb cook her famous meatballs stuffed into vegetables. She was making them for Friday night dinner, to serve with couscous. Though I had expected a quiet, grandmotherly woman, I found her to be a trim, stylish lady who had taken the Dale Carnegie course on public speaking. She is the president of the French version of the Jewish Federation in Nice, and the representative of B'nai B'rith on the Côte d'Azur.

These days, Madame Taïeb, who has lived alone since her husband's death, invites people in for Sabbath dinner. "In Tunisia, you have the same foods as in Nice—fish, vegetables, spices—so it is not difficult to make the recipes," she told me. "But you have to use your hands to judge, not your eyes, when making meatballs."

For Madame Taïeb, couscous with meatballs stuffed into peppers, artichoke bottoms, and eggplants, one of my favorite dishes, is symbolic of family, remembrance, and Friday night dinners.

M YIELD: ABOUT 3 DOZEN VEGETABLES STUFFED WITH MEATBALLS

8 frozen artichoke bottoms, thawed
Juice of 1 lemon
2 small eggplants
2 small zucchini
3 small green or red bell peppers
1 onion, chopped
¼ stale baguette, or 1 matzo
1 pound ground lamb or beef

Stuffing peppers

First, prepare the vegetables for stuffing. Put the artichoke bottoms in a large bowl with the lemon juice and water to cover. Cut the eggplants once down the center lengthwise, and then across the width. Scoop out some of the pulp from each piece, making sure you don't go all the way through the skin. You should end up with four cuplike pieces for each eggplant, plus the pulp. Cut the zucchini into three cylinders. With an apple corer, remove the center, saving the pulp. Cut the bell peppers in half widthwise, removing the pith, seeds, and stem. Cut each half in two, then cut across, to make eight pieces. Separate the rings.

To make the meatballs, first soak the bread or matzo in water for a few seconds, and then squeeze to drain. Break up the bread or matzo. Put the bread in a medium bowl with the meat, the cilantro, dill, parsley, onions, garlic, coriander, allspice, *harissa,* salt, pepper, and two of the eggs, and mix well. Roll the meat mixture into balls of about 2 tablespoons each. Press the meat into the artichoke bottoms, the hollowed-out eggplants, the pepper pieces, the onion and the zucchini. Don't try to stuff too much into them.

Heat 2 inches of the vegetable oil in a frying pan.

Put the flour or matzo meal in a bowl. Break the remaining egg into a second bowl, and mix well with the 2 tablespoons of vegetable oil. Dip the open part of each stuffed vegetable first in the flour and then in the egg. This will help keep the meat together while frying, but you still have to be gentle when handling.

Fry the stuffed vegetables in batches in the oil until the meat is golden brown. Remove and drain on paper towels. Finish cooking in the tomato sauce (see page 226) with the reserved eggplant and zucchini pulp.

2 bunches of fresh cilantro, finely chopped (about 2 cups)

½ bunch of fresh dill, finely chopped (about ½ cup)

1 bunch of fresh parsley, finely chopped (about 1 cup)

3 small onions, grated

2 cloves garlic, minced

3 teaspoons ground coriander

½ teaspoon allspice

1½ teaspoons *harissa* (see page 33)

1 teaspoon salt

½ teaspoon freshly ground pepper

3 large eggs

2 tablespoons vegetable oil, plus more for frying

3 cups flour or matzo meal

Savory meat-filled vegetables over couscous

Membre d'Agneau à la Judaïque

(ROAST LAMB JEWISH STYLE)

THE OLDEST RECIPE FOR LAMB I could find is for a shoulder of mutton or lamb—a *membre de mouton à la judaïque*—which comes from Pierre de Lune's 1656 cookbook, *Le Cuisinier, où Il Est Traité de la Véritable Méthode pour Apprester Toutes Sortes de Viandes . . .* This recipe calls for lots of garlic and anchovies to be embedded in a shoulder of lamb with *herbes de Provence*. The pan juices are reduced with the juice of an orange and enhanced with white pepper and orange peel. The title of this recipe is one of the first known uses of "*judaïque*" ("Jewish style") in a French recipe. Don't forget that, "officially," no Jews lived in France at this time. Here is my adaptation 350 years later.

 YIELD: 6 TO 8 SERVINGS

One 3-pound top-round or
  shoulder roast of lamb,
  without the bone
Salt and freshly ground pepper
  to taste
3 anchovy fillets, cut into
  3 pieces each
6 cloves garlic, peeled and cut
  into slivers
3 sprigs fresh rosemary, or
  1 teaspoon dried rosemary
3 sprigs fresh thyme, or
  1 teaspoon dried thyme
3 sprigs fresh sage, or
  1 teaspoon dried sage
8 small potatoes
1 pound green beans or
  zucchini, cut into chunks
2 tablespoons olive oil
Juice and grated peel of
  1 orange

Preheat the oven to 450 degrees, and season the roast with salt and pepper. Then pierce the lamb with a sharp knife, and insert the anchovy fillets and the garlic bits in the slits. Place in a small roasting pan with the herbs and about a cup of water. Scatter the potatoes and the green beans or zucchini around the lamb, and toss the vegetables with a little olive oil.

Place in the oven, and roast for 20 minutes. Then turn the oven down to 350 degrees, and continue cooking for about another 1½ hours, or until done and a meat thermometer measures 140 degrees, basting occasionally.

Remove the lamb from the oven and the pan. Add the orange juice and grated peel. Then cook, stirring, until the juices are reduced by about a half. Degrease the sauce, sprinkle with pepper, adjust seasonings, and serve.

Provençal Lamb with Garlic and Olives

MICHEL KALIFA IS ONE OF THE FEW butchers in France who go through the laborious process of removing the many veins in a leg of lamb, a process that is integral to koshering. Because of the difficulties in koshering a leg of lamb, most people will use the shoulder, which he loves as well. Glancing lovingly at his wife, he said, "A thigh of a woman is as nimble and light as a shoulder of lamb."

Here is an old Jewish Provençal recipe for a shoulder of lamb. Make it, as Michel Kalifa would, with a caress of garlic.

YIELD: AT LEAST 8 SERVINGS

Roll up and tie the roast with twine. Make about six small incisions with a sharp knife in the lamb, then insert half the garlic slivers way into the meat. Season the skin liberally with salt and pepper.

Heat the olive oil in a Dutch oven. Brown the lamb on all sides, then remove and set aside.

Sauté the onions, carrot, and remaining garlic in the Dutch oven until the onions are lightly golden. Add the tomato paste, the tomatoes, and the broth. Bring to a gentle simmer.

Put the lamb gently back in the pot, with the thyme or *herbes de Provence.* If the broth does not almost cover the lamb, add a little water. Cover with a lid, and cook very gently for about 2 hours, turning the lamb after 40 minutes.

After 2 hours, add the olives, and continue simmering slowly for another 20 minutes, or until tender when pierced with a fork.

Remove the lamb, and transfer to a platter. Discard the thyme sprigs, and return the liquid in the pot to a boil, scraping up any browned bits from the pan bottom. Reduce to a sauce consistency, strain and press, reserving the juice, and adjust the seasonings. Skim off the fat, and pour the sauce into a small bowl. Carve the lamb, and serve surrounded with the olives and vegetables.

One 5-pound shoulder of
  lamb, without the bone
6 cloves garlic, peeled, each cut
  into about 6 slivers
Salt and freshly ground pepper
¼ cup olive oil
2 onions, peeled and diced
1 carrot, peeled and diced
2 tablespoons tomato paste
3 large tomatoes, peeled,
  seeded, and cut into large
  chunks, or half a 28-ounce
  can peeled tomatoes
3 cups beef broth
4 large sprigs fresh thyme, or
  1 teaspoon dried thyme
  or *herbes de Provence*
1½ cups green olives, pitted

NOTE   If you'd like to make the dish in advance, refrigerate the lamb in the sauce overnight. Remove the fat that accumulates from the top, carve the lamb when cool, return the sliced lamb to the pot with the sauce, and simmer until warm, surrounded with the olives and vegetables.

Moroccan Braised Lamb with Couscous

My father, an Algerian Jew, saw my mother, a Catholic from Normandy, in the *métro* for the first time. *Par amour,* my mother converted to Judaism. Her couscous was a mixture of Jewish and Normandy. I have so many memories of her couscous. It was the best of my life. She was absolutely extraordinary and unique, and her food was full of love.

—Filmmaker Claude Lelouch, in an interview with the author

FOR CLAUDE LELOUCH AND OTHER FRENCH JEWS from North Africa, couscous (a term that refers both to the stew and to the grain) is comfort food. When Suzon Meymy started cooking as a young bride living in Paris, her native Morocco seemed terribly far away, so she wrote to her mother, asking for recipes. "My mother was so unhappy that I was in France, so she sent me cooked chicken and flans. What she didn't know was that they didn't travel well, so we couldn't eat them when they arrived." When Suzon cooks lamb couscous today, in her small apartment in a Paris suburb, she uses her mother's techniques. "My mother, who was the couscous-maker of Mogador, spent all her time in the kitchen," she told me. "I watched her and my sisters cook for every festival in our town. They were exhausted from so much cooking. I saw them falling apart with fatigue." Suzon, a very good cook, takes the time to make this lamb stew only when her whole family is present.

What I like about this amazing recipe for couscous is that the vegetables are not overcooked. Serve the lamb with couscous (see page 270) and a delicious Moroccan squash dish (see page 302).

YIELD: AT LEAST 12 SERVINGS

2 shoulders of lamb (about 5 pounds each, including the bone)

Salt and freshly ground pepper to taste

4 tablespoons vegetable oil

1 leek, cleaned and diced

2 onions, peeled and diced

The day before serving, season the meat heavily with salt and pepper, and sear it in a frying pan with one tablespoon of the oil. Then preheat the oven to 250 degrees. Put the meat in a pot, add a little water, and braise, covered, for about 2 hours, or until tender. Set aside to cool, and then refrigerate overnight.

Also the day before serving, heat the remaining oil in another pot, and sauté the leek and the onions. When the onions are translucent, add the turnips, carrots, ginger, cinnamon, turmeric, *ras el hanout,* salt and freshly ground pepper to taste, and garlic. Cover the vegetables and spices with water, and simmer, covered, until the carrots are tender.

The next day, cut the lamb into 2-inch chunks, and put it in the pot with the vegetables. Add the zucchini. Simmer slowly until the zucchini is just cooked but still bright green. Adjust seasonings, and stir in the *harissa* sauce. (I also serve more at the table, so that people can adjust the heat to their taste.)

4 turnips, halved

4 carrots, peeled and cut into rounds about ¼ inch thick

2 teaspoons grated fresh ginger

½ teaspoon ground cinnamon

1 teaspoon ground turmeric

½ teaspoon *ras el hanout*

4 or 5 cloves garlic, diced

4 zucchini, each cut into 4 pieces

1 to 2 tablespoons *harissa* sauce, or to taste (see following recipe)

Suzon and her husband with their couscous

NOTE If using a boneless cut of lamb, decrease the braising time by a half hour.

Suzon's *Harissa* Sauce

HARISSA IS AVAILABLE IN supermarkets all over the country, or you can make your own (see page 33).

Stir together the *harissa,* couscous broth, salt and freshly ground pepper to taste, cinnamon, and Spanish pepper in a small bowl. Serve with the couscous.

YIELD: ABOUT 1 CUP

1 tablespoon *harissa* (see page 33)

1 cup couscous broth (see page 270)

Salt and freshly ground pepper to taste

1 heaping teaspoon ground cinnamon

1 hot Spanish pepper, diced

Marcel Marceau, the Son of the
Kosher Butcher of Strasbourg

One afternoon in Strasbourg, I went to Simon and Gerta Loinger's apartment, over-looking the Parc du Contade, named for an aristocrat whose chef brought *pâté de foie gras* with truffles to Strasbourg. Simon, who is in his late eighties, told me that all Americans know two Frenchmen: Jacques Cousteau and Simon's cousin Marcel Marceau. When they were youngsters at their grandmother's camp, Marcel was a counselor, enchanting the children with his mimes. Always an admirer of Charlie Chaplin, Marcel dressed up in his father's clothes to mimic the great Charlot, to portray characters from the fables of La Fontaine, and even to do an impersonation of Adolf Hitler.

The son of Polish Jews who came to France before World War I, Marcel Marceau (born Marcel Mangel) grew up in Strasbourg, where his father worked as a kosher butcher, loved opera, and raised pigeons as a hobby. At the start of World War II, Marcel's father, Charles, stayed in Strasbourg, but when it became more dangerous for Jews, he moved his family to Limoges, in France's interior, where he worked for another kosher butcher. One day, while he was hard at work, the Gestapo came and took him away. Disappearing like so many others, he presumably perished in Auschwitz.

The war broke out when Marcel was seventeen. Disguised as a boy scout, he fled. "At that age, one doesn't truly realize when you are in danger," he said later in an article. "I entered the Resistance with the spirit of conscience, not only because I was a Jew. There reigned there a great spirit of tolerance, openness, and respect for France, the land of welcome. After the war, I never invoked the persecutions that my family was a victim of. I kept silent for I had above all the need to be recognized individually."

But Marcel, through his character Bip, created in 1947, imbued his art with the sounds of the street, the howls of drunkenness, the cries of beaten women, the deportation of his father, and a childhood that ended during his years of resistance. And all the while, he remembered his mother's square noodles cooked in goose fat, the strudel she stretched at the table, and the beef, chickens, and veal his father brought home from his butcher shop.

Römertopf

(LAMB WITH POTATOES, ZUCCHINI, AND TOMATOES)

A *RÖMERTOPF,* A POROUS CLAY POT developed in the 1960s by a German company, is often used in Alsace and southern Germany for long-simmering stews. These stews may be akin to Alsatian *baecke-offe,* a pot of meat (usually beef, pork, and veal along with calf or pig feet) mixed with potatoes, marinated in white wine, and cooked in the oven all day long, on Mondays, when the women traditionally do the wash. Agar Lippmann (see page 258) remembers her mother in Alsace making the Sabbath stew in a *baeckeoffe,* using a mix of flour and water to make a kind of glue to really seal the lid.

When I was having lunch at Robert and Eveline Moos's house in Annecy, they used a *Römertopf* to make a similar lamb stew for me. Eveline ceremoniously brought the dish to the table, and in front of all of us, took off the top so that we were enveloped in the steam and aromas of the finished dish.

Marinate the lamb in the white wine overnight. Drain, saving the marinade.

Soak the *Römertopf,* if using, in cold water for about ½ hour. Then drain but don't dry.

Preheat the oven to 375 degrees.

Place half the onions and potatoes in a Dutch oven or *Römertopf* pan. Cover them with half the zucchini, half the tomatoes, 3 cloves of garlic, and a bay leaf. Add the lamb, and cover with the remaining onion, potatoes, zucchini, tomatoes, garlic, and bay leaf.

Add the wine marinade, sprinkle on the spices, and salt and freshly ground pepper to taste, cover, and bake for 3 hours. Bring to the table in the pot, and then cut the meat and serve.

YIELD: 4 TO 6 SERVINGS

1 5-pound shoulder of lamb, deboned

2 cups white wine

2 onions, cut into chunks

4 pounds potatoes, peeled and thinly sliced

4 zucchini, cut into chunks

4 tomatoes, peeled and quartered

5 cloves garlic

2 bay leaves

1 teaspoon curry powder

1 teaspoon sweet paprika

2 tablespoons chopped fresh basil, or 1 teaspoon dried basil

Salt and freshly ground pepper to taste

Eveline Moos serves a lamb stew cooked in a *Römertopf.*

Kugelhopf, the Alsatian dessert par excellence

Quiches, Kugels, Omelets, and Savory Soufflés

Quiche à l'Oignon (Onion Tart Lorraine)

Quiche Savoyarde à la Tomme (Savoyard Tomato and Cheese Quiche)

Crustless *Quiche Clafoutis* with Cherry Tomatoes, Basil, and Olive Oil

A Jewish Twist on *Tarte Flambée*

Alsatian Pear Kugel with Prunes

Nudel Schaleth (Noodle Kugel with Apples)

Grumbeerekugel or *Kougel aux Pommes* (Potato Kugel)

Gretchenes Latkes (Buckwheat Onion Latkes)

Roquefort Soufflé with Pears

Metz Matzo Kugel

Omelette de Pâque (Passover Omelet)

Omelette aux Herbes (Spinach Omelet with Mint and Cilantro)

A Kosher Cheese Maker in Aix-les-Bains

Shimon Bellhasen is a character straight out of *Fiddler on the Roof*. His office is in great disarray, with holy books piled near lists of cheese orders. And, like Tevye, he loves cows.

Born in Tunisia, Shimon went to a small town near Geneva to be a veterinarian. Because he liked nature, he supplemented his income as a shepherd in the nearby Alps, tending the cows and milking them. He enjoyed the occupation because it worked well with living life as a religious Jew, allowing him to study the Torah and the Talmud while the cows grazed in the meadows.

After completing his studies, he thought of going to live in Israel. In preparation, he studied at a religious community in Aix-les-Bains (see page 212), over the border from Switzerland, in France. When he told the rabbi in charge that he wanted to go to Israel, the rabbi suggested to Shimon that he stay in the community instead and produce kosher cheese.

Apprenticing with local cheese-makers in this land of Reblochon and Tomme de Savoie, Shimon learned the trade, first mastering the art of making Gruyère from the milk of black-and-white Holstein cows. He then transposed his newly acquired knowledge to making kosher cheese by curdling the milk with fungi, bacteria, or plant by-products, as opposed to the usual rennet, which might have come from the stomach of a nonkosher animal or one that was not killed in a kosher manner.

Since Shimon, as a trained veterinarian, had taken care of their cows, the normally suspicious local farmers trusted him. Now he gets all of his milk from farmers who understand that for religious reasons he cannot produce cheese on the Sabbath. Today he makes over twenty different kinds of French cheeses, including Tomme de Savoie and Reblochon, distributing them throughout France.

Not only did the rabbi find him a profession, but he also found Shimon a Jewish bride from Beirut, and they now have eleven children. As he patted one of his cows, the oldest in all of Haute-Savoie, he said, *"J'ai la vie qu'il me faut. J'ai trouvé mon métier des shamayim. Baruch ha Shem."* ("I have the life that I should have. I found my job from the heavens. Blessed be the Name of God.")

Quiche à l'Oignon

(ONION TART LORRAINE)

THE EVER-POPULAR *LARDON*-LACED *quiche Lorraine* is off limits for Jews who eschew pork. In an effort to adapt the regional specialty to fit their dietary limitations, the Jews of Alsace and Lorraine created this onion tart, which I find delicious. I learned how to make it from the great chef André Soltner, who, before he came to America, worked for a kosher caterer in his native Alsace. Trust me, you won't miss the bacon.

To make the crust, put the flour, butter, vegetable shortening, and salt in a food processor fitted with a steel blade, and pulse until crumbly. Gradually add 2 tablespoons cold water, pulsing until the dough forms a ball. Remove, cover in plastic wrap, and refrigerate for 30 minutes.

On a floured surface, roll out the dough to about 10 inches in diameter. Gently lay it in an ungreased 9-inch tart pan with a removable bottom, pressing the dough into the sides and trimming off any excess dough. Cover the dough closely with aluminum foil, and refrigerate for a few hours or overnight.

To make the filling, heat the butter in a frying pan. Add the onions, sugar, and salt to taste, and sauté over low heat, covered, for about 30 minutes, or until the onions are golden and soft. Set aside to cool.

Preheat the oven to 450 degrees. Fill the foil-lined crust with enough dried beans to cover the bottom. Bake for 10 minutes. Reduce the temperature to 375 degrees, and cook for 5 more minutes. Remove the foil and the beans.

Put the eggs, cream, nutmeg, and salt and pepper in a mixing bowl, and beat them together until blended. Fold in the onions, then transfer the filling to the pie crust and scatter the chives on top. Return it to the oven, and bake for 30 minutes, or until the center is set and custardlike. Serve warm or at room temperature.

NOTE You can substitute prepared puff pastry for the crust.

 YIELD: 6 SERVINGS

CRUST

2 cups all-purpose flour, plus more for the work surface

5 tablespoons cold unsalted butter, cut into small cubes

5 tablespoons vegetable shortening

Pinch of salt

Dried beans for weighting the crust

FILLING

2 tablespoons unsalted butter

1 pound (about 4 small) onions, peeled, and thinly sliced in rings

2 teaspoons sugar

Salt to taste

3 large eggs

3 tablespoons heavy cream

¼ teaspoon grated nutmeg

Freshly ground pepper to taste

A handful of chives

Quiche Savoyarde à la Tomme

(SAVOYARD TOMATO AND CHEESE QUICHE)

AFTER GETTING REACQUAINTED over a game of Ping-Pong with Caroline and Philippe Moos, cousins I had not seen in many years, I joined them for a dairy dinner with four of their nine children in their house in Aix-les-Bains (see page 212). The meal was delicious, consisting of a vegetable soup, an apricot tart for dessert, and this Savoyard tomato-and-cheese quiche as the main course. This is one of those great recipes in which you can substitute almost any leftover cheese you may have in your refrigerator.

 YIELD: 6 TO 8 SERVINGS

2 cups all-purpose flour, plus
  more for the work surface
2 teaspoons baking powder
Pinch of salt, plus more to taste
6 tablespoons cold unsalted
  butter, cut into small cubes
2 large tomatoes (about
  1 pound)
Freshly ground pepper to taste
1 tablespoon Dijon mustard
8 ounces sliced Tomme de
  Savoie, Cantal, or Cheddar,
  crumbled goat cheese, or
  cubes of feta
A handful of black Niçoise
  olives, pitted and roughly
  chopped
2 tablespoons olive oil
1 teaspoon dried oregano,
  or 2 tablespoons chopped
  fresh oregano leaves
2 tablespoons grated Parmesan
  cheese

Preheat the oven to 425 degrees.

Put the flour, baking powder, and a pinch of salt in the bowl of a food processor fitted with a steel blade. Add the butter, and pulse in short spurts until crumbly. Drizzle in ⅓ cup ice water, and continue to pulse until the dough comes together into a ball. Wrap the dough in plastic wrap, and refrigerate for at least 30 minutes.

Cut the tomatoes into ⅛-inch-thick rounds. Remove the seeds, then put the tomatoes in one layer on a large plate, and sprinkle with salt and freshly ground pepper to taste. Let sit for a few minutes.

On a floured surface, roll out the dough to about 10 inches in diameter. Gently lay it in an ungreased 9-inch tart pan with a removable bottom, pressing the dough into the sides and trimming off any excess.

Using a rubber spatula, spread the mustard over the bottom of the crust, and put the cheese on top.

Drain and discard any liquid that has seeped out of the tomatoes, and then blot them dry with paper towels. Arrange the slices on top of the cheese, and scatter the olives over. Drizzle the olive oil over all, and sprinkle with the oregano, Parmesan cheese, and more freshly ground pepper to taste.

Put the tart in the oven, and bake for about 30 minutes, or until the crust is golden.

Another Moos family, in Aix-les-Bains

Tomato *clafoutis* in the shop window

Crustless *Quiche Clafoutis* with Cherry Tomatoes, Basil, and Olive Oil

SOMETIMES I DISCOVER DISHES that are perfectly in accord with the laws of kashrut in unlikely places. Walking around a neighborhood market in Paris one day, I wandered into a small delicatessen shop called Partout et Tout Mieux, which translates as "Everywhere and Better." An alluring cherry-tomato-and-basil tart sitting invitingly in the window caught my eye. So I went in and complimented Marie Le Bechennec, the shop owner, on the lovely-looking quiche. I explained that I was writing a cookbook on Jewish food in France and this crustless quiche would fit perfectly into a dairy meal. She replied that she and her husband, Serge, are from Brittany and have many Jewish customers. During the war, her father-in-law was taken prisoner by the Germans because he had hidden Jews who were being mistreated. She paused for a moment. "You know, I think my son is tolerant because he heard this strong voice growing up. That is the only way that tolerance will be translated from generation to generation."

Mary calls this dish a *quiche clafoutis*. In French cuisine, a quiche is a custard of eggs and milk or cream baked in a pastry crust. And *clafoutis* comes from the verb *clafir,* meaning "to fill up" or "puff up." In this case, the bright-red tomatoes and green basil puff up to the top of the custard.

I vary this dish by adding Parmesan and goat cheese; in winter try sautéed mushrooms or one package of frozen spinach and a handful of chives.

YIELD: 6 TO 8 SERVINGS

1 tablespoon olive oil, plus more for greasing pan

¼ cup whole fresh basil leaves

6 large eggs

3 heaping tablespoons crème fraîche

1 cup milk

⅓ cup crumbled goat cheese

4 tablespoons grated Parmesan cheese

3 tablespoons all-purpose flour

1 teaspoon salt

Freshly ground pepper to taste

2 pints cherry or grape tomatoes

Grease and line the bottom and sides of a 10-inch quiche mold or springform pan with parchment paper.

Put the basil leaves in a small cup, and coat with the tablespoon of olive oil, letting them macerate while you prepare the quiche.

Whisk the eggs in a medium bowl. Then stir in the crème fraîche, milk, goat cheese, Parmesan cheese, flour, salt, and freshly ground pepper to taste, making sure there are no lumps of flour.

Put the cherry tomatoes in the prepared pan, cover with the egg mixture, and poke the basil leaves in throughout.

Put the quiche in a cold oven, and then turn up the heat to 350 degrees. Cook for about 45 minutes, or until a toothpick comes out clean and the quiche starts to turn slightly golden on top. Serve immediately or at room temperature.

A Jewish Twist on *Tarte Flambée*

IF ANYTHING IS TYPICAL OF ALSACE, it is *tarte flambée,* a pizzalike flat bread covered with runny white and tangy cheese (a thin mixture of farmer's cheese, crème fraîche, heavy cream, and *fromage blanc* or Gruyère, depending on your preference) and a sprinkling of diced onions and *lardons.* Dating back hundreds of years, *tarte flambée* is served everywhere in Alsace, with connoisseurs arguing about their favorite versions. In the old days, the farmers would take leftover bread dough, roll it out paper-thin, spread some heavy cream mixed with egg over it, scatter some *lardons* or ham and onions on top, put it in a hot, wood-burning oven, and—*voilà!*—dinner was ready. The tradition still stands today, and *tarte flambée* is particularly enjoyed accompanied by a green salad as a simple Sunday night dinner.

At the end of a late Sunday afternoon in April, I was driving Yves Alexandre, a traveling salesman who loves to cook, near fields resplendent with signs of spring—white asparagus and rhubarb, and yellow rapeseed flowers (more commonly known in the United States as the flowers that produce canola). We stopped at Le Marronnier, a charming *winstub* in Stutzheim, a little town about ten miles from Strasbourg. It was here that I tasted my first *tarte flambée.* Most of the patrons were seated at outdoor tables in the cobblestoned courtyard with wisteria climbing over the brick walls. A *marronnier,* a sprawling chestnut tree, stood smack in the center of the patio.

"You have to eat the tart hot," Yves told me as tarts were being rushed to tables near us. The two Mauritian *tarte-flambée* bakers make a few hundred every Sunday, with a topping of farmer's cheese and crème fraîche. This Jewish version, with leftover challah dough as a base, of course omits the ham or bacon. At Passover, Yves told me, some Alsatian Jews use matzo for their Sunday night *tarte flambée.*

Preheat the oven to 500 degrees, and sprinkle a baking sheet with semolina.

Roll out the dough on a floured surface into a paper-thin circle measuring about 18 inches in diameter. Carefully fold in quarters, transfer, and unfold on the baking sheet.

Mix the farmer's cheese and the crème fraîche in a small bowl, and spoon over the dough. Then scatter the onions or shallots over the cheese. Drizzle the oil on top, season with salt, pepper, and nutmeg to taste, and, if you like, scatter the Gruyère cheese over all.

Bake in the oven for about 10 minutes, or until it is golden and the onions or shallots have softened.

D   YIELD: 6 TO 8 SERVINGS

Semolina for the baking pan
1 pound leftover challah
    dough (see page 128)
½ cup farmer's cheese
¼ cup crème fraîche
1 cup very finely chopped
    onions or shallots
1 tablespoon canola oil
Salt and freshly ground pepper
Grated nutmeg to taste
½ cup shredded Gruyère

Kugel Is the King of the Sabbath Meal

■

> I had Shabbes dinner with Cohn. He served kugel and it was with a guilty conscience that I ate this holy national dish, which has done more to preserve Judaism than all three issues of the *Zeitschrift*.
>
> —Heinrich Heine, letter to Moses Moser, December 19, 1825

The poet Heinrich Heine was not the only one who liked kugel. It was the nineteenth-century Alsatian writer Alexandre Weill who called it the king of the Sabbath meal. In his memoir, *Ma Jeunesse,* he said that on Friday night his family would also have a *schaleth*, which he called "the first cousin of a kugel." He said that Sarah in the Bible invented the *schaleth* in honor of the angels who visited her but continued that the "*schaleth* was still the vassal of Seigneur Kougel."

Kugel originated in Alsace-Lorraine and the Rhineland of southern Germany, since the word comes from the Germanic root meaning "ball" or "globe." Kugel, here put in a shallow terra-cotta vessel, was baked in the oven next to a pot of *choucroute* or *pot-au-feu,* and another pot of beans for the Sabbath. People passing through Alsace-Lorraine and southern Germany on their exodus out of France during expulsions learned about kugels and took them eastward, to Poland and Russia. Originally made of leftover bread and suet, they eventually included dried or fresh pears and/or prunes and sometimes onions. As potatoes and homemade noodles became popular, and industrial rectangular pans came into existence, Jews adapted them to this Sabbath side dish.

Alsatian Pear Kugel with Prunes

BOSC PEARS AND ITALIAN BLUE PLUMS (dried for use in the winter) are fruits that were most often put into kugel. This very old Alsatian Sabbath kugel uses leftover bread that is soaked in water, squeezed to remove any excess moisture, and then mixed with the dried or fresh fruit and left to stew in the oven overnight. Some, like this version, include onions, which add a savory dimension to the sweetness of the fruit and the dough. I love this dish, which I serve in my home for Rosh Hashanah and the Sabbath as a side dish with brisket.

One of the oldest and most delicious kugels

Alsatian Pear Kugel continued

 YIELD: 6 TO 8 SERVINGS

5 tablespoons vegetable oil

2 pounds (4 cups) ripe Bosc
    pears

2 small onions (about
    ½ pound), peeled and cut
    into 1-inch dice

½ teaspoon salt

½ loaf white bread (about
    7 ounces)

¾ cup sugar

6 tablespoons butter or *pareve*
    margarine, melted

3 large eggs

1½ cups pitted prunes

1 teaspoon ground cinnamon

Juice of 1 lemon

Preheat the oven to 350 degrees, and grease a 9-inch springform pan with 2 tablespoons of the oil.

Peel the pears, and cut all but one of them into 1-inch cubes.

Heat the remaining 3 tablespoons of the oil over medium-high heat in a skillet. Lightly sauté the onions until they are translucent. Remove from the heat, salt lightly, and allow them to cool slightly.

Soak the bread for a few seconds in lukewarm water, and squeeze dry. Put in a large bowl and, using a wooden spoon or spatula, mix with ¼ cup of the sugar, and the butter or *pareve* margarine. Stir in the eggs, the onions, and half of the diced pears, setting aside the remaining pears for the sauce.

Pour the batter into the springform pan, and bake for 1½ to 1¾ hours.

While the kugel is cooking, make the sauce. In a heavy saucepan set over medium-high heat, put 1 cup water, the remaining ½ cup sugar, the prunes, cinnamon, lemon juice, and the remaining diced pears. Cook this compote mixture uncovered for 30 minutes.

Finely grate the reserved whole pear and stir it into the cooked compote.

When the kugel is done, remove from the oven and set on a rack to cool for about 20 minutes. Unmold from the pan onto a serving platter, and spoon half of the compote over it. Serve the remaining compote on the side.

A perfect slice of kugel

NOTE You can make this kugel using only prunes or plums in place of the pears, and use them in the sauce as well.

Nudel Schaleth

(NOODLE KUGEL WITH APPLES)

WHEN THE FRENCH MAKE NOODLE KUGEL, it is more delicate and savory than the rich, creamy confections that Americans know. This *nudel schaleth* or pudding is derived from the Sabbath pudding baked in the oven overnight. Here is where linguistic immigration gets all mixed up—some call it noodle *schaleth,* others noodle kugel.

Preheat the oven to 375 degrees and grease a 6-cup soufflé dish or equivalent baking dish with butter or oil.

Cook the noodles in boiling salted water until *al dente,* slightly less than recommended by the package instructions. Drain in a colander.

Put the egg whites in the bowl of an electric mixer and beat until stiff but not dry.

Put the egg yolks in another bowl, and whisk in the sugar, ½ teaspoon salt, the vanilla, raisins, rum, apples, and melted butter or oil. Gently fold in the noodles and then the beaten egg whites. Spoon the mixture into the prepared soufflé pan, and bake for 50 minutes.

 YIELD: 4 TO 6 SERVINGS

4 tablespoons melted butter
  or vegetable oil, plus more
  for greasing the dish
8 ounces egg noodles
Salt to taste
4 large eggs, separated
¼ cup sugar
1 teaspoon vanilla extract
¼ cup raisins or currants
¼ cup rum
3 large apples, peeled, cored,
  and cut into 1-inch pieces
  (about 3 cups)

Grumbeerekugel or *Kougel aux Pommes*

(POTATO KUGEL)

"I WAS LUCKY DURING THE WAR," Albert Jacobs, a tiny man whose personality belied his stature, told me at his home in Ingwiller. "When war broke out, I was eighteen years old and was mobilized into the French army. I left Ingwiller with my knapsack on my back, marching in the middle of the road. My beret and wooden shoes gave me the air of youth." Instead of taking the train he was supposed to take, he and his comrades had a picnic and took the following one. As luck would have it, the Germans bombed the first train. Later, when it got dangerous for the Jews in the army, Monsieur Jacobs had to go into hiding. "Here too I was lucky," he told me. "An old grandmother who owned eight farms let me stay with her. She never told anybody that I was there."

Until he was almost ninety, Monsieur Jacobs dressed up three days a week, drove his car slowly into town, and ate lunch at the Cheval Blanc, where he also often dined with the local priest. "Everybody knows that I don't eat pork," he told me shortly before his death. When I asked him why he didn't move to a larger city, like Strasbourg, his response was quick: "Here I am someone, and there I would be just an old Jew."

At Monsieur Jacobs's home, a virtual museum of Alsatian Jewish history, the jewels were the old cookbooks in the attic and basement libraries. The books contained some handwritten recipes and were those of his late wife. "Books were her life," he said. She collected all the old recipes from her mother, who lived with them until she died at ninety-five.

When I looked through her handwritten book, I saw recipes like *grimserle,* which I know as *krimsel* or *chremslach,* a Passover fritter with nuts and raisins (which I wrote about in *Jewish Cooking in America*), *schaleth* (see page 251), *cou d'oie farci* (stuffed goose neck), *gemarti supp* (see page 76), and this *grumbeerekugel,* a potato kugel with onions, eggs, and soaked bread—all humble dishes of country Jews who used the food that was available.

In the old days, they cooked with goose, chicken, or veal fat. In the recipe that follows, I have substituted vegetable oil or butter for those not serving a meat meal, and I often mix the potatoes with celeriac and sometimes cooked peas or green beans. By microwaving the grated potatoes for a minute, I cut down the cooking time from 2½ hours to 45 minutes. This kugel is crisp and very delicious.

Preheat the oven to 375 degrees, and grease and flour a 9-by-9-inch baking pan.

Heat 2 tablespoons of the oil or butter in a frying pan. Add the onions, and sauté until they are golden, almost caramelized. Set aside to cool.

Grate the potatoes into a microwavable bowl. Add about a tablespoon of water, and set on high for 1 minute. Remove from the microwave.

Stir the onions into the potatoes, and add 3 tablespoons of the oil or butter, the salt, a liberal amount of pepper, 2 tablespoons of the parsley, and the egg. Tear the bread into little pieces, and stir into the potato mixture.

Spoon into the baking dish, brush with the remaining tablespoon of oil, and bake for 45 minutes to an hour, or until the top is golden. Sprinkle the remaining parsley on top, and serve.

6 tablespoons vegetable oil or butter, plus more for greasing the pan

2 onions, diced

1 pound baking potatoes (about 2), peeled

1 teaspoon salt

Freshly ground pepper to taste

3 tablespoons diced fresh parsley

1 large egg, beaten

2 slices white bread, dipped in water and drained very well

An antique egg holder
found in a French kitchen

Gretchenes Latkes

(BUCKWHEAT ONION LATKES)

PEOPLE OFTEN ASK ME what kind of latkes were eaten before potatoes came to the Old World from the New. This onion pancake gives us a taste of that past. Buckwheat, called *farine aux Sarrazins* or *blé noir* in French, is used for this recipe. Although rendered goose fat was traditionally the oil used in Alsace and elsewhere in Europe, oils made from safflower, walnuts, and other nuts and seeds were also used, probably pressed by the farmers who brought them to markets where they were sold. The recipe, although attributed as Alsatian in one cookbook, is clearly from eastern Europe, as the word "*gretchenes*" means buckwheat in Polish.

 YIELD: 8 LATKES

1 cup buckwheat flour
1 teaspoon salt
1 teaspoon baking powder
2 large eggs
2 cups grated onions (about 2 medium)
Vegetable oil for frying
Sour cream or applesauce for garnish

Stir the flour, salt, and baking powder together in a small bowl. Beat in the eggs, mixing well. Then stir in the onions.

Heat a nonstick frying pan and add a film of oil. Ladle about 2 tablespoons of the flour mixture into the frying pan and heat, frying until golden, then flip and cook the second side. Eat alone or with sour cream or applesauce.

An old postcard of the synagogue in Cavaillon

Roquefort Soufflé with Pears

WHEN I ATE LUNCH AT THE ELABORATE Hôtel Daniel, located between the Champs-Élysées and the Faubourg Saint-Honoré, I felt as though I were transported to a salon in Proust's Paris. I met the young chef, Denis Fetisson, who brought out an array of dishes. Among them was this wonderful Roquefort soufflé, which Denis serves to vegetarians and to his kosher clientele. It is easy and elegant and makes a wonderful meal when served with a large salad.

Preheat the oven to 400 degrees, and grease a 6-cup soufflé mold.

Melt the butter over medium-low heat in a heavy sauté pan. Whisk in the flour and salt, and continue stirring until there are no more lumps and the mixture has darkened slightly, about 2 minutes.

Slowly pour in the milk while whisking, and bring to a boil. Remove from the heat, and stir in the cheese and then the egg yolks.

Put the egg whites in the bowl of an electric mixer, and beat until stiff peaks form. Gently fold the whites into the cheese mixture. Pour into the soufflé pan, and bake for 20 minutes, or until slightly golden on top. Serve immediately, garnished with the pear pieces and with a nice green salad on the side (see page 90).

D   YIELD: 4 TO 6 SERVINGS

4 tablespoons unsalted butter, plus more for greasing dish

⅓ cup all-purpose flour

Dash of salt

1 cup milk

6 ounces Roquefort cheese, broken up into little bits

2 egg yolks, plus 5 egg whites

1 ripe pear, peeled and chopped

Pain Azyme (Unleavened Bread), or Matzo, in France

> Young people go from one house to another, helping one another make matzo. Some knead the dough with distilled water, others make thin cakes that they pierce with holes to stop them from rising; others put the matzos in the oven, counting and classifying them. These matzo-baking parties go to every house that has an oven and a room large enough for fifty or sixty workers, and the houses remain open for fifteen days.
>
> —Alexandre Weill, *Couronne,* 1858

Matzo, or *pain azyme,* has always been popular, as shown in the quotation above from a novel about an Alsatian village in the early nineteenth century.

But even earlier, in the Provençal town of Cavaillon, whose Jewish community dates at least to the thirteenth century, matzo, round and poked with holes, was baked for the Jews at Passover in an oven in the basement of the beautifully preserved

Matzo oven in the basement of the Cavaillon synagogue

eighteenth-century synagogue. For years before mechanization, Jews bought their matzo from their synagogues. Because the demand for the unleavened bread was so great even within the gentile community, Christian bakers, according to Professor René Moulinas, an authority on Provençal Jews, entered the Jewish *carrière,* or quarter, to buy what they called *coudolles* or *condoles,* and dispensed them as a special treat to their customers.

The Jews of nearby Carpentras also made money for their community by shipping round matzo all over the world until the early twentieth century, when machine-made matzo came into existence.

In 1838, an Alsatian Jew named Alex Singer invented the first mechanized matzo-dough-rolling machine, which cut down on the dough's preparation time and made mass production possible. At first rabbis were wary of this industrial matzo, which they did not approve as being kosher for Passover. But by 1920, mechanization had prevailed, and the Neymann family, in the matzo business since 1850 in Alsace, started producing rectangular matzo by machine.

To this day, when Frenchwomen want to go on a diet, they often eat *pain azyme,* which is healthy and *"bio."* And they buy it from several companies, including Neymann, located in Wasselonne, Alsace; Paul Heumann in Soultz-sous-Forêts, Alsace; Rosinski, near Paris; and Biscuiterie d'Agen in Agen, in the southwest of France, which makes a more elaborate Algerian Sephardic version. At Passover, these companies go kosher, producing kosher-for-Passover *pain azyme,* known to the Jewish community as matzo.

Entrance to the *carriere* at Cavaillon, where Jews were locked in at night

Metz Matzo Kugel

AGAR LIPPMANN, AGE EIGHTY-TWO, is a living encyclopedia of Alsatian Jewish food. Born Agar Lippmann in a little town near Colmar, and raised in Bollwiller, she married another Lippmann (no kin) and moved to Lyon during World War II. When her son Henri opened a kosher catering company there almost thirty years ago, she started out helping in the kitchen, and has been helping him ever since. Now, using local chefs—some Jewish and some not—the two cater kosher events all over Lyon and as far away as Besançon, bringing their kosher pots and pans and sometimes portable ovens. For Passover they take over a hotel in nearby Aix-les-Bains, where French Jews can have their Seder while enjoying the baths. Today most of the Lippmanns' cooking is North African and modern French. Only for the holidays do they make traditional Alsatian and Ashkenazic food for their clients.

"At holidays, people come back to their roots," she told me in her catering office, just steps away from the Grande Synagogue. Recipes like this savory matzo kugel predate noodle kugels in general, and certainly the noodle kugels we eat in America today. Although the original recipe called for veal fat, I substitute melted butter or vegetable oil.

D OR P   YIELD: 4 TO 6 SERVINGS

½ cup melted butter or
    vegetable oil
6 sheets of matzo, broken up
6 large eggs
3 to 4 tablespoons matzo meal
Salt and freshly ground pepper
    to taste
¼ cup chopped parsley

Preheat the oven to 350 degrees, and grease a 6-cup heavy soufflé dish or casserole with some of the butter or oil.

Dip the matzo in warm water, let sit a minute or so, drain, and pat dry.

Beat the eggs in a large bowl. Add the matzo, all but 2 tablespoons of the remaining butter or vegetable oil, the matzo meal, salt and freshly ground pepper to taste, and the parsley. Stir until the ingredients are just mixed together, and then pour them into the prepared pan.

Smear the top with the remaining butter or vegetable oil, and bake, uncovered, for 50 minutes to an hour. Serve with horseradish sauce (see page 158) or a compote as a garnish, and with vegetables.

Omelette de Pâque

(PASSOVER OMELET)

THESE DAYS, THERE ARE ALL SORTS of packaged Passover cereals and baked goods, even in France. But every Jewish family has a Passover breakfast dish to break the monotony of matzo and butter. I like this typically French omelet, served as is or sprinkled with cinnamon sugar.

Put the egg whites in a bowl, and whip until stiff peaks form.

In a separate bowl, whisk the egg yolks with the sugar, salt, matzo meal, and milk. Gently fold in the egg whites.

Heat the butter or oil in a 10-inch omelet pan. Pour in the eggs, and, with a spatula, push the edges of the egg mixture in, allowing the uncooked eggs on top to flow underneath. Carefully repeat at a few places around the edges of the eggs. This should take about 2 minutes, until the omelet is set. Then carefully remove with a spatula to a serving dish.

YIELD: 4 SERVINGS

4 large eggs, separated
4 teaspoons sugar
½ teaspoon salt
4 teaspoons matzo meal
½ cup milk
2 tablespoons butter or oil
   for frying

Omelette aux Herbes

(SPINACH OMELET WITH MINT AND CILANTRO)

IF JEWISH-ARAB RELATIONS ARE BETTER in Marseille than in any other city in France, it is in part due to people like Martine Yana. A Moroccan-born Jewish sociologist married to a Tunisian, she is the head of the Centre Culturel Juif (Jewish Cultural Center), near the Grande Synagogue in downtown Marseille.

When La Radio de la Communauté Juive (Radio of the Jewish Community) went on the air in 1981, Martine hosted a weekly talk show in which she invited Jews to chat about their culinary customs. "We followed people's holiday traditions in Tétouan, Salonika, Turkey, and Marseille," she told me in her office. "And we got their stories." This was the period when people were beginning to open up about their experiences in World War II and their Jewishness in general.

Like many other French people, Martine thinks philosophically about food. She asks the guests on her programs why they eat certain foods and about the symbolism surrounding them. "I was surprised that so many people didn't see the greater meaning in what they were doing," she told me.

As head of the cultural center, she has taken it upon herself to present Jewish traditions in France proudly to the outside world. When the mayor of the city of Marseille chose to feature the country of Algeria at a city exhibition, for example, she made sure that there was a Jewish presence and set up a pavilion featuring traditional handmade costumes and cuisine.

Last year, during the annual Ramadan festival in Marseille, she suggested to the head of the Arab Cultural Center that there be a Jewish booth. He agreed, and her team of assistants joined her in organizing Hanukkah games for the children and distributing pamphlets on Jewish religion and customs. To their

Martine Yana in her office
in Marseille

surprise, the curiosity about Judaism made the booth a huge success. Clearly, the time was right.

In her cookbook, *Trésors de la Table Juive,* Martine gathers stories and recipes that cover the breadth of Judaism in France. She includes dishes like this old Provençal spinach-and-herb omelet. The omelet, often served cold, is similar to the North African omelets called *m'hemmer,* flavored sometimes with chicken and calves' brains, sometimes with vegetables. Today they are mostly eaten cut into small squares as an hors d'oeuvre on special occasions, such as weddings and Bar Mitzvahs. I love this rendition, with its bright-green color, served hot or cold as an appetizer, or as a main dish for brunch. Use the recipe as a guide, and vary the greens and herbs seasonally, according to your whim.

Preheat the oven to 350 degrees.

Wash and dry the greens and herbs thoroughly. Save a sprig or two of the herbs for garnish. Put the rest in a food processor, and pulse until the greens and herbs are finely chopped, but not puréed. You can also mince them, and then grind them with a large pinch of salt in a mortar and pestle. The goal is to extract the juices from the greens.

Beat the eggs in a medium bowl with 3 tablespoons water and the teaspoon of salt. Then gently fold the greens into the eggs. The mixture should be a vivid shade of green.

Heat a thin film of olive oil in a large ovenproof skillet over low heat. Add the beaten eggs, and cook just a minute or so, to brown the bottom a bit. Then put the pan in the oven, and cook for about 10 minutes, until set. Put a plate the size of the skillet on top of the eggs, flip, and then slide the top side onto a platter and serve, sprinkled with some more herbs; or serve the omelet straight from the pan.

 YIELD: 4 TO 6 SERVINGS

½ pound baby spinach, Swiss
   chard, or beet greens
½ cup mixed chopped fresh
   mint, sage, marjoram,
   cilantro, parsley, and/or dill
10 large eggs
1 teaspoon salt, or to taste
2 tablespoons olive oil for
   frying

Herb omelet, a great brunch dish

Sacks of overflowing goods at Le Monde des Épices

Grains, Pulses, Couscous, and Rice

Reisfloimes (Alsatian Rice with Prunes)

Tunisian *Orisa* (Wheat Berry Pilaf)

Spiced Lentils with Mint and Cilantro

Sweet Couscous

Moroccan Couscous from Mogador

Southwestern Saffron Risotto with Meat and Mushrooms

Spaghetti with Bottarga, Preserved Lemon, and *Harissa*

Policeman's Lasagna

Riz au Safran (Saffron Rice Pilaf)

Macaroni and Cheese à la Mathias

Kitniyot (Legumes) at Passover

> You shall not sow your field with two kinds of seeds.
>
> —Leviticus 19:19

> Seven days you shall eat unleavened bread: on the very first day you shall remove leaven from your houses. For whoever eats leavened bread from the first day to the seventh day, that person shall be cut off from Israel.
>
> —Exodus 12:15

Everybody knows that at Passover, Jews are supposed to eat matzo (unleavened bread), which can only be made out of the true biblical grains: wheat, barley, spelt, rye, and oats.* But aside from the unleavened matzo, all grains should be removed from the home to cleanse it before the holiday. In addition, observant Ashkenazic Jews also remove legumes such as rice, corn, chickpeas, and lentils, seeds, and any grains that can be cooked and baked like matzo and "confused" with the biblical grains, a ruling made in the twelfth and thirteenth centuries in the strong rabbinic centers of Languedoc by Rabbi Isaac ben Joseph of Corbeil, son-in-law of the Rabbi of Paris.

In the Middle Ages, rice, lentils, chickpeas, and fava beans were all ground into flour, which in that state could be confused with the true grains. The list continued to grow after corn and beans came to the Old World from the New. In France, where mustard seeds grow, mustard was added to the list, because the seeds could be intertwined and confused with other plants.

Even though Languedoc rabbis disagreed about this ruling—Rabbi Samuel of Falaise referred to it as a "mistaken custom," and Rabbi Yerucham Peretz of Corbeil called it a "foolish custom"—the prohibition spread to other countries in the world of Ashkenazic Jews. The rabbis of Spain never followed this custom. It is only now, eight hundred years later, with so much intermarriage between Sephardic and Ashkenazic Jews, that these customs are being reevaluated.

---

*Some scholars believe that rye was imported from colder places, while others think rye and oats refer to other forms of barley.

Reisfloimes

(ALSATIAN RICE WITH PRUNES)

THIS OLD ALSATIAN DISH of rice and fruit sautéed in veal fat is typical of so many simple, seasonal recipes. It is adapted from *La Cuisine Juive en Alsace* by Freddy Raphaël. The dried fruit, mixed with an onion and sautéed in a little veal fat with prunes and raisins, transforms the rice into a magnificent dish. I have substituted vegetable oil for the suggested veal fat, and I usually serve this rice dish alongside a meat dish.

Pour the oil into a medium saucepan or a deep sauté pan. Toss in the onion, and sauté over medium heat until translucent.

Add the rice, and continue sautéing for a minute or two, or until the rice is coated with the oil. Stir in the prunes, raisins, salt, and cinnamon, and add 8 cups water. Bring to a boil, cover, and simmer for 20 minutes, or until the rice is done.

YIELD: 8 SERVINGS

¼ cup vegetable oil

1 medium onion, peeled and diced

3 cups long-grain rice

1 cup prunes, pitted and halved

1 cup raisins

1 tablespoon salt, or to taste

½ teaspoon ground cinnamon

Tunisian *Orisa*

(WHEAT BERRY PILAF)

WHILE I WAS HAVING LUNCH AT Au Rendez-vous/La Maison de Couscous in Paris (see page 112), the owner brought out some of the magnificent Tunisian Sabbath stew he was cooking for that evening. It was made with a special North African kind of wheat berries, meat, a large amount of oil, onions, and a mixture of coriander, caraway, and *harissa,* the spice combination of peppers and garlic. This is certainly a later variation of the thirteenth-century recipe for *orisa,* a famous nutritious porridge brimming with soaked wheat berries, chickpeas, pounded meat, melted mutton fat, and cinnamon, found in the *Manuscrito Anonimo,* an Arabic-language Andalusian cookbook. Among the Jews of Tangier it was a simple meatless dish consisting of crushed wheat spiced with red pepper. I have made a vegetarian version that can accompany any meat dish or be served alone.

Au Rendez-vous/La Maison de Couscous in Paris

1 pound wheat berries, picked over to
    remove any pebbles

4 to 5 tablespoons olive oil

1 large onion, thinly sliced

3 cloves garlic, minced

4 carrots, peeled and cut into ½-inch
    pieces

3 to 4 stalks celery, cut into ½-inch
    pieces

½ teaspoon ground turmeric

1 teaspoon honey or sugar

1 teaspoon *harissa* (see page 33), or
    more to taste

1 teaspoon ground coriander

½ teaspoon ground caraway seeds

½ teaspoon freshly ground black
    pepper

¾ teaspoon coarse salt

About 2 cups chicken, beef,
    or vegetable broth or bouillon cube

The day before making this dish, put the wheat berries in a large bowl. Cover with cold water, and soak overnight.

The day of serving, heat the olive oil in a heavy casserole or Dutch oven. Scatter in the onion and garlic, and sauté until the onion is translucent. Add the carrots, celery, turmeric, honey or sugar, *harissa,* coriander, caraway, black pepper, and coarse salt. Drain the wheat berries, and add them to the pot along with enough broth to cover the wheat berries by 2 inches.

Bring to a boil, cover, and simmer over low heat for at least 1 hour, or until most of the water has evaporated. Season with additional *harissa,* if you like, or serve more on the side.

NOTE You can transfer the wheat berries and seasonings to a slow cooker, adding more water, if needed, to cover them by 2 inches. Cook overnight. By lunch on Shabbat morning, they will be a nice golden color and will have a concentrated nutty flavor.

Spiced Lentils with Mint and Cilantro

WHEN VIOLETTE CORCOS ABULAFIA TAPIERO BUDESTCHU makes this spice-scented lentil dish, its subtle flavors bring back memories of the Morocco of her childhood. Now, when her grandchildren or great-grandchildren prepare it, it smells like afternoons and evenings they spent when they were growing up, visiting her in her apartments in Jerusalem or near Avenue Victor Hugo in Paris. Born in Mogador, Madame "Granny" Budestchu, a fabulous cook, is descended from Kabbalists, prominent merchants, and royal counselors to the sultans and kings of Morocco. Her recipes, traveling from country to country, like the path of the Jews, can be traced back at least to twelfth-century Spain. When she makes this dish, she grinds each spice separately with the mortar and pestle that she brought with her to Paris in the 1940s, enlivening the spices with the fresh tastes of mint and cilantro leaves.

P YIELD: 4 TO 6 SERVINGS AS A SIDE DISH, OR 6 TO 8 SERVINGS AS ONE OF MANY APPETIZERS

1 teaspoon freshly ground coriander

1 teaspoon freshly ground cumin

1 teaspoon freshly ground cinnamon

1 small handful of fresh mint

1 small handful of fresh cilantro

2 cups black lentils

5 tablespoons olive oil

Sea salt to taste

Put the coriander, cumin, and cinnamon in a little bowl. Pluck a few of the mint and cilantro leaves, and nestle them into the spices.

Soak the lentils in water for 30 minutes. Then steam them for 40 to 50 minutes, until cooked but still firm. You can boil them for 15 to 20 minutes if you do not have a steamer. Put the lentils in a bowl, and toss with the olive oil and sea salt.

Sprinkle the spice mixture liberally over the lentils, stirring them in. Season with salt to taste. Chop the remaining cilantro and mint, and sprinkle liberally over the lentils.

The Corcos family

Sweet Couscous

THIS COUSCOUS DISH, originally made especially by Moroccans at the *Maimouna,* a post-Passover celebration, has become pan–North African in France now that Tunisians and Algerians are preparing it. They also make this dish, using butter and accompanying it with yogurt, at Shavuot, a late-spring holiday celebrating the giving of the Torah on Mount Sinai and the abundance of milk in the springtime. Sweet couscous can be made with either couscous or rice, although I prefer the texture of the couscous with the raisins and nuts.

In a frying pan, sauté the onions in the oil or butter over medium heat until translucent. Add the sugar and saffron, and continue to cook until caramelized and jamlike. Add the raisins and almonds, cooking until the almonds are golden.

Prepare the couscous according to the package instructions, seasoning it with salt and freshly ground pepper to taste. Mound the couscous in the middle of a plate, and surround with the onions, raisins, and almonds.

P OR **D**   YIELD: 6 TO 8 SERVINGS

4 pounds onions, peeled and thinly sliced in rings

4 tablespoons vegetable oil or butter

1 tablespoon sugar

Pinch of saffron

¼ cup raisins

½ cup sliced or roughly chopped blanched almonds

1 pound (about 2 cups) couscous

Salt and freshly ground pepper to taste

Moroccan Couscous from Mogador

WHEN SUZON MEYMY RUBS THE GRAINS of ready-made couscous between her fingers to separate them, she thinks about her mother, the couscous-maker of Mogador. Unlike Suzon, her mother prepared couscous from scratch. First she would take a kilo or so of coarse semolina, moisten it with a little water, and carefully separate the grains. Then she would rake the fingers of her right hand through the semolina in sweeping circular movements, creating the tiny pellets of couscous. She would rub them against the weave of a fine basket to shape them, and they were then laid out to dry. Afterward, she would pass the couscous several times through a wood-handled sieve to obtain granules of uniform size. Finally, she would steam the couscous twice in a *couscoussier,* a special pot similar to a double-level steamer, which was filled with different kinds of hearty meat-and-vegetable stews.

A North African Jewish woman makes couscous.

Today, with the availability of presteamed "instant" couscous, the process is much easier. Even so, Suzon mimics the gestures she learned from her mother, rubbing her fingers through the grains. Each time she makes this dish, it is a return to her childhood, her family, and a life that is no more in a small coastal town in Morocco.

Although with instant couscous you really don't need to steam the couscous, I still do, to fluff it up and make it lighter. If you do not have a *couscoussier,* use a regular stockpot with a vegetable steamer. If the holes are too big, simply line the steamer with cheesecloth to prevent the couscous grains from falling through.

Bring about 3 cups water to a boil. Put the couscous in a bowl, sprinkle with the salt, and cover with enough of the boiling water to cover by about an inch. Let sit for about 30 minutes, or until the liquid is absorbed. If you are short on time, you can skip the last step of this recipe and merely sprinkle the couscous with water and put it in the microwave for a minute or two, always separating the grains with your fingers before serving.

Drizzle the oil over the grains, and gently rub them with your fingers to break apart any lumps. Let sit for another 15 minutes.

Then, if you want, steam the couscous. Set a *couscoussier* or a cheesecloth-lined vegetable steamer in a stockpot with a few inches of simmering water, broth, or soupy stew. The couscous should sit not in the liquid but, rather, a few inches above it. Try to keep the steam from escaping from the sides of the pot. Set a timer for 15 minutes once you start seeing steam rise through the couscous.

2 pounds couscous (about 4 cups)
1 tablespoon salt, or to taste
2 tablespoons vegetable oil

Southwestern Saffron Risotto
with Meat and Mushrooms

THIS RISOTTO RECIPE FROM Natan Holchaker, a retired dentist and food hobbyist in Bordeaux, includes smoked goose breast. If you cannot find a kosher version, substitute smoked turkey breast.

 YIELD: 4 TO 6 SERVINGS

Pinch of saffron

2 cups chicken broth

4 tablespoons rendered goose fat or olive oil

1 large onion, diced

½ cup dry white wine

1¼ cups Arborio rice

5 ounces smoked goose or turkey breast, diced

1 cup diced porcini, morels, or some other, more readily available mushrooms

2 tablespoons fresh thyme leaves

Salt and freshly ground pepper to taste

2 tablespoons roughly chopped fresh parsley

Soak the saffron in 3 tablespoons warm water.

Bring 4 cups water and the chicken broth to a boil in a small saucepan. Keep warm but not boiling, and stir in the saffron with its water.

Heat 3 tablespoons of the goose fat or olive oil in a heavy frying pan, such as a Dutch oven, toss in the onion, and sauté until golden. Pour in the white wine, and cook until the liquid is reduced by half. Scatter the rice over the onion, and stir until it becomes pearly white and shiny. Ladle on a quarter of the warm bouillon, and simmer while stirring until it is absorbed.

Continue cooking the rice while stirring, adding a ladleful of the liquid at a time and letting it be absorbed before adding another ladleful, about 20 minutes total.

Heat the remaining goose fat or olive oil in a small frying pan. Add the diced goose or turkey breast and mushrooms, and stir while cooking until the mushrooms are cooked through. Stir in the fresh thyme, and set aside until the risotto is done.

Fold the meat and mushrooms into the risotto, add salt and freshly ground pepper to taste, cover, and let sit for a minute or two. Sprinkle with the parsley, and serve warm.

Bottarga, the Mediterranean Caviar

On Boulevard Voltaire, in the Eleventh Arrondissement of Paris, in the midst of a block of bakeries, butchers, grocery stores, and Japanese, Italian, and hamburger restaurants—all kosher—is Koskas & Fils. This tiny Tunisian shop, billed as the "bottarga specialist," sells kosher bottarga, the Mediterranean caviar. Bottarga is dried mullet roe, here already grated and sold in small bags or sold whole cased in wax. The family-owned shop, which has a branch in Marseille, sells different grades of the eggs, as well as *boukha,* a fig brandy also from Tunisia.

Because of bottarga's high price, shoppers tend to buy this caviar for special occasions or for the Sabbath, serving it as an appetizer in thin slices on bread or alone with a little garlic, lemon and/or olive oil on top. Some serve it with pasta (recipe follows) or scrambled eggs. One shopper, Simha Cohen, was bringing it to her sister who lives in Nantes, "*pour lui faire plaisir*" ("to give her pleasure"), she said. "My father cured the eggs himself in Tunis. First he salted them heavily for five hours. Then he washed the salt off with water and dried the fish eggs in our house, behind a screened-off window. He also made caviar out of tuna eggs. Now bottarga is so expensive that we can only eat it on special occasions."

Spaghetti with Bottarga, Preserved Lemon, and *Harissa*

BOTTARGA, DRIED MULLET ROE, is absolutely delicious grated and sliced in thin strips in this simple spaghetti dish with *harissa* and tiny Tunisian *beldi* (meaning traditionally produced) preserved lemons.

Marc Berrebi, an entrepreneur and food hobbyist who makes this dish that originated in his native Tunisia but is influenced by Italy, says, "It is interesting to taste the melding of three strong ingredients: preserved lemon, *harissa,* and bottarga in small quantities." Bottarga is also available at bottarga.net or koskas-fils.com.

 YIELD: 4 TO 6 SERVINGS

8 ounces spaghetti

Salt to taste

4 to 6 tablespoons olive oil

2 cloves garlic, crushed

4 tiny *beldi* or 1 normal-sized preserved lemon, finely chopped, with seeds removed

1 tablespoon *harissa* (see page 33), or to taste

3 ounces bottarga

3 to 4 tablespoons grated dried bottarga

Fill a pot with water, and heat to boiling. Add the spaghetti and salt, and cook according to the package instructions.

While the spaghetti is cooking, heat the olive oil in a small frying pan. Add the garlic, preserved lemons, and *harissa,* and toss together until heated through.

Peel the wax from the bottarga, and cut crosswise into very thin slices.

When the spaghetti is *al dente,* drain, saving a bit of cooking water. Toss spaghetti with the garlic, *harissa,* and preserved lemon in a large bowl, adding water if needed to thin out. Mix the spaghetti with the sliced and the grated bottarga.

A kosher bottarga shop on Boulevard Voltaire

Waiting for Dad's spaghetti dish with bottarga

Policeman's Lasagna

WHEN I MET LIONEL BARRIEU, practically the only Jew living in Auch, a small town in the sparsely inhabited department of Gers, in the southwest of France, I thought he was an ordinary Jewish policeman. But as his story unfolded, his saga became more complicated. Lionel, who also goes by his Hebrew name, Ariel, is the grandson of a Roman Catholic Paris-born police inspector. When the Germans took

A Jewish policeman at work in Auch

over Paris in 1940, the other policemen encouraged his grandfather to help round up the Jews living in the capital. As Lionel tells the story, his grandfather smelled a rat and, not wanting to be part of this witch hunt, went underground.

Lionel, in his early forties, followed in his grandfather's footsteps, going to the police academy while also studying theology, Greek, and Latin at the University of Strasbourg. "When I discovered the biblical texts in Hebrew and French," he told me in his office, "I realized the two Bibles were different. The Hebrew was richer and more spiritual." After moving to Auch, he converted to Judaism with the help of the rabbi in Toulouse, about one and a half hours away, even getting circumcised at the age of thirty-nine. Today Lionel leads a Jewish life with his wife, also a police officer, who does not follow his religious practices. "I go to buy kosher meat at a little store in Toulouse," he told me. "I feel as if I can now respect the animal."

For the Jewish Sabbath every week, which he observes, Lionel makes challah. He used to bake it on Friday, during his lunch hour, but too many police emergencies disturbed his bread-making. Now, to be extra careful, he makes it on Thursday evening, after work.

One of the dishes that he missed most after taking on the obligation of keeping kosher was his meat lasagna. To satisfy his craving, he created this version, using soy milk instead of cow's milk in the béchamel sauce. It is hearty and rich, and can fool almost anyone.

Preheat the oven to 375 degrees.

Heat 2 tablespoons of the vegetable oil in a large sauté pan over medium-high heat. Add the ground beef, breaking it apart with a wooden spoon as it cooks. Once it begins to brown, add the minced garlic and the *herbes de Provence.* Stir the tomato sauce into the meat, bring it to a simmer, and remove from the heat. Add salt and freshly ground pepper to taste.

To make the béchamel sauce, heat the margarine or oil in a saucepan over medium heat. Once the margarine has melted, add the flour all at once, and stir with a wooden spoon until the mixture has no lumps and begins to turn golden, about 5 minutes. Whisk in the soy milk, 1 cup at a time, keeping in mind that you might not need the whole quart. Stir in a good pinch of salt and freshly ground pepper to taste, and remove from the heat when creamy.

Cook the lasagna sheets in a pot of boiling, salted water until they are almost cooked through but still a bit chewy. Drain, and coat with the remaining 2 tablespoons oil to prevent them from sticking together.

To assemble the lasagna, pour about 1 cup of the béchamel into the bottom of an 8-by-11-inch ovenproof baking dish. Put a layer of lasagna sheets on top. Spread about 1 cup of the meat sauce on top of the lasagna. Then cover the meat sauce with another cup of the béchamel, followed by a layer of lasagna sheets. Repeat with the meat sauce and the béchamel until you have four layers, or until you run out of meat sauce. Finish with a layer of lasagna sheets covered with béchamel.

Bake in the oven for 40 minutes, or until the top is golden brown.

M YIELD: 6 TO 8 SERVINGS

4 tablespoons vegetable oil
1 pound ground beef
2 cloves garlic, minced
¼ teaspoon *herbes de Provence*
One 24-ounce jar (about 3 cups) prepared tomato sauce
Salt and freshly ground pepper to taste
1 stick *pareve* margarine, or ½ cup vegetable oil, for béchamel sauce
6 tablespoons all-purpose flour
3 to 4 cups plain soy milk
12 ounces dried lasagna sheets

NOTE The lasagna can be assembled in advance and frozen, unbaked. When ready to bake, place frozen lasagna in 375-degree oven, and cook for about 1 hour, or until the top is golden brown.

Riz au Safran

(SAFFRON RICE PILAF)

THIS SABBATH RICE DISH, typical of Provence, reveals the history both of *pilau* or *pilaf,* as it is called in French, and of Persian Jews who settled in the area near the Camargue, the rice-growing area of southwestern Provence located on the triangle of land between the two major tributaries of the Rhône River. Jews, first by barge and later by boat, used the river to bring goods here from the Mediterranean.

The word and the dish *pilau* come from Persia, taking various forms as the dish traveled around the world. In India, it became *pulao;* in modern-day Iran, it is called *polo;* and in Provence, *pelau* or *pilaf.*

Rice, and therefore pilaf, traveled with the Jews to Provence, where many Persian Jewish merchants and scholars settled and lived until the end of the fourteenth century or even later. These Jews, who traded rice, cooked it for the Sabbath with fragrant spices like nutmeg, garlic, cumin, cinnamon, and saffron. Some scholars believe that Jews brought saffron to Europe from Asia Minor for their Sabbath rice. The late Karen Hess, author of *The Carolina Rice Kitchen,* repeatedly told me that Jews first brought rice to the Camargue. In their *Inventory of the Culinary Patrimony of France,* Philip and Mary Hyman relate that emigrants from the Piedmont paid a *dîme* of rice to noblemen in the year 1497. And although *pilau* and *riz au safran* are no longer particularly Jewish dishes in Provence, they are clearly rooted in the Sabbath tradition.

This simple recipe is typically eaten on Rosh Hashanah, alongside a symbolic whole roasted fish with a Sephardic sweet-and-sour greengage-plum sauce (see my *Jewish Holiday Kitchen*), and goes very well with the sea bream with tamarind (see page 170).

YIELD: 4 SERVINGS

Pinch of saffron
3 tablespoons olive oil
1 large onion, finely chopped
½ cup pine nuts, almonds, or pistachios
1 cup long-grain rice
¼ teaspoon freshly grated nutmeg
1 bay leaf
1 teaspoon salt, or to taste
Freshly ground pepper to taste

Stir the saffron into 2 tablespoons hot water in a bowl, and set aside.

Heat the olive oil in a heavy-bottomed ovenproof pan. Add the onion and pine nuts, and cook over medium heat, stirring, for about 5 minutes, or until the onion is translucent and the nuts are fragrant and beginning to change color. Lower the heat, and stir in the rice. Add the saffron and its water, the nutmeg, the bay leaf, the salt, freshly ground pepper to taste, and 2 cups water.

Bring to a boil, reduce the heat to a slow simmer, cover, and cook for 15 to 18 minutes, or until the liquid is absorbed and the rice is tender. Fluff the rice with a fork, removing the bay leaf. Taste, and adjust the seasoning. Serve warm.

Macaroni and Cheese à la Mathias

MATHIAS LAURENT, THE COOK IN HIS FAMILY, makes this simple dish for his children in his sleek kitchen. With leftovers, he adds lots of Comté cheese. You can use any grated cheese you like.

Bring a large pot half full of water to a boil. Add the macaroni and salt, cooking the pasta according to the directions on the package.

Meanwhile, heat a sauté pan with the olive oil. Sauté the tuna and the lemon peel for a minute or two. Then add the tomato sauce, and continue to cook until the sauce is heated through. When the pasta is cooked, drain and add to the tomato-tuna sauce.

Just before serving, top with some grated cheese.

YIELD: 6 TO 8 SERVINGS

8 ounces penne or other
  macaroni
½ teaspoon salt
3 tablespoons olive oil
⅔ pound fresh tuna, cubed
Peel of 3 small or 2 large
  preserved lemons, diced
10 ounces good tomato sauce
Grated Comté or other cheese
  of your choice

Outside the kitchen where Mathias makes his macaroni and cheese

Cèpes for sale at a roadside stand near Bordeaux

Vegetables

Tomates à la Provençale

Ratatouille of Zucchini, Tomatoes, Eggplant, and Peppers

Tian of Zucchini, Spinach, and Rice

Carpentras's *Tian* of Spinach and Salt Cod for Purim

Papeton d'Aubergines (Eggplant Gratin)

Gratin d'Aubergines à l'Algérienne (Algerian Eggplant Gratin)

Le Tian d'Aubergines Confites (*Tian* of Eggplants, Tomatoes, and Onions)

Fried Artichokes, Jewish Style

Choux-fleur Sauce Persillée (Cauliflower with Parsley and Garlic)

Épinards Tombés (Dropped Spinach with Zucchini)

Sautéed *Haricots Verts et Poivrons Rouges* (Green Beans and Red Peppers)

Sautéed Porcini Mushrooms with Shallots

Stir-Fry of Fennel and Fennel Seeds

White Beans and Carrots

Cassolita (Winter Squash with Caramelized Onions)

Marrons aux Oignons et aux Quetsches (Chestnuts, Onions, and Prunes)

Red Cabbage with Chestnuts

Potato *Chremslach*

Palets de Pommes de Terre (Potato Pancakes)

Brandade Potato Latkes

Gratin Dauphinois (Scalloped Potatoes with Milk, Cheese, and Garlic)

Pommes de Terre Sarladaises (Stir-Fried Potatoes with Parsley and Garlic)

Asparagus with *Mousseline* Sauce

Haricots à l'Ancienne aux Pommes de Terre (Friday Night Green Beans with Onions and Potatoes)

Carottes Confites (Candied Carrots with Preserved Lemon)

Braised Endives

A Sacred Secular Sukkah Sanctuary

> Swinging majestically above the door [of a *sukkah*] as a safeguard against the evil eye, is the glorious, indispensable and infallible red onion, covered completely with rooster feathers inserted into it. No evil spirit in Jewish Alsatian memory has ever been able to penetrate, by day or by night, into a *sukkah* equipped with such a precious bulb.
>
> —Daniel Stauben, *Scenes of Jewish Life in Alsace,* 1860

One recent October, my family was staying at a friend's house in Vence, one of the picturesque hilltop villages in the south of France. Dana Sardet, a documentary filmmaker, invited us for lunch at her home in La Gaude, a nearby quaint hilltop village. We walked past the old stone houses with red-tiled roofs, entered through a gate, and emerged in her garden, where pots of rosemary and climbing vines still heavy with zucchini and tomatoes basked in the autumn sun.

Dana's home, she told us, was one of the original houses in this village created after the plague. In 1920, the Jewish artist Chaim Soutine, who at the time was very poor and struggling, rented one room from the woman who owned the house. According to Dana, Soutine supposedly paid his rent by giving some of his paintings to the landlady, who used them to build a chicken coop!

When we sat down to dinner, Dana casually mentioned that it was the holiday of Sukkot. "Radical atheists, my parents were secular Jews, NYU-trained architects, who were in reaction to most of their Brooklyn upbringing," she said. "I was not brought up on religion except for the food stuff. That was the way into the culture for us."

Although church bells were pealing in the background, I felt that the umbrella shading us from the hot Riviera sun, together with the arbor of grapes growing nearby, created something like a *sukkah,* the hut where observant Jews eat during the fall harvest. It is traditional to hold a *lulav* (a palm frond held together with myrtle and willow branches) in the right hand and an *etrog* (citron) in the left, reciting a blessing before waving them. For at least fifteen hundred years, the Jews of Provence have sold the *lulav* and the *etrog* to communities in France, bringing them from the Middle East.

Dana, who is making a film on olive oil, explained to us that five thousand years ago olives grew wild in the eastern Mediterranean. Cultivation began in Syria and Palestine around 3000 B.C.E., and spread. Olives have been cultivated in the region of Nice for the past few hundred years. Olives and oil, at first sustenance crops for the local farmers, have had a "renaissance" in the Nice area. Many people, like Dana and her family, have restored orchards, or are planting new ones, and spend the weekends in December harvesting olives by hand. "Olives need the hand of man to graft them, to hybridize them," she said. "For that, human beings are ingenious."

Besides cooking with the fruits and vegetables that grow nearby, Dana makes jams from the orange and cherry trees that surround her home. At a table covered with the bright colors of a Soleidado tablecloth, Dana served us our first course, of three salads: beet, carrot, and end-of-the-summer tomato splashed with the family's own olive oil. Our main course was a delicious roast lamb with quinoa, toasted like couscous and sprinkled with carrots and chickpeas. For dessert we had a simple chocolate cake.

As we plucked grapes from the arbor surrounding our table to accompany the cake, I couldn't imagine a more perfect secular *sukkah*.

Tomates à la Provençale

NOTHING TASTES SO GOOD TO ME as the intense flavor of a fresh tomato, picked at the height of summer, cooked down and seasoned with fresh parsley, garlic, and olive oil. This recipe exemplifies southern-French vegetable cooking at its best. I have served these tomatoes as an accompaniment to roast lamb (see page 234) or, in the summer, as a scrumptious first course. They are also great with lox, bagels, and cream cheese to break the fast of Yom Kippur.

YIELD: 6 TO 8 SERVINGS

6 ripe but firm tomatoes (beefsteak are great for this), cored and cut in half horizontally

Coarse salt and freshly ground pepper to taste

½ cup olive oil

2 tablespoons sugar

5 cloves garlic, minced

¾ cup chopped fresh flat-leaf parsley

Set a strainer in a bowl, and carefully squeeze the juice and the seeds out of the tomatoes, letting the juice drop into the bowl and reserving it. Discard the seeds. Season the cut sides of the tomatoes with coarse salt and freshly ground pepper.

Heat the oil in a large nonstick skillet. When very hot and beginning to smoke, carefully place the tomatoes, skin side down, in the oil. You may have to do this in batches so as not to crowd the pan. The tomatoes should not be touching. Sear until the skin starts to brown, about 10 minutes.

Sprinkle the sugar over the cut sides, and flip, continuing to cook over high heat. When the tomatoes are caramelized and beginning to turn very dark, remove to a serving plate, and sprinkle the garlic and parsley over the top.

Pour the reserved tomato juice into the pan, and reduce by half. Pour the reduced juice over the tomatoes, and serve warm or at room temperature.

Friday Night in Paris

Wherever I visit Jewish homes in different countries, the tables may be set differently and the accents of the Hebrew prayers may vary, but the spirit of the meal is fundamentally the same. I felt this particularly one night in Paris, at the home of Hélène Goldenberg and my cousin Richard Moos, as we sat down to dinner in their top-floor apartment in the Eighteenth Arrondissement, looking over the Lubavitcher center, the Eiffel Tower, and the famous church of Sacré-Coeur.

Hélène Goldenberg prepares for Shabbat dinner

Hélène, a pediatric anesthesiologist, lit the candles and recited the blessing. Then Richard said the prayer over the wine and the two baguettes. Tearing the bread into little pieces, he dipped them in salt, a tradition that has various explanations. One is that salt accompanied every offering that was brought to the altar in the Temple of Jerusalem. Another is that salt never spoils and is used to preserve food, therefore making it symbolic of the eternal covenant with God. And, finally, salt adds flavor, reminding us that every moment in our lives should be meaningful and flavorful. After Richard passed the morsels of bread to the guests, we all said *"Shabbat shalom"* ("Sabbath peace") to one another and exchanged kisses on both cheeks.

Hélène was born in Toulouse, though her parents are originally from Poland. During the war, her parents and her uncle escaped the Nazis and were hidden by a Christian family. Her uncle fell in love with the daughter of the family, and they later married.

As we sat around their table, Hélène brought out course after course of simple and beautiful food, including a fillet of salmon with lemon butter, rice, and a special ratatouille. Afterward, she served a salad simply dressed with lemon, mustard, and cilantro, followed by a Manchego cheese from Spain served with a jam of black cherries, typical of the southwestern region, from which Hélène hails, and a Reblochon, produced in the Alps, near Richard's home in Annecy.

For dessert, Hélène baked an apple *schaleth,* which Richard used to have every Friday night growing up.

Ratatouille of Zucchini, Tomatoes, Eggplant, and Peppers

THE SECRET OF HÉLÈNE'S RATATOUILLE is to cook the vegetables separately in the oven, intensifying their individual flavors. This may seem like using a lot of pans, but it is mostly waiting time. She assured me, "You can just let vegetables cook themselves and gently stir them all together."

The word "ratatouille" is related to the word *touiller* and the Latin *tudiculare,* meaning "to stir," "crush," or "toss." After being cooked, the vegetables were originally assembled in a rectangular earthenware *tian* casserole, then gratinéed, and served hot or cold on the Sabbath. Now the cooked eggplant, pepper, zucchini, and tomato may be served together, or separately as individual salads. Ratatouille is similar to the Middle Eastern and North African dish *tchoukchouka* (see page 94), meaning "to shake up," in both Hebrew and Arabic, and to other very old Mediterranean dishes of zucchini and eggplant. Hélène seasons her version with a hot but not fiery Basque pepper called *piment d'Espelette,* from Espelette, a town near her native Toulouse. If you don't have *piment d'Espelette,* you can use hot paprika or New Mexico red chili powder.

A new way of making ratatouille

Preheat the oven to 325 degrees.

Heat the olive oil in a large skillet. Add the onions, the garlic, and the salt, and cook over medium-high heat until the onions are just translucent, 5 to 7 minutes. Remove three-quarters of the onions to a bowl. Add the zucchini to the pan with the remaining quarter of the onions, season with a little salt and freshly ground pepper to taste, and cook for a few minutes, until the zucchini begin to brown. Transfer the zucchini-and-onion mixture to an 8-inch square or circular baking pan.

Sauté the red and green peppers separately just until they begin to brown, with a third of the remaining onions, then the eggplant with another third of the onions, and then the tomatoes with the remaining onions. Transfer each vegetable to its own baking pan.

Cover the four pans with aluminum foil, and bake in the preheated oven for 1 hour. Uncover the pans, sprinkle each with a teaspoon of the sugar and a bit of hot pepper, and stir. Cook for an additional hour, uncovered. If there is any liquid in the pans after the second hour, drain the vegetables and reserve that liquid. Gently toss the vegetables together.

Place the reserved liquid in a small saucepan, bring to a boil, and reduce until it is thick and can coat the back of a wooden spoon. Stir this reduction into the ratatouille. Taste, and adjust the seasoning if necessary. Serve at room temperature.

 YIELD: 8 TO 10 SERVINGS

¼ cup olive oil

5 medium yellow onions, cut into ½-inch pieces

5 cloves garlic, peeled and minced

2 teaspoons salt

4 small zucchini, cut into ½-inch pieces (about 2 pounds)

Freshly ground pepper to taste

1 red bell pepper, cut into ½-inch pieces

1 green bell pepper, cut into ½-inch pieces

2 pounds eggplants, preferably small ones, cut into ½-inch pieces

2 pounds tomatoes, cut into ½-inch pieces

4 teaspoons sugar

1 teaspoon *piment d'Espelette,* hot paprika, or New Mexican ground red chili

Tian of Zucchini, Spinach, and Rice

WHEN I WAS VISITING THE LUBÉRON, we wound our way up to the top of the hillop village of Bonnieux and stopped at the Musée de la Boulangerie. There, in an ancient house, the history of bread and baking is traced. Among the ancient pots and pans were shallow unglazed earthenware bowls called at the museum "*tians,*" which were and are used much like Dutch ovens for cooking vegetables in the embers of a fire.

In the south of France, there are many recipes for *tians,* layered casseroles of vegetables sometimes mixed with eggs and sometimes with rice and served in the Jewish way as a main course for a dairy meal. In this recipe, a nice substitute for the spinach would be Swiss chard, also a vegetable used since antiquity.

YIELD: 6 TO 8 SERVINGS

1 cup long-grain white rice

Salt to taste

4 zucchini, in rounds

6 tablespoons olive oil

1 medium onion, sliced

¼ cup pine nuts

2 bags (about 20 ounces) spinach

¼ cup raisins

Freshly ground pepper to taste

6 ounces Gruyère cheese, grated

¼ cup bread crumbs or panko

In a medium saucepan, bring 2 cups water to a boil. Add the rice with ½ teaspoon salt. Cover, and simmer slowly for 15 to 20 minutes, or until the rice is cooked and the water absorbed.

Bring a large pot of water to a boil. Add the zucchini and a little salt, and boil for 1½ minutes. Using a pair of tongs, transfer the zucchini to an ice-water bath. You can also microwave the zucchini for 2 minutes instead of blanching it, if you prefer.

Sauté the onion and the pine nuts in 3 tablespoons of the oil in a sauté pan over medium heat until the onion is translucent. Stir the spinach and the raisins into the onion and the pine nuts, cooking until the greens are wilted. Then stir in the cooked rice, mixing well.

Preheat the oven to 400 degrees, and grease a 9-by-13-inch *tian* or other baking dish with another tablespoon of the olive oil.

Spoon half the spinach mixture into the prepared baking pan. Then lay the zucchini in overlapping layers in the pan. Season with salt and pepper, and sprinkle half the cheese over the zucchini. Repeat, layering the remaining spinach and zucchini, ending with the cheese. Sprinkle with the bread crumbs or panko, and drizzle the remaining 2 tablespoons of olive oil over all. Bake in the oven for 20 to 25 minutes, or until the top is golden brown.

L'Isle-sur-la-Sorgue

"Turn left at the pastry shop and you will find La Place de la Juiverie," a young man told me as I strolled through this charming Provençal town on the Sorgue River, known for its antiques stores. Very few people who visit this *brocantes* center know that it was one of the four towns in the Vaucluse where the Jews were protected by the Italian Popes who broke with the papacy in Rome in the fourteenth century. The other three were the nearby towns of Carpentras, Cavaillon, and Avignon, all of which have synagogues and old Jewish cemeteries.

Across the street from a new, widely acclaimed chocolate shop, in the old city, with narrow streets, is a sign that reads "Ancienne Rue Hebraïque." Farther on, the center of the Jewish community, once a square, is now a parking lot with plane trees, their outstretched arms shading the cars. Houses built in the nineteenth and twentieth centuries surround the lot. The only remnant of the *carrière,* which housed about 250 people, is the façade of a four-story stone building, attesting to the extensive community that lived here, protected by the cathedral nearby. Beginning in 1650, the Jews were locked in the *carrière* from dusk until the morning. By the eighteenth and nineteenth centuries, members of the Jewish community, despite

L'Isle-sur-la-Sorgue, an antiques center in the Vaucluse, once one of four towns where Jews lived

these confinements, were the leading silk merchants of the town. After the Revolution, the ghettolike existence ended, and the Jews left L'Isle-sur-la-Sorgue and the three other towns for larger cities in France.

A few miles outside of town, on the main road, a small sign indicates "Le Chemin du Cimitière Israëlite." It winds through fields dotted with bright-red poppies. Across from asparagus and tomato fields is a large fenced-in cemetery with a stone door. Inside, the few remaining graves are family tombs. Most of the other stones were pillaged long ago to make houses in the area.

Carpentras's *Tian*
of Spinach and Salt Cod for Purim

GÉRARD MONTEUX, WHO IS A DESCENDANT of the Juifs du Pape, told me that this was a very famous dish from Carpentras, eaten at Purim. (It is also a Lenten dish.) In this town, which had an oven in the Jewish quarter, cooks prepared the dish at home, putting it in an earthenware *tian*. They then brought it to the public oven and baked it, fetching it when it was done. Our modern-day casserole dishes have evolved from this tradition.

YIELD: 6 TO 8 SERVINGS

1¼ pounds salt cod, preferably from the front half of the fish

1 bay leaf

3 cloves garlic, minced

A few sprigs fresh thyme, or 1 teaspoon dried thyme

3 peppercorns

3 pounds spinach

1 tablespoon flour

2 hard-boiled eggs

4 tablespoons olive oil, plus more for greasing pan

1 yellow onion, diced

½ cup bread crumbs

Freshly ground pepper to taste

Soak the salt cod about 8 hours, or overnight, in cold water to cover, changing the water several times.

Then remove the skin and any bones from the fish. Cut into 1-inch cubes, and put in a saucepan with the bay leaf, 2 cloves of the garlic, the thyme, and peppercorns. Add water to cover, and bring to a boil. Remove from the heat and let rest.

Clean and blanch the spinach in a large pot of boiling water for a minute. Then drain, roughly chop the leaves, and toss in a bowl with the flour.

Peel and dice the hard-boiled eggs, and mix with the spinach.

Preheat the oven to 375 degrees. Grease an 8-inch *tian* or equivalent casserole with 1 tablespoon of the olive oil.

Heat 2 tablespoons of the olive oil in a frying pan, and sauté the onions and the remaining garlic until the onions are golden.

Transfer the onions to the *tian* pan with half the spinach and eggs. Stir in the salt cod, and top with the remaining spinach. Toss the bread crumbs evenly on top, and finish with a good sprinkle of the remaining olive oil and pepper to taste.

Bake for 25 minutes, and then put under the broiler for a few minutes, until golden.

Papeton d'Aubergines

(EGGPLANT GRATIN)

EGGPLANT CAME TO EUROPE from India sometime around the eighth century, possibly with seeds carried by Jewish merchants. Often called the Jew's apple, the eggplant has played an important role in Jewish cooking since early times.

The old recipes found in the Vaucluse, such as the Ladino *almodrote de berenjenas,* are present today throughout the Sephardic world in the Mediterranean.

Although the eggplant is sometimes sautéed in this dish, I prefer roasting it over a fire to bring out the smoky flavor, and then chopping it into chunks with two knives, a technique I learned from Sephardic French cooks. You can also roast the eggplant in an oven then pulse it in the food processor.

With the increasing number of vegetarians even in France, this dish is becoming very popular, "modernized" with pesto, crème fraîche, or anchovies, or covered with tomato sauce. A purist, I like to serve it the old way—simply, with a salad.

Preheat the oven to 350 degrees, and grease a 6-cup gratin dish with some of the oil.

If grilling the eggplants over a gas stove, make small slits all over the outside. Using tongs, hold them over the open flame, rotating them every few minutes, until they are soft and collapsed. If roasting them in the oven, cut them in half lengthwise. Brush the cut sides with olive oil, and place them, cut sides down, on a baking sheet. Roast for about 30 minutes, or until very soft.

Place the cooked eggplant in a sieve over a large bowl, sprinkle with a teaspoon of salt, and let cool and drain for about 15 minutes. Peel, discarding the skin and any liquid that has accumulated, and, using two knives (see headnote), chop the eggplant in a sieve over a bowl.

Stir together the feta and Gruyère cheeses, the thyme, the oregano, 3 tablespoons of the bread crumbs, a few sprinklings of pepper, and all but a tablespoon of the remaining oil. Beat the eggs in a small bowl, and stir into the eggplant mixture. Then pour everything into the gratin dish. Brush with the remaining oil, and sprinkle with the Parmesan cheese and the remaining bread crumbs. Bake for an hour, or until golden on top.

YIELD: 4 TO 6 SERVINGS

¼ cup olive oil

3 large eggplants (about 4 pounds)

1 teaspoon salt, or to taste

1 cup crumbled feta or goat cheese

1 cup grated Gruyère, kashkaval, or mozzarella

1 sprig fresh thyme, or ½ teaspoon dried thyme

1 sprig fresh oregano, or ½ teaspoon dried oregano

4 tablespoons bread crumbs or matzo meal

Freshly grated pepper to taste

3 large eggs, lightly beaten

4 tablespoons Parmesan cheese

Gratin d'Aubergines à l'Algérienne

(ALGERIAN EGGPLANT GRATIN)

LIKE MANY FRENCH JEWS TODAY, Jocelyne Akoun (see page 28) is a cultural amalgam. She grew up in a Turkish-Spanish family that lived in Algeria for many years before immigrating to Marseille. This dish could as easily be Provençal as Algerian, the tomatoes having been added when they came to the Old World with the discovery of the Americas.

YIELD: 6 SERVINGS

2½ tablespoons olive oil, plus more for greasing

2 pounds eggplant (3 or 4 small)

About 6 ounces Gruyère cheese, grated

Salt and freshly ground pepper to taste

1 large tomato, cut into thin round slices

Preheat the oven to 375 degrees, and grease an ovenproof 9-by-12-inch casserole.

Cut the eggplants in half lengthwise. Steam them for 5 minutes, or microwave them in a bowl for 5 to 8 minutes, depending on the size, until the interior is soft. When the eggplants are cool enough to handle, scoop out the pulp with a spoon into a colander, pressing out and discarding the water. Be careful to keep the shells intact.

Chop the eggplant pulp, transfer it to a large bowl, and mix in all but ¼ cup of the cheese. Taste, seasoning with salt and pepper. Spoon the eggplant-and-cheese mixture into the shells, cover each with a thin slice of tomato, sprinkle the remaining cheese on top, and drizzle with olive oil.

Place in the prepared casserole, and bake for 30 minutes. If the tops of the eggplants are not golden brown, put them under the broiler for a few minutes. Serve hot, accompanied by a big salad.

NOTE The gratin can also be made without using the eggplant shells. Simply spread the eggplant-and-cheese mixture in a smaller greased casserole, top with the tomato slices and the cheese, and bake as above.

Le Tian d'Aubergines Confites

(*TIAN* OF EGGPLANTS, TOMATOES, AND ONIONS)

IN THE MOVIE *RATATOUILLE,* the rat made a *tian* of eggplant and other vegetables, set vertically in a baking dish.

A similar dish came down in the family of Gérard Monteux, whose ancestors have made this dish since tomatoes came to Provence. The keys to the recipe are to make sure that the tomatoes and onions are of the same diameter as the eggplant, and to use a square or rectangular baking dish. I have made it in a French *tian,* but you can use any pan about 9 inches square. Good any time of year, it is spectacular in the summer, when tomatoes are at their best.

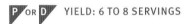 YIELD: 6 TO 8 SERVINGS

Preheat the oven to 400 degrees, and rub 1 tablespoon of the olive oil into a 9-by-9-inch or equivalent casserole dish.

Tightly layer the eggplants, onions, and tomatoes vertically upright, starting and ending with the eggplant. Make three or four rows, depending on the size of your pan, until the dish is filled tightly with vegetables.

Crush the garlic, basil, salt, pepper, and 4 tablespoons of the olive oil together, and gently and generously rub into the stacked vegetables. Then scatter the bay leaves and thyme all over.

Bake in the oven for 20 minutes, then remove the pan, and carefully pour out the water that has accumulated.

Sprinkle with the remaining olive oil, and return to the oven for another 30 minutes, or until the eggplant is cooked. You can also, if you wish, top it with grated cheese for the last 15 minutes.

6 tablespoons olive oil

3 long eggplants, about
   2 pounds, sliced in ¼-inch
   rounds

3 onions, about 1½ pounds,
   sliced in ¼-inch rounds

3 or 4 tomatoes, about
   2 pounds, sliced in ¼-inch
   rounds

5 cloves garlic, sliced thin

¼ cup chopped fresh basil

Salt and freshly ground pepper
   to taste

3 bay leaves

3 sprigs fresh thyme, or
   1 teaspoon dried thyme

2 tablespoons grated
   Parmesan cheese (optional)

Fried Artichokes, Jewish Style

I USED TO THINK THAT THIS DISH, called *carciofi alla giudea,* originated in Rome. But now I am not so sure. When I was visiting Barcelona last spring, it seemed as if every restaurant, every bar, every street vendor was selling this crispy delicacy of deep-fried artichoke flavored with herbs and garlic and served cold. I love it. This is a recipe that has come down in the family of Violette Corcos Abulafia Tapiero Budestchu of Paris.

YIELD: 8 OR MORE SERVINGS

12 small artichokes, or four 10-ounce boxes of frozen artichoke hearts or artichoke quarters

Juice of 1 lemon

Coarse salt to taste

Olive oil for frying

6 cloves garlic, crushed

3 tablespoons chopped fresh chives

3 tablespoons chopped fresh cilantro

3 tablespoons chopped fresh parsley

Coarsely ground pepper to taste

If using fresh artichokes, snap off the outer leaves, leaving only the pale inner leaves. Trim the stems, and cut off the thorny tops about ¾ inch down. Take a sharp knife, and smash the artichokes so that the leaves look as if they are blooming like a flower. Put the trimmed artichokes in a bowl, and cover with cold water and the juice of half a lemon (the juice keeps them from turning brown). If using frozen artichokes, defrost them in the refrigerator the night before. The next morning, sprinkle with salt and let sit for an hour or so.

Line two cookie sheets with paper towels or parchment paper. Heat the olive oil in a deep-fryer, heavy pan, or wok to 375 degrees. Pat dry the artichokes, and lower a few at a time into the hot oil. Fry until golden brown, crispy, and puffed up. Using a wire strainer, transfer them to the paper-towel- or parchment-lined pans to drain of all the excess oil. Gently press out any excess oil, but don't crush the artichokes! Continue frying the rest of the artichokes in batches.

Toss while still warm with the remaining lemon juice, crushed garlic, and fresh chives, cilantro, and parsley. Season with salt and pepper to taste. Serve at room temperature.

Choux-fleur Sauce Persillée

(CAULIFLOWER WITH PARSLEY AND GARLIC)

THIS DELICIOUS CAULIFLOWER DISH comes from Michelle Cahen Bamberger, whose family had lived in Lorraine since "forever," as she told me, until World War II brought her to the south of France, where she was forced into hiding. Madame Bamberger says that she feels and cooks French. And she feels French first and Jewish second, despite all that she went through during the war. "One day, I was going home with a bottle of wine under my arm to the place we were hiding in Lyon during the war," she told me in the parlor of the apartment in Toulon where she and her husband now live. "I saw the Gestapo coming, so, instead of going into the house, I kept walking and saved myself. When we were in hiding, our life wasn't bad compared with others. Because my parents were in the clothing industry, we traded fabric for butter and rabbits. I remember one day we received a lamb roast. That was really something."

Her cauliflower dish, with its crunchy golden exterior, is similar to ones I have tasted in Israel and elsewhere.

To cook the cauliflower, place it in a large bowl with 1 cup water and salt to taste, cover with plastic wrap, and microwave for 4 minutes, or until barely cooked. Or cook it on top of the stove in boiling salted water for about 5 minutes. Drain.

Heat the olive oil in a skillet over medium heat, and stir in the garlic, cooking until just fragrant. Add the cauliflower, and sauté until golden all over. Sprinkle in the parsley, and continue to cook for another minute. Remove from the heat, season with salt and pepper, and serve warm.

YIELD: 4 TO 6 SERVINGS

1 head of cauliflower, cut into flowerets
Coarse salt to taste
¼ cup olive oil
2 cloves garlic, minced
1 cup finely chopped fresh parsley
Freshly ground pepper to taste

Épinards Tombés

(DROPPED SPINACH WITH ZUCCHINI)

I TASTED THIS SIMPLE BLENDING of two green vegetables at Irene Weil's home in Nice (see page 170). Always a big hit, it is colorful, delicious, and a perfect vegetable dish, particularly for Passover. "You can make this dish with fresh peas, green asparagus tips, fava beans—the list is endless," said Irene.

 YIELD: 6 TO 8 SERVINGS

1¼ pounds or 3 bags fresh
   baby spinach
3 tablespoons olive oil
3 cloves garlic, minced
Sea salt to taste
2 zucchini
¼ cup pine nuts
4 teaspoons dried mint,
   or 4 tablespoons chopped
   fresh mint

Wash the spinach well, and leave some water on the leaves. Put in a pot, heat, and stir until the spinach is just wilted, or "tombé." Then add 1 tablespoon of the oil and the garlic, heat, and stir. You may have to work in batches. Sprinkle with sea salt, and heap everything, liquid included, together in a casserole and keep warm.

Slice the zucchini in rounds, heat the frying pan with a little oil, and sauté for a few minutes. When soft, mash.

Toast the pine nuts in a dry frying pan over medium heat for a few minutes, or until golden.

Drain some of the liquid from the spinach, transfer the spinach to a serving platter, top with the zucchini pieces, and sprinkle with the pine nuts and the mint.

Sautéed *Haricots Verts et Poivrons Rouges*

(GREEN BEANS AND RED PEPPERS)

VISITING THE MARKETPLACE OF CARPENTRAS, near Avignon, we almost missed the synagogue, the oldest still-functioning one in France, dating back to 1367 and renovated in the eighteenth century. The façade, like that of all synagogues in France, was nondescript, whereas inside it was a jewel box of eighteenth-century Greek Corinthian columns, and all around, the interior was decorated in rose, green, blue, and yellow. As in the synagogue in nearby Cavaillon, the rabbi's pulpit was perched upstairs, above the congregants.

"In 1358, the provincial town of Carpentras was known as La Petite Jérusalem," Jennie Lévy told us during a tour. "A yellow cloth on their coats and on the women's bonnets indicated that they were Jewish."

Today about eighty Jewish families live in Carpentras and the surrounding area, most of them emigrants from Morocco. Madame Lévy, who came from Safi, Morocco, in 1964, showed me the basement, which has a *mikveh* (ritual bath), fed by a natural spring, and an oven used for baking Sabbath bread, as well as another for matzo. As I listened to Madame Lévy's eloquent history of this French synagogue, I was aware again of how Sephardic Jews are rekindling Jewish life in France.

Since it was on Friday when we visited, Madame Lévy was anxious to go home to prepare her Sabbath dinner of vegetable soup, meatballs, and sautéed red peppers and *haricots verts,* the thin French green beans that are so absolutely delicious.

YIELD: 4 TO 6 SERVINGS

¼ cup olive oil

2 large shallots, diced

1 pound *haricots verts* (thin green beans), cut into 1-inch pieces

2 red bell peppers, seeded and cut into 1-inch pieces

2 teaspoons drained capers

6 black picholine olives, pitted and roughly chopped

Salt and freshly ground pepper to taste

Put the olive oil in a large skillet, and sauté the shallots until translucent.

Add the green beans and peppers, stir-frying over medium heat for about 30 minutes, or until the beans are very soft. Stir in the capers and black olives and heat until warm, and add salt and pepper to taste. Serve at room temperature.

Sautéed Porcini Mushrooms with Shallots

The Holchakers staking out porcini mushrooms at a roadside stand

In season, I would go into the nearby woods in the morning and gather mushrooms, one of the rare items that the Germans had not succeeded in rationing. How proud I was to come home, before leaving for school, with my basket half full of *coulemelles* and *rosés des prés*. My mother would be ecstatic. She could exchange them for eggs or cream—gold, so to speak.

—Michel Goldberg, *Namesake,* 1982

LIKE MICHEL GOLDBERG, NATAN HOLCHAKER was a little boy during the Nazi occupation. When the war started, his father moved to a small village in the Dordogne with a little garden and a well. One day his father told him to "disappear," and he and his brother left to live with peasants in the countryside. Two days later, the Germans attacked. Throughout the war, he and his brother lived on farms, helping to pick crops and learning how to find porcini mushrooms, which they gathered for the farmers.

This delicious recipe comes from Natan and his wife, Josiane Torrès-Holchaker. Josiane's ancestors came to Bordeaux from Portugal in the sixteenth century. Although they lived outwardly as Marranos, or New Christians, the Torrès-Vedras family continued to live as Jews at home. In 1790, the National Assembly decreed that all the Portuguese and Spanish Jews in France would enjoy the rights of active citizens.

As we were driving with Natan and Josiane toward the Médoc wine country in Bordeaux, they suddenly stopped the car, jumped out, and looked at the cèpes (porcini mushrooms) that were being sold by the road. They were so excited, as only the French can be, in anticipation of cooking the mushrooms.

"See how fresh these are," said Josiane. "They are shiny and white, the cap is closed, and they aren't green inside, a sign of their being too old." She told me that sometimes she just serves the mushrooms raw, dicing and marinating them first in lemon juice. Then she described the way her mother prepared porcini.

Detach the caps from the stems of the mushrooms. Wipe the caps clean with a damp dish towel to get rid of any dirt. Clean the stems, and cut into two or three pieces each, lengthwise. If the caps are small, leave them whole; if not, cut them into large chunks.

Coat a large frying pan with a thin film of oil. Put over medium heat, and sauté the large pieces of mushroom for a few minutes before adding any smaller pieces. Toss periodically, cooking until they turn golden brown and their liquid has been released. Drain on paper towels.

Return the drained mushrooms to the skillet, and add the parsley and garlic or shallot. Sauté over medium heat for a minute or two, and serve sprinkled with salt and pepper to taste.

P YIELD: 4 SERVINGS

2 pounds fresh porcini
  mushrooms
Peanut or vegetable oil
½ cup chopped fresh parsley
3 cloves garlic, thinly sliced,
  or 1 large shallot, thinly
  sliced
Salt and freshly ground pepper
  to taste

Stir-Fry of Fennel and Fennel Seeds

THE FRENCH ARE CRAZY ABOUT seasonal vegetables, and particularly, I am happy to say, about fennel. A flavoring that is mentioned in the Mishnah around 200 C.E., fennel is used in both sweet and savory preparations. This particular dish was served as an accompaniment to fish with *beurre-blanc* sauce at a Bat Mitzvah that I attended in Geneva. I especially like its intense, sharp flavor.

YIELD: 4 TO 6 SERVINGS

2 fennel bulbs, including fronds
¼ cup olive oil
2 tablespoons fennel seeds
2 shallots, thinly sliced
Salt and freshly ground pepper to taste
A handful of pomegranate seeds (optional)

Remove the fronds from the tops of the fennel, roughly chop them, and set them aside. Remove the tough outer layers of the fennel, then cut the bulb into quarters. Thinly slice the quartered fennel bulbs, using a sharp knife or a mandoline.

Heat the olive oil in a medium skillet. Add the fennel seeds, and cook, stirring, for about 2 minutes, or until they turn just a shade darker. Stir in the shallots, and sauté until translucent. Add the fennel bulbs, season with salt and freshly ground pepper to taste, and sauté until the fennel is beginning to wilt but is still crunchy, about 5 minutes. Add the fronds to the pan, and stir-fry for another minute. Remove from the heat, and toss in the pomegranate seeds, if using. Serve warm as a bed for roasted chicken or grilled fish.

White Beans and Carrots

WHEN I WAS IN THE SOUTHWEST OF FRANCE in mid-October, the farmers' markets had an abundance of large dried white beans. These lima beans, which came to Spain from the New World, have now become an integral part of the Old World's cuisine. Before the discovery of the Americas, only fava beans, chickpeas, and lentils were to be had. My cousin Richard Moos's wife, Hélène, cooked her white beans with carrots in goose fat rather than lard. The day before, I had eaten the same combination in a soup at a farm nearby. Either way, this is a great fall dish.

Cover the beans with cold water, and soak overnight. Drain the beans, put them in a large pot, and cover them with fresh cold water. Bring to a boil, and cook them for 5 minutes, then skim any foam that may have accumulated, and drain them in a colander.

In the same pot, sauté the onion and the carrots in the vegetable oil or goose or duck fat until the onion is translucent. Add the beans and about 8 cups water, or enough to cover the beans by 3 inches. Bring to a boil, and add salt and freshly ground pepper to taste. Lower the heat, and simmer, covered, for 1 hour, or until the beans are soft. Adjust the seasoning, and garnish with the parsley. Serve drained as a vegetable, or with the cooking liquid as a soup. If serving as a soup, you can also purée it in batches in a blender or food processor fitted with a steel blade.

P OR **M**   YIELD: 6 TO 8 SERVINGS

1 pound dried lima beans or other large white beans (such as Greek gigantes)

1 large onion, diced

2 large or 3 small carrots, peeled and cut into ¼-inch-thick rounds

2 tablespoons vegetable oil, goose fat, or duck fat

Salt and freshly ground pepper to taste

2 tablespoons chopped fresh parsley

Garlic and carrots in the Belleville market

Cassolita

(WINTER SQUASH WITH CARAMELIZED ONIONS)

THE WORD *CASSOLITA* COMES FROM the Spanish word *cassola* or *cazuela,* which refers both to a round clay pot and that which is cooked in it. A Sephardic squash dish from Tétouan, Morocco, this *cassolita* is scented with cinnamon and caramelized onions and gets a nice crunch from the almonds. It is typically served with lamb couscous (see page 236), although it goes well with any hearty meat dish. When I made it for a dinner party for my editor, Judith Jones, all the high-powered foodies attending asked me for the recipe. It can be made ahead and then reheated before serving.

 YIELD: 8 SERVINGS

2 pounds butternut, calabaza, or kabocha squash, halved lengthwise and seeded
3 tablespoons vegetable oil
½ cup slivered almonds
2 pounds onions, peeled and sliced thinly in rounds
Salt to taste
1 bunch of fresh flat-leaf parsley, finely chopped
2 teaspoons plus (optional) 1 tablespoon sugar
1 teaspoon ground cinnamon
½ cup raisins
Freshly ground pepper to taste

Preheat the oven to 350 degrees.

Place the squash, cut side down, on a rimmed baking sheet. Add ¼ cup water, cover with aluminum foil, and bake until the squash is very soft, about 30 minutes. Remove from the oven, and once it's cool enough to handle, scoop out the pulp into a large bowl.

Heat the oil in a large skillet, toss in the almonds, and cook until golden. With a slotted spoon, remove to a plate, and set aside. Sauté the onions in the same pan over medium heat until translucent. Then add salt to taste, 2 tablespoons of the parsley, 2 teaspoons of the sugar, the cinnamon, and the raisins, and continue to cook, stirring occasionally, for about 30 more minutes, or until the onions are caramelized.

Gently fold the onions into the squash. Season with pepper and more salt, if necessary, and sprinkle with the remaining parsley, the almonds, and, if you wish, the extra tablespoon of sugar. Serve immediately, or make ahead and reheat.

Marrons aux Oignons et aux Quetsches

(CHESTNUTS, ONIONS, AND PRUNES)

WINTER IN FRANCE MEANS CHESTNUTS, particularly roasted in a long-handled frying pan in the coals. Ever since my mother introduced me to the nuts as a child, they have had a special place in my heart. This winter melding of chestnuts, onions, and prunes is a common Alsatian dish. You can add celeriac to the delicious mix, or, if you like it a little sour, increase the vinegar or lemon juice.

Place the chestnuts and the prunes in a large pan in a single layer. Add water just to cover, and 1 tablespoon of the sugar. Bring to a boil, then reduce to a simmer, and cook for 5 minutes. Drain, cool, and halve both the chestnuts and the prunes.

Meanwhile, sauté the onions in the oil or butter in a frying pan until golden.

Add the 4 remaining tablespoons of sugar to the onions, as well as salt and freshly ground pepper to taste, the lemon juice or vinegar, and the cinnamon. Then stir in the chestnuts and prunes, and cook for 5 more minutes. Serve warm or at room temperature.

P OR D YIELD: 6 TO 8 SERVINGS

1 pound canned, bottled,
    or fresh peeled chestnuts
    (see note)
1 pound pitted prunes
5 tablespoons sugar
4 medium onions, peeled and
    thinly sliced in rounds
4 tablespoons vegetable oil or
    unsalted butter
Salt and freshly ground pepper
    to taste
Juice of ½ lemon or
    2 tablespoons vinegar
½ teaspoon ground cinnamon

NOTE To prepare fresh chestnuts, freeze them for 24 hours. Pour boiling water over them, and let sit for 5 minutes. Using a sharp knife, shell and skin them.

Red Cabbage with Chestnuts

THIS IS ONE OF MY FAVORITE WINTER Alsatian vegetable combinations, and a common winter vegetable dish of French Jews. It is best made a day in advance and left to meld the flavors. Serve as an accompaniment to roast goose, chicken, or duck.

 YIELD: 10 TO 12 SERVINGS

2 large onions, diced

3 tablespoons rendered goose fat or vegetable oil

1 red cabbage, about 3 pounds, the white core removed and the cabbage shredded

2 cups dry red wine, such as Côtes du Rhône

1 clove

1 bay leaf

Salt and freshly ground pepper to taste

2 apples, such as Fuji or Gala, peeled, cored, and grated

1 pound canned, bottled, or fresh peeled chestnuts (see note to preceding recipe)

1 tablespoon red-wine or sherry-wine vinegar

Sauté the onions in the goose fat or vegetable oil in a large casserole or Dutch oven for about 5 minutes, or until translucent. Add the cabbage, sauté for a few minutes, and then stir in the wine.

Add the clove, the bay leaf, salt, and pepper. Bring to a boil, lower the heat, cover, and simmer for 30 minutes.

Stir in the apples, cover, and let cook for another 45 minutes. Finally, add the chestnuts, and cook for 15 more minutes. Just before serving, fish out the bay leaf and stir in the vinegar. Adjust seasonings to taste.

Oil at Hanukkah, the Festival of Lights

And you shall command the children of Israel, and they shall take to you pure olive oil, crushed for lighting, to kindle the lamps continually.

—Exodus 27:20

As Rashi (see page 7) wrote in his commentary on the Old Testament, only pure oil, "without sediment" could be used to light the Temple lamps in Jerusalem. This scholar and farmer also gave some advice for picking the best olives for the oil. "Pick olives that have ripened at the top of the olive tree," he advised. "Crush them in a mortar, but don't grind them in a mill, so that they will not contain sediment. After extracting the first drop [of oil], place [the olives] into a mill and grind them. The [resulting] second oil is unfit for the menorah but is fit for meal offerings." Then he explained that the light must burn "continually" from Sabbath to Sabbath. In other words, it is clear that the best oil was used for the lamps, and the second-best for cooking and eating.

I thought about Rashi and his commentary when I was staying in a fourteenth-century house in Vence, built next to one of the town's early stone olive presses. Cultivated in the south of France for thousands of years, olives, growing on trees that seem never to die, were used to give light and also for cooking. They also symbolize fecundity and peace.

The holiday of Hanukkah celebrates light, and the fried foods that we eat at that time of year serve as a reminder of the oil necessary to light the lamps. In France, for the most part, Hanukkah is a holiday when children play games and receive *gelt* or coins as a gift from their parents. The fun, not the food, is the highlight of this minor holiday, as is the lighting of the menorah, representing the miracle of the light that burned in the Temple of Jerusalem for eight days although there was only enough olive oil for one night.

Even so, many French Jews, coming from other countries, bring their customs with them. They have also created new ones. One custom in France today, for example, is to celebrate Hanukkah with *fondue bourguignonne,* cooking the meat in the hot oil. Potato pancakes have also become a tradition, as you will see from the selection of recipes that follows.

Potato *Chremslach*

THIS RECIPE, MADE FROM MASHED POTATOES fried in little patties, came from Poland to Metz a century ago. I have tasted different versions of Passover and Hanukkah *chremslach,* whose name refers to the well in the pan in which they were traditionally formed before frying. Sometimes stuffed with meat, they should be eaten piping hot, as directly from the pan as your fingers and tongue can stand.

 YIELD: ABOUT 24
CHREMSLACH, SERVING
6 TO 8

3 large potatoes (about
1½ pounds), peeled
2 large eggs, separated
Salt and freshly ground pepper
to taste
Peanut or vegetable oil for
frying

Put the potatoes in a pot, cover with cold water, and boil for about 20 minutes, or until easily pierced with a knife. Drain them, and when they are cool enough to handle, press them through a potato masher or ricer.

Mix the potatoes with the egg yolks, and season with salt and freshly ground pepper to taste.

Using a standing mixer, beat the egg whites to stiff peaks, and fold into the potato mixture.

Fill a wok or deep pot with about 4 inches of oil, and heat to about 375 degrees. Take about a tablespoon of potato batter at a time and form carefully into a ball. Then gently drop about three at a time into the oil. Fry for about 2 minutes, or until golden and crisp. Continue until the batter is used up. Drain on paper towels, and serve immediately.

Palets de Pommes de Terre

(POTATO PANCAKES)

ALTHOUGH POTATO PANCAKES (OR LATKES) go by many names in France—*palets de pommes de terre, pommes dauphines,* the Alsatian *grumbeerkischle,* and *matafans,* a mashed-potato latke typical of Savoie—a latke by any other name is still a latke. In Poland, these egg-free latkes are made with older potatoes, whose increased starch helps bind them together. You can just dress the traditional latke with a dollop of applesauce, or you can try a variation made with apples and sugar.

Using a box grater or the shredding blade of a food processor, grate the potatoes. Toss them with the flour, and add salt and pepper to taste.

Heat enough oil in a large skillet over medium-high heat just to cover the bottom of the pan. Gently drop about 2 tablespoons of the potato mixture into the pan. Repeat with two or three more. Then flatten each with the back of a spoon to ¼ inch thick and allow the pancakes to brown on one side before flipping them over. Once they are brown on both sides, drain them on a paper towel, and serve warm sprinkled with sugar.

YIELD: 8 TO 10 PANCAKES

1 pound Yukon Gold or russet
  potatoes, peeled
¼ cup all-purpose flour
Salt and freshly ground pepper
  to taste
Peanut or vegetable oil for
  frying
Sugar for sprinkling

Brandade Potato Latkes

OLD COOKBOOKS OF JEWISH FAMILIES from Provence and descendants of the Juifs du Pape contain a famous dish combining spinach and *morue* (salt cod; see page 290).

Morue is also blended with mashed potatoes to make *brandade,* a typical dish of the south of France. The preserved fish is rehydrated in milk or water, and then grilled, fried, or baked. Fritters were particularly common, and are still prevalent throughout Spain and Portugal.

This recipe, a modern interpretation of a traditional salt-cod-and-potato *brandade,* was created by Chef Daniel Rose (see page 68). He uses fresh cod, salting it briefly to remove the excess moisture, seasons it with thyme and garlic, and then cooks it in milk and olive oil. Mixed with mashed potatoes and fried, the result yields a sort of latke that can be served as an appetizer, a side dish, or a main course, with the fennel-and-citrus salad on page 110.

YIELD: ABOUT 16 LATKES, SERVING 8 AS A MAIN COURSE OR 32 AS AN APPETIZER

2 pounds fresh cod, skin and bones removed
Sea salt to taste
½ cup olive oil
1 cup milk
5 sprigs fresh thyme, or 1 teaspoon dried thyme
8 cloves garlic, crushed
2½ pounds russet potatoes, peeled and halved
1 large egg, well beaten
2 cups matzo meal or fine, dry bread crumbs, plus more if needed for batter
Freshly ground pepper to taste
Vegetable oil for frying

Preheat the oven to 300 degrees.

Liberally coat each side of the cod with sea salt, about 3 tablespoons in all, and let rest for 15 minutes. Rinse the cod with cold water, and pat dry with paper towels.

Place the cod in an 8-by-12-inch baking dish or rimmed jelly-roll pan. Pour the olive oil and the milk over it, and lay the thyme sprigs and garlic on top. Cover with aluminum foil, and cook for 20 minutes, or until the fish is just cooked and begins to flake apart. When the fish has cooked, remove it, reserving the thyme and the cooking liquid; discard the garlic.

Meanwhile, put the potatoes in a large pot of cold water and season with 2 tablespoons sea salt. Bring the water to a boil, and cook the potatoes until a knife passes effortlessly through them. Strain in a colander and return to the pot, cooking over very low heat for about 4 minutes to get rid of any excess moisture. Remove from the heat, and mash in the pot until smooth.

Lightly beat the egg in a large bowl. Stir the mashed potatoes, little by little, into the egg. Add the leaves of the reserved thyme. Using a fork, flake the cod, and then fold it into the mashed potatoes. If the batter is too stiff, mix ¼ cup to ½ cup of the reserved cod-cooking liquid into the batter. On the other hand, if the batter does not hold together, add up to ¼ cup matzo meal. Season with salt and freshly ground pepper if needed. Cover and refrigerate for 30 minutes.

Heat about ¼ inch of vegetable oil in a large skillet. Scoop up ¼ or ½ cup of the cod-potato mixture. Form into a ½-inch-thick disk, and roll it in the matzo meal or bread crumbs. Fry in batches of two or three for about 2 minutes on each side, or until golden. Drain on paper towels. Repeat with the remaining cod-potato mixture. Reheat, if necessary, on a baking sheet in a 350-degree oven.

Brandade Potato Latkes

Gratin Dauphinois

(SCALLOPED POTATOES WITH MILK, CHEESE, AND GARLIC)

THE EARLIEST KNOWN FRENCH POTATO DISH is *pommes de terre dauphinoises,* which originated in Switzerland in 1600. I tasted this divine dish of scalloped potato, cheese, and milk, a specialty of the region near Annecy, at the home of Ruth Moos (see page 3), who made it as an evening dairy meal served with a salad and vegetables. Instead of covering the potatoes and the cheese with the traditional beef bouillon or broth, Ruth makes it kosher style using only cream or milk.

YIELD: 6 SERVINGS

1 clove garlic, halved
4 tablespoons unsalted butter
6 medium potatoes (about
   2½ pounds)
Salt and freshly ground pepper
   to taste
A few gratings of nutmeg
1½ cups grated Gruyère cheese
2 cups milk or cream

Preheat the oven to 375 degrees. Rub the garlic around in a 9-by-12-inch shallow fireproof baking dish, then smear the dish with 2 tablespoons of the butter.

Peel the potatoes, and slice them ⅛ inch thick. Keep them in cold water until ready to use. Dry the potatoes well, and then layer half of them on the bottom of the dish, season with salt and pepper, grate some nutmeg on top, and then scatter half the grated cheese over all. Arrange a second layer of potatoes on top, season again with salt, pepper, and nutmeg, and scatter the remaining cheese on top. Heat the milk or cream, and pour over the potatoes, barely to cover them. Dot with the remaining butter. Heat the pan on top of the stove until it comes to a boil.

Bake in the oven for 45 minutes, or until the milk has been completely absorbed, the potatoes are tender when tested with a knife, and the top is nicely browned.

NOTE You can cook this dish in advance, but if you do, cook for only 30 minutes and reheat until the liquid is dissolved and the top is golden.

Pommes de Terre Sarladaises

(STIR-FRIED POTATOES WITH PARSLEY AND GARLIC)

WITH MY FIRST BITE OF potatoes *sarladaises,* I fell in love with the dish. Originating in the town of Sarlat, it is served everywhere in the Dordogne. Cooks sometimes include *lardons* (a kind of bacon) or giblets, and sometimes, depending on the season, truffles or porcini mushrooms. I was delighted when Anne-Juliette Belicha (see page 47) offered to give me a potatoes-*sarladaises* lesson at her home in Montignac. I guarantee that this dish will be a crowd pleaser.

Heat the goose fat or vegetable oil in a heavy frying pan or wok. Add the potatoes, and sauté, tossing frequently with a wooden spoon, until they start to brown and become golden about 25 minutes.

Sprinkle with salt and freshly ground pepper, the garlic, and the parsley. Serve warm.

 YIELD: 6 SERVINGS

4 tablespoons rendered goose fat or vegetable oil

10 russet or Yukon Gold potatoes (about 3 pounds), peeled and cut into ½-inch pieces

Salt and freshly ground pepper to taste

4 cloves garlic, minced

1 cup chopped fresh flat-leaf parsley

Potatoes *sarladaises,* from the Dordogne

NOTE You can save time by half cooking the potatoes, peeled but left whole, in boiling salted water for about 5 minutes, or until almost cooked. Drain them completely, then proceed to sauté in the goose fat or oil until they brown, about 5 minutes.

White Asparagus

■

In Alsace, the white-asparagus season arrives in mid-April, about the time of
Passover. The luxurious stalks, originally brought here in the eighteenth century
from Holland, are sold all over France, and are also exported to the United States
and elsewhere in Europe. They are usually served with a mayonnaise, a *sauce verte*
(an herbed vinaigrette), or a sauce *mousseline* (a mayonnaise lightened with a
beaten egg white), but sometimes, when you're particularly lucky, three sauces
accompany them at once. White asparagus are so sweet and so sumptuous that I
eat them fresh at every opportunity.

While visiting an asparagus farm, I learned that you have to get up very early to
pick white asparagus right away. They grow under mounds of sandy, lime-rich soil,
and during the harvest season, they are picked in the morning and at night. The
spears can grow as much as ten inches in one day! As soon as the white-asparagus
tip pops its head up from the earth, the stalk is gently dug up and picked.

White asparagus are the same plant as green asparagus and have been cultivated in France since the third century B.C.E., but because they are grown underground, they don't produce chlorophyll, which is what gives green asparagus their
vibrant color.

Asparagus with *Mousseline* Sauce

THE FIRST TIME I ATE ASPARAGUS the correct way was as a student in Paris in the 1960s. Whenever I had lunch with Camille and her husband, René Dreyfus, a doctor who was the physician to Charles de Gaulle, I was confronted with the complexities of elegant French dining. Luckily, their butler, probably having pity on me, helped me navigate the many knives and forks, finger bowls, doilies, etc. Because a huge flower arrangement usually sat at the center of their round table, I couldn't see how the Dreyfuses ate . . . and, fortunately for me, they couldn't see how I ate. Once, during the asparagus season, the butler served me white-asparagus spears, which I ate with my fork, cutting them as daintily as I could. To my surprise, Dr. and Madame Dreyfus, the most proper people I knew in Paris, gingerly ate the spears, one by one, with their fingers. They then washed their hands in the finger bowls.

Years later, I ate dinner in Strasbourg at the home of Pierre and Martine Bloch at the start of the local asparagus season. The minute I entered their apartment, I could smell the asparagus being steamed in the kitchen. Then Martine shared her trick for cooking white asparagus: put a little sugar in the water, to bring out the flavor.

Snap the ends off the asparagus. Then, using a vegetable peeler, peel about 2 inches off the thickest part of the stems.

Bring a big pot of water, with the salt and the sugar, to a boil. Drop in the asparagus, and cook for about 15 minutes, depending on the thickness. Pierce with a fork to see if they are tender; white asparagus should be cooked softer than green asparagus. Drain, and set aside.

Meanwhile, to make the *mousseline,* separate the egg, and put the yolk in the bowl of a food processor fitted with a steel blade. Add the mustard, red-wine vinegar, and salt and freshly ground pepper to taste. Pulse to combine. With the motor running, gradually drizzle in the oil until it emulsifies and you have a thick, creamy mayonnaise.

Beat the egg white to stiff peaks. Mix half of the beaten egg white into the mayonnaise, then gently fold in the other half to make a very fluffy *mousseline.* Serve the hot asparagus with the *mousseline* on the side.

YIELD: 6 SERVINGS

2 pounds white asparagus
1 teaspoon coarse salt, plus
  more to taste
1 teaspoon sugar

MOUSSELINE

1 large egg
1 teaspoon Dijon mustard
1 tablespoon red-wine vinegar
Freshly ground pepper to taste
¾ cup vegetable oil

René Dreyfus and Pierre Bloch's family establishment
in a village in old Alsace

Boys with menorah, post World War II

Haricots à l'Ancienne aux Pommes de Terre

(FRIDAY NIGHT GREEN BEANS WITH ONIONS AND POTATOES)

THIS IS ONE OF THOSE SIMPLE French vegetable combinations that just taste really good, especially for Friday night dinner, next to a well-roasted chicken. Although it has become popular to cook green beans for a short time, I still prefer them when they are meltingly tender!

Preheat the oven to 350 degrees.

Heat the vegetable oil in an ovenproof frying pan. Add the onion, and sauté until soft and golden. Add the green beans to the frying pan, stir to coat with the oil, and season with salt and pepper. Place in the oven for 30 minutes.

Toss in the potatoes, and bake for another 30 minutes, or until the potatoes are cooked through and the beans are very tender.

YIELD: 4 TO 6 SERVINGS

3 tablespoons vegetable oil
1 large onion, roughly chopped
1 pound green beans, trimmed and cut into 1-inch pieces
Salt and freshly ground pepper to taste
1 pound potatoes, peeled and cut into 1-inch cubes

Carottes Confites

(CANDIED CARROTS WITH PRESERVED LEMON)

THIS SOPHISTICATED Algerian-Parisian carrot dish, another from Jacqueline Meyer-Benichou, goes perfectly with fish or roast chicken. The sweetness of the carrots marries well with the preserved lemon.

YIELD: 6 TO 8 SERVINGS

2 pounds carrots, peeled

3 tablespoons olive oil

Salt and freshly ground pepper
   to taste

¼ cup honey

Peel of 2 preserved lemons
   (see page 171), diced

4 tablespoons sesame seeds,
   for garnish

Cook the carrots in boiling salted water for about 15 minutes, or until just tender. Drain, and when cool enough to handle, cut into ½-inch-thick rounds.

Heat the oil in a large frying pan. Add the carrots, salt and freshly ground pepper, the honey, and the preserved lemon. Toss to coat. Add ¼ cup water, and continue to cook over medium heat for 5 minutes, or until the carrots begin to caramelize.

Remove from the heat, and spoon onto a serving plate. Scatter the sesame seeds all over the carrots, and serve warm or at room temperature.

Braised Endives

THIS IS ONE OF THE RECIPES that show how Jews have adapted a local French dish to conform to their dietary laws. Though often sautéed with *lardons*, braised endives are also frequently served without the bacon in Jewish homes in France, as a first course or as a vegetable side dish.

Wash off the endives, but do not dry: just shake off the water. Season with salt and pepper.

Put the butter and olive oil in a frying pan, and set over medium heat. Add the endives with their water, cover, and simmer for 30 minutes, turning them occasionally with tongs.

D or P   YIELD: 6 SERVINGS

6 Belgian endives
½ teaspoon salt
Freshly ground pepper to taste
1 tablespoon butter or *pareve* margarine
1 tablespoon olive oil

Gâteau de Hannouka

Desserts

Chocolate Almond Cake

Molten Chocolate Cake

Mousse au Chocolat et à l'Huile
(Chocolate and Olive Oil Mousse)

Gâteau de Savoie (Sponge Cake)

Charlotte or *Schaleth aux Cerises*
(Cherry Bread Pudding)

Frou-Frou Chalet (Apple Upside-Down
Cake for Erev Yom Kippur)

Gâteau de Hannouka (Apple Cake)

Tarte au Fromage (Cheesecake)

Compote de Pommes (Applesauce)

Tarte à la Compote de Pommes
(Applesauce Tart)

Gratin de Figues (Figs Gratinée)

Kugelhopf (Raisin and
Almond Coffee Cake)

Frozen Soufflé Rothschild

Baba au Rhum

Nougatine (Caramel-Based Candy)

Gâteau à la Crème de Marron
(Chestnut Cream Cake)

Citrus-Fruit Soup with Dates and Mint

Parisian Passover Pineapple Flan

Compote de Pruneaux et de Figues
(Poached Prunes à la Alice B. Toklas)

Tarte au Citron (Lemon Tart)

Tarte à la Rhubarbe Alsacienne
(Alsatian Rhubarb Tart)

Torte aux Carottes de Pâque
(Passover Carrot Torte)

Tarte aux Quetsches (Italian Plum Tart)

Galettes de Cherbourg de Mamine
(Cherbourg Butter Cookies)

Butterkuchen (Butter Cookies)

Biscuits de Gingembre et de Cardamome
(Candied Ginger Cookies)

Passover Almond Macaroons

Flavored French Macaroons

Hamantashen (Poppy-Seed-and-Fruit-
Filled Purim Cookies)

Beignets de Carnaval
(Purim Doughnuts)

Montecaos de Mamine (Grandmother's
Melt-Away Cookies)

Manicottes au Miel Maison (Tunisian
Rosh Hashanah Fritters)

Pignolats de Nostredame
(Nostradamus's Pine Nut Pralines)

Rosquettes Égyptiennes

Truffes (Chocolate Truffles)

Bayonne:
The French Cradle of Chocolate

We certainly believe that the production of chocolates by the master choco-latiers of Bayonne will be of a higher quality than that of the Jews; but if a bour-geois from Bayonne cares so little for his own self interest and is such an enemy of his own stomach as to prefer the chocolate of a Jew, why should one prevent him from having the Jew come to his home to make it?

—From a 1763 ordinance, in Susan J. Terrio,
Crafting the Culture and History of French Chocolate

To learn about the history of chocolate in France, there is only one place to go—Bayonne. Standing on the northern bank of the Adour River, in Saint-Esprit, you can feel the Jewish presence in this quarter of Bayonne. It was here that King Henri IV welcomed the Jews fleeing from the Inquisition in the sixteenth century. They came to France to save their culture and their lives, and brought with them spices, textiles, tobacco, leather, and cocoa beans, then called *fèves de cacao* (chocolate beans).

Most important, these refugee Jews, called *marchands portugais,* Marranos, or New Christians, brought the traditions of chocolate-making to Bayonne, and over the years chocolate became a central part of the Jewish livelihood in that region. Many Jews became chocolate- and candy-makers. And those who became doctors used the cocoa for its aphrodisiac, nutritional, and curative powers.

At first, cocoa beans were used only to make a drink prescribed by doctors as a remedy for many ailments. An early cookbook describes the formula: "The principal base [of the remedy] is cacao: the other drugs which are in its composition are vanilla, sugar, cinnamon, Mexican pepper, and cloves; some add orange flower, nutmeg, or ambergris [a waxy substance produced in the digestive system of sperm whales]. Chocolate, warmed, fortifies the stomach and the chest, supports and reevaluates natural warmth of the body: it nourishes, changes bad moods, fortifies and repairs the voice."

As the demand for chocolate moved from purely as medicine to a luxury to be enjoyed, Jews were integral in satisfying that demand: they were not only the most revered makers of the product, but also the largest exporters of the raw materials. A network of Jews living in the Caribbean were already active in the sugar and cocoa markets, and developed refineries for vanilla and rum. They did this despite the 1685 Code Noir, which banned Jews from living on the French islands because they were "enemies of the Christian faith." Sephardim of Bordeaux, Bayonne, and Marseille imported the spices and chocolates from their connections in the Caribbean and rose to even greater prominence.

The reputation of Bayonnais chocolate spread because of the quality of the cocoa beans and the Portugese Jews' expertise in blending chocolate, sugar, and other spices according to the formulas brought from nearby Spain. But little by little, other Bayonnais learned how to make chocolate, and their numbers increased so much that in 1691 Christian chocolate-makers banned the Jews from the trade. The Jews, long the only experts in this craft, were forced to make their chocolate in the shops of Bayonnais grocers, and even took their tools to individual homes.

At L'Atelier du Chocolat in Bayonne, you can see the process that Jews used to make chocolate by hand in those early days. They would roast the cocoa beans by placing them on a concave granite stone and heating them in the middle of a *brasero*. A kneeling artisan would then grind the beans and heat them with sugar and spices. The mass was shaped by hand, then cooled.

At the end of a visit to the museum, one can taste all kinds of chocolate, including a dark-chocolate *ganache* flavored with cinnamon and African pepper, a reminder of the medicinal spices used by the original chocolate-makers. As I bit into the bittersweet bar made from an ancient recipe, I had to laugh at the latest advertisements extolling the "newly discovered" health properties of chocolate.

Chocolate Almond Cake

THIS RECIPE FOR CHOCOLATE-ALMOND CAKE is four hundred years old, and was passed down orally in one Bayonne family from mother to daughter in Spanish, Ladino, and then French. The accent of rum was probably introduced in the seventeenth century. My guess is that at first the eggs would have been whole, and later separated, the whites whipped to give it more height, probably in the eighteenth century. This cake can be made with matzo cake meal for Passover.

D OR P   YIELD: 1 CAKE, SERVING 8 PEOPLE, OR TWENTY-FOUR 1-INCH CIRCLES OR SQUARES

7 tablespoons unsalted butter or *pareve* margarine, plus more for greasing

8 ounces bittersweet chocolate, chopped

¾ cup granulated sugar

¼ teaspoon salt

3 large eggs, separated

1 teaspoon vanilla extract

1¼ cups finely chopped blanched almonds

½ cup all-purpose flour or matzo cake meal

6 tablespoons confectioners' sugar

1 tablespoon rum

Optional garnish: raspberries and whipped cream

Preheat the oven to 350 degrees, and grease a 9-inch springform or cake pan.

Melt the chocolate in the top of a double boiler over low heat. Let cool slightly.

Cream the butter or margarine with the granulated sugar and salt in the bowl of an electric mixer equipped with a paddle.

Mix the cooled, melted chocolate into the butter. Then add the egg yolks, one at a time, beating well after each addition. Finally, mix in the vanilla, almonds, and flour or cake meal.

In a clean bowl, with clean beaters, beat the egg whites to stiff peaks. Fold the egg whites into the cake batter.

Pour into the springform pan, and bake for 30 to 35 minutes, inserting a cake tester or toothpick to make sure it is done. Cool on a rack, and unmold.

To make the glaze, dissolve the confectioners' sugar in the rum and 1 tablespoon water. Mix well. Pour the glaze over the cooled cake. This cake can also be cut into 1-inch circles or squares before glazing. If you wish, garnish with raspberries, and serve with a dollop of whipped cream.

Molten Chocolate Cake

RECENTLY, A NUMBER OF STYLISH kosher restaurants have opened in Paris. One is the super-chic Osmose, which calls itself a fusion and health-food restaurant. When I dined there, it was packed with well-dressed young French couples who could clearly afford the steep prices. The food, prepared by French-born Jewish Tunisian chef Yoni Saada, is delicious and sophisticated. Our meal began with a long, narrow plate filled with cumin-roasted almonds, fava beans, and tiny olives, and a tasty carrot-and-mango soup served in a champagne glass. And for dessert: an extravagant plate with that now classic molten chocolate cake and little marshmallow lollipops.

Molten chocolate cake began as a simple French birthday cake that everyone's grandmother made until the Alsatian chef Jean-Georges Vongerichten accidentally undercooked one. To his surprise, the guests loved it. An instant classic was born, now found just about everywhere, even at this chic kosher restaurant in Paris. The beauty of this cake is that the batter can be made ahead, poured into a cake pan or muffin tins, refrigerated, and baked 10 minutes before serving.

Preheat the oven to 450 degrees. Grease a 9-inch round cake pan or eighteen muffin cups with butter or margarine, and lightly dust them with cocoa powder. Tap out the excess cocoa.

Melt together the butter and the chocolate in the top of a double boiler. Remove from the heat, and let cool for about 10 minutes.

Beat together the eggs and granulated sugar in the bowl of an electric mixer set on medium-high speed until pale yellow. Lower the speed, and pour in the chocolate. Add the flour and salt, and mix gently until just combined. Do not overbeat.

Pour the batter into the cake pan, or divide evenly among the muffin tins, filling them about half full. (At this point, you can cover and refrigerate the batter for several hours or overnight; make sure to leave time to bring to room temperature before baking.)

Bake for about 10 minutes for the muffins or about 20 for the cake. The center should still be soft, but the sides dry and set. Let cool for a few minutes before running a knife around each tin and inverting the cakes onto a cookie sheet. Quickly turn each cake onto a large platter or individual serving plates. Serve sprinkled with confectioners' sugar, and garnish with fresh berries.

D or P   YIELD: ONE 9-INCH OR 18 INDIVIDUAL CAKES

2 sticks unsalted butter or *pareve* margarine, plus more for greasing

Cocoa powder for dusting

10 ounces bittersweet chocolate

6 large eggs

1⅓ cups granulated sugar

½ cup all-purpose flour

Pinch of salt

Confectioners' sugar for garnish

Strawberries or raspberries for garnish

Mousse au Chocolat et à l'Huile d'Olive

(CHOCOLATE AND OLIVE OIL MOUSSE)

EVER SINCE ANA BENSADÓN MOVED to Madrid from her native Tangier in the 1950s, she has been writing to Sephardic Jews all over the world asking for recipes. "My idea is to leave a legacy for the young women," she told me, while visiting her daughter in Florida. "It is very important to maintain fidelity to our traditions and to transmit them to the new generation." Many recipes, like *fijuelas* (see page 360) and *flan,* are commonly known, but others, like this chocolate mousse using olive oil instead of cream, is a fascinating adaptation of a local French delicacy to comply with the laws of kashrut.

YIELD: 8 TO 10 SERVINGS

11 ounces 60-percent-cacao bittersweet chocolate

8 large eggs, separated

¾ cup sugar

½ cup extra-virgin olive oil

2 tablespoons kosher-for-Passover brandy

Melt the chocolate over low heat in the top of a double boiler. Cool slightly.

Beat the egg yolks in an electric mixer with ½ cup of the sugar until light. Whisk in the olive oil, brandy, and melted chocolate.

Beat the egg whites in the clean bowl of an electric mixer until soft peaks form. Then beat in the remaining ¼ cup sugar, continuing until stiff peaks form. Fold the whipped egg whites into the chocolate mixture, gently continuing to fold until no streaks of white remain. Cover and refrigerate for 24 hours before serving.

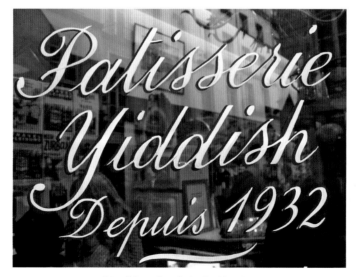

A Jewish patisserie in the Marais

Gâteau de Savoie

(SPONGE CAKE)

Look at those young, graceful girls in their holiday dresses, holding green and brown faience plates covered by white napkins. They are the daughters of the village bourgeoisie carrying *shalach mones* to their families. . . . The theme is a cake called *gâteau de Savoie*. . . . stars, cones, cubes, and round biscuits, and pyramids or domes cut up into slices. The custom of exchanging *shalach mones* plates allows one to give alms to needy people in a delicate way, without hurting their feelings.

—Daniel Stauben, *Scenes of Jewish Life in Alsace*, 1860

GÂTEAU DE SAVOIE IS ONE OF THE EARLIEST French cakes to use whipped egg whites as a leavener. Savoie is the mountainous area between Italy and France, long used as a travel route, and home to many Jews from the twelfth century on. The area was first integrated into France in 1792.

The similarity between the *gâteau de Savoie, pan d'España,* and Italian ladyfingers (also known as *savoiardi*) leads me to believe that the recipe may have traveled throughout the Mediterranean with Sephardic Jews and other travelers. This sponge cake tends to dry out after only a day, but it can also absorb a large amount of liquid. Serving it with a homemade fruit syrup, or just fresh strawberries with a little sugar, will keep it moist.

YIELD: 8 TO 10 SERVINGS

7 large eggs, separated
1 cup granulated sugar
⅛ teaspoon salt
1 teaspoon vanilla extract
1 teaspoon grated lemon zest
¾ cup potato starch or cornstarch
⅔ cup all-purpose flour or matzo cake meal
Confectioners' sugar for dusting

Preheat the oven to 325 degrees, and grease a 10-inch Bundt pan.

Mix together the egg yolks, granulated sugar, and salt in the bowl of an electric mixer, and beat until they are pale yellow and make a thick ribbon, about 3 minutes. Mix in the vanilla and the lemon zest.

Stir the potato starch or cornstarch with the flour or matzo cake meal in a bowl, and then gently fold it into the egg-yolk mixture.

Beat the egg whites to stiff peaks in a clean bowl with clean beaters. Mix a third of the egg whites into the egg-yolk batter, and then gently fold in the remainder of the egg whites.

Pour the batter into the greased pan, and bake for 35 to 40 minutes, or until a toothpick inserted into the middle of the cake comes out dry. Unmold the cake immediately onto a rack, and allow to cool completely. Dust with confectioners' sugar, and serve as is or with fruit syrup, strawberries, whipped cream, or ice cream.

Charlotte or *Schaleth aux Cerises*

(CHERRY BREAD PUDDING)

THIS CLASSIC *charlotte* or *schaleth aux cerises* is adapted from Françoise Tenenbaum, a deputy mayor in Dijon who is responsible, among other things, for bringing meals on wheels to the elderly poor. At a luncheon in the garden of a fifteenth-century building where the film *Cyrano de Bergerac,* with Gérard Depardieu, was filmed, Françoise described this Alsatian version of an apple, pear, or cherry bread pudding that she makes for her family. Starting with stale bread soaked in brandy, rum, kirsch, or the Alsatian mirabelle liqueur, it is baked in an earthen *schaleth* mold or, as Escoffier calls it, a "greased iron saucepan, or a large mold for *pommes Anna.*" Earlier recipes were baked in the oven, for 4 to 5 hours. Françoise bakes hers in a heavy cast-iron skillet or pot for less than an hour, at Passover substitutes matzo for the bread, and, except during cherry season, makes hers with apples.

 YIELD: 8 SERVINGS

2 tablespoons unsalted butter
   or *pareve* margarine, plus
   more for greasing pan
½ cup rum, mirabelle liqueur,
   or kirsch
¼ cup raisins
5 ounces stale challah, or
   3 matzos
6 large eggs, separated
¾ cup sugar
Grated zest of 1 lemon
1 teaspoon ground cinnamon
¼ cup chopped walnuts
   (optional)
2 pounds cherries, pitted

Preheat the oven to 350 degrees, and grease a springform pan.

Mix the rum, mirabelle, or kirsch with the raisins in a small bowl, and macerate for a few minutes.

Tear the challah or break up the matzo, and put in a bowl. Cover with water, soak, squeeze dry, and put the bread back in the bowl. Stir in the egg yolks, all but 2 tablespoons of the sugar, the grated lemon zest, ¾ teaspoon of the cinnamon, and the nuts. Fold the cherries into the bread or matzo mixture. Then add the rum and the raisins, mixing well.

Beat the egg whites until stiff peaks form, and fold into the cherry mixture.

Spread the batter evenly in the baking pan, dot with the butter or margarine, and bake for about an hour, or until the crust is golden. Serve warm, sprinkled with the remaining sugar and cinnamon.

NOTE   You can substitute 2 pounds diced Jonathan or pippin apples for the cherries.

Frou-Frou Chalet

(APPLE UPSIDE-DOWN CAKE FOR EREV YOM KIPPUR)

ONE OF THE COOKS HIGHLIGHTED in a day celebrating Jewish food history and the presence of the Jews in France was Huguette Uhry. I first noticed her intriguing recipe for *frou-frou chalet* on the Web site www.LeJudaïsmeAlsacien.com. Similar to a light, caramelized apple *tarte Tatin,* it is traditionally served at the dinner prior to the fast of Yom Kippur. When I called Madame Uhry, she walked me through the recipe and told me that *frou-frou* means "the rustling of silk" or "to make a fuss," and a *charlotte*— or, as she spells it, *chalet*—means a kind of apple cake. You can substitute Passover cake meal for the flour.

Preheat the oven to 350 degrees, and line a 9-inch springform or cake pan with parchment paper.

Mix 1 cup of the sugar with ⅓ cup water in a heavy saucepan set over medium-low heat. Stir until the sugar dissolves. Increase the heat to medium-high, and cook without stirring. Periodically swirl the pan and brush down the sides with a wet pastry brush. Cook until dark amber in color. Watch carefully! When it browns, this caramel can burn very quickly. Pour the caramel into the bottom of the cake pan, and cool for about 15 minutes.

Whisk together in a medium bowl the egg yolks and the remaining cup of sugar until pale yellow. Add the brandy or *eau-de-vie,* and continue whisking until incorporated. Stir in the flour, the salt, and the almonds, and then fold in the apples.

In a separate bowl, beat the egg whites to stiff peaks, and gently fold them into the apple mixture.

Pour the batter over the caramel, and bake in the oven for 35 to 40 minutes, or until a toothpick inserted in the center of the cake comes out clean. Remove from the oven, flip the *chalet* over onto a serving plate, and serve warm, with the caramel side up.

P   YIELD: 6 TO 8 SERVINGS

2 cups sugar

6 large eggs, separated

1 tablespoon brandy or *eau-de-vie*

¼ cup all-purpose flour

Dash of salt

½ cup almonds, roughly chopped

4 flavorful apples such as Jonathan, Gala, or pippin, peeled, cored, and thinly sliced

Gâteau de Hannouka

(POLISH HANUKKAH APPLE CAKE)

DANIELLE FLEISCHMANN BAKES THIS apple cake in the same beat-up rectangular pan that her mother used. Known as a "Jewish apple cake" because oil is substituted for butter, it is called *gâteau de Hannouka* in France. When Danielle makes the cake, she uses very little batter, and half sweet and half tart apples, a combination that makes a really tasty version of this simple Polish cake. Although her mother grated the apples, Danielle cuts them into small chunks. I often make it in a Bundt pan and serve it sprinkled with sugar.

 YIELD: 8 TO 10 SERVINGS

1 cup vegetable oil, plus more for greasing pan

5 apples (3 Fuji and 2 Granny Smith, or any combination of sweet and tart apples), peeled, cored, and cut into ½-inch pieces (about 6 cups)

Grated zest and juice of 1 lemon

⅓ cup walnut halves, roughly chopped

1½ teaspoons ground cinnamon

2 cups all-purpose flour

1 teaspoon baking powder

⅛ teaspoon salt

2 tablespoons chopped almonds

1¼ cups plus 2 tablespoons sugar

4 large eggs

¼ teaspoon almond extract

Preheat the oven to 350 degrees, and grease a Bundt pan or a 9-by-13-inch baking pan.

Toss the apples in a large bowl with the zest and juice of the lemon, the walnuts, and the cinnamon.

Pulse together the flour, baking powder, salt, almonds, and 1¼ cups of the sugar in the bowl of a food processor fitted with a steel blade. With the food processor running, add the eggs, oil, and almond extract, processing until just mixed.

Spoon ⅓ of the batter over the bottom of the pan. Scatter the apples on top, and cover the apples with the remaining batter. Sprinkle the top with the remaining 2 tablespoons sugar (you'll need less if using a Bundt pan).

Bake for 45 to 60 minutes, or until golden and cooked through. The cake will take a shorter time to bake in the shallow rectangular pan than in the Bundt pan.

Tarte au Fromage

(CRUSTLESS POLISH CHEESECAKE)

NO LARGE SIGN—JUST A PLAQUE next to a simple security button—tells you that this is the gate to a simple building housing the Cercle Bernard Lazare. The center was named in memory of Bernard Lazare, who, during the Dreyfus Affair, was a left-wing literary critic, anarchist, Zionist, and newspaper editor. He bravely defended Captain Dreyfus, and won over Jewish artists such as Camille Pissarro to the cause. The center sponsors Jewish cultural events, choosing not to advertise its location because of previous anti-Semitic attacks.

When I entered this very bare-boned building, it was full of activity. Jeanine Franier came out of the kitchen to greet me, bringing along a waft of the delicious aromas from her oven. Every Thursday, before the center's weekly lectures, she cooks. She believes that people listen to lecturers more attentively if they know a little food will be served. Regardless of what her staff cooks as a main course, this cheesecake from her Polish past is served for dessert. It has become an integral part of the lectures, and was published in the Cercle's cookbook, called *Quand Nos Boubés Font la Cuisine* (*When Grandmothers Cook*), which she wrote in part as a fund-raising device, in part as a way of preserving a culture that is rapidly being forgotten.

The cheesecake reminds me of many I ate all over France, including the one at Finkelsztajn's Delicatessen in Paris. It tastes clearly of its delicate component parts, unlike the creamy block of cheesecake with a graham-cracker crust we find in the United States.

YIELD: 8 TO 10 SERVINGS

Butter for greasing the pan
½ cup milk
16 ounces farmer's or ricotta cheese
1 cup crème fraîche
5 large eggs, separated
⅔ cup sugar
Zest and juice of 1 lemon
1 teaspoon vanilla extract
¼ teaspoon salt
½ cup all-purpose flour
½ cup raisins (optional)

Preheat the oven to 350 degrees, and butter a 10-inch springform pan.

Beat together the milk, farmer's or ricotta cheese, crème fraîche, egg yolks, sugar, lemon zest and juice, vanilla, and salt in the bowl of an electric mixer or another large bowl. Toss the flour with the raisins, if using, and add to the cheese mixture.

Beat the egg whites to stiff peaks in a clean bowl with clean beaters. Gently fold them into the cheese batter in three batches. Pour into the greased pan, and bake for 40 minutes, or until golden and firm in the center. Allow to cool for at least 20 minutes before unmolding.

Compote de Pommes

(APPLESAUCE)

I LOVE THIS CHUNKY APPLESAUCE for its texture and the fact that it uses grapes as a sweetener. The key is good, flavorful apples. Take a bite out of one of the apples to determine the tartness.

P YIELD: 2 CUPS APPLESAUCE

2 pounds sweet apples, such as Jonathan, Gala, King of the Pippins, Jonagold, or Fuji, cored, peeled, and cut into 1-inch chunks
¾ cup halved white grapes

NOTE At Rosh Hashanah, I often add ½ pound Italian blue plums to the apples instead of the grapes. It gives the applesauce a rosy color.

Put the apples and the grapes in a heavy saucepan.

Cover, and cook over low heat for 20 to 30 minutes, stirring occasionally, until the apples are mushy. This applesauce will be chunky.

A few grapes or plums are the key ingredient to great applesauce.

Tarte à la Compote de Pommes

(APPLESAUCE TART)

MY FIRST TASTE OF A French applesauce tart was in a convent in Jerusalem many years ago. When I was visiting Biarritz recently in late autumn, I was delighted to taste it again, at the home of Nicole Rousso. She learned how to make the tart from her grandmother, who came from the Vosges Mountains. Nicole has a penchant for *bio* and healthy products, and uses fresh grapes as a sweetener in the applesauce. I love her elegant French touch of thinly slicing an apple and arranging it on top of the applesauce before baking.

 YIELD: 8 SERVINGS

1½ cups all-purpose flour, plus more if needed

½ teaspoon salt

1 tablespoon sugar

9 tablespoons cold unsalted butter or *pareve* margarine, cut into small cubes, plus more for greasing pan

2 cups thick applesauce (see preceding recipe)

1 Gala apple, peeled and thinly sliced

Put the flour, salt, and sugar in the bowl of a food processor fitted with a steel blade. Add the butter or margarine little by little, and pulse until crumbly. Add 2 tablespoons ice water, and pulse until the dough comes together in a ball, adding a bit more flour if necessary. Remove the dough, shape it into a disk, wrap in plastic wrap, and refrigerate for at least 30 minutes.

Preheat the oven to 425 degrees, and roll out the chilled dough to a circle about 10 inches in diameter. Press it evenly into a greased 9-inch tart pan with a removable bottom, bringing the dough up the sides almost to the top of the pan, and keeping an even thickness throughout. Prick the bottom and sides of the shell with the tines of a fork, and bake for 8 to 10 minutes, or until it is lightly browned. Remove from the oven, and let cool slightly.

Lower the oven temperature to 400 degrees. Spread the prepared applesauce in the pie crust, putting the sliced apple in a circular pattern on top. Return the pie to the oven, and bake for 30 minutes more.

Gratin de Figues

(FIGS GRATINÉE)

Chef Jean Ramet of Bordeaux with his wife, Raymonde

WHEN ELIE WIESEL STOPPED IN BORDEAUX to give a speech, he asked members of the Jewish community for suggestions on where to eat. They told him to go to Jean Ramet, a marvelous thirty-seat southwestern-French restaurant. Run by a Jewish chef, it is located right down the street from the eighteenth-century Grand Théâtre.

Raised in a Polish Jewish home in France, Jean doesn't have many culinary memories from his childhood. He grew up in Vichy, where his parents, like so many other Jews returning to France after the war, had priorities other than food.

But food became a career for Jean. He apprenticed at the three-star Maison Troisgros in Roanne, learning pastry skills. "Pastry-making gives you discipline; it is very important for a chef," he told me. "You need the rules of pastry first."

In the 1970s, Jean met Tunisian-born Raymonde Chemla on a youth trip to Israel. They have now been married for more than thirty years, living mostly in Bordeaux, where they run the restaurant.

On vacations, they often travel to Morocco, because they love the food of North Africa. "Moroccan food is sincere," said Jean. "When I met Raymonde, I fell in love with North African spices, such as cinnamon, mint, and cloves."

This gratin of figs with a zabaglione sauce and a splash of orange-flower water is a dish that celebrates North African flavors and classic French techniques. It also captures the essence of the flavor of fresh fig. As the French Jewish sage Rashi so beautifully stated in his commentaries on the Bible, "Summer is the time of the gathering of the figs and the time when they dry them in the fields, and it [the dried fig] is summer."

To make the syrup, bring the red wine, the granulated sugar, and the cinnamon stick to a boil in a saucepan. Reserve a few tablespoons each of the mint, cilantro, and verbena, if using, and put all the rest in the boiling sugar and wine. Continue boiling for 2 minutes.

While the syrup is cooking, score each fig with an X on the stem end. Plunge the figs in the syrup, and let the fresh figs cook for about 2 minutes and the dried for 5 minutes. Remove them with a slotted spoon, and cool. Then cut each fig lengthwise into two pieces.

To make the sauce, stir together the confectioners' sugar and the eggs in a small pan over medium heat, stirring vigorously until the mixture is thick and frothy. Pour in the Sauternes, Marsala, or Prosecco and continue to beat for another minute or two, until thickened.

When ready to serve, preheat the broiler. Put the figs in a shallow ovenproof dish. Delicately spoon on the sauce, and put the dish under the broiler for 3 to 5 minutes, or until the figs begin to brown. Then sprinkle with the slivered almonds, a pinch of cinnamon, and the remaining chopped mint, cilantro, and verbena.

 YIELD: 6 SERVINGS

4 cups red wine
¼ cup granulated sugar
1 cinnamon stick
1 cup chopped fresh mint
1 cup chopped fresh cilantro
1 cup chopped fresh verbena (optional)
12 ripe fresh or dried figs
1 cup confectioners' sugar
4 egg yolks
1½ cups Sauternes, Marsala, or Prosecco
½ cup toasted slivered almonds
½ teaspoon ground cinnamon

Kugelhopf

(RAISIN AND ALMOND COFFEE CAKE)

KUGELHOPF, SEEN IN EVERY BAKERY in Alsace, is the regional special-occasion cake par excellence. The marvelous nineteenth-century illustration by Alphonse Lévy shows how this tea cake, which he calls *baba,* was also revered by the Jews of Alsace. *Kugel* means "ball" in German, and *hopf* means "cake" in Alsatian. This cake is found all over Germany, Austria, Hungary, and parts of Poland. According to food historians Philip and Mary Hyman, a *Kugelhopf* is first mentioned in German texts in the 1730s, where it is described as a cake baked in a mold shaped like a turban. I suspect that this cake went back and forth throughout the Austro-Hungarian Empire with travelers and cooks, and possibly came back to Lorraine as *baba,* also a turbaned cake in its original form. Sometimes *kugelhopf* is raised with yeast; some later versions use baking powder. It may contain raisins, or a combination of raisins and almonds. *Kugelhopf* molds are as varied as the myriad recipes.

You can easily find *kugelhopf* molds at fine kitchen-supply stores, or you can use a small-capacity Bundt pan. Be careful to watch the cake as it cooks, since baking time will vary depending on the size and material of your pan, and you do not want to let the cake dry out.

YIELD: 10 TO 12 SERVINGS

1½ teaspoons active dry yeast

½ cup warm milk

2 cups all-purpose flour

¼ teaspoon salt

2 large eggs

¼ cup granulated sugar

1 stick (8 tablespoons) unsalted butter, at room

Put the yeast and the milk in the bowl of an electric mixer fitted with a dough hook. When the yeast has dissolved, add the flour and salt, and mix on low speed. The dough will not come together at this point. Add the eggs, one at a time, then pour in the granulated sugar, and continue to mix on low speed for about 7 minutes.

Add the butter bit by bit, making sure to incorporate each piece before adding the next. Increase the mixer speed to medium, and mix for 10 minutes, scraping down the bowl every 2 minutes. Transfer the dough to a clean, greased bowl, cover with plastic wrap, and let rise for 2 hours at room temperature.

Gently punch down the dough, and incorporate the raisins.

Butter an 8-cup *kugelhopf* mold or Bundt pan. Place the almonds in the crevices of the pan. Form the dough into a 20-inch log, and then lay it in a ring on top of the almonds. Cover the pan with a piece of plastic wrap, and let the dough rise for 3 hours at room temperature.

Preheat the oven to 375 degrees, remove the wrap, and bake for 35 to 45 minutes, or until golden brown.

When cool, unmold onto a cooling rack. Just before serving, dust with confectioners' sugar.

temperature, plus more for greasing bowl and mold
½ cup golden raisins
¼ cup blanched slivered almonds
Confectioners' sugar for dusting

Man with *baba*

Rothschild's Chef Antonin Carême

Today the Rothschild name conjures up images of wealth and wine. Indeed, during the agricultural crisis in the mid-nineteenth century, this family bought Château Brane Mouton and renamed it Mouton Rothschild.

James Rothschild came to Paris in 1831, and, fancying fine food, he hired Antonin Carême, who had been the chef to the King of England. This famous nineteenth-century chef enjoyed finishing his career, as he said, "in the good family of Monsieur le Baron." James and his wife and cousin Betty greatly respected the artist-chef, rejoicing in the extraordinary refinements that characterized his food. Since the Rothschilds entertained lavishly and often, Carême had plenty of opportunity to show off his culinary prowess. Cooking for the Rothschilds, he had access to the best cooking technology in a time of great advancement and change that included the development of the gas stove.

Soufflé Rothschild from Le Nôtre

Frozen Soufflé Rothschild

THE ORIGINAL SOUFFLÉ ROTHSCHILD, created for James Rothschild by Antonin Carême, was a baked soufflé embellished with gold leaf. Since then, there have been all kinds of "Rothschild" soufflés, salads, and other dishes—the name is used to denote extravagance or richness.

This frozen soufflé Rothschild was conceived by the famous pastry chef Gaston Le Nôtre, for a grand dinner at the home of one of the Rothschilds. It was served to me at a dinner party in Paris, and is one of the most delicious desserts I have ever tasted. Neither an ice cream nor a sorbet, it is technically a *bavaroise glacée,* a frozen parfait based on eggs and cream. The best part of this recipe is that it is quite quick to make. Just watch—your guests will sneak back for seconds and thirds!

Put the candied fruit in a small bowl, and cover with 3 tablespoons of Grand Marnier or other orange liqueur.

Cut a strip of parchment paper the full circumference of a 10-cup soufflé dish. Ring the inside edge of the dish all the way to the bottom with the paper, creating a collar that extends a few inches above the rim, and secure the end of the paper with tape.

Whip the egg whites with the lemon juice in the bowl of an electric mixer until foamy. Gradually add 3 tablespoons of the sugar, and whip until stiff peaks are formed. Remove to a large bowl, and fold in the remaining ½ cup of Grand Marnier.

Clean the mixer bowl and beaters, and whip the cream until it holds soft peaks. Fold the cream into the egg whites.

Clean the bowl again, and, using the mixer, beat the egg yolks and the remaining 6 tablespoons sugar until very thick and pale yellow. Then fold into the whipped cream and egg whites.

Fill a third of the soufflé dish with the batter. Drain the candied fruit, and sprinkle half of it, along with the cookie pieces, over the surface of the batter. Pour in the rest of the batter, and top with the remaining candied fruit.

Cover tightly with plastic wrap, and freeze for at least 3 hours and up to 8 days. Before serving, remove to the refrigerator, and when half frozen, sprinkle the *nougatine* over the soufflé. Remove the paper collar before serving.

YIELD: 8 TO 10 SERVINGS

½ cup candied orange or ginger, finely chopped

3 tablespoons plus ½ cup Grand Marnier or other orange liqueur

6 large egg whites, plus 9 large egg yolks

1 teaspoon lemon juice

9 tablespoons sugar

1½ cups heavy cream

5 ounces almond cookies (or any other kind of flavorful crunchy cookies), cut up into bite-sized pieces

1 cup *nougatine* (see page 339) or other crackly caramel-based candy, such as praline (see page 361), finely chopped

Baba au Rhum

BABA IS THE YEAST PASTRY that became familiar in Lorraine in the early nineteenth century and is eaten, as described above, by the Jews of Alsace for Purim breakfast; it was sometimes confused with *Kugelhopf.* The French gilded the lily, dousing the dry *baba* with rum—a novelty from America. Today *babas* are baked and served two ways, in either a large or a tiny bulbous mold.

I adore *baba* soaked in rum and order it whenever I can. After tasting an especially light *baba* in a tiny sixteen-seat restaurant called Les Arômes in Aubagne, I asked the chef, Yanick Besset, if he would give me his recipe, and here it is. As you can see, a good *baba* dough itself contains very little sugar, the sweetness coming from the sugar-rum bath spooned on after baking.

 YIELD: 8 TO 10 SERVINGS, OR 12 SMALL *BABAS*

2 sticks (8 ounces) unsalted butter, at room temperature, cut into small pieces, plus more for greasing molds

⅔ cup warm milk

3 tablespoons plus 1 cup sugar

2 teaspoons active dry yeast

1 teaspoon salt

4 large eggs

2⅔ cups all-purpose flour

½ to 1 cup good-quality dark rum

Berries for garnish

Whipped cream or vanilla ice cream for serving

Generously butter one large or twelve small *baba* molds or muffin cups.

Pour the milk in a small bowl, and stir in 3 tablespoons of the sugar. Sprinkle the yeast over the milk and sugar, and let stand for 10 minutes.

Using an electric mixer equipped with a beater, cream the butter. Add the salt and the eggs, one at a time, mixing well between additions. Add the milk-yeast mixture, blending until smooth.

On a low speed, add the flour little by little, mixing until you have a thick, creamy batter. Pour it into the prepared pan, gently spreading it out. If using greased muffin cups or small *baba* pans, scoop out about a half cup of batter, roughly the size of a golf ball, and put it in one of the cups or pans. Repeat with the rest of the batter. Allow to rise at room temperature for 1½ to 2 hours.

Preheat the oven to 375 degrees, and bake the big *baba* for 25 to 30 minutes and the little ones for 20 minutes, or until a skewer inserted in the center comes out clean.

While the *baba* is cooking, make the syrup. Mix 1½ cups water and the remaining 1 cup sugar in a saucepan. Stir until the sugar is dissolved, bring to a boil, remove from the heat, and stir in half a cup of the rum. Pour the rum mixture over the large *baba* in the baking pan. If making mini-*babas,* turn them out into a large bowl. Prick the *babas* all over with a skewer or a fork, then spoon the syrup all over them. It may seem like a lot of syrup, but *babas* can really drink. Refrigerate for at least 4 hours, or up to 2 days, before they are to be eaten. Just before serving, unmold the large *baba* onto a rimmed serving plate and spoon on more rum as you wish. Serve with berries, whipped cream, or vanilla ice cream.

Nougatine

(CARAMEL-BASED CANDY)

WHEN I WAS TRYING TO FIGURE OUT how to make *nougatine,* I consulted pastry chef Ann Amernick, who has perfected *nougatine* and makes it effortlessly. This recipe is adapted from her latest book, *The Art of the Dessert.*

Coat an 18-by-13-inch rimmed jelly-roll pan with vegetable oil. Have a pastry brush ready, along with a cup of cold water.

Put the sugar, ¼ cup water, the vanilla, and the corn syrup in a heavy medium-sized saucepan, and stir over low heat until the sugar melts. Then raise the heat to medium, and cook, stirring constantly, until the sugar comes to a boil. Dipping a pastry brush in cold water, quickly wash down the side of the pan to rinse away any sugar that is still crystallized.

Continue to boil, without stirring, but gently agitate the pan to distribute the heat. When small puffs of smoke begin coming from the sugar, which should be a rich dark brown but not burned, remove the pan from the heat. Quickly stir in the almonds and spread the *nougatine* on the jelly-roll pan. Cool completely.

Break the *nougatine* into 4-inch pieces. Loosely wrap several pieces together in plastic wrap, and store in an airtight container. When ready to use, leave the *nougatine* in the plastic wrap and hammer it into little pieces, being careful not to pulverize it.

YIELD: 2 CUPS

1¼ cups sugar
1 teaspoon vanilla extract
1 tablespoon light corn syrup
1½ cups blanched sliced
   almonds

Gâteau à la Crème de Marron

(CHESTNUT CREAM CAKE)

DURING WORLD WAR II, Claudine Moos's family hid in Lyon, which was the center of the Free Zone and considered to be a slightly safer city for the Jews. One day, her father, a socialist and Resistance fighter, was distributing leaflets against the Germans at the railroad station. The French police, helped by the German SS officer Klaus Barbie, caught him and others, and they were dispatched on the last train to Auschwitz. As they were escorted away, they sang the "Marseillaise," the French national anthem, at the top of their lungs. Claudine, who was five years old at the time, has memories of their singing voices fading off into the distance. She was raised by her mother, who had also lost her father at a young age. Despite a difficult life, having lost her father and her husband, Claudine's mother's last words were "Life is good."

Even in a good life, food could be a challenge. "During and after the war, food was rationed," Claudine told me in her kitchen in Annecy. "We got ration cards for the milk and eggs. Of course there was no chocolate. I remember my mother coming home with the first tablet of chocolate she could get after the war. How excited we all were!"

Regardless of the shortages during the war, chestnuts still fell from trees throughout France in autumn. This rich uncooked cake would have been made from the chestnuts that were collected on the street. The recipe comes from a handwritten cookbook that Claudine's grandmother gave her when she got married in 1960. The original recipes were measured in interesting ways, calling for a "glass of mustard" and a "nut of butter."

Peeling chestnuts used to be a laborious task. Her grandmother would collect or buy them whole, score them a quarter of the way down, boil them to loosen the skin, and then peel them. For Claudine, it is so much easier these days to make this cake, because she can buy frozen or jarred chestnuts, already peeled. Best made a day in advance, this rich cake should be served in small portions, topped with dollops of whipped cream.

Put the chestnuts in a saucepan with the milk and the salt, and simmer, uncovered, for about 15 minutes, or until soft.

Drain the chestnuts, discarding the milk, and put them in a food processor fitted with a steel blade. Add the sugar and the stick of butter or margarine, and purée them. Add the rum, pulsing until smooth.

Spoon the chestnut mixture onto a long, shallow platter, forming it into a narrow loglike rectangle measuring about 3 by 10 inches. Cover, and refrigerate overnight.

The next day, melt the chocolate over a double boiler. Add the remaining teaspoon butter or margarine, the confectioners' sugar, and a teaspoon of water, and mix well. Using a spoon or fork, drizzle the chocolate glaze over the cake. Garnish with walnut halves, slice, and serve with a dollop of whipped cream, if using.

D OR P   YIELD: 8 TO 10
          SERVINGS

2½ cups peeled chestnuts
2 cups milk or soy milk
⅛ teaspoon salt
6 tablespoons granulated
    sugar
1 stick (8 tablespoons) plus
    1 teaspoon unsalted butter
    or *pareve* margarine, at room
    temperature
¼ cup rum
4 ounces bittersweet chocolate
1 tablespoon confectioners'
    sugar
Walnut halves for garnish
Whipped cream for serving
    (optional)

A street vendor roasts chestnuts.

Citrus-Fruit Soup with Dates and Mint

WHEN I INTERVIEWED GILLES CHOUKROUN, one of the darlings of a new generation of French chefs who are injecting playfulness into French food, he had just opened the Mini Palais, a beautiful restaurant in Paris's newly renovated Grand Palais exhibition hall, across from Les Invalides. In addition to his nascent restaurant empire, Gilles is also the father of Generation C, which stands for "Cuisines et Culture," a group of chefs who teach cooking to the disadvantaged in Paris.

Gilles, whose father is a Jew from Algeria, experiments with the spices and flavors of North Africa to accent his French food. One of his signature desserts is this refreshing citrus-fruit soup. It makes the perfect ending to a North African meal, especially with cookies on the side.

 YIELD: 6 TO 8 SERVINGS

4 tangerines

1 grapefruit

4 blood or other oranges

1 cup orange juice

2 to 4 tablespoons sugar

6 dried dates or figs, roughly chopped

1 pint lemon or tangerine sorbet

6 tablespoons orange-blossom water

6 tablespoons extra-virgin olive oil

½ teaspoon ground cumin

6 mint leaves, cut in chiffonade

¼ cup shelled and peeled pistachio nuts, roughly chopped

¼ cup toasted almonds, roughly chopped

Cut off the tops and bottoms of the tangerines, grapefruit, and oranges with a sharp knife. Slice off the peel and the white pith, and cut in between the white membranes to extract individual segments. Put in a large bowl with the orange juice and enough sugar to make it slightly sweet. Add the dates or figs, cover with plastic wrap, and refrigerate. You can do this a day in advance.

Just before serving, ladle some of the citrus juice into a glass dessert bowl or individual snifters. Add a small scoop of the sorbet, some of the citrus slices, and a few pieces of fig or date. Splash some orange-blossom water and olive oil on top. Then sprinkle with cumin and mint leaves, and scatter a few pistachios and almonds on top.

Parisian Passover Pineapple Flan

THIS QUICK PASSOVER-FLAN RECIPE came recently to Paris with North African Jews and has stayed. A quick dessert usually made with canned pineapple, it is even better with fresh. Because it can be prepared two days in advance, and left in the mold until serving, the flan is popular for Sabbath-observant Jews.

Stir 1 cup of the sugar with the juice of one of the lemons in a small saucepan. Heat the pan, stirring constantly, until the syrup begins to bubble. Stop stirring, and allow the pan to sit over the flame until the syrup begins to turn golden at the edges. Remove from the heat. Brush down any sugar crystals with a brush dipped in cold water. Occasionally rotate the pan to mix the syrup without stirring it. Continue doing this until the syrup is evenly golden.

Carefully pour the resulting caramel into an ungreased 10-inch flan mold or round cake pan, making sure you swirl the caramel up the sides of the pan.

Preheat the oven to 350 degrees, and put fifteen pineapple slices in the food processor. Pulse until chunky but not puréed. Set aside in a bowl.

Mix ½ cup of sugar and the pineapple juice in a saucepan and simmer slowly for a few mintes to dissolve the sugar. Then pour into the bowl with the chopped pineapple. Taste, and add ¼ cup more sugar if needed. Let cool slightly, and whisk in the eggs, remaining lemon juice, and potato starch.

Pour the pineapple mixture into the flan mold, and set the mold in a *bain-marie,* a larger pan filled with hot water to come about halfway up the side of the mold. Bake in the oven for 45 minutes, cool, and refrigerate at least a couple of hours. Before serving, run a sharp knife around the edge of the pan. Cover with a plate, and carefully flip over to release.

YIELD: 8 SERVINGS

1½ to 1¾ cups sugar
Juice of 2 lemons
15 flavorful pineapple slices, either fresh or canned*
1½ cups unsweetened pineapple juice, fresh or reserved from the can
10 large eggs
⅓ cup potato or corn starch

*Two 20-ounce cans of rings of unsweetened pineapple

Compote de Pruneaux et de Figues

(POACHED PRUNES AND FIGS À LA ALICE B. TOKLAS)

IN THE EARLY TWENTIETH CENTURY, a Jewish woman named Geneviève Halévy Bizet, the mother of Marcel Proust's friend Jacques, held one of the most popular women's salons in Paris, depicted in Proust's work.

Gertrude Stein, the Jewish writer, along with her partner, Alice B. Toklas, hosted another famous salon, conversing with and cooking for writers and artists during the many years when they lived together in France. One of the recipes Alice liked to serve to their guests was very similar to this prune-and-fig compote.

In Alsace and southern Germany, prune compote is eaten at Passover with crispy sweet *chremslach*, doughnutlike fritters made from matzo meal (there is a recipe for them in my book *Jewish Cooking in America*).

 YIELD: 6 SERVINGS

½ pound prunes

½ pound dried figs

2½ cups dry red wine, or more
  if necessary

3 cinnamon sticks

Grated zest and juice of
  1 orange

Grated zest of ½ lemon

3 peppercorns

3 cloves

3 tablespoons sugar, or to
  taste

Whipped cream for serving
  (optional)

Put the prunes and figs, wine, cinnamon sticks, orange zest and juice, lemon zest, peppercorns, and cloves in a wide saucepan. If necessary, add more wine so that the fruit is just covered. Bring to a boil, and simmer, covered, for about an hour. Stir in the sugar, adding more to taste if you like.

Using a slotted spoon, transfer the fruit to a bowl. Strain the liquid, and pour it over the fruit. Cover with plastic wrap, and let sit in the refrigerator overnight. Serve at room temperature, with or without the whipped cream.

Figs growing in the south of France

Tarte au Citron

(LEMON TART)

WHEN I WAS A STUDENT IN PARIS, I became hooked on intensely tart yet sweet French lemon tarts, and sampled them at every pastry shop I could find. I still love them, especially when they are bitingly tart.

To make the crust, cut the butter into small pieces, and toss into a food processor fitted with a steel blade, along with the flour, sugar, and salt. Pulse until the texture is like very coarse meal. Pour in the milk or water a tablespoon at a time, pulsing until the dough comes together in a ball. Be careful not to add too much liquid, or the dough will be impossible to roll out. Shape the dough into a disk, cover with plastic wrap, and refrigerate for at least 45 minutes.

Roll out the piecrust, and line an ungreased 9-inch tart pan with it. Prick it all over with a fork, and bake in a preheated 400-degree oven for 15 minutes, or until golden brown. (This can be done ahead of time.)

To make the filling, pour 2 cups water into a heavy medium-sized saucepan. Add 1 cup of the sugar, and bring to a boil.

Slice one of the lemons into thin circles, drop them into the boiling sugared water, lower the heat, and simmer for about 30 minutes, uncovered. Drain, and discard the liquid.

Grate the zest of the remaining 3 lemons to get 2 tablespoons of zest, then juice the lemons to get about ¾ cup juice. Whip the eggs and remaining sugar in the bowl of an electric mixer at medium speed. Gradually add the lemon juice and zest. Pour the filling ingredients into a medium saucepan, add the butter or margarine, and cook over medium heat, stirring constantly, being careful not to boil, until the lemon thickens into a curdlike custard, about 5 minutes.

Spoon the filling into the prebaked crust. Lay the lemon slices all over, and refrigerate until firm.

D OR **P** YIELD: 8 SERVINGS

FOR THE CRUST
½ cup (1 stick) unsalted butter or *pareve* margarine
1 cup all-purpose flour
2 tablespoons sugar
⅛ teaspoon salt
About 2 tablespoons cold milk or water

FOR THE FILLING
2 cups sugar
4 lemons
3 large eggs
4 tablespoons unsalted butter or *pareve* margarine

Tarte à la Rhubarbe Alsacienne

(ALSATIAN RHUBARB TART)

"I'M NOT MUCH OF A COOK," Michèle Weil told me as she ushered me into her charming kitchen in a residential section of Strasbourg. Fresh basil was growing on her kitchen windowsill, and paintings from the Jewish School of Paris adorned the walls. "But," she continued, "I have to cook. All French women cook."

A full-time pediatrician and the mother of three boys, Michèle is smart enough to know she can't do it all. On medical call before we arrived for dinner, she quickly pulled from the freezer a package of hunks of frozen salmon and cod, bought at Picard Surgelés. Then she boiled some potatoes, put the fish in the oven, and opened a carton of prepared Hollandaise sauce, which she microwaved and poured over the baked fish. Putting this together with a green salad with tomatoes and her homemade vinaigrette, she had made a quick and balanced dinner.

Like all working women, Michèle has to make compromises. "My mother would never have given you frozen food," she apologized. "But, no matter how busy I am, I would never buy desserts. I always make them," she told me as she presented a free-form rhubarb tart that she had made before going to work.

It seemed that every Jewish cook I visited in Alsace served me rhubarb, the sour-tasting sign of spring. Unlike Americans, who almost always marry tart rhubarb with strawberries and lace the two with large quantities of sugar, French cooks make a less sweet tart using only rhubarb.

They peel the stalks first, which I do not. I think it might be one of those French fetishes, like always serving radishes with butter, or tomato juice with celery salt. Alsatian home cooks also serve their tart with a delicious custard topping made from cream and eggs.

 YIELD: ABOUT 8 SERVINGS

FILLING

6 cups ½-inch pieces of rhubarb (about 2 pounds), peeled if stringy

1¼ cups sugar

2 large eggs

½ cup heavy cream

¼ teaspoon vanilla extract

Put the rhubarb and ¾ cup of the sugar in a heavy medium saucepan set over medium heat. Cook, stirring occasionally, for about 30 minutes, or until the rhubarb is jamlike. This can be done a day ahead.

To make the crust, cut the butter into small pieces, and toss into a food processor fitted with a steel blade, along with the flour, salt, and sugar. Pulse until the texture is like very coarse meal. Gradually add 3 tablespoons ice water, pulsing until the dough comes together in a ball. Shape the dough into a disk, cover with plastic wrap, and refrigerate for at least 45 minutes.

Preheat the oven to 375 degrees, and roll out the dough. Carefully fit it into an ungreased 9-inch tart pan with a removable bottom, or make it freeform on a cookie sheet of approximately the same size. Prick it all over with a fork, and bake for 15 minutes. Remove from the oven, and cool slightly.

In the meantime, beat the eggs in a small bowl. Whisk in the cream, the vanilla, and the remaining ½ cup sugar.

Spread the rhubarb on the bottom of the tart. Pour the custard over the rhubarb, and bake for about 25 minutes, or until golden brown and set. Serve warm or at room temperature.

CRUST

6 tablespoons unsalted butter
1¼ cups unbleached all-
   purpose flour
¼ teaspoon salt
2 tablespoons sugar

NOTE If you like strawberries in your tart, reduce the rhubarb to 4 cups and add 2 cups of strawberries. For a dairyless pie, make the crust with *pareve* margarine and top with meringue. Beat 3 egg whites to a fluff, add ½ cup sugar, and beat to a shiny meringue. Bake as above, for about 15 minutes, then remove from the oven, spoon the meringue over, and bake for another 10 minutes, until golden.

Tea time in Paris

Torte aux Carottes de Pâque

(PASSOVER CARROT TORTE)

I HAVE ALWAYS FELT THAT COOKING is the time to tell stories. In the sixties, when I learned to make this Passover carrot torte from Ruth Moos in Annecy, we talked about lots of things, but never about World War II. When I cook this torte now, after her death, I tell the story of how brave she was during the occupation.

Not only did she help so many Jews trying to flee, but she had a narrow escape herself once. When the Annecy police warned the Mooses that the Gestapo was looking for her husband, Rudi, he went underground, hiding between the pork sausages and hams in a butcher's smokehouse. Looking for him, the Gestapo went to the hotel where the Mooses had been hiding in nearby Talloires. Ruth, walking outside for a quick breath of fresh air while her tiny daughter was sleeping upstairs, turned around to see the Gestapo agents entering the lobby. In order to sneak past the guards, she grabbed some sheets from a chambermaid and, posing as a maid herself, climbed the stairs, passing the Gestapo. Terrified, she snatched her baby and fled to safety.

P YIELD: 8 TO 10 SERVINGS

Vegetable oil or spray for
  greasing the pan
7 large eggs
1 cup sugar
½ teaspoon ground cinnamon
¼ teaspoon salt
1 teaspoon vanilla extract
Grated zest and juice of
  1 lemon
5 large carrots, peeled and
  grated (about 2½ cups
  grated)
1½ cups ground hazelnuts or
  almonds

Preheat the oven to 350 degrees, and grease a 9-inch springform pan.

Separate five of the eggs. In the bowl of an electric mixer, beat the five egg yolks with the two remaining whole eggs, the sugar, cinnamon, salt, vanilla, and the lemon zest and juice. Mix in the carrots and hazelnuts.

Beat the five egg whites to stiff peaks in a clean bowl with clean beaters. Gently fold in batches into the carrot batter. Pour into the prepared pan, and bake for 50 minutes, or until a tester inserted in the center of the cake comes out clean. Allow to cool before unmolding.

Tarte aux Quetsches

(ITALIAN PLUM TART)

I CAN NEVER DECIDE WHAT I LIKE BETTER about this Alsatian and southern-German tart: the *quetsches* (similar to Italian blue plums, which are available for a short time in the fall) or the butter crust (called *sablé* in French and *Mürbeteig* in German). On a recent trip to France, I learned a trick for making it: if you bake the tart with no sugar over the fruit, you won't get a soggy crust. Just sprinkle on a small amount of sugar after baking. Italian blue plums are only available in the early fall, so I tend to serve this tart at Rosh Hashanah.

 YIELD: 8 SERVINGS

To make the crust, pulse the flour, sugar, salt, and butter or margarine together in the bowl of a food processor fitted with a steel blade until crumbled. Then add the egg yolk, and pulse until the dough comes together.

Put the dough in the center of an ungreased 9-inch tart pan with a removable bottom. Dust your fingers with flour, and gently press out the dough to cover the bottom and sides of the pan. Refrigerate for at least 30 minutes.

Preheat the oven to 450 degrees, and bake the crust for 10 minutes. Reduce the oven to 375 degrees, and bake for another 5 minutes. Remove the crust from the oven, and let cool slightly. Reduce the oven temperature to 350 degrees.

Mix the jam with the brandy in a small bowl, and spread over the bottom of the crust. Pit the plums, and cut them into four pieces each. Starting at the outside, arrange the plums in a circle so that all the pieces overlap, creating concentric circles that wind into the center of the pan. Sprinkle with the cinnamon and lemon zest.

Return the tart to the oven, and bake for about 30 minutes, or until the crust is golden brown and the plums are juicy. Remove the tart from the oven, sprinkle on the sugar, and serve warm or at room temperature.

CRUST

1 cup all-purpose flour

1 tablespoon sugar

⅛ teaspoon salt

1 stick (8 tablespoons) unsalted butter or *pareve* margarine, cut into 8 pieces

1 egg yolk

FILLING

3 tablespoons plum or other fruit jam

1 tablespoon brandy

1½ pounds Italian blue plums

½ teaspoon ground cinnamon

1 teaspoon grated lemon zest

¼ cup sugar

Galettes de Cherbourg de Mamine

(CHERBOURG BUTTER COOKIES)

THIS COOKIE WAS ONE THAT "MAMINE" — an affectionate name for Maryse Weil, the matriarch of the Weil family from Besançon—baked as a young girl for family gatherings. Her granddaughter Martine Trèves makes it now in her kitchen. She showed me the recipe from a handwritten book that suggested adding a "grain of salt" to the batter.

 YIELD: ABOUT 4 DOZEN COOKIES

1¼ sticks (10 tablespoons) unsalted butter or *pareve* margarine

¾ cup sugar

1½ teaspoons vanilla extract

¼ teaspoon salt

1 large egg

2 scant cups all-purpose flour

1 cup slivered almonds or whole pine nuts

Put the butter or margarine and the sugar in the bowl of a standing mixer, and cream with the paddle until smooth. Add the vanilla, salt, egg, and flour, continuing to mix until well blended and smooth. Pull the dough away from the paddle, and stir in the almonds or pine nuts. Remove from the mixer, pat together into a round, and refrigerate for ½ hour.

Preheat the oven to 350 degrees, and line two cookie sheets with parchment paper.

Roll out the dough to about ⅛ inch thick, and make 2-inch rounds with a cookie cutter. Transfer to the cookie sheets, and bake for about 20 minutes, turning once.

Butterkuchen, the madeleine of Alsatian Jews

Butterkuchen

(BUTTER COOKIES)

WHEN RESEARCHING THIS BOOK, I talked about Jewish food with Pierre Dreyfus, a great-grandson of Captain Alfred Dreyfus, the Jewish officer on the French General Staff who was falsely accused of being a German spy. The one recipe that Pierre remembered from his childhood was for *butter,* or *butterkuchen,* simple shortbread butter cookies sprinkled with cinnamon and sugar.

A century ago, *butterkuchen,* similar to *sablés* in Brittany, were made by using equal weights of eggs in their shells, butter, sugar, and flour. Sometimes cooks would add a little kirsch or vanilla sugar. Some used a glass to cut round pieces from the cookie dough; others pressed the dough into pans and cut it into tiny squares or rectangles after baking. One elderly lady I interviewed told me how her grandmother would make butter in the summer from the fresh, unpasteurized cream of their cows and store it in a stone jar on a ledge outside their house all winter long. Then, when she wanted to use the butter for *butter,* it was right there.

One day when I was visiting Sandrine Weil (see page 181), she and her daughters showed me how to make a tender *butter.* This is her take on the *butterkuchen,* made with rich French butter, which has a low water and high fat content, and is cut after baking into the traditional 1-inch squares.

Put the flour, salt, 1 cup of the granulated sugar, and ½ teaspoon of the cinnamon in the bowl of a food processor fitted with a steel blade. Pulse until well mixed, then add the eggs, one at a time, followed by the butter pieces. Process until the dough comes together in a ball. Wrap in plastic wrap, and refrigerate for 2 hours, or until firm.

Preheat the oven to 350 degrees. Lightly flour a piece of parchment paper that is as big as a baking sheet. Roll out the dough on the floured parchment paper. It should be about 12 by 18 inches and about ⅛ inch thick. You will have to work quickly, because the butter will get too soft. If the dough gets too soft and sticky, put it back in the refrigerator for 15 minutes. Sprinkle the brown sugar, the remaining ½ cup granulated sugar, and the remaining cinnamon over the dough.

Bake for about 15 minutes, until golden brown around the edges. Remove from the oven, and, using a sharp knife, cut in little squares, about 1 inch or a little larger.

YIELD: 4 DOZEN COOKIES

3 cups unbleached all-purpose flour

⅛ teaspoon salt

1½ cups granulated sugar

1 teaspoon ground cinnamon

2 large eggs

2 sticks unsalted European butter with high fat content, slightly softened, cut into little pieces

3 tablespoons brown sugar

NOTE   You can also use cookie cutters to make this recipe.

Biscuits de Gingembre et de Cardamome

(CANDIED GINGER COOKIES)

SHEILA MALOVANY-CHEVALLIER is a typical Parisian expat, one who lives a fascinating life. She and her husband, Bill, reside in a bohemian artist's apartment in the Latin Quarter during the week, and in the countryside, near Dijon, on weekends. Spending her work time teaching English at the Institute d'Etudes Politiques, and doing a new translation of Simone de Beauvoir's *Second Sex,* she would seem unlikely to have time to cook. But not only have she and her writing partner, Constance Borde, also an American living in Paris, written several American cookbooks in French, with all the Jewish recipes with which Sheila grew up, but when she is invited to dinner, she makes a point of bringing every hostess an elegantly packaged sweet she has made herself. These ginger cookie clusters are one of her and my favorites.

 OR YIELD: 40 TO 50 COOKIE CLUSTERS

½ cup sugar

1 stick unsalted butter or *pareve* margarine

1 tablespoon honey

1¼ cups all-purpose flour

1 teaspoon baking powder

Pinch of salt

1 heaping teaspoon ground cardamom

¾ cup finely chopped candied ginger

Preheat the oven to 350 degrees, and line a baking sheet with parchment paper.

Put the sugar, butter, and honey in a saucepan and heat. When the sugar is melted and well mixed, stir in the flour, baking powder, salt, cardamom, and candied ginger. Remove from the heat, and cool for a few minutes.

Drop teaspoons of the batter onto the baking sheets. Flatten them slightly, so that they resemble small disks. Bake for about 10 minutes, or until they are golden. They will harden as they cool, so do not overcook.

Sheila and her friend Alex Miles in her kitchen in the country

Passover Almond Macaroons

IN JEWISH HOMES IN FRANCE and all around the world, recipes for macaroons have been handed down from mother to daughter for centuries. Jewish macaroons are descended from the Ladino *marunchinos* and *almendredas,* both terms for almond cookies. In fact, during the Inquisition, historian David Gitlitz told me, crypto-Jews were accused of having bought almond cookies from the Jewish quarter in Barbastro, in Aragón.

The modern Jewish macaroon is specifically associated with Boulay, a town about twenty-five miles north of Nancy. It seems that a Jewish wine salesman named Bines Lazard opened in 1854 Maison Lazard, along with his wife, Françoise, and their son Léopold, where they sold macaroons, matzo, and wholesale wine. In 1898, the folklorist Auricoste de Lazarque tasted their macaroons, and proclaimed them the best in France, making the company enormously successful. During World War I, the Lazard family sold the wine business, and in 1932, they abandoned the matzo trade. Some thirty years later, the business, which included its secret recipe for macaroons, was sold to Jean Alexandre, who opened a shop in Boulay where *macarons de Boulay* are baked and sold to this day. Made from the traditional mixture of almonds, sugar, and egg whites, they are slightly robust, a departure from the flat and shiny French macaroons that are so popular today.

Although the Alexandres would not give me their secret recipe, Yves Alexandre (no relation), from Strasbourg, had me taste his, which are very similar but made by hand, rather than machine.

YIELD: ABOUT 7 DOZEN

4 large egg whites

1¼ cups sugar

2 cups ground almonds or almond flour

¼ teaspoon almond extract

Preheat the oven to 300 degrees, and line a baking sheet with parchment paper.

Whip the egg whites to almost-stiff peaks in the bowl of an electric mixer. In another bowl, stir together the sugar, ground almonds, and almond extract. Fold the sugar-and-almond mixture gently into the egg whites in three batches.

Drop teaspoons of the batter onto the baking sheet, and bake for about 15 minutes, or until just dry.

Flavored French Macaroons

TO LEARN HOW TO MAKE THE French macaroons that I tasted at many bakeries and homes in Paris, I asked Sherry Yard, executive pastry chef at Wolfgang Puck's Spago, for guidance. Spending a day with Sherry and her staff, I had the opportunity to witness how American pastry chefs are learning from the macaroon-crazy French. The first of these dainty macaroon sandwiches filled with chocolate *ganache* was developed by the pastry chef Pierre Desfontaines Ladurée at the beginning of the twentieth century. Today almost every pastry shop in France makes them in a dizzying array of flavors and colors with jam, chocolate, and buttercream fillings. Some pastry shops make certified kosher versions.

Here is a master recipe for the chocolate macaroon, with suggestions for making them vanilla- or raspberry-flavored. I have given a recipe for chocolate-mocha filling as well. You can also fill them with good-quality raspberry jam or almond paste. After you have made a few macaroons, use your own imagination to create others. And do serve them for Passover.

D OR **P** YIELD: 24 TO 30 SANDWICHED MACAROONS

CHOCOLATE MACAROONS

4 large eggs

2 cups confectioners' sugar*

1 cup blanched almonds

¼ cup good unsweetened cocoa powder

¾ teaspoon cream of tartar

¼ cup granulated sugar

*At Passover, use kosher-for-Passover confectioners' sugar, made with potato starch.

An hour before making the macaroons, separate the eggs and let the whites sit in the bowl of an electric mixer to reach room temperature. Line two baking sheets with parchment paper.

Put the confectioners' sugar and the almonds in a food processor fitted with a steel blade. Pulse them together until they become a fine powder. Add the cocoa powder, and pulse until well mixed.

Whip the egg whites at low speed until they start to foam. Add the cream of tartar, and increase the speed to medium. After 2 minutes, gradually add the granulated sugar. Continue to beat until stiff and shiny peaks form.

Put the almond-sugar mixture in a large bowl, and, using a rubber spatula, fold in the egg whites. This will take about forty strokes (after twenty strokes, the egg whites will deflate; after another twenty, the batter will be mixed and runny).

Fill a pastry bag with the batter (it is easiest to use a ½-inch-diameter tip). Pipe out 1 tablespoon, or enough batter to make silver dollar–sized circles, an inch apart on the lined cookie sheets. The best way to do this is by holding the pastry bag straight up and squeezing until about 1½ inches of batter runs out for each macaroon. Let the macaroons sit at room temperature, uncovered, on the baking sheets for 1 hour, or until they dry and are less glossy.

While the macaroons are drying, make the mocha filling. Stir together the butter or margarine, honey, and coffee in a small saucepan. Bring to a boil, and remove from the heat. Stir in the chocolate, and, using a hand mixer or a whisk, beat until slightly stiff. Set aside.

Preheat the oven to 275 degrees, and arrange the racks in the two lower thirds of the oven. Put the sheet pans in the oven, and bake for 15 minutes. Switch the positions of the baking sheets, and continue to bake for 5 to 10 minutes more, or until the macaroons are no longer wobbly and sticky.

Allow to cool. To serve, spoon about a heaping teaspoon of filling on one cookie, and top with another.

MACAROON VARIATIONS

For white macaroons, omit the cocoa powder and proceed as above.

For raspberry-flavored macaroons, replace the cocoa powder with 2 tablespoons raspberry powder, and add a few drops of red food coloring when you whip the egg whites. Alternatively, you can make your own raspberry, strawberry, blackberry, or cherry powder by pulverizing a few dehydrated (not dried) berries in the food processor. Dehydrated fruits and raspberry powder are available from www.justtomatoes.com and are also sold at many supermarkets. Although the Just Tomatoes products are not certified kosher, they are processed in a facility that is purely vegetarian.

FILLING VARIATIONS

Chocolate-*ganache:* Heat ¾ cup heavy cream with 8 ounces bittersweet chocolate, and stir until the chocolate melts and the mixture thickens slightly.

Chocolate-orange: Substitute ¼ cup orange juice for the coffee.

CHOCOLATE MOCHA FILLING

2 tablespoons unsalted butter
   or *pareve* margarine
3 tablespoons honey
¼ cup strong brewed coffee
6 ounces semisweet chocolate

The French are crazy for macaroons.

NOTE The unfilled macaroon cookies can be stored in an airtight container in the freezer for up to 2 months. Sandwiched, they can be stored in the refrigerator for 3 days.

Hamantashen

(POPPY-SEED-AND-FRUIT-FILLED PURIM COOKIES)

Games and parties at Purim in Paris

AS A CHILD, I LOVED THE HOLIDAY of Purim, the time when my mother would make *hamantashen,* filled with apricot jam or dried prune fillings. As a young adult, when I was living in Jerusalem, I discovered a whole new world of *hamantashen* fillings, and the magic of the *shalach manot,* the gift baskets stuffed with fruits and cookies. Traditionally, these were made to use up the year's flour before the beginning of Passover as well as to make gift offerings.

Strangely enough, *hamantashen* are little known in France, except among Jews coming from eastern European backgrounds. The North African Jews don't make them, nor do the Alsatian Jews, who fry doughnuts for Purim (see following recipe). French children who do eat *hamantashen* like a filling of Nutella, the hazelnut-chocolate spread. You can go that route, or opt for the more traditional apricot preserves, prune jam, or the filling of poppy seeds, fruit, and nuts that I've included here.

To make the dough, cream the butter or margarine with the sugar in the food processor. Add the egg, vanilla, and orange juice, and continue to mix until smooth.

Add 2½ cups flour, the baking powder, and the salt. Process until smooth. Flour your hands, remove the dough from the food processor, and cover it in plastic wrap. Chill in the refrigerator for a few hours or overnight.

Meanwhile, make the filling. Put the poppy seeds in a small saucepan. Cover with the milk, and simmer for a few minutes, stirring occasionally. Turn off the heat, and cool.

Add the poppy seeds and milk to the sugar, dates or figs, raisins, walnuts, almonds, lemon zest, and egg yolk. Transfer to a food processor equipped with a steel blade, and pulse until just combined. Refrigerate until the batter is chilled.

When ready to make the cookies, remove the cookie dough from the refrigerator, preheat the oven to 375 degrees, and grease two cookie sheets.

Divide the dough into four pieces. Roll one ball out on a lightly floured board to a thickness of ⅛ inch. Cut the dough into 3-inch circles. Place 1 teaspoon of filling in the center of each circle. To shape the *hamantashen,* first brush water around the rim of the circle with your finger. Lift the edges of the dough up to form a triangle around the filling, pinching the three corners together, leaving a small opening in the center. Transfer to the cookie sheet, and bake in the oven for 10 to 15 minutes, or until the tops are golden. Repeat with each of the remaining dough balls.

YIELD: ABOUT 40 COOKIES

COOKIE DOUGH

1¼ cups (2½ sticks) unsalted butter or *pareve* margarine, at room temperature

½ cup sugar

1 large egg

½ teaspoon vanilla extract

1 tablespoon orange juice

2½ to 3 cups unbleached all-purpose flour

1 teaspoon baking powder

½ teaspoon salt

FILLING

½ cup poppy seeds

½ cup milk

½ cup sugar

10 pitted dates or figs, chopped

¼ cup raisins

10 walnuts, roughly chopped

¾ cup ground almonds

Grated zest of 1 lemon

1 egg yolk

Poppy-seed *hamantashen*: a Purim treat

Beignets de Carnaval

(PURIM DOUGHNUTS)

WHEN THE WRITER MARCEL PROUST was a little boy, he played a game with Jeanne Weil, his mother. She would read one line from her favorite play, *Esther* by Racine, and Marcel would read the next. In the play, the Jewess Esther marries Ahasuerus, the good king of Persia. Proust's mother also married a non-Jew, a Catholic doctor named Achille Proust.

Madame Proust's love of *Esther* may have extended beyond the text—a favorite sweet was these doughnuts from her childhood, eaten by Jews at Purim, which celebrates Queen Esther. The doughnuts are the same as the *beignets de Carnaval* eaten by Catholics around the same time of year, just before Lent. These doughnuts and *Butterkuchen* (see page 351) probably evoked more memories for Proust than did the *madeleine* dunked in tea in the fictional *Swann's Way*. Curiously enough, in an early version of the opening pages of the manuscript, the *madeleines* were *biscottes* (dry toast, zwieback, or rusks). The change to *madeleines* was made later by Proust.

D OR P YIELD: ABOUT 2 DOZEN

1½ tablespoons active dry yeast

4 cups all-purpose flour

3 large eggs

½ teaspoon salt

¼ cup granulated sugar

7 tablespoons unsalted butter or *pareve* margarine, at room temperature

Vegetable oil for frying

Confectioners' sugar

Dissolve the yeast in ½ cup warm water in the bowl of an electric mixer fitted with the dough hook. Stir in the flour, eggs, salt, granulated sugar, and the butter or margarine, and knead until you have the consistency of a smooth dough. Turn it out, clean and grease the bowl, and put dough back in. Allow dough to rest, covered, for 1½ to 2 hours, or until doubled in volume. Punch down, and knead again.

Roll out the dough with a rolling pin to a thickness of about ¼ inch. With a sharp knife, cut the dough into roughly equal 2-inch triangles or rectangles. Allow to rise for 45 minutes.

Heat about 2 inches of the oil to 375 degrees in a deep pan or a wok. Lower three or four pieces of the dough at a time into the hot oil, and fry until they are golden on both sides. Extract them with a slotted spoon, and drain on paper towels. Repeat with the rest of the dough. Sprinkle with confectioners' sugar before serving.

Montecaos de Mamine

(GRANDMOTHER'S MELT-AWAY COOKIES)

THIS MELT-IN-YOUR-MOUTH COOKIE, also called *ghouribi,* comes from Oran, Algeria, but is widely used across North Africa. I love its soft, crumbly texture, made from crushed nuts and sugar. It reminds me of Mexican wedding tea cakes or Greek *kourambiedes.* You can substitute butter for the oil if you like. These irresistible and simply made drop cookies are eaten on Purim, Hanukkah, and Shabbat, when Moroccan Jews decorate the table with flowers and sweets. They are also one of the symbolic cookies that women gather together today in France to make for weddings and other life-cycle events.

Preheat the oven to 325 degrees, and line two baking sheets with parchment paper.

Pour the oil or butter into a mixing bowl. Stir in the confectioners' sugar and almonds, mixing well.

Mix together the flour, salt, baking powder, and half the cinnamon. Add to the oil mixture, and stir until blended. Cover the batter with plastic wrap, and refrigerate for at least 30 minutes.

If, when you remove the batter from the refrigerator, it is a bit runny, then just add a little more flour to make it hold its shape. Scoop up a level tablespoon of cookie dough and mold it with your hands into a ball. Repeat, using all the dough. Arrange the balls about 2 inches apart on the baking sheet, and sprinkle with the remaining ½ teaspoon cinnamon.

Bake for 15 to 20 minutes, or until beige-colored, changing the position of the cookie sheets halfway through.

P OR D YIELD: ABOUT 30 COOKIES

1 cup vegetable, canola, or safflower oil, or melted butter
1 cup confectioners' sugar
1 cup finely ground almonds
2 cups all-purpose flour
¼ teaspoon salt
½ teaspoon baking powder
1 teaspoon ground cinnamon

Manicottes au Miel Maison

(TUNISIAN ROSH HASHANAH FRITTERS)

THESE ROSETTE-SHAPED FRITTERS can be seen these days in bakeries all over Paris. Variously called *fijuelas* (Moroccan) and *zeppole* (Italian), they are a special-occasion food for happy celebrations, especially Rosh Hashanah. I tasted them at a wedding ceremony recently. Although they look difficult to make, they are quite easy.

YIELD: ABOUT 10 *MANICOTTES*

2 cups sugar
1 teaspoon lemon juice
2 heaping teaspoons honey
1 teaspoon vanilla extract
2 cups all-purpose flour
2 large eggs
¼ teaspoon salt
Vegetable oil for frying

North African *manicottes*
for Rosh Hashanah

To make the sugar-and-honey syrup, put the sugar in a small heavy saucepan with 4 cups water. Bring to a boil, and add the lemon juice. Lower the heat, and simmer for 20 minutes, uncovered. Stir in the honey and the vanilla. Set aside.

To make the dough, put the flour, eggs, and a pinch of salt in a small mixing bowl, and knead with your hands until the dough can be formed into a ball. You can also use a food processor. Divide the dough in half, and cover with a towel. Let rest for at least 15 minutes.

Roll out the dough as thin as possible, less than ⅛ inch thick. Using a sharp knife or a pizza cutter, cut the dough into long strips, about 1 inch by 12 inches.

Pour about 4 inches of oil into a heavy pot and heat to 375 degrees.

Wrap each strip of dough carefully and loosely around three fingers into a spiral, keeping the center ring very wide and very loose. Carefully slip the dough off your fingers and into the hot vegetable oil, turning with tongs for a few minutes as the dough cooks. The tongs will help keep the round shape. First the ring will puff up like a rose, and then it will start to turn golden. Once it is golden, carefully remove from the oil and drain on paper towels. Repeat with the rest of the dough, one strip at a time.

Put the warm fritters on a serving plate, and spoon the syrup over all. Serve warm.

Pignolats de Nostredame

(NOSTRADAMUS'S PINE NUT PRALINES)

IN THE QUAINT WALLED TOWN OF Saint-Rémy-de-Provence, I passed the birthplace of Michel de Nostredame—called Nostradamus by most—a physician and astrologer best known for his prophecies, not for his recipes. Nearby is a small bakery called Le Petit Duc. Owned and operated by Anne Daguin and her husband, Hermann van Beeck, the bakery, which has a branch in Paris called La Grande Duchesse, specializes in Renaissance recipes. They include those of the prominent Nostradamus, who came from a Jewish family that converted to Catholicism in 1504, when he was just under a year old.

When I spoke with Anne, whose mother is Jewish, she told me that she had wanted to open her shop in Saint-Rémy but felt that there was no real pastry tradition there. So she turned to old books for inspiration, and found many recipes, some by Jewish physicians like Nostradamus, who came from a long line of men skilled in mathematics and medicine. As a healer, he often used foods and herbs as treatments for various illnesses, such as this praline with pine nuts.

Preheat the oven to 350 degrees, and line two baking sheets with parchment paper.

Toast the pine nuts in the oven or in a sauté pan until they are dry and fragrant and lightly browned.

In a heavy-bottomed saucepan, heat ½ cup water with the sugar and the rose water. Stir until the sugar is just dissolved, and let cook over medium heat without stirring for 20 minutes, or until the syrup reaches 250 degrees. Add the pine nuts and the crushed fennel seeds, and mix quickly with a wooden spoon until the sugar becomes white. Remove from the heat.

Using two teaspoons and working quickly, make small disks by dropping heaping teaspoons of the pine-nut mixture on the lined baking sheets. They will flatten themselves. Allow them to dry for a few hours before peeling them off of the paper and serving. The pralines can be decorated, as Nostradamus explains, with little pieces of gold leaf.

YIELD: ABOUT 40 PINE-NUT PRALINES

2 cups pine nuts
2 cups sugar
2 tablespoons rose water
2 tablespoons crushed fennel seeds*

*If you don't have a mortar and pestle, the easiest way to crush the fennel seeds is to put them in a zip-top bag and bang them with the bottom of a measuring cup or a rolling pin.

Rosquettes Égyptiennes

VISITING EIGHTY-FIVE-YEAR-OLD AIMÉE BERESSI and ninety-one-year-old Lydia Farahat is like crawling into a cozy casbah. Friends since they left Egypt in the late 1950s, they get together once a week at Lydia's apartment on Rue Dragon, right near Saint-Germain-des-Prés. For more than forty years, the two have been discussing recipes, current events, and the Egypt of their childhood.

When Aimée was growing up in Cairo, there was no school on Thursday, so she helped her mother and aunt make the cakes and cookies for the Sabbath. The word *rosquettes*, which comes from the Spanish *rosquillas*, refers to round cookies with a hole. Aimée still bakes a batch each week to bring to her friend of so many years.

 YIELD: 70 *ROSQUETTES*

½ cup sugar

Grated zest of 1 lemon

3 eggs

½ cup vegetable oil

2⅓ cups all-purpose flour, plus more if needed

1 teaspoon baking powder

⅛ teaspoon salt

Mix the sugar, lemon zest, two of the eggs, and the oil in the bowl of an electric mixer. Lower the speed, and carefully add 1 cup of the flour, the baking powder, and the salt. Slowly add the remaining 1⅓ cups of flour, until the dough comes together. Turn it out onto a floured surface, and mold the dough into a ball, adding enough extra flour so that it will not stick to your hands but retains the imprint of your finger. Knead until the dough is supple and smooth. If it continues to stick to your hands or the surface, add more flour.

Preheat the oven to 375 degrees. Sprinkle an ungreased cookie sheet with flour, and lightly flour the work surface.

Take a piece of dough about the size of a golf ball, and roll it into a long snake that is ¼ inch in diameter. Cut the long roll into 4-inch pieces. Bring the two ends of each piece together to form a doughnut, and gently pinch them together. Put on the baking sheet. Repeat with the remaining dough. Beat the remaining egg, and brush the *rosquettes* with it.

Put the *rosquettes* close together on the floured cookie sheet. Bake them for 10 to 12 minutes, or until golden.

Truffes

(CHOCOLATE TRUFFLES)

WHAT WOULD A FRENCH or any festive meal be without a little chocolate? Françoise Tenenbaum, a deputy mayor of Dijon, shared her entire recipe book with me. When she has time in her busy schedule, she rolls these chocolate truffles at home to serve for parties. They are also perfect for Passover.

Melt the chocolate in the microwave or the top of a double boiler. Let cool slightly. Put the cocoa in a shallow bowl or pie plate.

Mix the egg yolks, sugar, and butter together in a mixer equipped with a paddle, and gradually add the melted chocolate. Scoop into a small bowl, and leave in the refrigerator a few hours, or until firm.

Remove from the refrigerator, and let sit at room temperature until slightly softened. Scoop out level teaspoons of dough, and drop them into the cocoa powder. Gently roll into little balls, and chill until hard. Remove from the refrigerator, and roll a second time in the cocoa. Keep chilled until serving.

D OR P   YIELD: 50 TRUFFLE
BALLS

8 ounces dark bittersweet chocolate
½ cup unsweetened cocoa for dipping
2 large egg yolks
3 tablespoons sugar
1 stick unsalted butter or *pareve* margarine, softened

Aimée Beressi and Lydia Farahat, lifelong friends from Egypt who meet for coffee and cookies each week in Paris

A Sampling of French Jewish Menus

*Signifies recipes in the book

FRIDAY NIGHT DINNERS

Pan-French

Rabbi's wife's challah*
Green pea soup with tarragon*
Chicken fricasse*
Saffron rice pilaf*
Ratatouille*
Green salad dressed with lemon, mustard, and cilantro
*Tarte à la compote de pommes**

Alsatian

Alsatian *barches**
Chicken soup with *knepfle**
Stuffed breast of veal* with roasted potatoes
Compote de pruneaux et de figues (poached prunes and figs)*

Tunisian

At least three and as many as ten salads, such as roasted beet;* shaved fennel with celery, cucumber, lemon, and pomegranates;* and Tunisian carrots*
Tunisian vegetables stuffed with meat*
Couscous*
Fresh fruit
Montecaos (*ghouribi* cookies)*

Old Provençal

*Fougasse**
Carpentras's *tian* of spinach and salt cod*
*Papeton d'aubergines**
Lettuce with classic vinaigrette*
Pignolats de Nostredame (pine-nut pralines)*

UPSCALE FRENCH FRIDAY NIGHT DINNER

Rabbi's wife's challah*
Scrambled eggs with truffles

Roast chicken stuffed with truffles*
Roasted potatoes
Citrus-fruit soup with dates and mint*
*Biscuits de gingembre**

SABBATH LUNCH

Alsatian

Herring*
*Choucroute garni**
Boiled potatoes
Alsatian pear kugel with prunes*
In-season fruit tart (rhubarb,* apple,* or *quetsche**)

North African

Pain pétri (Moroccan challah)*
Shaved fennel with celery, cucumber, lemon and pomegranate*
*Tchoukchouka**
Eggplant caviar*
Avocado with lemon and cilantro
*Adafina**
Strawberries and raspberries on a meringue

ROSH HASHANAH

Alsatian

*Pain au pavot**
*Carpe à la juive**
Alsatian *pot-au-feu**
Potato salad*
Schaleth with cherries or apples*

Pan-French

Moroccan *salade de blettes**
Chicken with cinnamon and apples from Metz*
*Riz au safran**
*Tarte aux quetsches**

EREV KOL NIDRE DINNER

Eggplant caviar*
Poulet au riz
Lettuce with classic vinaigrette*
*Frou-frou chalet**

BREAK THE FAST

Alsatian Dairy

Large cheese platter
Herrings in cream with apples and radishes*
Oatmeal bread with fig, anise, and walnuts*
*Kugelhopf** or lemon cake

Alsatian Meat

Sweet and sour fish*
Alsatian *choucroute* (with sausage and corned beef)*
Boiled potatoes
*Raifort**
*Tarte aux quetsches**

PURIM PROVENÇAL

*Soupe de poisson**
*Membre d'agneau à la judaïque**
Green beans and red peppers*
Tunisian carrots with caraway and *harissa**
*Beignets de Carnaval**

PASSOVER

Alsatian

Spring chicken broth with *knepfle**
Asparagus with *mousseline* sauce*
Roasted kid, lamb, or turkey
Wine mousse
Passover almond macaroons*

Tunisian

*Haroset**
Fennel salad*
Carrot salad*
Artichoke and orange salad*
Tunisian winter-squash salad with coriander*
*Harissa**
*M'soki**
Fruit
Macaroons*

MOROCCAN

*Salade juive**
Artichoke and orange salad with saffron and mint*

Shad with fava beans and red peppers*
Tagine of chicken with prunes, apricots, and almonds*
Rice
Fresh fruit
Passover almond macaroons*

WARM WEATHER BRUNCH

*Salade juive**
*Omelette aux herbes**
Ratatouille*
Citrus-fruit soup with dates and mint*
*Schaleth aux cerises**

ELEGANT LUNCH

Terrine of chicken flavored with pistachio nuts, curry,
    and hazelnuts*
Artichoke and orange salad with saffron and mint*
Molten chocolate cake*

SOUTHWESTERN BIARRITZ LUNCH

Cold lettuce and zucchini soup*
Salmon with pearl onions, lettuce, and peas*
Rice
Lettuce with classic vinaigrette*
Applesauce tart*

LIGHT SUMMER LUNCH

French cold beet soup*
Shaved fennel salad with celery, cucumber, lemon, and
    pomegranate*
Babka à la française with olive tapenade
Citrus-fruit soup with dates and mint*

THURSDAY NIGHT DINNER

*Gemarti supp**
Honey-coated baked chicken with preserved lemon*
French potato salad with shallots and parsley*
Fennel and citrus salad*

JEWISH ENGAGEMENT DINNER
AT TROISGROS

Salade nouvelle au foie gras de canard
*Saumon à l'oseille**
Pavé de chocolat à la feuille d'or
Petits fours
Kir Royal
Blanc de Blanc

Glossary of Terms and Ingredients

adafina—Moroccan Sabbath stew with chickpeas, meat, and rice or barley

Ashkenazim—Central and eastern European Jews and their descendants, including Yiddish speakers

babka or *baba*—a yeast cake originally from Poland

bain-marie—a hot-water bath in which you insert the cooking pan for delicate desserts and other dishes to bake in the oven

barches, berches—literally, "twisted"; a type of braided bread for the Sabbath, made from flour and sometimes cooked potatoes

bavaroise glacée—a frozen parfait based on eggs and cream

Beth Din—religious governing board that certifies kosher foods and eating establishments

beurre blanc—a French butter sauce with an acid reduction of lemon or vinegar, often made with shallots

blini—small pancakes, often leavened with yeast and made of buckwheat flour

bottarga—dried pressed fish eggs, usually from mullet, a delicacy called "Mediterranean caviar"

boulangerie—French for "bakery"

bouquet garni—a bundle of herbs tied together, often including bay leaf, rosemary, thyme, savory, and parsley, used to flavor stocks and stews

bourride—a French fish stew similar to bouillabaisse but without shellfish

brandade—puree of salt cod, olive oil, milk, and sometimes potato, eaten in the south of France

brik—a North African pastry, with a thin dough wrapped around a savory filling

brisket—a cut of beef consisting of the breast muscles and other tissues, with the bones removed, and best served braised

butterkuchen—an Alsatian butter cookie, often called *butter*

cameline—a French sweet-and-sour sauce with cinnamon and vinegar, first mentioned in print in the thirteenth and fourteenth centuries

carpe à la juive—an Alsatian Sabbath dish of carp cooked "in the Jewish style" and served cold, either with a parsley or a sweet-and-sour sauce

cassolita—Spanish for a round clay pot and that which is cooked in it

cassoulet—a stew of white beans and meat

charcutier—a butcher specializing in smoked meats and sausages

chiffonade—a technique of cutting leafy green vegetables or herbs in which the leaves are rolled and sliced to resemble "chiffon" or rags

cholent—long-simmering eastern European Sabbath stew of meat, potatoes, and beans

chremslach—a doughnutlike fritter made from matzo meal

clafoutis—a custardlike baked French dessert with cherries or other fruits

confit—a process of preserving and flavoring food by immersing it in a fat

consommé nikitouche—a Tunisian chicken soup with dumplings

coriandre—the French word for the leaves and seeds of the cilantro plant

côte de boeuf—a rib-eye beefsteak with the bone in

coudelle—old French for "matzo"

cou d'oie farci—stuffed goose or chicken neck

couscous—small pellets made of semolina flour, or the dish of the grains with vegetables, broth, and a meat or fish

couscoussier—a special pot similar to a double-level steamer, used to make couscous

crème fraîche—a naturally soured French cream, thicker and less sour than American sour cream

dafina—also called *adafina*, a North African Jewish Sabbath meat stew with chickpeas and rice eau-de-vie—a light, clear fruit brandy

farfel—noodle dough or matzo in the form of small pellets or granules

fèves de cacao—cocoa beans

fijuelas—Moroccan deep-fried pastry for Rosh Hashanah and other holidays

flanken—beef short ribs

foie gras—the liver of a duck or goose that has been specially fattened

foie haché—chopped liver

ganache—a thick, syrupy mass made by mixing chopped chocolate with heated heavy cream

gavage—the process of fattening geese for foie gras

gefilte fish—poached patties of ground white fish, such as carp, pike, or whitefish

gehackte leber—Alsatian for "chopped liver"

gemarti supp—Alsatian homemade vegetable soup

gretchene—buckwheat in Alsatian

grumbeerekugel—Alsatian for potato "kugel"

hamantashen—a triangle-shaped cookie eaten at Purim

harissa—a North African hot sauce made with chili peppers and garlic

haroset—a pastelike mixture of fruit, nuts, cinnamon, and wine eaten during Passover Seder, symbolic of the mortar the Israelites used in building during Egyptian slavery

herbes de Provence—a mixture of dried herbs including rosemary, marjoram, basil, bay leaf, thyme, and sometimes lavender

Juifs du Pape—Jews protected by the Pope in Avignon

julienne—a long, thin cut of vegetables

kashrut—the Jewish dietary laws

kirsch—an Alsatian and southern-German fruit brandy, made from cherries, also known as kirschwasser

knepfle or knopfle—Alsatian for "matzo balls"

knoblewurst—Alsatian for "garlic sausage"

kosher—sanctioned by Jewish law, ritually fit, clean, or prepared for use according to the laws of kashrut

kugel—baked sweet or savory casserole or pudding made of noodles, potatoes, bread, or vegetables, often served on the Sabbath or festivals

kugelhopf mold—a type of baking mold, like a Bundt pan

lardons—French term for narrow strips of pork fat, or diced bacon that has been blanched and then fried

lungenwurscht—an Alsatian wurst made out of lungs, heart, and onions

Maimouna—an end of Passover North African celebration

maror—bitter herbs, usually horseradish or romaine, eaten at Passover as a symbol of the bitterness of slavery

mechouia—means "grilled" in Arabic; also the name of a salad

mellah—"salt" in Arabic; Mellah is the Jewish quarter of Fez

merguez—a spicy sausage of beef or lamb, common in Morocco, France, and Algeria

mérou—type of grouper

mezuzah—piece of parchment in a decorative case, in fulfillment of the biblical mitzvah of having "Shma Yisrael," "the Lord our God is one," on the doorpost

mikveh—Judaism understands that ritual impurities can be washed away by immersion in a mikveh. This applies to women following the cessation of their monthly menstrual cycle. Even dishes can be made kosher through immersion in a mikveh.

minyan—the quorum of ten men necessary for communal worship

mitzvoth—commandments in the Torah; also, acts of human kindness or goodwill

morue—French for "salt cod"

mousseline—a mayonnaise lightened with a beaten egg white

nougatine—crackly caramel-based candy

orisa—Tunisian baked stew with wheat berries

pain au pavot—French for Alsatian challah with poppyseeds

pain de campagne—French country bread, similar to a sourdough

pain pétri—Morrocan kneaded bread for the Sabbath

pareve—made without milk, meat, or their derivatives

pastis—an anise-flavored liqueur

pâté—a paste of minced meats, often liver, and fat, sometimes baked with a crust

pavot—French for "poppy seeds"

petits fours—from the French for "small oven," a small cake served at the end of a meal

pickelfleisch—corned beef made in Alsace

pied-noir—term for French nationals living in Algeria before Algeria's independence *piment d'Espelette*—hot but not fiery Basque pepper from a village near Toulouse

pistou—French for "pesto," a blend of basil, garlic, pine nuts, olive oil, and sometimes cheese

pletzl—a Yiddish term for the central square in the Marais as well as a flatbread from Poland flavored with poppy seeds and chopped onions

pot-au-feu—French for "pot on the fire," a dish of boiled meats

quetsche—a dark-skinned Alsatian German plum similar to Italian blue plums

raifort—French for "horseradish"

ras el hanout—a Moroccan spice mixture of thirty spices, including cinnamon, cumin, cardamom, cloves, and paprika

ratatouille—a Provençal dish made of eggplant, zucchini, tomatoes, and onions

reis floimes—a rice dish with prunes

riouttes—French for ancient anise-flavored bagel-like bread

rose water—a sweet liquid made from rose petals, often used in desserts

rosquettes—French for round Sephardic cookies with a hole

rouget—French for "red mullet"

rouille—a French sauce made with olive oil, bread crumbs, herbs, garlic, and red pepper

roux—a cooked mixture of flour and fat, in Jewish cooking often of oil, but usually butter, often becoming a reddish-brown color

sablé—a butter crust

sauce verte—a green herb sauce, usually used for fish

savoiardi—Italian ladyfingers

schaleth—an Alsatian pudding traditionally made with soaked bread or matzo or, later, ladyfingers with fruit, often called *charlotte,* traditionally served on the Sabbath and holidays

Seder—home or community service and ceremonial dinner on the first and second nights of Passover, commemorating the Exodus from Egypt

Sephardim—Jews and their descendants who settled in Spain and Portugal at an early date and later spread to Greece, the Levant, England, the Netherlands, and the Americas

Shabbat—Hebrew for "Sabbath"

shalach manot—Hebrew for gifts of sweets presented at Purim

shmaltz—rendered chicken fat

shmatteh—Yiddish word for "rags" or "headscarf"

shofar—ritual ram's horn traditionally blown to usher in the New Year

shtetl—Yiddish word for a small town in eastern Europe

skeena—an Arabic stew, similar to *cassoulet* or *adafina*

soufflé—a sweet or savory baked dish that rises because of beaten egg whites folded into the batter and quickly falls after coming out of the oven

Sukkot—fall harvest celebration, during which meals are taken out-of-doors, in an arbor, or *sukkah*

tabbouleh—a salad that is a mixture of bulgur and chopped herbs

tarte flambée—French for an Alsatian onion flatbread usually served on Sunday nights

tchoukchouka—a North African salad of tomato, eggplant, and pepper

terrine—a covered clay pot, and dishes cooked inside

tian—a Provençal earthenware cooking dish; the term also denotes what is baked in the dish

tierfleisch—Alsatian for "smoked meat"

winstub—Alsatian wine bar

A Source Guide

Cash Cacher Naouri
Locations throughout France
Tel: 01 40 35 01 46

Florence Finkelsztajn's (now Kahn)
Traiteur Delicatessen
24 Rue des Écouffes
75004 Paris, 4th arr
Tel: 01 48 87 92 85
florencefinkelsztajn.free.fr/

Geismar Traiteur, Boucherie,
Charcuterie
21 Grand Rue
68230 Turckheim
Tel: 03 89 27 14 12

Koskas & Fils
276 Boulevard Voltaire
75011 Paris, 11th arr
Tel: 01 40 09 00 60
www.koskas&fils.com

La Grande Duchesse
13 Rue Castellane
75008 Paris, 8th arr
Tel: 01 42 66 12 57
www.lagrandeduchesse.com

Le Monde des Épices
30 Rue François-Miron
75004 Paris, 4th arr
Tel: 01 42 72 66 23

Lenôtre
Locations throughout Paris
Tel: 01 53 90 24 50
http://www.lenotre.fr

Le Petit Duc
7 Boulevard Victor Hugo
13210 Saint-Rémy-de-Provence
Tel: 04 90 92 08 31
contact@petit-duc.com
www.petit-duc.com

Picard Surgelés
Locations throughout France
http://www.picard.fr

RESTAURANTS

Abbaye de Collonges
Quai de la Jonchère
69660 Collonges au Mont d'Or
Tel: 04 72 42 90 90
http://www.bocuse.fr/accueil.aspx

Au Rendez-vous/La Maison de
Couscous (kosher)
14 Avenue de Wagram
75008 Paris, 8th arr
Tel: 01 42 27 23 57

Chez Paul (kosher)
23 Rue Saint-Saëns
13001 Marseille
Tel: 04 91 33 07 43

Cordeillan-Bages in Pauillac
Route des Châteaux
33250 Pauillac
Tel: 05 56 59 24 24
http://www.cordeillanbages.com/

Daniel Hôtel
8 Rue Frédéric Bastiat
75008 Paris, 8th arr
Tel: 01 42 56 17 00
http://www.hoteldanielparis.com/

D'Choucrouterie
20 Rue Saint-Louis
67000 Strasbourg
Tel: 03 88 36 07 28

Jean Ramet
7–8 Place Jean Jaurès
33000 Bordeaux
Tel: 05 56 44 12 51

La Tupina
6 Rue de la Porte de la Monnaie
33800 Bordeaux
Tel: 05 56 91 56 37
http://www.latupina.com/

Le Crocodile
10 Rue de l'Outre
67000 Strasbourg
Tel: 33 3 88 32 13 02
http://www.au-crocodile.com/

Le Marronnier
18 Route de Saverne
67370 Stutzheim
Tel: 03 88 69 84 30

Le Mas Tourteron
Chemin de Sainte-Blaise-les-
    Imberts
84220 Gordes
Tel: 04 90 72 00 16
http://www.mastourteron.com/

Les Arômes
8 Rue Moussard
13400 Aubagne
Tel: 04 42 03 72 93

Mini Palais
Avenue Winston Churchill
(entrance: Pont Alexandre III)
75008 Paris, 8th arr
Tel: 01 42 56 42 42
http://www.minipalais.com/

Osmose (kosher)
31 Avenue de Versailles
75016 Paris, 16th arr
Tel: 01 45 20 74 12
http://www.osmose-paris.com/

La Maison Troisgros
Place Jean Troisgros
42300 Roanne
Tel: 04 77 71 66 97
http://www.troisgros.fr/

Spring Restaurant
28 Rue de la Tour d'Auvergne
75009 Paris, 9th arr
Tel: 01 45 96 05 72
http://www.springparis.blogspot
    .com/

Sushi West (kosher)
169 Boulevard Saint-Germain
75006 Paris, 6th arr
Tel: 01 08 26 88 26 88
http://www.sushiwest.fr/

Wistub Brenner
1 Rue Turenne
68000 Colmar
Tel: 03 89 41 42 33
http://www.wistub-brenner.fr/

SOURCES

Biscuiterie d'Agen
132 Avenue Michelet
47000 Agen
Tel: 05 53 96 17 24

Les Macarons de Boulay
Maison Alexandre
13 Rue de Saint-Avold
57220 Boulay
Tel: 03 87 79 11 22
info@macaronsdeboulay.com

Les Spécialités Paul Heumann
Matzo
67259 Soulz-sous-Forêts
Tel: 02 88 80 40 61
http://www.matsot.com/

René Neymann Matzo
46 Rue du 23 Novembre
67310 Wasselonne
Tel: 03 88 87 03 57
info@neymann.com

Bibliography

Abrahams, Israel. *Jewish Life in the Middle Ages.* London, 1896.

Ali-Bab. *Gastronomie Pratique: Études Culinaires Suivies du Traitement de l'obésité des Gourmands.* Paris: E. Flammarion, 1907.

Asserolette, C. *Ma Cuisine.* Paris: E. Plon, Nourrit and C'e, 1890.

Bahloul, Joëlle. *Le Culte de la Table Dressée: Rites et Traditions de la Table Juive Algérienne.* Paris: Éditions A. M. Métailié, 1983.

Benbassa, Esther. *Cuisine Judéo-Espagnole: Recettes et Traditions.* Paris: Éditions du Scribe, 1984.

——. *The Jews of France.* Princeton, N.J.: Princeton University Press, 1999.

Berr, Hélène. *Le Journal d'Hélène Berr.* Paris: Chez Talandier, 2008.

Bloch-Dano, Eveline, and Alice Kaplan. *Madame Proust: A Biography.* Chicago: University of Chicago Press, 2007.

Bohan, Eben, editor. *Kalonimos ben Kalonimos d'Arles.* Tel Aviv: A. M. Haberman, 1956.

Carter, William C. *Marcel Proust: A Life.* New Haven, Conn.: Yale University Press, 2000.

Chiche-Yana, Martine. *La Table Juive.* Aix-en-Provence: Édisud, 1992, volumes 1 and 2.

Choinska, Frida. *Cent Recettes de Cuisine Juive.* Paris: R. Laffont, 1967.

Cohen, Albert. *Livre de Ma Mère.* Paris: Gallimard, 1991.

——. *The Psalms.* London: Soncino Press, 1977.

Conseil National des Arts Culinaires. *Lorraine: Produits du Terroir et Recettes Traditionnelles.* Paris: Albin Michel, 1995.

——. *Provence-Alpes-Côte d'Azur: Produits du Terroir et Recettes Traditionnelles.* Paris: Albin Michel, 1995.

——. *Rhône-Alpes: Produits du Terroir et Recettes Traditionnelles.* Paris: Albin Michel, 1995.

The Complete Jewish Bible with Rash Commentary, chabad.org/library.

Cooper, John. *Eat and Be Satisfied: A Social History of Jewish Food.* Northvale, N.J.: Jason Aronson, Inc., 1993.

David, Elizabeth. *French Provincial Cooking.* New York: Penguin Press, 1974.

Dictionnaire de l'Acadèmie Française.

Encyclopaedia Judaica. New York: Macmillan, 1972.

Endelman, Todd M., editor. *Comparing Jewish Societies.* Ann Arbor: University of Michigan Press, 1997.

Escoffier, Auguste. *Escoffier's Cook Book of Desserts, Sweets, and Ices.* New York, Crescent Books Inc., 1941.

Escudier, Jean-Noel. *La Véritable Cuisine Provençale et Niçoise.* Paris: Éditions Allia, 1953.

Ezratty, Harry A. *500 Years in the Jewish Caribbean: The Spanish and Portuguese Jews in the West Indies.* Baltimore: Omni Arts, Inc., 2002.

Fagan, Brian. *Fish on Friday.* New York: Basic Books, 2006.

Farmer, Jean. *Messieurs les Fabriciens.* Paris: Bernard Grasset, 1911.

Favre-Vassas, Claudine. *The Singular Beast.* New York: Columbia University Press, 1999.

Flandrin, Jean-Louis, and Massimo Montanari, editors. *Food: A Culinary History.* New York: Columbia University Press, 1999.

Gérard, Charles. *L'Ancienne Alsace à Table.* Paris: Berger-Levraulet, 1877.

Gil, Moshe. "The Radhanite Merchants and the Land of Radhan." *Journal of the Economic and Social History of the Orient,* vol. XVII, pt. 3.

Ginor, Michael. *Foie Gras: A Passion.* New York: John Wiley & Sons, 1999.

Ginsburger, Moses. *Les Juifs à Ribeauvillé et à Bergheim: Conférence Faite à la Société d'Histoire et d'Archéologie de Ribeauvillé et des Environs.* Strasbourg: Sostralib, 1939.

Green, Nancy. *The Pletzel of Paris: Jewish Immigrant Workers in the Belle Epoque.* New York: Holmes and Meier, 1986.

——. *Ready to Wear and Ready to Work: A Century of Industry and Immigrants in Paris and New York.* Durham, N.C.: Duke University Press, 1997.

Grivetti, Louis E., and Howard-Yana Shapiro, editors. *Chocolate: History, Culture, and Heritage.* Hoboken, N.J.: John Wiley & Sons, 2009.

Hallie, Philip. *Lest Innocent Blood Be Shed.* New York: Harper and Row, 1975.

Hazan-Arama, Fortunée. *Saveurs de Mon Enfance.* Paris: Éditions Robert Laffont, 1987.

Heine, Heinrich. *Jewish Stories and Hebrew Melodies.* Princeton, N.J.: Markus Wiener Publishers, Inc., 1987.

Herbst, Sharon Tyler. *Food Lover's Companion.* New York: Barron's Educational Series, 2001.

Hertzberg, Arthur. *The French Enlightenment and the Jews.* New York: Columbia University Press, 1990.

Herz, Juliette, and WIZO-Strasbourg. *La Tradition de la Cuisine Juive.* Strasbourg: Bon & Casher, 1969.

Hinkel-Rudrauf, Marguerite. *El sässisches Kochbuch.* Strasbourg: Heitz, 1939.

Husson, C. *Étude sur les Épices.* Paris: Dimd, 1883.

Hyman, Paula E. *The Emancipation of the Jews of Alsace.* New Haven, Conn.: Yale University Press, 1991.

———. *The Jews of Modern France.* Berkeley: University of California Press, 1998.

Isnard, Léon. *La Cuisine Française et Africaine.* Paris: Albin Michel, 1949.

Jaffin, Léone. *150 Recettes et Mille et un Souvenirs d'une Juive d'Algérie.* Paris: Encre, 1980.

Kamins, Toni L. *Jewish Guide to France.* New York: St. Martin's Griffin, 2001.

Kamm, Henry. "Jewish History in Provence." *New York Times,* 15 Sept. 1991.

Kluger, Daniel. *Vigtor le Rebelle: La Résistance d'un Juif en France.* Paris: L'Harmattan, 1999.

Kraemer, David. *Jewish Eating and Identity Through the Ages.* New York: Routledge, 2007.

Laurioux, Bruno. *Manger au Moyen Âge.* Hachette Littératures, 2002.

Lazarque, E. Auricoste de. *La Cuisine Messine.* Nancy, France: Presses Universitaires de Nancy, 1898.

Lewi, Monique. *Histoire d'une Communauté Juive, Roanne: Étude Historique et Sociologique d'un Judaïsme.* Paris: Horvath, 1976.

Lune, Pierre de. *Le Cuisinier, où Il Est Traité de la Véritable Méthode pour Apprester Toutes Sortes de Viandes . . .* Paris, 1656.

Lunel, Armand. *J'ai Vu Vivre la Provence.* Paris: A. Fayard, 1962.

Malcolm, Janet. *Two Lives: Gertrude and Alice.* New Haven, Conn.: Yale University Press, 2007.

Malino, Frances. *The Sephardic Jews of Bordeaux.* Tuscaloosa: University of Alabama Press, 1978.

Marin, François, *Suite des Dons de Comus ou l'Art de la Cuisine, Réduit en Pratique.* Paris: Pissot, 1742.

Marrus, Michael R., and Robert O. Paxton. *Vichy France and the Jews.* New York: Basic Books, 1981.

Massialot, François. *Nouveau Cuisinier Royal et Bourgeois.* Paris: Joseph Saugrain, 1748.

Meyer, Charles. "Le Choc et les Échanges," *Historia,* special no. 4, *consacré aux croisades,* March–April 1990.

Moulinas, René. *Les Juifs du Pape en France.* Toulouse: Privat, 1981.

Pirenne, Henri. *Medieval Cities: Their Origins and the Revival of Trade.* Princeton, N.J.: Princeton University Press, 1969.

Plaut, W. Gunther. *The Torah: A Modern Commentary.* New York: Union of American Hebrew Congregations, 1981.

Pomiane, Édouard de. *Cuisine Juive Ghettos Modernes.* Paris: Albin Michel, 1929.

Rabinowitz, Louis. "The Routes of the Radanites." *Jewish Quarterly Review,* vol. 35, no. 3, January 1945.

———. *Jewish Merchant Adventurers: A Study of the Radanites.* London: Edward Goldston, 1948.

Raphael, Freddy. *La Cuisine Juive en Alsace.* Strasbourg: La Nuée Bleue, 2005.

Reboul, J. B. *La Cuisinière Provençale.* Marseille: Tacussel, 1991.

Robb, Graham. *The Discovery of France.* New York: W. W. Norton & Co., 2007.

Roden, Claudia. *The Book of Jewish Food.* New York: Alfred A. Knopf, 1996.

Roukhomovsky, Suzanne. *Gastronomie Juive.* Paris: Flammarion, 1929.

Roumi, Marcelle. *La Cuisine de Ma Mère.* Paris: Agrandir, 1984.

Samuels, Maurice. *Inventing the Israelite: Jewish Fiction in Nineteenth-Century France.* Palo Alto, Calif.: Stanford University Press, 2009.

Schlienger, Jean-Louis. *Le Mangeur Alsacien: 2000 Ans de Gastronomie.* Strasbourg: La Nuée Bleue, 2000.

Serrao, Joaquim Verissimo. "L'Exode des Juifs Portugais aux XVIe Siècle, le Cas Spécifiquement Bayonnais." In *L'Exode des Juifs d'Espagne vers Bayonne: Des Rives de l'Ebre et du Tage à Celles de l'Adour,* Colloque International, Faculté Pluridisciplinaire de Bayonne-Anglet-Biarritz, 7–9 Avril 1992, pp. 73–84.

Serventi, Silvano. *Le Foie Gras.* Paris: Flammarion, 2005.

Shereshevsky, Esra. *Rashi: The Man and His Word.* Northvale, N.J.: Jason Aronson Inc., 1996.

Stauben, Daniel, translated by Rose Choron. *Scenes of Jewish Life in Alsace* (1860). Malibu: Pangloss Press, 1991.

Stouff, Louis. *Ravitaillement et Alimentation en Provence.* Paris: Mouton & Co., 1970.

———. "Isaac Nathan et les Siens: Une Famille Juive d'Arles des XIVe et XVe Siècles." *Provence Historique,* vol. 37, no. 150, 1987.

———. *La Table Provençale.* Avignon: Éditions A. Barthelomy, 1996.

Sypeck, Jeff. *Becoming Charlemagne.* New York: HarperCollins, 2006.

Taïeb, Daisy. *Les Fêtes Juives à Tunis Racontées à Mes Filles.* Nice: Simonot, 1998.

Terrio, Susan. *Crafting the Culture and History of French Chocolate.* Berkeley: University of California Press, 2002.

Tigay, Alan. *The Jewish Traveler: Hadassah Magazine's Guide to the World's Jewish Communities and Sights.* Northvale, N.J.: Aronson Inc., 1998.

Touitou, Odette. *Tunisie: La Cuisine de Ma Mère.* Geneva: Minerva, 2003.

Tudela, Benjamin of. *The Itinerary of Benjamin of Tudela: Travels in the Middle Ages.* London: A. Asher & Co., 1841.

Turner, Jack. *Spice: The History of a Temptation.* New York: Alfred A. Knopf, 2004.

Visson, Lynn. *The Russian Heritage Cookbook: A Culinary Heritage Preserved in 360 Authentic Recipes.* New York: Overlook, 2004.

Wheaton, Barbara Ketcham. *Savoring the Past: The French Kitchen and Table from 1300 to 1789.* New York: Touchstone, 1996.

Wygoda, Georgette. *La Gastronomie Cashèr.* Ingersheim, France: Saep, 1996.

Yana, Martine. *Trésors de la Table Juive.* Aix-en-Provence: Édisud, 2005.

Zana-Murat, Andrée. *De Mère en Fille: La Cuisine Juive Tunisienne.* Paris: Albin Michel, 1998.

Zeitoun, Edmond. *250 Recettes Classiques de Cuisine Tunisienne.* Paris: J. Grancher, 1977.

Index

Illustrations Credits

A Note About the Author

Joan Nathan was born in Providence, Rhode Island. She graduated from the University of Michigan with a master's degree in French literature and earned a master's in public administration from Harvard University. For three years she lived in Israel, where she worked for Mayor Teddy Kollek of Jerusalem. In 1974, working for Mayor Abraham Beame in New York, she cofounded the Ninth Avenue Food Festival. Guest Curator of Food Culture USA for the 2005 Smithsonian Folklife Festival, she was a founding member of Les Dames d'Escoffier. Ms. Nathan is a frequent contributor to the *New York Times* and other publications. She is the author of numerous books including *Jewish Cooking in America* and *The New American Cooking,* both of which won the James Beard Award and the IACP Award. She was the host of the nationally syndicated PBS television series *Jewish Cooking in America with Joan Nathan,* based on the book. She is the recipient of numerous awards, including James Beard's Who's Who in American Food and Beverage and *Food Arts* magazine's Silver Spoon Award, and she received an honorary doctorate from the Spertus Institute of Jewish Culture in Chicago. The mother of three grown children, Ms. Nathan lives in Washington, D.C., and Martha's Vineyard with her husband, Allan Gerson.